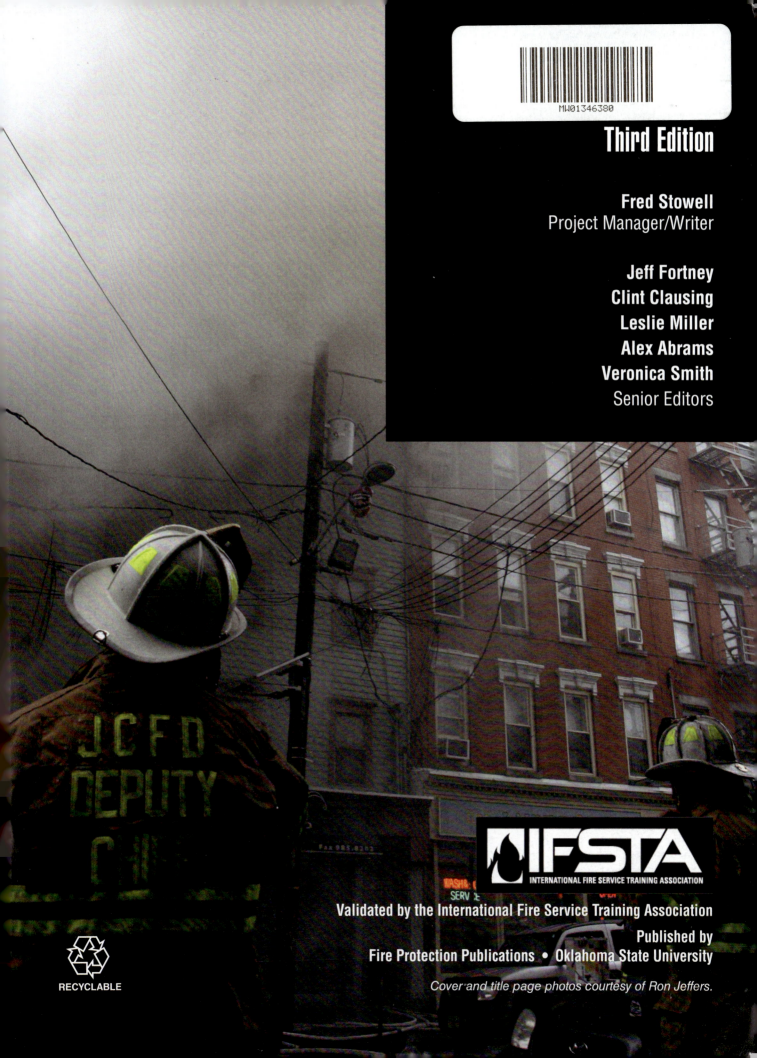

Third Edition

Fred Stowell
Project Manager/Writer

**Jeff Fortney
Clint Clausing
Leslie Miller
Alex Abrams
Veronica Smith**
Senior Editors

Validated by the International Fire Service Training Association

Published by
Fire Protection Publications • Oklahoma State University

Cover and title page photos courtesy of Ron Jeffers.

The International Fire Service Training Association (IFSTA) was established in 1934 as a *nonprofit educational association of fire fighting personnel who are dedicated to upgrading fire fighting techniques and safety through training*. To carry out the mission of IFSTA, Fire Protection Publications was established as an entity of Oklahoma State University. Fire Protection Publications' primary function is to publish and distribute training materials as proposed, developed, and validated by IFSTA. As a secondary function, Fire Protection Publications researches, acquires, produces, and markets high-quality learning and teaching aids consistent with IFSTA's mission.

IFSTA holds two meetings each year: the Winter Meeting in January and the Annual Validation Conference in July. During these meetings, committees of technical experts review draft materials and ensure that the professional qualifications of the National Fire Protection Association® standards are met. These conferences bring together individuals from several related and allied fields, such as:

- Key fire department executives, training officers, and personnel
- Educators from colleges and universities
- Representatives from governmental agencies
- Delegates of firefighter associations and industrial organizations

Committee members are not paid nor are they reimbursed for their expenses by IFSTA or Fire Protection Publications. They participate because of a commitment to the fire service and its future through training. Being on a committee is prestigious in the fire service community, and committee members are acknowledged leaders in their fields. This unique feature provides a close relationship between IFSTA and the fire service community.

IFSTA manuals have been adopted as the official teaching texts of many states and provinces of North America as well as numerous U.S. and Canadian government agencies. Besides the NFPA® requirements, IFSTA manuals are also written to meet the Fire and Emergency Services Higher Education (FESHE) course requirements. A number of the manuals have been translated into other languages to provide training for fire and emergency service personnel in Canada, Mexico, and outside of North America.

Copyright © 2014 by the Board of Regents, Oklahoma State University

All rights reserved. No part of this publication may be reproduced in any form without prior written permission from the publisher.

ISBN 978-0-87939-568-1   Library of Congress Control Number: 2014942512

Third Edition, First Printing, July 2014   *Printed in the United States of America*

10   9   8   7   6   5   4   3   2

If you need additional information concerning the International Fire Service Training Association (IFSTA) or Fire Protection Publications, contact:

Customer Service, Fire Protection Publications, Oklahoma State University
930 North Willis, Stillwater, OK 74078-8045
800-654-4055   Fax: 405-744-8204

For assistance with training materials, to recommend material for inclusion in an IFSTA manual, or to ask questions or comment on manual content, contact:

Editorial Department, Fire Protection Publications, Oklahoma State University
930 North Willis, Stillwater, OK 74078-8045
405-744-4111   Fax: 405-744-4112   E-mail: editors@osufpp.org

Oklahoma State University in compliance with Title VI of the Civil Rights Act of 1964 and Title IX of the Educational Amendments of 1972 (Higher Education Act) does not discriminate on the basis of race, color, national origin or sex in any of its policies, practices or procedures. This provision includes but is not limited to admissions, employment, financial aid and educational services.

Chapter Summary

Chapter 1 World of the Chief Officer 10
2 Human Resources Management 42
3 Community and Government Relations 96
4 Emergency Services Administration 136
5 Fire Inspection and Safety Planning 212
6 Emergency Services Delivery 234
7 Emergency Services Health, Safety, and Wellness 272
8 Emergency Management 298

[Handwritten note: Exclude 114-135]

Appendices

A NFPA® 1021 Job Performance Requirements (JPRs) with Chapter and
Page References 318
B 16 Firefighter Life Safety Initiatives 320
C Sample Justification Form 321
D SCBA Survey Form 322
E Sample RFP/RFQs 325
F Equipment Evaluation Form 328
G Model Building and Fire Codes 330
H Formula for Calculating Frequency and Severity 331

Glossary 335
Index 337

Table of Contents

Acknowledgments xi
Introduction xv
Background 2
Requirements 3
Purpose and Scope 4
Key Information 5
Metric Conversions 6

1 World of the Chief Officer 10
Case History 13
Making the Transition 13
Characteristics of a Successful Chief Officer ... 14
    Ethics 14
        Ethical Conduct 15
        Personal Ethics Origins 15
        Causes of Unethical Conduct 15
        Personal Justifications 16
        Ethical Issues 18
    Leadership 18
        Leadership vs. Management 19
        Leadership Theory: The Principled Leader ... 20
        Applying Leadership Theory 20
        Good Leader Traits 22
    Challenges and Solutions 23
        Proactive Leadership 24
        Problem Solving 24
        Politics 24
        Foresight 24
        Criticism 25
        Decisions 25
Professional Standards of Conduct 25
Education and Training 27
Experience vs. Experiences 29
    Experience 29
    Experiences 29
Best Practices Application 29
    Current Management Theory 29
        Quantitative Management 30
        Organizational Behavior 30
        Systems Theory 30
        Contingency Theory 30
        Total Quality Management 31
        Organizational Culture 32
    Fire Service Leadership Best Practices ... 32
        Forecasting and Trending 32
        Environmental Scanning 32
        Technology Awareness 33
        Innovation 33
        Research, Analysis, and Evaluation 34
Successful Change Management 34
        Change Types 35
        Resistance to Change 35
        Process Implementation 36
        Follow-up Program Plan 38
Executive Level Communications 38
    Keys to Good Communications 39
    Controversy Avoidance 40
Chapter Summary 40
Review Questions 40

2 Human Resources Management 42
Case History 45
Emergency Services Staffing 45
    Planning 46
        Projecting Needs 46
        Anticipating Challenges 47
    Staffing Requirements 48
    Staffing Assignments 49
Employment Practices 50
    Laws Affecting Employment 50
    Human Resources Policies and Procedures ... 51
    Employee Disabilities and Accommodations ... 52
        Legal Requirements and Reasonable Accommodations 52
        Fitness for Duty Considerations 52
    Job Analyses and Position Descriptions ... 53
    Recruitment 54
        Recruiting Sources 54
        Recruiting and Attracting Diverse Workforces ... 55
        Position Marketing and Posting 56
        Employment Process 58
        Application Form 58
        Background Screening/Investigation and Reference Check 58
        Tests 58
        Interview 59
        Medical-fitness examination 62
    Applicant Selection 62
    Promotions 63
    Employee Benefits 65
        Benefit Needs Analysis 66
        Improving or Modifying Benefits 67
Separation and Termination 67
        Line-of-Duty Death 67
        Disability 68

   Termination 68
   Retirement 69
   Exit Interview 69
Professional Development and Continuing Education 70
  Higher Education 70
   Levels of Education 70
   Types of Degree Programs 71
  Professional Organizations 72
  Personal Professional Development 73
  Succession Planning 73
  Credentialing 73
   Executive Fire Officer Program (EFOP) 74
   Chief Officer Designations 74
  Continuing Education 74
   Training Program Development 74
   Agency Mission and Goals 75
   Needs Assessments 75
IV Human Resources Demographics Appraisal 76
  External Community Demographics 76
  Internal Organizational Demographics 77
  Diversity Barriers 78
  Affirmative Action Programs 78
  Workplace Diversity Initiative 79
   Organize for Change 80
   Identify the Current Organizational Culture 80
   Raise Cultural Awareness 80
   Manage Diversity 81
   Evaluate Program Progress and Success 81
Labor Relations 82
  Negotiation Process 82
   Open Communications 83
   Bargaining Session Schedule 84
   Contract Content 84
   Representation 85
   Preparation 85
   Proposal Presentation 85
   Contract Issues 85
   Impasses 86
   Employee Involvement and Participation 87
  Incentive Programs 88
Training and Education Goals 89
  Determining Needs 89
  Assessing Resources 90
Member Assistance Services 91
  Behavioral Health Program 91
  Member Assistance Programs 92
  Local, State/Provincial, and Federal Regulations 93
  Program Appraisal 93

Chapter Summary 93
Review Questions 94

3 Community and Government Relations ... 96
Case History 99
III Service Delivery 100
  Systems-Model Approach 100
  Comprehensive-Risk Approach 101
  Types of Fire and Emergence Services 101
  Monitoring Service Delivery 103
Community Awareness Programs 103
  Community Relations Strategies 104
   Language Barriers 104
   Cultural Customs 105
   Cultural Values 105
  Public Relations 105
   Public Information Officer 105
   Media Relations 107
   Social Media 109
  Public Fire and Life Safety Education 109
   Purpose and Scope 109
   Group Presentations 111
   Media Programs 111
  Concerns/Complaints/Inquiries 112
   Concern/Complaint Resolution 113
   Member Act/Omission Resolutions 113
   Public Inquiries 114
   Customer Service 114
IV Participation in the Political Arena 114
  Public Awareness and Acceptance 115
  Government Acceptance 116
  Interagency Relations 117
   Jurisdictions 118
   Fire and Emergency Services Organizations 118
   State/Provincial and Local Law-Enforcement Agencies 119
   Federal Law Enforcement Agencies 120
   Federal Agencies 121
  Intergovernmental Agreements 122
Political Decision-Making Process 122
  Political Processes 112
   Responsibility of Government Officials 123
   Concept of Governing 124
   Influence of the Public 124
  Political Relationships 126
   Political Neutrality 126
   Guidelines for Dealing with Government Officials 126

Political Resources 127
    Communication *127*
    Public Relations *127*
    Educational Information *128*
Legislation Monitoring **128**
  Local 129
  State/Provincial 129
  Federal 129
Community Involvement **130**
  Community Leadership 130
  Decision-Making and Goals-Setting
    Functions 130
  Partnerships and Programs 132
    Partnerships *132*
    Programs *132*
Chapter Summary **134**
Review Questions **135**

4   Emergency Services Administration 136
Case History **139**
III Public Budgeting and Finance **140**
  Budget Systems and Types 140
    Budget Systems *140*
    Budgets Types *142*
  Budget Considerations 144
    Facilities *144*
    Equipment *145*
    Apparatus *145*
    Maintenance *145*
    Personnel *145*
    Training and Professional Development *145*
  Revenue Sources 145
    Taxes *146*
    Memberships/Subscriptions *147*
    Trust Funds *147*
    Enterprise Funds *148*
    Bonds *148*
    Grants/Gifts *148*
    Fund-Raisers *149*
  Budget Development and Management 149
    Plan *150*
    Prepare *150*
    Implement *153*
    Monitor *154*
    Evaluate *155*
    Revise *155*
Purchasing **155**
  Needs Assessment 156
  Research 157
    Survey Other Jurisdictions *157*
    Review Manufacturers' Business Histories *157*
    Request References *158*
    Review Standards and Regulations *158*
    Review Industry Trends *158*
    Compare Various Products *158*
    Determine Equipment Compatibility *159*
    Review Purchasing Ordinances and Laws *159*
    Develop Request for Proposal, Qualifications,
      or Information *159*
  Product Evaluation 160
  Review Product Data 161
  Acquisition Process 162
    Funding Sources *163*
    Bid Specifications *164*
    Evaluate and Score Proposals *166*
    Award *166*
  Standardization 167
Record-Keeping Function **167**
  Record Types 167
    Budget *167*
    Inventory *168*
    Maintenance *168*
    Activity *168*
    Personnel *169*
  Record Development 170
    Define Requirements *170*
    Plan *171*
    Testing and Implementation *171*
    Complete *172*
  Evaluation 172
  Revision 172
  Legal Requirements 172
    Record Types *173*
    Retention *173*
    Privacy *173*
    Public Access *174*
  Data Analysis and Interpretation 175
Organizational Improvement **176**
  Needs Analysis 176
    Community Needs *176*
    Department Capabilities *176*
  Gap Analysis 176
  SWOT Analysis 177
  Planning 178
    Benchmarks *178*
    Code Requirements *179*
    Staffing *179*
    Response Times *180*
    Local, State/Provincial, and Federal
      Regulations *180*

IV Strategic Planning 180
- Planning Process 180
- Development 181
- Implementation 182
- Monitoring 182
- Evaluation 182
- Annual Reports 183
- Revisions 183

Operational Planning 183
- Short-Term 184
- Intermediate-Term 184
  - *Preventive Maintenance* 185
  - *Reorganization* 185
  - *Resource Allocation* 185
  - *Equipment Replacement* 185
- Long-Term 185
  - *Codes and Standards* 186
  - *Capital Improvements* 186
  - *Real Estate* 186
  - *Apparatus Replacement* 187
  - *Staffing Needs* 188

Training Requirements 188
- Evaluation of Requirements 188
  - *Legal Mandates* 189
  - *Building and Fire Codes* 189
  - *Training Standards* 189
  - *Community Needs* 189
  - *Hazards Assessment* 189
  - *Risk Analysis* 190
- Program Development 190
  - *Program Design* 191
  - *Course Selection* 194
  - *Facility Types* 195
  - *Personnel* 201
  - *Scheduling* 202
- Sources of Funding 204
- External Training Sources 204
  - *Colleges/Universities* 204
  - *North American Fire Training Associations* ...205
  - *Regional Training Programs* 205
  - *Seminars* 205
  - *National Courses/Curriculum* 205
  - *Private Sources* 206
- Training Program Evaluation 206

Community Risk Assessment and Reduction 206
- Hazard Categories 207
  - *Behavioral* 207
  - *Intentional* 208
  - *Natural* 208
  - *Occupancy Related* 208

- High Value/Priority Exposures 209
- Creating a Written Analysis 209
- Creating a Community Risk Reduction Program 210

Chapter Summary 210
Review Questions 211

5 Fire Inspection and Safety Planning 212
Case History 215
III Fire Prevention and Life Safety Planning 216
- Needs Identification 218
- Program Selection 220
  - *Legal Mandates* 221
  - *Data Collection* 221
- Program Design 222
  - *Approvals* 222
  - *Alternatives* 223
- Implementation 223
  - *Organizational Structure* 223
  - *Resource Allocation* 223
  - *Personnel Selection* 224
- Evaluation 224
  - *Data Monitoring* 224
  - *Indicators* 225

Fire Inspection Programs 226
- Selection and Design 227
  - *Inspection/Enforcement* 227
  - *Plans Review* 228
  - *Building Code Enforcement* 229
- Alternatives 229
- Implementation 230
- Evaluation/Revision 231
- Public Awareness and Acceptance 231

Chapter Summary 232
Review Questions 232

6 Emergency Services Delivery 234
Case History 237
III Resource Planning 239
- Mutual and Automatic Aid Agreements 239
  - *Mutual Aid* 239
  - *Automatic Aid* 239
- Joint Training Requirements 239

Incident Action Plan 240
- IAP Development 242
  - *Understand the Situation* 242
  - *Identify the Incident Priorities* 242
  - *Determine the Incident Objectives* 243
  - *Develop the Plan* 243

  Prepare and Disseminate the Plan 243
  Execute, Evaluate, and Revise the Plan..........243
 IAP Forms 243
Post Incident Analysis 244
 Types of Post Incident Analysis 245
  Informal 245
  Formal 245
 Development Procedures 246
  Implementation 246
  Monitor, Evaluate, Revise 246
 Incident Data 247
  Evolution of the Incident 247
  Safety Issues 247
 PIA Critique 248
 Recommended Changes 248
 Documentation 248
  Incident Reports 248
  Informal Debriefing Records 248
  Critique Records 248
  Reimbursement Logs 248
  Records Management 249
 Final Reports 249
IV Comprehensive Disaster Plan 249
 Disaster Types 250
  Natural 251
  Human-Caused 252
  Technological 254
 Interagency Relations 254
 Jurisdictional Authority 254
 Emergency Operations Center 256
 Resource Allocation 256
 Plan Implementation 257
 Incident Termination 258
 Recovery and Rehabilitation 259
  Security 259
  Debris Removal 259
  Restoration of Services 259
Incident Management System 260
 Components/Operational Positions 260
  Command 261
  Operations 262
  Planning 262
  Logistics 262
  Finance/Administration 263
 Integrated Communications 263
 Unified and Area Commands 263
  Developing Unified Command Systems 265
  Implementing Unified Command Systems.....267
  Monitoring, Evaluating, Revising Unified
   Command Systems..................................268

  Reporting on Unified Command Systems.......269
  Operating within Unified Command
   Systems 269
Chapter Summary 270
Review Questions 270

7 Emergency Services Health, Safety, and Wellness 272
Case History 275
III Health and Safety Program Development 276
 Occupational Safety and Health Committee ... 277
 Health and Safety Officer Roles and
  Responsibilities 278
 Health and Safety Program Components 278
Accident, Injury, and Illness Prevention
Program 279
 Hazards/Corrective Measures
  Identification 279
  Fatalities 280
  Injuries 282
  Occupational Illness 283
  Motor Vehicle-Related Incidents 283
  Hearing Loss 284
  Respiratory Injury or Illness 285
  Hazardous Materials Exposure 286
 Program Implementation 286
 Program Monitoring, Evaluation,
  and Revision 288
IV Risk Management Plan 288
 Risk Management Model 289
 Occupational Hazards Analysis 290
 Personnel Risk Analysis 291
  Risk Identification 291
  Risk Evaluation 291
  Risk Prioritization 292
  Risk-Control Techniques 292
Plan Implementation Procedures 293
 Implementation 293
 Monitoring 294
 Evaluation 294
 Revision 295
 System Safety Program 295
Chapter Summary 296
Review Questions 296

8 Emergency Management......................... 298
Case History 301
III Principles of Emergency Management 302
 Emergency Management Concepts 303
  Interagency 303
  Intergovernmental 304

Interoperability *304*
　　　Interdisciplinary *305*
　Four Phases of Emergency Management 305
　　　Mitigation *305*
　　　Preparedness *307*
　　　Response *308*
　　　Recovery *309*
　Emergency Declaration Process 310
Resource Integration **310**
　Types of Resources 311
　　　Fire Service *311*
　　　Law Enforcement *312*
　　　Emergency Medical Services (EMS) ...*312*
　　　Public Works *312*
　　　Community Resources *312*
　　　State/Provincial Resources *313*
　　　Federal Resources *313*
　Integration Planning 314

Emergency Operations Centers (EOCs) 314
Chapter Summary 316
Review Questions 316

Appendices **317**
A　NFPA® 1021 Job Performance Requirements (JPRS) with Chapter and Page References... 318
B　The 16 Firefighter Life Safety Initiatives....... 320
C　Sample Justification Form............................. 321
D　SCBA Survey Form.. 322
E　Sample Request for Proposal 325
F　Equipment Evaluation Form.......................... 328
G　Model Building and Fire Codes..................... 330
H　Formula for Calculating Frequency and Severity of Risk 331

Glossary **335**
Index **337**

List of Tables

Table 6.1	Common ICS Forms and Their Purposes	244
Table 7.1	On-duty Firefighter Fatalities (1977-2012)	282
Table 7.2a	Fire-Related Firefighter Injuries by Cause of Injury (2006-2008)	284
Table 7.2b	Percent of Fire-Related Firefighter Injuries by Gender (2006-2008)	284
Table 8.1	Emergency Support Functions and Primary Responsible Federal Departments/Agencies	308
Table 8.2	Federal Resources Deployable in a Disaster	315

Acknowledgements

The third edition of the IFSTA **Chief Officer** manual is written to assist fire and emergency services personnel in meeting the job performance requirements of National Fire Protection Association® (NFPA®) 1021, *Standard for Fire Officer Professional Qualifications* (2014). This manual is intended to provide the basic level of knowledge that is required for Level III and Level IV Fire Officers who perform the duties of administrative and department chief. It should be understood that this manual is intended to be the foundation for professional development and that additional reading and course work is highly recommended for those officers who aspire to upper level chief officer ranks of the fire and emergency services.

Acknowledgement and special thanks are extended to the members of the IFSTA validating committee. The following members contributed their time, wisdom, and knowledge to the development of this manual:

IFSTA Chief Officer, Third Edition
IFSTA Validation Committee

Committee Chair
Dennis Compton
Mesa, Arizona

Committee Members

Stephen M. Ashbrock
Madeira and Indian Hill Joint Fire District
Cincinnati, Ohio

Shawn Bayouth
Ames Fire Department
Ames, Iowa

Roxanne Bercik
Los Angeles Fire Department
Long Beach, California

Jason Caughey
Laramie County Fire District #2
Cheyenne, Wyoming

Glenn Davis
Helena (MT) Fire Department
Helena, Montana

Richard Dunn
South Carolina Fire Academy
Columbia, South Carolina

CJ Haberkorn
Denver Fire Department
Denver, Colorado

Anthony Huemann
McHenry Township Fire Protection District
McHenry, Illinois

Tom Jenkins
Rogers Fire Department
Rogers, Arkansas

Kevan Jess
Government of Alberta
Edmonton, Alberta, Canada

Scott Kerwood
Hutto Fire Rescue
Hutto, Texas

Danny Kistner
McKinney Fire Department
McKinney, Texas

Frank Kodzis
Boston Fire Department
Dorchester, Massachusetts

Robert Kronenberger
Middletown Fire Department
Middletown, Connecticut

IFSTA Chief Officer
Third Edition IFSTA Validation Committee
continued

Dean Maggos
Village of La Grange Park
La Grange Park, Illinois

Laurent McDonald
Monson Fire Department
Monson, Massachusetts

Michael McLaughlin
City Of Merced Fire Department
Merced, California

Mark Pare
Massachusetts Department of Fire Services
Plainville, Massachusetts

Edward Richards
Enfield Fire District No. 1
Enfield, Connecticut

Thomas Saxton
North Slope Borough Fire Department
Barrow, Alaska

Steve Westermann
Central Jackson County Fire Protection District
Blue Springs, Missouri

Lynn Wojcik
Yuma, Arizona

The following individuals contributed their assistance and comments as reviewers for this manual:

Niko King, Assistant Chief
Sacramento Fire Department
Sacramento, CA

Earl Provencher, Chief
North Thompsonville Fire Department
Enfield, CT

The following individuals and organizations contributed information, photographs, and other assistance that made completion of this manual possible:

Bob Esposito
Ron Jeffers
Mike Wieder

Edmond Fire Department, Edmond, Oklahoma
    Jake Rhoades, Fire Chief
    Jon Neely, Chief Training Officer /Assistant Fire Chief
    Joe Elam, Training Officer
    Doug Hall, Battalion Chief
    Jerry Harwell, Captain
    Jason Hazzard, Lieutenant
    Benjamin A. Young, Lieutenant
    John D. Block
    Dustin Bowman
    Jeff Fountain
    Lindall Wood

International Association of Fire Chiefs (IAFC)
    Jacqueline S. Garnier

National Fire Protection Association® (NFPA®)

New Orleans Fire Department, New Orleans, Louisiana
    Chris Mickal, District Chief

Oklahoma State University Fire Service Training, Stillwater, Oklahoma
    Jason Louthan

Owasso Fire Department, Owasso, Oklahoma
    Chris Garrett, Fire Chief
    Mark Stuckey, Assistant Fire Chief
    Bruce Kelly, Emergency Medical Services Manager
    Matthew Morton, Captain/Acting Battalion Chief
    Mickey Lewis, Captain
    Danise Stanley, Administrative Assistant
    Joshua Berk
    Patrick Bladen
    Scott Graybill
    David Huist
    Kip A. Jennings
    Daniel Johnson

Kevin Lawson
Jarrod Linthiccim
Matt Trout
Steph Wagner
Eric York

Perkins Fire Department, Perkins, Oklahoma
    Bill Hunt, Assistant Chief
    John Konrad, Captain

Stillwater Fire Department, Stillwater, Oklahoma
    Tom Bradley, Fire Chief
    Rick Hauf, Assistant Fire Chief
    Robert Black, Training Officer
    Mike Eytcheson, Captain
    Mike Wilda, Lieutenant
    Dustan Portman
    Greg Scheihing
    Josh Spence

Tulsa Fire Department, Tulsa, Oklahoma
    Steve Gage, Deputy Chief
    Stacy Belk, Chief of Training
    Mike Mallory, Chief of Physical Resources
    Mike Bailey, Assistant Chief
    Glenn Brigan, District Chief
    Nate Morgans, District Chief
    Lee A. Horst, Jr., Captain
    Stan May, Captain
    Chad Meyer, Captain
    Robert Peters, Captain
    Alec Ridener, Captain
    Ben Weaver, Captain
    Jon T. Wintle, Captain
    Heather Greenwood, EMS Officer
    Jerry Camp, FireFighter
    Bennie Jay Herring, FireFighter
    Scott Moeller, FireFighter
    Lisa Mosley, Administrative Assistant

United States Fire Administration

Additionally, gratitude is extended to the following members of the Fire Protection Publications **Chief Officer Project Team** whose contributions made the final publication of this manual possible:

Chief Officer Project Team

Project Managers/Staff Liaison/Writer
Fred Stowell, Senior Editor
Jeff Fortney, Senior Editor
Mike Sturzenbecker, Senior Editor

Editors
Jeff Fortney, Senior Editor/Photographer
Clint Clausing, Senior Editor
Leslie Miller, Senior Editor
Alex Abrams, Senior Editor/Photographer
Veronica Smith, Senior Editor/Photographer

Lead Instructional Developer
Brad McLelland

Technical Reviewers
Niko King, Assistant Chief
Sacramento Fire Department
Sacramento, CA

Earl Provencher, Chief
North Thompsonville Fire Department
Enfield, CT

Proofreader
Veronica Smith, Senior Editor

Production Manager
Ann Moffat

Illustrators and Layout Designers
Errick Bragg, Senior Graphic Designer
Missy Hannan, Senior Graphics Designer
Clint Parker, Senior Graphic Designer

Library Researcher
Susan F. Walker, Librarian

Editorial Assistant
Tara Gladden

Indexer
Nancy Kopper

The IFSTA Executive Board at the time of validation of the **Chief Officer, 3rd Edition**, was as follows:

IFSTA Executive Board

Executive Board Chair

Steve Ashbrock
Fire Chief
Madeira & Indian Hill Fire Department
Cincinnati, OH

Vice Chair

Bradd Clark
Fire Chief
Ocala Fire Department
Ocala, FL

IFSTA Executive Director

Mike Wieder
Associate Director
Fire Protection Publications at OSU
Stillwater, OK

Board Members

Steve Austin
Past President
Cumberland Valley Volunteer FF Association
Newark, DE

Claude Beauchamp
Director
Institute of Emergency and Judicial Services
Ottawa, Canada

Roxanne Bercik
Deputy Chief of Training and Support Bureau
Los Angeles Fire Department
Los Angeles, CA

Mary Cameli
Assistant Chief
City of Mesa Fire Department
Mesa, AZ

Chief Dennis Compton
Chairman
National Fallen Firefighters Foundation
Mesa, AZ

John Cunningham
Executive Director
Nova Scotia Firefighter's School
Waverly, NS, Canada

John Hoglund
Director Emeritus
Maryland Fire & Rescue Institute
New Carrollton, MD

Wes Kitchel
Assistant Chief
Sonoma County Fire & Emergency Services
Cloverdale, CA

Brett Lacey
Fire Marshal
Colorado Springs Fire Department
Colorado Springs, CO

Lori Moore-Merrell
Assistant to the General President
International Association of Fire Fighters
Washington, DC

Jeff Morrissette
State Fire Administrator
State of Connecticut Commission on Fire Prevention
and Control
Windsor Locks, CT

Josh Stefancic
Assistant Chief
City of Largo Fire Department
Largo, FL

Paul Valentine
Senior Engineer
Nexus Engineering
Oakbrook, IL

Steven Westermann
Fire Chief
Central Jackson County Fire Protection District
Blue Springs, MO

Introduction

Introduction Contents

Introduction 1	Purpose and Scope 4
Background 2	Key Information 5
Requirements 3	Metric Conversions 6

Introduction

The National Fire Protection Association® (NFPA®) Standard 1021, *Standard for Fire Officer Professional Qualifications* (2014), defines the skills and knowledge needed to perform the tasks generally assigned to fire and emergency services officers. Ranks normally associated with these officer levels vary throughout North America. For instance, a Fire Officer I in one department may be referred to as a Lieutenant while another department uses the term Captain. Likewise, a Battalion/District Chief may be a Level II or even a Level III, depending on the size and organization of the department.

Because of these variations, the title of *Chief Officer* may not match the levels described in NFPA® 1021. Even the path that a fire service member takes to attain the position of chief officer will vary. For the purpose of this manual, Chief Officer will be associated with the duties assigned to the NFPA® Level III and Level IV Fire Officer.

The environment in which the fire and emergency services operate continues to change drastically. Fire and emergency service organizations of all types must continually find ways to meet the challenges of this new environment. The fire and emergency service must prepare for changing economic, political, cultural, demographic, social, and technological circumstances. In addition, the expectations of the public make it imperative that the fire and emergency service becomes proactive in its approach to involving the community in planning new initiatives. The department chief and other chief officers of the administrative, operational, and management teams are responsible for ensuring that the organization stays ahead of the changes faced by the fire service. It is essential that members who hold positions as chief officers have the experience, knowledge, skills, and leadership ability to effectively manage their fire and emergency services organizations.

The reasons that motivate individuals to become chief officers are as wide and varied as the makeup of the fire and emergency service. A few reasons that are mentioned are as follows:

- ***Desire to make a difference*** — Being an agent of change both in the community and in the organization
- ***Desire to serve others*** — Motivation that may have influenced the initial decision to join the fire and emergency service organization
- ***Desire to succeed*** — Continuing advancement to higher ranks (a sign of success in the fire service)

- ***Commitment to the fire and emergency service organization and the community*** — Sense of professionalism that tends to develop over the career of a firefighter or emergency service responder
- ***Desire to do the right thing*** — Opportunity the chief officer position provides to do what is viewed as ethically correct
- ***Feeling of loyalty and responsibility*** — Strong motivator: loyalty to the membership, the organization, the profession, and the community or service area
- ***Desire for personal growth*** — Promotion into the chief officer ranks results in a sense of personal fulfillment
- ***Sense of stewardship*** — Understanding that being a chief officer involves taking responsibility for the organization, maintaining and improving it, and leaving it better than it was before
- ***Desire to meet new challenges*** — First in the physical challenges of the emergency scene and later in the organizational challenges of management (the fire and emergency service is a challenging career)

Each of these reasons, along with others, can play a major role in the decision to become a chief officer. Some reasons are the result of a strong self-awareness, while others are based on a sense of purpose or duty. They may also be a function of Maslow's Hierarchy of Need that describes the development of the individual through stages. Many of the chief officers in the fire and emergency service share these motivations. They also share something else: They are dedicated leaders.

Competent, committed leaders are essential to the current and future success of the fire service. *Leadership* involves a consistent commitment to a vision held by the chief officer and shared with the rest of the organization and community. The *vision,* a statement that is focused on future results, is based on integrity and ethical conduct. Leadership does not occur alone; followers who believe in the vision, the organizational leadership, and the ability to fulfill that vision must support it. Without this foundation, the vision will remain only a dream.

The primary purpose of this manual is to provide all chief officers (regardless of the type of organization or position held within the organization) with a framework for the basic knowledge and skills necessary to lead their organizations and fulfill the vision. This manual's purpose is also to provide company officers and chief officer candidates with the motivation and tools to achieve promotions and ensure a professional and well-trained officer corps. Finally, this manual can provide any fire and emergency services organization with an overview of the knowledge and skills required to lead and manage it.

Background

The selection and promotion of chief officers who have the education, experience, and training necessary to manage and lead the organization are critical elements to success in the fire and emergency service. Whether volunteer, combination, or career fire and emergency service organizations, selecting chief officers for reasons other than their abilities to lead and manage the organization is not in the best interest of the organization, the membership, or the service area it protects. The selection or promotion of anyone who does not have these abilities is also not beneficial to the fire and emergency services. Over the past 70 years, the shift toward a more professional and institutionalized fire and emergency service has resulted in changes in how chief officers are selected and promoted. The motivations for these changes include the following:

- Expansion of service demands beyond fire suppression
- Increased emphasis on education
- Effects of economic recessions
- Demand for better business practices in public sector organizations
- Influence of organized labor groups
- Emphasis on increased credibility and validity of the promotional process
- Emphasis on better government
- Requirement to provide equal access to promotions

Positive changes in the promotional process have developed within the fire and emergency service. In particular, the joint initiatives developed by the International Association of Fire Fighters (IAFF) and the International Association of Fire Chiefs (IAFC) have produced positive effects. In addition, the principles of fairness and equal opportunity in the hiring and promotional processes have developed, and groups who were formerly excluded from full participation (such as women and racial and ethnic minorities) have increasingly filled the ranks of the fire service. The performance of chief officers has been enhanced by educational criteria, promotional examinations, assessment centers, annual fitness and performance reviews, and time-in-grade requirements. Many of these changes are due to the development of NFPA®1021, *Standard for Fire Officer Professional Qualifications*, one of the fire and emergency services professional qualifications documents. Originally produced in 1976, the standard has evolved to its current form. NFPA® 1021 establishes the job performance requirements (JPRs) for all fire officers from company officer to the department chief. This standard has provided the guidelines for a transition from the company officer who is responsible for tactical operations and single-company supervision to the chief officer who focuses on strategic objectives and large-scale operations and projects.

Requirements

To meet the requirements of NFPA® 1021, chief officers and chief officer candidates must possess certain prerequisite knowledge and skills to perform the job performance requirements contained in the six duties or functions outlined in the standard. These duties or functions include the following:

- Human resources management
- Community and government interaction
- Administration
- Inspection and investigation
- Emergency services delivery
- Health and safety awareness

Each of these duties is a broad category that contains one or more JPRs. To fulfill the JPRs, the chief officer must have a knowledge base that is specific to the local jurisdiction. The authority having jurisdiction requires candidates for chief-officer positions to acquire this knowledge. The candidates may acquire the knowledge through experience or self-directed studies of the jurisdiction's laws, codes, ordinances, policies, and procedures. No single manual or textbook could provide this type of knowledge due to the wide variations found in communities across North America.

The skills that a chief officer must possess are also general but can be reduced to the following seven basic skills:

- Interacting interpersonally
- Writing
- Speaking
- Researching
- Analyzing
- Evaluating
- Organizing

While these are topics normally found in formal educational programs (usually at the college level), some general concepts can be provided in a single document. When applied to the JPRs, they can give the chief officer or candidate the foundation needed to efficiently perform the duties of the respective position. This manual provides a general overview of some these skills. **Appendix A** contains the complete listing of NFPA® 1021 Job Performance Requirements for Levels III and IV. In addition, other topics not included in the JPRs are also discussed, including ethics, management, leadership, and decision-making. Each chapter includes appropriate case histories, key information, and personal experiences. Appendices and a glossary that contain additional information and samples of materials that support the topics are also included.

Purpose and Scope

The *purpose* of IFSTA **Chief Officer, 3rd** edition, is to provide the necessary basic skills for Fire Officer III and IV personnel and candidates to meet the minimum job performance requirements as defined in NFPA® 1021, *Standard for Fire Officer Professional Qualifications* (2014), Levels III and IV.

The *scope* of this manual is to provide chief officers and chief officer candidates with the basic skills and knowledge to supervise, manage, and administer fire and emergency services organizations.

Key Information

Various types of information in this book are given in shaded boxes marked by symbols or icons. See the following definitions:

Case History

A case history analyzes an event. It can describe its development, action taken, investigation results, and lessons learned.

Information

Information boxes give facts that are complete in themselves but belong with the text discussion. It is information that needs more emphasis or separation. (In the text, the title of information boxes will change to reflect the content.)

A **key term** is designed to emphasize key concepts, technical terms, or ideas that chief officers need to know. The key terms are listed at the beginning of each chapter and the definition is placed in the margin for easy reference. An example of a key term is:

Two key signal words are found in the book: **CAUTION** and **NOTE.** Definitions and examples of each are as follows:

- **CAUTION** indicates important information or data that chief officers need to be aware of in order to perform their duties safely. See the following example:

Management — Process of accomplishing organizational objectives through effective and efficient handling of resources; official, sanctioned leadership.

CAUTION
The fire chief should be aware that manufacturer's specifications may be restrictive and violate the AHJ's competitive bidding requirements.

- **NOTE** indicates important operational information that helps explain why a particular recommendation is given or describes optional methods for certain procedures. See the following example:

NOTE: Organizations, such as the Insurance Services Office (ISO) Fire Suppression Rating Schedule (FSRS), the Fire Underwriter's Survey (in Canada), the National Institute of Standards and Technology (NIST), and the Center for Public Safety Excellence (CPSE), can assist with determining needed staffing requirements.

Metric Conversions

Throughout this manual, U.S. units of measure are converted to metric units for the convenience of our international readers. Be advised that we use the Canadian metric system. It is very similar to the Standard International system, but may have some variation.

We adhere to the following guidelines for metric conversions in this manual:

- Metric conversions are approximated unless the number is used in mathematical equations.
- Centimeters are not used because they are not part of the Canadian metric standard.
- Exact conversions are used when an exact number is necessary such as in construction measurements or hydraulic calculations.
- Set values such as hose diameter, ladder length, and nozzle size use their Canadian counterpart naming conventions and are not mathematically calculated. For example, 1½ inch hose is referred to as 38 mm hose.
- Add metric notes particular to your manual.

The following two tables provide detailed information on IFSTA's conversion conventions. The first table includes examples of our conversion factors for a number of measurements used in the fire service. The second shows examples of exact conversions beside the approximated measurements you will see in this manual. **(Tables on pp. 7 and 8.)**

U.S. to Canadian Measurement Conversion

Measurements	Customary (U.S.)	Metric (Canada)	Conversion Factor
Length/Distance	Inch (in) Foot (ft) [3 or less feet] Foot (ft) [3 or more feet] Mile (mi)	Millimeter (mm) Millimeter (mm) Meter (m) Kilometer (km)	1 in = 25 mm 1 ft = 300 mm 1 ft = 0.3 m 1 mi = 1.6 km
Area	Square Foot (ft^2) Square Mile (mi^2)	Square Meter (m^2) Square Kilometer (km^2)	1 ft^2 = 0.09 m^2 1 mi^2 = 2.6 km^2
Mass/Weight	Dry Ounce (oz) Pound (lb) Ton (T)	gram Kilogram (kg) Ton (T)	1 oz = 28 g 1 lb = 0.5 kg 1 T = 0.9 T
Volume	Cubic Foot (ft^3) Fluid Ounce (fl oz) Quart (qt) Gallon (gal)	Cubic Meter (m^3) Milliliter (mL) Liter (L) Liter (L)	1 ft^3 = 0.03 m^3 1 fl oz = 30 mL 1 qt = 1 L 1 gal = 4 L
Flow	Gallons per Minute (gpm) Cubic Foot per Minute (ft^3/min)	Liters per Minute (L/min) Cubic Meter per Minute (m^3/min)	1 gpm = 4 L/min 1 ft^3/min = 0.03 m^3/min
Flow per Area	Gallons per Minute per Square Foot (gpm/ft^2)	Liters per Square Meters Minute (L/(m^2.min))	1 gpm/ft^2 = 40 L/(m^2.min)
Pressure	Pounds per Square Inch (psi) Pounds per Square Foot (psf) Inches of Mercury (in Hg)	Kilopascal (kPa) Kilopascal (kPa) Kilopascal (kPa)	1 psi = 7 kPa 1 psf = .05 kPa 1 in Hg = 3.4 kPa
Speed/Velocity	Miles per Hour (mph) Feet per Second (ft/sec)	Kilometers per Hour (km/h) Meter per Second (m/s)	1 mph = 1.6 km/h 1 ft/sec = 0.3 m/s
Heat	British Thermal Unit (Btu)	Kilojoule (kJ)	1 Btu = 1 kJ
Heat Flow	British Thermal Unit per Minute (BTU/min)	watt (W)	1 Btu/min = 18 W
Density	Pound per Cubic Foot (lb/ft^3)	Kilogram per Cubic Meter (kg/m^3)	1 lb/ft^3 = 16 kg/m^3
Force	Pound-Force (lbf)	Newton (N)	1 lbf = 0.5 N
Torque	Pound-Force Foot (lbf ft)	Newton Meter (N.m)	1 lbf ft = 1.4 N.m
Dynamic Viscosity	Pound per Foot-Second (lb/ft.s)	Pascal Second (Pa.s)	1 lb/ft.s = 1.5 Pa.s
Surface Tension	Pound per Foot (lb/ft)	Newton per Meter (N/m)	1 lb/ft = 15 N/m

Conversion and Approximation Examples

Measurement	U.S. Unit	Conversion Factor	Exact S.I. Unit	Rounded S.I. Unit
Length/Distance	10 in	1 in = 25 mm	250 mm	250 mm
	25 in	1 in = 25 mm	625 mm	625 mm
	2 ft	1 in = 25 mm	600 mm	600 mm
	17 ft	1 ft = 0.3 m	5.1 m	5 m
	3 mi	1 mi = 1.6 km	4.8 km	5 km
	10 mi	1 mi = 1.6 km	16 km	16 km
Area	36 ft^2	1 ft^2 = 0.09 m^2	3.24 m^2	3 m^2
	300 ft^2	1 ft^2 = 0.09 m^2	27 m^2	30 m^2
	5 mi^2	1 mi^2 = 2.6 km^2	13 km^2	13 km^2
	14 mi^2	1 mi^2 = 2.6 km^2	36.4 km^2	35 km^2
Mass/Weight	16 oz	1 oz = 28 g	448 g	450 g
	20 oz	1 oz = 28 g	560 g	560 g
	3.75 lb	1 lb = 0.5 kg	1.875 kg	2 kg
	2,000 lb	1 lb = 0.5 kg	1 000 kg	1 000 kg
	1 T	1 T = 0.9 T	900 kg	900 kg
	2.5 T	1 T = 0.9 T	2.25 T	2 T
Volume	55 ft^3	1 ft^3 = 0.03 m^3	1.65 m^3	1.5 m^3
	2,000 ft^3	1 ft^3 = 0.03 m^3	60 m^3	60 m^3
	8 fl oz	1 fl oz = 30 mL	240 mL	240 mL
	20 fl oz	1 fl oz = 30 mL	600 mL	600 mL
	10 qt	1 qt = 1 L	10 L	10 L
	22 gal	1 gal = 4 L	88 L	90 L
	500 gal	1 gal = 4 L	2 000 L	2 000 L
Flow	100 gpm	1 gpm = 4 L/min	400 L/min	400 L/min
	500 gpm	1 gpm = 4 L/min	2 000 L/min	2 000 L/min
	16 ft^3/min	1 ft^3/min = 0.03 m^3/min	0.48 m^3/min	0.5 m^3/min
	200 ft^3/min	1 ft^3/min = 0.03 m^3/min	6 m^3/min	6 m^3/min
Flow per Area	50 gpm/ft^2	1 gpm/ft^2 = 40 L/(m^2.min)	2 000 L/(m^2.min)	2 000 L/(m^2.min)
	326 gpm/ft^2	1 gpm/ft^2 = 40 L/(m^2.min)	13 040 L/(m^2.min)	13 000 L/(m^2.min)
Pressure	100 psi	1 psi = 7 kPa	700 kPa	700 kPa
	175 psi	1 psi = 7 kPa	1225 kPa	1 200 kPa
	526 psf	1 psf = 0.05 kPa	26.3 kPa	25 kPa
	12,000 psf	1 psf = 0.05 kPa	600 kPa	600 kPa
	5 psi in Hg	1 psi = 3.4 kPa	17 kPa	17 kPa
	20 psi in Hg	1 psi = 3.4 kPa	68 kPa	70 kPa
Speed/Velocity	20 mph	1 mph = 1.6 km/h	32 km/h	30 km/h
	35 mph	1 mph = 1.6 km/h	56 km/h	55 km/h
	10 ft/sec	1 ft/sec = 0.3 m/s	3 m/s	3 m/s
	50 ft/sec	1 ft/sec = 0.3 m/s	15 m/s	15 m/s
Heat	1200 Btu	1 Btu = 1 kJ	1 200 kJ	1 200 kJ
Heat Flow	5 BTU/min	1 Btu/min = 18 W	90 W	90 W
	400 BTU/min	1 Btu/min = 18 W	7 200 W	7 200 W
Density	5 lb/ft^3	1 lb/ft^3 = 16 kg/m^3	80 kg/m^3	80 kg/m^3
	48 lb/ft^3	1 lb/ft^3 = 16 kg/m^3	768 kg/m^3	770 kg/m^3
Force	10 lbf	1 lbf = 0.5 N	5 N	5 N
	1,500 lbf	1 lbf = 0.5 N	750 N	750 N
Torque	100	1 lbf ft = 1.4 N.m	140 N.m	140 N.m
	500	1 lbf ft = 1.4 N.m	700 N.m	700 N.m
Dynamic Viscosity	20 lb/ft.s	1 lb/ft.s = 1.5 Pa.s	30 Pa.s	30 Pa.s
	35 lb/ft.s	1 lb/ft.s = 1.5 Pa.s	52.5 Pa.s	50 Pa.s
Surface Tension	6.5 lb/ft	1 lb/ft = 15 N/m	97.5 N/m	100 N/m
	10 lb/ft	1 lb/ft = 15 N/m	150 N/m	150 N/m

World of the Chief Officer

Chapter Contents

CASE HISTORY ... 13	Best Practices Application ... 29
Making the Transition ... 13	Current Management Theory ... 29
Characteristics of a Successful Chief Officer ... 14	Fire Service Leadership Best Practices ... 32
Ethics ... 14	Successful Change Management ... 34
Leadership ... 18	Executive Level Communications ... 38
Challenges and Solutions ... 23	Keys to Good Communications ... 39
Professional Standards of Conduct ... 25	Controversy Avoidance ... 40
Education and Training ... 27	Chapter Summary ... 40
Experience vs. Experiences ... 29	Review Questions ... 40
Experience ... 29	
Experiences ... 29	

Chapter 1

Key Terms

Leadership 13	Needs Assessment 34
Management 17	Risk Assessment 34

World of the Chief Officer

Learning Objectives

After reading this chapter, students will be able to:

1. Recognize various factors that influence the selection of a chief officer.
2. Identify characteristics of a successful chief officer.
3. Describe professional standards of conduct to which a chief officer must adhere.
4. Explain the roles that education and training play in preparing a chief officer to manage responsibilities.
5. Describe the differences between experience and experiences as they relate to the chief officer.
6. Identify various methods for applying best business practices as a chief officer.
7. Explain various skills needed for successful communication at the executive level.

Chapter 1
World of the Chief Officer

Case History

Leadership requires Fire Chiefs to continually evaluate current processes and procedures to verify that they are not only efficient and effective but meeting the overall goals of the organization. Recruit training is one of those areas.

A fire chief evaluated the overall recruit training program and noted 47 percent failure rate of entry level firefighters within the training academy. Training the average recruit firefighter was estimated to cost $35,000 for each recruit. Since 25 recruits failed, the deficient training cost the department approximately $875,000. Concerned with the financial loss, the Fire Chief took a proactive stance, directed staff to assess the current training practices, and determined a more effective methodology aimed to produce a higher graduation rate while still maintaining the department standards for training.

The new training methodology used a group interactive classroom format, scenario based emergency simulations, and adult learning concepts. The instructors at the academy were trained on the new teaching method. The academy instructors then trained the field training officers where the recruits would be assigned upon graduation. Additionally, a Quality Assurance unit was established for oversight of progress during the academy and the entire one year probationary period. Based on this new method, the graduation/retention rate increased to 85%.

Your first step toward becoming a chief officer occurred when you decided to be a firefighter. Your motivation may have been a desire to serve your community or make a career in a secure, yet challenging profession. Regardless of your reason, you have now decided to advance in rank, authority, and responsibility. You begin developing your **leadership** skills as a company officer. Other skills you used as a firefighter or company officer won't necessarily translate into being a good chief officer **(Figure 1.1, p. 14)**.

Leadership — Knack of getting other people to follow you and to do willingly the things that you want them to do.

This chapter introduces you to the roles and functions of a chief officer and provides fundamental knowledge that will help you make the transition. It also recognizes the need for and sources of requisite knowledge and minimizes the challenges that are associated with higher levels in the fire service.

Making the Transition

A major influence on your career will be the type of fire and emergency services organization to which you belong. Career and combination organizations promote chief officers through competitive internal examinations or through an external selection process based on an assessment of skills. Policies may determine who is eligible for promotion based on a number of factors: Total

Figure 1.1 Leadership skills are often developed when personnel serve as company officers.

service time, time in rank, education/training achievements, and time in certain divisions. Volunteer organizations may use competitive examinations, a selection process, or an election process.

Closely associated with the organization's policies is the table of organization (T/O) or organizational chart. Generally, all types of organizations have an established T/O that defines:

- Chain of command
- Authorized positions
- Relationships to superiors, subordinates, and peers
- Succession from one level to the next

Local laws and ordinances may regulate the promotion, selection, or election process. Fire and emergency services organizations may be subject to Civil Service laws or be exempt from them. In many municipalities, the fire department is specifically created, authorized, and organized by an article of the city charter. State/provincial laws may regulate volunteer organizations in a similar fashion.

Throughout your time in the fire service, you should continue to grow and strive for the next objective or goal. In order to accomplish this, you must have the right skills, knowledge, and abilities that you will need for each level. First, you should learn the characteristics of a successful chief officer.

Characteristics of a Successful Chief Officer

Like successful members of society, a successful chief officer must possess certain personal traits. We must be aware of these characteristics and continually develop them. Some of these characteristics are learned through exposure to role models found in family, peers, and observing our mentors and heroes. Others are developed through study and practice, or you may be born with them. We must be aware of the traits that define an exceptional chief officer and continually develop them.

Ethics

The members of society use ethics as a philosophical principle to determine correct and proper behavior. Without ethics, there would be chaos and civilization (or society) would dissolve. Unfortunately, the examples that tend to appear in the news media are often examples of the lack of ethical conduct. Compromising employment practices, improper vendor negotiations, inappropriate use of funds, criminal actions, sexual harassment, and racial/ethnic/gender discrimination are just some of the unethical activities that appear to have become commonplace in society.

Because the fire and emergency services are not immune to these activities, it is essential that you understand the importance of ethics. This section deals with ethical conduct in the fire and emergency services.

Ethical Conduct

Ethical standards express the level of conduct all members of society are expected to follow. They are statements of what is right and proper conduct for the individual in all relationships and activities. This conduct may involve relationships with others, the decision-making process, or simply choosing between *right* and *wrong*. Few decisions are as clear, and most involve many choices that fall into the *gray* range between the two extremes.

Because of the position of respect, honor, and public trust that fire and emergency service members hold, all such personnel should uphold a higher standard of ethical conduct than the general public. Negative headlines involving firefighters tend to get lots of public attention and can adversely affect the fire department's image.

Personal Ethics Origins

Ethics and ethical behavior are learned traits. They are transmitted to an individual from many sources. The primary source is the family, which instills personal values and morals. Other sources are organized religions, educational institutions, society, and peers **(Figure 1.2)**. The values that are instilled by these sources remain with us for life unless we consciously alter them. Examples of ethical values include the following:

- Honesty
- Integrity
- Impartiality
- Fairness
- Loyalty
- Dedication
- Responsibility
- Accountability
- Perseverance
- Frugality
- Faithfulness
- Heroism
- Patriotism

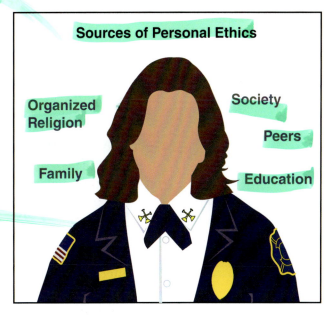

Figure 1.2 Personal ethics are derived from a variety of sources.

Causes of Unethical Conduct

There are many reasons for unethical conduct. The most common reasons include the following:

- ***Basic needs*** — Actions or statements that are intended to gain objects that fulfill an individual's basic needs.

- ***Affiliation*** — Actions or statements that are intended to create, prolong, or avoid social relationships.

- ***Self-esteem*** — Actions or statements that increase the perceived competence of an individual in the eyes of others.

- ***Self-gratification*** — Actions or statements that are intended to increase an individual's personal enjoyment.

Chief officers and other fire service leaders must understand what contributes to unethical behavior and consistently set a positive example for others to follow. The potential for unethical conduct is limitless and is often found in private enterprise. Researchers in private industry have documented the causes of unethical behavior in organizations. Some of these causes are summarized as follows:

- ***Behaviors that violate ethical standards*** — Bribery or payoffs to ensure that an organization is awarded a contract or is rewarded in the form of promotions, bonuses, gifts, trips, or employment. It is also unethical if the violations are not addressed in a prompt and effective manner.
- ***Bottom-line mentality*** — Making a profit does not motivate fire and emergency services; however, staying within the constraints of budgets can influence them. Examples:
    — Making the organization *look good on paper* to the political authority can create situations where unethical conduct may occur.
    — The *political bottom line* is where decisions are intended to influence the electorate in favor of a politician at the expense of the voters.
    — *Pork-barrel projects* are government expenditures that may have little or no real value other than to enhance the image of a politician and gain more votes.
- ***Exploitive mentality*** — An attitude that encourages people to use others in order to succeed. Examples include: telling lies about people, starting and spreading rumors, or taking credit for the labors of another person.

Personal Justifications

When an organization or society rewards unethical conduct, it is easy to understand how individuals engage in these activities. The individual accepts the benefits of such actions and then justifies them internally. Common justifications for unethical conduct include the following:

- Pretending that the action is legal or ethical
- Believing that the action is really in the best interest of the organization or individual
- Believing that the action is okay because no one will ever find out about it
- Expecting that the organization will support the action if it is ever discovered
- Believing that the action is acceptable because everyone else is doing it
- Believing that the end (result) justifies the means (method) even if the means are unethical

When the individual has justified or rationalized the unethical action internally, then it becomes easier to commit the action and any similar subsequent actions. To overcome these attitudes, the organization must create a culture that encourages and rewards ethical conduct and enforces a clear set of consequences for unethical conduct.

Code of Ethics: Fire Chiefs

The purpose of the International Association of Fire Chiefs (IAFC) is to actively support the advancement of the fire service. It is dedicated to the protection and preservation of life and property against fire and the provision of emergency medical services and other emergencies. Towards this endeavor, every member of the International Association of Fire Chiefs shall represent those ethical principles consistent with professional conduct as members of the IAFC:

- Recognize that we serve in a position of public trust that imposes responsibility to use publicly owned resources effectively and judiciously.
- Not use a public position to obtain advantages or favors for friends, family, personal business ventures, or ourselves.
- Use information gained from our positions only for the benefit of those we are entrusted to serve.
- Conduct our personal affairs in such a manner that we cannot be improperly influenced in the performance of our duties.
- Avoid situations whereby our decisions or influence may have an impact on personal financial interests.
- Seek no favor and accept no form of personal reward for influence or official action.
- Engage in no outside employment or professional activities that may impair or appear to impair our primary responsibilities as fire officials.
- Comply with local laws and campaign rules when supporting political candidates and engaging in political activities.
- Handle all personnel matters on the basis of merit.
- Carry out policies established by elected officials and policy makers to the best of our ability.
- Refrain from financial investments or business that conflicts with, or is enhanced by our official position.
- Refrain from endorsing commercial products through quotations, use of photographs, or testimonials for personal gain.
- Develop job descriptions and guidelines at the local level to produce behaviors in accordance with the code of ethics.
- Conduct training at the local level to inform and educate local personnel about ethical conduct and policies and procedures.
- Have systems in place at the local level to resolve ethical issues.
- Orient new employees to the organization's ethics program during new employee orientation.
- Review the ethics management program in **management** training experiences.
- Deliver accurate and timely information to the public and to elected policymakers to use when deciding critical issues.

Source: *Policy Statements of the International Association of Fire Chiefs.*

Management — Process of accomplishing organizational objectives through effective and efficient handling of resources; official, sanctioned leadership.

Ethical Issues

Training employees in the importance of making ethical decisions, how to make those decisions, and how to recognize and respond to unethical actions on the part of others provides valuable tools for dealing with such issues. However, you must be able to manage issues when they arise. Use the following steps when dealing with an ethical dilemma:

- ***Recognize and define the situation*** — Answer the following questions: *What is it? What has caused it? Who is involved? What are the potential results?*

- ***Obtain all the facts surrounding the situation*** — Conduct an objective inquiry or investigation to gather the details of the event.

- ***Identify all possible options necessary to respond to the situation*** — Brainstorm with members of the department and develop options. In emergency situations, the officer may have to rely on personal experience to identify possible options.

- ***Compare each option to established criteria*** — Use benchmarks such as legality, morality, benefit, and justification as criteria.

- ***Select the best option that meets the criteria*** — Make the decision.

- ***Double check the decision*** — Ask more subjective questions such as *How would I feel if my family/spouse/friends found out about this?* And *How would I feel if this decision was reported in the local/national media?*

- ***Take action and implement the decision*** — The best decision is made if the factual foundation is firm, criteria are met, and potential for exposure is minimized.

Chief officers lead primarily by example and the most important example they can provide to their organization and community is ethical decision-making and action. They must be able to recognize and use ethical behavior in relationships, in decision-making, and as leaders. An organization's culture is only as sound as the example set by the chief of the department or organization and the chief officers who manage the organization. This example means that chief officers must establish and adhere to goals that are ethical. Those goals must be based on sound factual evidence and reasoning. Officers must be honest in their presentation of their decisions, both in communicating the decision and the results of the decision. Honesty generates acceptance for the decision and builds trust in the officer who made that decision.

Leadership

Leading is the act of controlling, directing, conducting, guiding, and administering through the use of personal behavioral traits or personality traits or characteristics that motivate members to the successful completion of the organization's goals. As a manager and supervisor, a chief officer is expected to exhibit leadership traits and characteristics. Not all chief officers may be strong leaders; they may struggle with effectively influencing their subordinates. Strong leaders may not be in the chief-officer ranks. For example, leaders of the labor organization have influence over employees as well as the ability to affect the operation of career organizations, management staff, and political officials of the governing body. Every organization has formal leaders, and most have informal leaders. Remember that rank does not necessarily translate to leadership: it empowers people but does not make them leaders. Informal leaders might influence the opinions of their fellow emergency responders and are sometimes the ones most sought after for information and advice. Sometimes chief officers are informal leaders; sometimes company officers and individual emergency responders are informal leaders. As a chief officer, you need to know who the informal leaders are, tap into their informal communication channels, and communicate with them frequently.

Leadership is one of the top five skills that employers look for when hiring new personnel. Other skills are communication, technical, teamwork, and interpersonal **(Figure 1.3)**. When combined with these skills, positive leadership produces results that benefit the organization and the community. Leaders are committed to a vision. They develop relationships that help to accomplish the vision by sharing it with others and seeking their input on how best to attain it. Finally, leaders have a high level of personal integrity that is at the core of all decisions and actions. Ethical leadership not only considers what is best for the organization but also what is best for the community. There are rare instances when doing what is best for the organization may not be in the best interest of the community. In these situations, the wisest ethical decision would be to choose what is best for the community.

Figure 1.3 Five common skills that employers look for in an employee.

Leadership vs. Management

Leadership is also an important part of the management process because it means the difference between an organization that is reactive to a situation and one that is proactive; meeting challenges as they develop and not after they occur. However, the most effective chief officers are those who are capable managers and also effective leaders. They have learned the importance of blending these two very critical requirements into their approach to carrying out their responsibilities.

Managers assign goals and tasks to people within the organization. They are responsible for planning, organizing, and directing activities and programs that result in the desired outcome. Managers tend to be focused on the work of the members and are responsible for addressing conflict, analyzing risk, and ensuring the effective operation of the department or work group.

Leaders are more concerned with the attitude, direction, and vision of the organization. Leaders inspire and guide subordinates and are sometimes charismatic, attracting followers who want to work with them. The goal of leadership is to instill in subordinates an intrinsic desire to perform assigned duties for their own personal fulfillment. Leaders need confidence to take responsibility for errors and give credit to followers for accomplishments, and be willing to take risks that help in the pursuit of their vision.

Leadership Theory: The Principled Leader

Many theories exist on what leadership is and how it affects an organization. Many of these theories are similar to each other, due to the cumulative effect of their development over time. One of the theories is referred to as either *principled* or *principle-centered* leadership and is based on the writings of Stephen Covey. It focuses on the use of basic values or principles to lead an organization. It suggests that there are certain core ethical values that the individual holds and transfers to others in the organization. These values may be the foundation for the mission statement or the code of ethics of the organization. In any case, these values must be held by other members of the organization for principled leadership to be effective. The theory states that the leader uses these values to guide internal and external personal relations, make decisions, create policy, and determine success. Examples of these values include the following:

- Integrity
- Excellence
- Respect
- Harmony
- Loyalty
- Faith
- Honesty
- Courage
- Trust
- Responsibility

Applying Leadership Theory

Chief officers must be able to compare their own personal traits to those listed above, determine what is lacking, and then work to generate the missing ones. Additionally, a chief officer must understand the types of problems that exist, nature and mood of employees, and methods used for making decisions. An understanding of the attitudes and behaviors typical of a leader is also important. This understanding of both employee and self provides a fair and equitable means of influencing the members of the organization without the use of coercion or force.

The first step in developing leadership skills and styles is to create a list of accepted leadership traits. This list becomes the criteria or benchmark standard that is compared to the individual. Next, a chief officer needs to complete a personal inventory of leadership traits. Next, a personality analysis like the Myers-Briggs Type Indicator® can be taken to complete an inventory of leadership traits. Another method would be to take the standard and use it as a checklist of personal leadership traits. A final method would involve an anonymous survey of the chief officer's subordinates, peers, and superiors in a 360-degree feedback evaluation that includes objective responses to questions about the chief officer's leadership traits. A third party like the organization's Human Resources Department typically compiles the results.

360 Degree Feedback Evaluation

The concept of a 360-degree feedback evaluation is to provide a performance evaluation based on the observations of people who are associated with the person who is being evaluated. The information is gathered from people who have direct professional contact with the person, which may include peers, subordinates, employees, members of other agencies, and members of the public who are in reasonably constant contact with the individual. The information gathered is based on the performance they observe. Responses must remain confidential to protect the people who are providing the information. It also ensures that they will speak freely and will not hesitate to provide constructive criticism. A professional trained in this evaluation technique should administer and interpret the feedback.

Once you have determined the characteristics that are present and those that are lacking, you need to develop a strategy for improving weaker skills. The fact that not all leaders are outstanding in all situations should be remembered. For example, while some military leaders have been exceptional field commanders, they have been less than adequate administratively or politically. You should remember that becoming a chief officer does not mean that your education has ended. You should continue to learn and develop by participating in courses, workshops, and other opportunities, such as the Executive Fire Officer Program at the National Fire Academy. Depending on the area that seems to need attention, you may choose to follow any number of paths to improve the area such as the following:

- *Courses* — Take a course in a specific subject such as interpersonal, intercultural, or oral communications. Courses on these topics focus on improving skills that are basic to the leadership function. These courses are usually offered through local colleges, universities, the National Fire Academy, or state/provincial training associations in classroom settings, workshops, or on-line.

- *Seminars/workshops* — Attend seminars or workshops on leadership, diversity, and decision-making.

- *Literature reading* — Read available literature on leadership and leaders to determine how to implement personal change **(Figure 1.4)**.

- *Counselors/mentors* — Work with a counselor on personal traits that help to change or reinforce values and beliefs. A mentor, particularly one who exemplifies positive leadership capabilities, can also be helpful in providing guidance and feedback on leadership traits.

- *Networking* — Connect with other chief officers and peers to discuss issues and ideas. Networking can consist of officers in your department, state, or region during periodic meetings and conferences. The Internet can be used to make contact with officers around the country and in other parts of the world **(Figure 1.5, p. 22)**.

Figure 1.4 Chief officers can help implement personal change by reading literature about leadership and leaders.

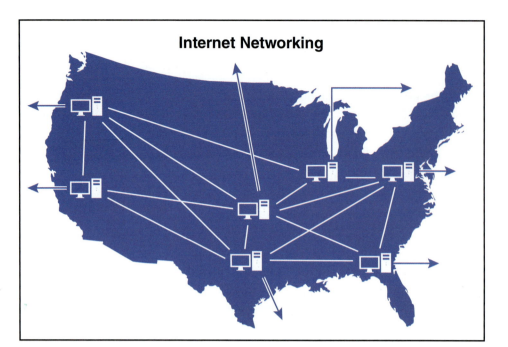

Figure 1.5 The Internet has become a common method for chief officers and their peers to network.

Good Leader Traits

While the traits of a leader mentioned previously may not exist in every individual, they can be developed and gathered into concepts that are fundamental to a good leader. A chief officer who has these traits will be able to lead the workgroup or organization on the road to success. Descriptions of these concepts are as follows:

- *Sees opportunities* — A chief officer will need a vision that views situations from all angles while still understanding that tradition can provide direction.

- *Identifies challenges* — A chief officer recognizes potential problematic situations that may confront the workgroup or organization, ranging from personality conflicts to political intrigue. This recognition monitors the internal and the external climate of the organization much as a meteorologist tracks potential storms on a radar screen.

- *Communicates* — Effective communication involves not only being able to express ideas clearly but also being able to listen to and interpret feedback from others who are either internal or external to the organization **(Figure 1.6)**. Without good communication skills, a chief officer will miss opportunities and challenges and**,** therefore, will serve only as an autocratic leader.

- *Plans for success* — A chief officer generates plans, implement those plans, and evaluate the effectiveness of the plans. Effective planning saves energy, time, resources, lives, and frustration and is the sign of an organized and confident leader.

- *Builds trust* – A chief officer creates an environment of mutual trust within the organization, within the service area, and the profession. To create this environment, a chief officer must do the following:

  — Lead by example and with integrity.

  — Place trust in the people who have earned it.

  — Respect others.

— Value fairness.
— Emphasize *personal leadership.*
— Support the political and administrative leadership.
— Grasp the importance of the overall situation.

Besides ethical and leadership traits, there are other traits that you should have to be successful. Some of them include the following:

- *Be loyal* — be loyal to the organization, the governing body, your personnel, and to yourself. However, remember that blind or unquestioning loyalty can result in inappropriate or unethical actions.
- *Be dedicated* — be dedicated to the organization, its vision, and its mission.
- *Be a good listener* — listening to your crew is the basis for situational awareness as a company officer. Listen to the public, your staff, your membership, and your peers, even if they voice an opinion that is opposed to your own.
- *Have a sense of humor* — enjoy life but realize that there is a time and place for laughter.
- *Be a mentor* — help members of your organization grow professionally.
- *Be decisive* — once you have gathered the facts, make the decision.
- *Be humble* — Share the credit with those who deserve it.
- *Be a team player* — you are the leader of a team and the member of a larger team of other departments and agencies. You all have the same goal and that is protecting the citizens.

Figure 1.6 This chief officer is using good listening skills to help him receive and understand feedback from his personnel.

Challenges and Solutions

Chief officers will always be challenged with situations that test their abilities. As Level I and II Fire Officers, you faced rapidly changing conditions at emergency scenes that have required changes in strategy and tactics. At the fire station, you had to deal with personnel issues from mediating minor disagreements to major labor/management issues. With each challenge, you had to analyze the problem, select the most appropriate action or response, and implement the response. When the outcome was not altogether satisfactory, you had to select an alternative response. In each case, you learned from the situation and became more experienced. Those experiences are now available to you as you advance in the fire and emergency service.

Proactive Leadership

One of the best solutions to challenges is to be proactive rather than reactive. The fire and emergency services have tended to operate in a reactive model. We respond after the hazard has already occurred. As a Level III or IV chief officer, the challenges that you face will give you the opportunity to respond before a situation becomes critical. You have the chance to analyze a potential challenge and gather information and resources to mitigate it. For instance, you may become aware that your municipality is planning to annex a large portion of land that contains existing high hazard occupancies. You can gather information on the fire and life safety risks that this action will generate and the resources needed to control these risks. Emergency response plans, budget requests, and future fire station locations can be created to protect the new acquisition.

Problem Solving

Whether large or small, problems can be addressed using the following process:

1. Define the problem.
2. Develop a set of solutions.
3. Evaluate the solutions based on resources.
4. Select the best solution.
5. Provide necessary training.
6. Implement the best solution.
7. Compare the actual results with the desired outcome.
8. Make required revisions and revisit the steps as necessary.

This problem solving is similar to the process that you used when commanding an emergency incident. One of the differences is that you may have more time to use it in administrative situations.

Politics

Some of the most challenging moments as a chief officer may involve your relationship with the world of politics. Political decisions will directly affect you as a Level III and a Level IV chief officer. The political arena may be the elected mayor and city council, county commissioners, or the board of directors/trustees of your organization. Your interactions and relationships with them can determine the support that your organization gets in the form of resources and revenue. It can also determine if you will continue in your position with the organization. You must not openly criticize, antagonize or display hostility toward the political leaders to whom you answer. If you disagree with a decision that affects your organization, you must respond with civility and state your opinion based on facts and not emotion.

Foresight

We cannot predict the weather, political change, or how other people will react to our decisions. We can, however, prepare for the worst possible situation. For example, history has shown that during part of the year, the Gulf Coast of the United States can expect moderate to severe storms and hurricanes. In response to that potential, one retail organization positions trailers containing emergency supplies in areas close to the coastal communities. This preplanning allows supplies to be distributed with as little delay as possible.

Criticism

Chief officers must be able to take criticism from below and from above. Not all decisions are popular with everyone. You must be able to justify your actions based on the decision-making process that you used to reach that decision. Realize that some people and organizations will find fault with your decision.

Decisions

You must have the will power to stand behind your decisions and the decisions of your subordinates if those decisions are appropriate and warrant your support. You may have already been faced with similar situations when you decided to use a defensive strategy rather than risk firefighter lives to save a vacant building. Remember, what is right is not always what is most popular.

Professional Standards of Conduct

State/provincial laws and organizational codes define professional standards of conduct **(See information box for sample state law)**. Enforcement of the standards can range from loss of certification, expulsion from the organization, or judicial action.

> ### Ohio Administrative Law
>
> **4765-22-01 Professional standards of conduct for fire service training certificate holders.**
>
> (A) A person issued a fire service training certificate shall not discriminate in the provision of fire services on the basis of race, color, religion, sex, sexual orientation, or national origin.
>
> (B) A person issued a fire service training certificate shall not misrepresent the person's professional qualifications or credentials.
>
> (C) Upon request by the division, a person issued a fire service training certificate shall accurately document and report all approved continuing education programs the certificate holder completes in accordance with Chapter 4765-20 of the Administrative Code and within the time parameters set forth by the executive director with advice and counsel of the committee.
>
> (D) A person issued a fire service training certificate shall, within fourteen days of the final sentencing of any misdemeanor involving moral turpitude, any misdemeanor committed in the course of practice, or any felony, provide written notification to the division of such offense. A person issued a fire service training certificate shall within sixty days of the final sentencing of any misdemeanor involving moral turpitude, any misdemeanor committed in the course of practice, or any felony, provide the division a certified copy of the judgment entry from the court in which the conviction occurred, a certified copy of the police or law enforcement agency report, if applicable, and a bureau of criminal identification and investigation (BCI&I) civilian background check.
>
> (E) A person issued a fire service training certificate shall not commit fraud or material deception in applying for or obtaining a certificate issued under section 4765.55 of the Revised Code.
>
> Effective: 01/24/2008

A fire and emergency services organization can codify its professional standard of conduct in the organization's Code of Ethics, Rules and Regulations, or the standard operating policies/procedures (SOP). A code of ethics is a more general statement of behaviors while the SOP is more detailed. The National Fire Academy (NFA) has proposed a sample code of ethics shown below.

Firefighter Code of Ethics

I understand that I have the responsibility to conduct myself in a manner that reflects proper ethical behavior and integrity. In so doing, I will help foster a continuing positive public perception of the fire service. Therefore, I pledge the following...

- Always conduct myself, on and off duty, in a manner that reflects positively on myself, my department and the fire service in general.
- Accept responsibility for my actions and for the consequences of my actions.
- Support the concept of fairness and the value of diverse thoughts and opinions.
- Avoid situations that would adversely affect the credibility or public perception of the fire service profession.
- Be truthful and honest at all times and report instances of cheating or other dishonest acts that compromise the integrity of the fire service.
- Conduct my personal affairs in a manner that does not improperly influence the performance of my duties, or bring discredit to my organization.
- Be respectful and conscious of each member's safety and welfare.
- Recognize that I serve in a position of public trust that requires stewardship in the honest and efficient use of publicly owned resources, including uniforms, facilities, vehicles and equipment and that these are protected from misuse and theft.
- Exercise professionalism, competence, respect and loyalty in the performance of my duties and use information, confidential or otherwise, gained by virtue of my position, only to benefit those I am entrusted to serve.
- Avoid financial investments, outside employment, outside business interests or activities that conflict with or are enhanced by my official position or have the potential to create the perception of impropriety.
- Never propose or accept personal rewards, special privileges, benefits, advancement, honors or gifts that may create a conflict of interest, or the appearance thereof.
- Never engage in activities involving alcohol or other substance use or abuse that can impair my mental state or the performance of my duties and compromise safety.
- Never discriminate on the basis of race, religion, color, creed, age, marital status, national origin, ancestry, gender, sexual preference, medical condition or handicap.
- Never harass, intimidate or threaten fellow members of the service or the public and stop or report the actions of other firefighters who engage in such behaviors.
- Responsibly use social networking, electronic communications, or other media technology opportunities in a manner that does not discredit, dishonor or embarrass my organization, the fire service and the public. I also understand that failure to resolve or report inappropriate use of this media equates to condoning this behavior.

Developed by the National Society of Executive Fire Officers.

Chief officers must adhere to their emergency services organization's professional standard of conduct. For instance, the local authority having jurisdiction (AHJ) generally regulates the use of public equipment: when and how you use a vehicle assigned to you, who you can transport in the vehicle, and where you may take that vehicle. It also includes the use of personal electronic equipment such as government owned telephones, pagers, computers, and other personal communications technology. You may have heard about fire officers and politicians that had to resign because they sent inappropriate e-mails or public employees who have lost their jobs because they used government vehicles for personal trips. These situations illustrate how important it is for you to be able to differentiate between professional and personal activities.

As a senior fire officer, you are a public figure. The media and the public scrutinize your life. You must consider how your actions and comments will be perceived and how they will reflect on you, your organization, and your community. A chief officer's conduct will be scrutinized more than other members of the organization.

Education and Training

Proper training is critical to safe, efficient, and effective fire and emergency services operations. It prepares you to manage the responsibilities of chief officer. State/provincial, local, and organizational requirements determine the knowledge, skills, and abilities you must have to be a firefighter or emergency responder. If the authority having jurisdiction (AHJ) has adopted NFPA® 1021, you must meet the Level III and IV job performance requirements (JPRs) listed in that standard. In order to perform those JPRs, however, you will need to know the prerequisite and requisite knowledge and skills listed for each JPR.

NFPA® prerequisite and requisite knowledge and skills are written broadly to be applicable to a wide variety of fire and emergency services organizations and jurisdictions. Some fire service organizations may not teach general subjects that support the JPRs. A few of the knowledge topics included are:

- Minimum staffing requirements
- Firefighter health and safety requirements
- Local policies and procedures
- Regulations and standards
- Applicable federal, state/provincial, and local laws
- Purchasing laws, policies, and procedures
- Local budget policies

Required skills mentioned in the standard include, but are not limited to:

- Research methods
- Evaluative methods
- Analysis
- Oral communications
- Written communications
- Interpersonal communications

Figure 1.7 Chief officers should be very familiar with the policies and procedures of the AHJ and their organization.

Your AHJ and organization maintain documents that you will be required to research **(Figure 1.7)**. The skills will require that you take courses or research the topics on your own. Community colleges, vocational schools, and universities, both onsite and online, can provide you with the courses that you need.

In addition to the NFPA® requirements, the United States Fire Administration (USFA) has established the Fire and Emergency Services Higher Education (FESHE) curriculum as a guide for college-level degree programs for the fire service. These programs currently cover Associates and Bachelor courses. Many FESHE-based programs are available online.

The USFA also provides advanced education through the Executive Fire Officer Program (EFOP). This program is administered through the National Fire Academy (NFA). Fire officers must meet both service and academic requirements to be selected for the program.

Chief officers who are accepted into the program enhance their professional development through a unique series of four graduate and upper division baccalaureate-equivalent courses. The EFOP spans a 4-year period with four core courses that are two weeks in length. EFOP participants must complete an Applied Research Project (ARP) that relates to their organization within six months after the completion of each of the four courses. A certificate of completion for the entire EFOP is awarded after the successful completion of the final research project.

The International Association of Fire Chiefs provides guidance for professional development in its Officer Development Handbook. The handbook provides a matrix for each category with the knowledge outcome, college course level, and recommended course subject. The handbook divides fire officers into categories comparable to the NFPA® fire officer levels. They are:

- Supervising Fire Officer (NFPA® Level I)
- Managing Fire Officer (NFPA® Level II)
- Administrative Fire Officer (NFPA® Level III)
- Executive Fire Officer (NFPA® Level IV)

The CPSE, through the Commission on Professional Credentialing (CPC), offers the Chief Officer Designation Program based on the FESHE supported National Professional Development Model. Attaining the designation of Chief Fire Officer indicates that the individual has demonstrated the completion of educational and technical competencies.

In addition to these national programs, state/provincial and regional training academies offer courses for chief officers. Local training programs may be available including internships for chief officer candidates. The AHJ mandates certification requirements for such programs.

Experience vs. Experiences

Successful chief officers depend on their experience and their experiences to guide them. Their experience can be defined as the positions they have held while their experiences are the things they have done and situations to which they have been exposed. Experience and exposure are not the same thing. Seniority does not necessarily equate to experience.

Experience

The NFPA® requisite knowledge and skills are examples of experience that chief officers need. The courses accumulate into a body of knowledge that you can draw on to make decisions and plans.

You may be required to gain experience based on local requirements such as service time and positions held. You may be required to work as a Fire Officer II for 5 years with a total of 12 years in the organization prior to being eligible to promote to a Level III. In some organizations, personnel who wish to promote must spend a specified amount of time in various divisions within the organization. Time served in the Fire and Life Safety, Training, Special Operations, or Suppression Division ensures that you will understand the operational requirements of each division. Even if AHJ does not mandate this type of experience, it is a wise choice to work in areas other than your primary field.

Experiences

Personal experiences are as important as your official work experience. Experiences are situations that you face daily. Your experiences add to the skills you need as a chief officer.

As a firefighter, driver/operator, and company officer, you observed your superiors and formed opinions on the type of leader you want to be. You also learned how to be a team member in both emergency and nonemergency situations. You experienced successful emergency operations that benefited from good decisions. You also observed management decisions that you questioned.

All of your experiences have allowed you to develop friendships and relationships that form a network you can access when you need it. Fire service professional organizations also provide a source for opinions, information, and assistance when making decisions.

Best Practices Application

Successful chief officers apply best business practices from both public and private arenas. They continue to read and follow emerging trends in management theory, business practices, research and analysis, and change management. They are never complacent and they always seek new methods to respond to potential challenges.

Current Management Theory

Current theory is based on the classical models but attempts to correct some of its inherent weaknesses. There are six contemporary theories currently in use, including:

- Quantitative Management
- Organizational Behavior

- Systems Theory
- Contingency Theory
- Total Quality Management
- Organizational Culture

Quantitative Management

The quantitative management theory uses mathematical equations to solve complex problems and make decisions. This theory has long been used for determining cost/benefit and forecasting trends, supplemented by other theories. The use of computer software has aided making quantitative management available for the fire service. Computer software can be used to determine response times, find station locations, and aid in the investigation of incendiary fires.

Organizational Behavior

Organizational behavior is a human relations approach to management, recognizing that human resources are the most important part of the organization. It focuses on management activities to encourage workers to be more effective and efficient. The theory did result in management decisions to enrich and change job designs for the benefit of the workers and the organization. However, it failed to consider the effect that external influences and technology have on workers.

Systems Theory

The systems theory views organizations as systems with interdependent parts. For example, a fire department takes input from the response area in the form of revenue and provides an output in the form of fire protection. To provide these fire protection services, the department hires and trains firefighters, purchases and maintains apparatus and equipment, adopts and enforces fire and life safety codes, and responds to emergencies within the community. Besides revenue, the system depends on the community to express its needs, wants, and expectations. The system also depends on other departments within the parent organization for support, such as the finance department or water department.

Contingency Theory

The contingency theory is based on the belief that there is no one best management or leadership style. This belief is based on the idea that every organization is unique. Organizational objectives and the composition of the workforce are different. Therefore, the organization's leadership must consider each situation or challenge to the organization as a different contingency. Contingencies include:

- Internal strengths and weaknesses
- Worker values, knowledge, skills, and abilities
- Types of technology used
- Organizational resources
- Complexity of the external environment
- Rate of change within the environment

This theory may not be applicable to all management situations or able to identify all contingencies that challenge the organization. It is still popular because of its flexibility and ability to adapt to changes in the organization and environment.

Total Quality Management

The primary focus of Total Quality Management (TQM) is to prevent problems rather than correct them later. The result of TQM is satisfaction for both internal and external customers. Moving an organization to a TQM structure can be very difficult. However, TQM has proven that quality in product and service can be managed and improved.

PERFORMANCE EXCELLENCE

Performance Excellence (PE) is a process used to generate defined results. It produces an organization that efficiently and continuously improves, and effectively executes its mission for the benefit of the customers that it serves.

PE includes a seven-criteria assessment and evaluation method and continuous improvement process. It enables organizations to take a fresh and systemic look at themselves from the perspective of employees who are continuously focused on increasing their ability organizationally, individually, and in teams to better serve customers. The seven assessment criteria are:

- Leadership
- Strategic Planning
- Customer Focus
- Workforce Focus
- Operations Focus
- Measurement/Analysis/Knowledge
- Management
- Results

The PE model values employee perspectives, ideas and contributions as being critical to the improvement of the organization as a whole. It does not hold that a small group of "traditional leaders" is the only source for ideas that can make the organization more effective and efficient. Equally valued is each employee's full potential in alignment with the organization's mission, strategic priorities, and action plans. As the individual grows, the organization will grow.

The Baldrige model of PE has proven to be successful in the fire service, in government agencies, in healthcare, in the private sector, and in education. Practitioners are happy to share bottom line results and methods that have been used to achieve them. The Baldrige Performance Excellence Program is affiliated with NIST (the National Institute of Standards and Technology).

Organizational Culture

One of the most recent management theories is based on research of successful Japanese companies. The organizational culture theory states that key cultural values within the organization are the foundation for successful management. The basic values of workers, owners/founders, and managers are critical in the decision making process. This approach has been shown to be unscientific and generally ignores elements of the system that do influence the organization's success.

Fire Service Leadership Best Practices

Chief officers also need to be aware of current business practices. Some suggestions for best practices include:

- Forecasting and trending
- Environmental scanning
- Technological awareness
- Innovation

Forecasting and Trending

Forecasts are projections of what may occur in the future. You use forecasts to plan the acquisition and allotment of resources. For instance, based on personal protective clothing manufacturer's recommendations of the service life of their equipment, you can project when you will need to replace it and budget for it.

Trending is the use of data from past events to determine what may occur in the future. For example, based on fire response data from the previous 10 years, we can predict that there will be an increase in chimney fires in the winter. Then we can plan fire and life safety education programs that target the safe use of fireplaces and the importance of having chimneys inspected and cleaned.

Environmental Scanning

Environmental scanning is the careful monitoring of your organization's internal and external environments. You are looking for early signs of opportunities and threats that may influence your operations, decision making, and planning. You can think of it as situational awareness about events, trends, issues, and community expectations. You gather internal information from your staff, membership, and stakeholders. You gather external information from members of the community and political leaders. You can also get it online, through the media, and at community meetings. Topics you should consider include:

- Political
- Economic
- Socio-cultural
- Technological
- Environmental
- Legal

Technology Awareness

As chief officers, we need to be aware of technological advances. Computer technology can help us develop budgets, predict the best locations for fire stations, deploy our resources efficiently, and recognize trends in emergency responses **(Figure 1.8)**.

To make it easier, evaluating potential equipment and software can be delegated to groups of members. Using environmental scanning can provide an initial concept of available items.

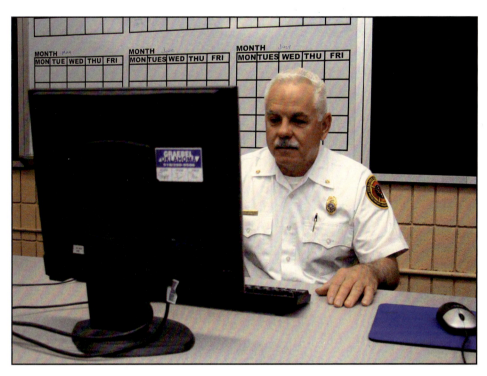

Figure 1.8 Chief officers need to stay current with technological advances such as the growing use of computers within the fire service.

Innovation

Innovation allows you to find new methods to respond to unexpected challenges or work within new constraints. If your organization depends on alternative funding sources such as fund raisers, you may want to find a different approach that allows you access to new donors. Diverse workforce recruitment can benefit from posting on social media web sites. You may need to apply an innovative approach when the AHJ asks you to make reductions in your operating budget and still maintain the same level of service. Innovation is very important in being able to effectively provide services and sustain the organization.

A good approach to being innovative is to form a task group and involve as many customers and stakeholders as possible, which provides a variety of potential options. The top ideas should be tested and the best one implemented. However, innovative ideas must be ethical, within the law, and accomplish the desired goal. An organization that supports innovation will be vulnerable to mistakes and must be willing to learn from them. Trying something new will not always work the first time.

> **Needs Assessment** — Analysis identifying life-support and critical infrastructure requirements.
>
> **Risk Assessment** — (1) Determining the risk level or seriousness of a risk. (2) Process for evaluating risk associated with a specific hazard defined in terms of probability and frequency of occurrence, magnitude and severity, exposure, and consequences. *Also known as* Risk Evaluation.

Research, Analysis, and Evaluation

Administrative chief officers spend a great deal of time doing research, analyzing data, and evaluating programs. Each of these activities takes time and must be done correctly if you are going to make the correct decision. You may decide to perform these activities yourself, form a committee, or hire an external organization.

The goal of research is to gather all the information from all relevant sources that will help you make informed decisions. Sources will depend on the decision you need to make. For instance, purchasing a new type of personal protective clothing will involve doing a **needs assessment** and a **risk assessment**. Good research is foundational to decision making and can also prevent you from reinventing the wheel or repeating the mistakes of others.

Analysis is the process of looking at the parts of a process, system, item, or situation and how they work together. In the example of the protective clothing, you would analyze the components of the clothing to determine if they meet NFPA® design criteria, if they interface with existing equipment, and if they will meet your organization's needs. Training in data analysis is available from numerous sources including the Center for Public Safety Excellence.

An evaluation, based on research and analysis, will lead you to a conclusion. Your evaluation of the protective clothing should result in justification for purchasing the clothing because it will do the intended job for the cost.

Each of these activities, research, analysis, and evaluation, will be described in the following chapters. You will learn how to apply them to the budget and purchasing process, personnel issues, fire and life safety education, and firefighter health and safety.

Successful Change Management

Change can have either a devastating effect or motivating effect on the organization. To successfully manage change, you must know the forces that create and cause change and the change process itself. Knowing the types of change, how to overcome resistance to change, how to implement the change process, and how to use a follow-up plan can lead to successful change management.

The forces of change can come from both internal and external sources. The first force comes from inside the organization and includes the delegation of responsibility, periodic performance reviews, organizational restructuring, and realignment of duties and tasks to meet the second or outside force of change.

The second force comes from outside the organization takes the form of political decisions, economic trends, community service demands, changes in technology, and changes in the demographics of the community, among others.

The prospect of change causes people to go through the following four change process stages:

- ***Denial*** — People refuse to believe that the change will affect them.
- ***Resistance*** — When the threat of change becomes real, people start to resist it, which can be manifested in anger and dissatisfaction with management or the organization.

- ***Exploration*** — People start to gain a better understanding of the potential change through training.
- ***Commitment*** — Increased understanding in the third stage leads to an increased commitment to the new process, procedure, or structure.

Change Types

Each type of change can be managed to create a new and effective organization as long as the chief officers involved are open to change. Support for change must come from the top down in order to be successful. However, those affected must take ownership through involvement and commitment or it will be a difficult and painful process. The types of change that an organization may have to undergo are as follows:

- ***Strategic*** — Change in the short or long range plan of the organization.
- ***Structure*** — Changes in organizational design.
- ***Technology*** — Change in the addition of new equipment, apparatus, communications systems, extinguishing agents, or computerization.
- ***People*** — Change in the skills, performances, attitudes, behaviors, or cultures of the workforce to meet the force of change.

Resistance to Change

Organizational change can fail because of employee resistance. To be a successful change agent, you must understand the reasons for employee resistance and the methods used to overcome those reasons. The following reasons cause resistance to change:

- ***Fear of the unknown*** — Employees' routines or environments are disrupted, which causes them to feel insecure and not know how the changes will affect them or other members of the workforce.
- ***Loss of control or power*** — Employees resent the feeling that they have lost control over their lives.
- ***Fear of loss*** — Employees experience layoffs, work-schedule changes, or transfers between workgroups.
- ***Self-interest*** — Employees are more concerned about their own situations than with the organization.
- ***Learning anxiety*** — Employees experience anxiety when they need to learn a new skill, technique, process, procedure, or equipment operation.
- ***Lack of trust*** — Employee distrust can be directed toward the organization's leaders and based on prior history or future concerns.

Recognize the resistance to change and take steps to reduce it; you can increase the opportunity for success in the process. Business analysts have determined that resistance to change can be overcome using seven basic steps:

- ***Create a climate for change*** — This step is founded on good human relations between the manager and the workgroup; they must have mutual trust and respect. Positive change can be a part of the organization's culture as the manager and employees look for better ways to accomplish tasks. Encourage employees to suggest changes and implement those changes. With this type of climate in place, the organization will be better prepared to face external changes.

- ***Plan for change*** — Have a plan and prepare to follow it in order to effectively implement change. First, analyze the current conditions. Next, identify the resistance factors. Define change objectives and clearly communicate them to the workgroup. Finally, identify, acquire, and provide the necessary resources for change to the workgroup.
- ***Communicate the advantages and effects of change*** — Communication is the basis for all good management practice and is essential in the change process. State the advantages and effects of change to prevent unfounded rumors from eroding the trust between the manager and employees **(Figure 1.9)**.
- ***Meet the needs of both the organization and employees*** — View the change from the employees' viewpoints. Then, focus on their concerns and try to balance the good of the employees with the good of the organization. Share benefits equally in order to create a win-win situation.
- ***Involve employees in the change process*** — Involve employees in the change process, keep employees informed, focus on their needs, and implement their suggestions. This involvement gives organizations a greater chance of success. Employees who participate in the change process are more likely to be committed to the change.
- ***Provide support for employees during the change*** — Make a firm commitment to the change; listen to employees' concerns, resistances, and suggestions. Provide the necessary resources, including training, and help employees cope with unexpected change.
- ***Seek the input and support of "opinion leaders" in the organization*** — Informal leaders of the organization can influence the opinions of others, such as leaders of the labor organization or spouses of members.

Figure 1.9 Change within an organization can be difficult. Chief officers must be able to communicate the advantages and effects of change to their subordinates.

Process Implementation

Even though change can come from both internal and external sources, establishing and following a specific change process benefits the organization. Having a policy for implementing change leads to success, and makes change a part of the department/organization's culture. That policy should include methods for analyzing the current processes used, methods for suggesting change from the bottom up and the top down, methods for implementing change, and a follow-up plan to ensure that the change met the needs it was intended to meet.

A current model for implementing change is based on the following five steps:

- **_Recognize the need for change_** — Clearly state the need for change and establish objectives. Consider the effects the change will have on other parts of the organization.

- **_Identify resistance and overcome it_** — Identify potential resistance to the change and determine the best method for overcoming it.

- **_Plan the change interventions_** — Recognize that a variety of change agents or interventions exist that can help in implementing the change. Some of those interventions are as follows:

  — *Training and development*: Use to develop skills, behaviors, and attitudes that will be used in the workplace; may include technical skills, interpersonal skills, or communication skills.

  — *Team building:* Focus on how to get the job done. The team approach allows for member involvement in defining the change and how to implement it.

  — *Sensitivity training*: Teach people to recognize their behaviors, the effects they have on others, and how to improve them.

  — *Job design*: Change the tasks that members of the organization perform. It includes enhancement, enrichment, simplification, rotation, or expansion of tasks to improve efficiency or effectiveness.

  — *Direct feedback*: Use an outside agent such as a manufacturer's representative to train members in the use of new equipment or techniques.

  — *Survey feedback*: Uses a written questionnaire that is designed to gather data from members of the organization. Analyze the data and determine recommended changes.

  — *Process consultation*: Focus on how people interact to get the job accomplished. Have an outside observer analyze the relationships within the group and make recommendations for change to the organization.

- **_Implement the change_** — Use the appropriate change agent, and put the change into operation.

- **_Control the change_** — Enforce, review, monitor, and analyze the change model. Take corrective action if change objectives are not met.

Periodic systems analysis of the organization and the service area (including demographics, political, environmental, and economic conditions) is necessary to determine two things: need for change and potential for change. First, the need for change must be determined. Having a baseline comparison with periodic analysis can determine trends that require a corresponding change. For example, the presence of an aging population may warrant a change in service delivery that shifts its primary focus from structural fire fighting to emergency medical services. Second, the potential for change due to anticipated future changes must be evaluated. An example of this change would be federal mandates that require a local organization to assume added responsibilities in the area of national security.

When systems analysis is a part of the organization's daily operation, it becomes commonplace and accepted as a preparation for change. It creates the climate of a proactive, change-oriented organization and not a reactive one. It is very important to maintain records that can illustrate trends, especially when justifying additional funding or requesting grants from other agencies.

Change is an opportunity for innovation. Innovation may include new types of extinguishing agents, new fire prevention and inspection programs, new forms of funding, or new staffing methods. Leaders anticipate industry and organizational changes and position their organizations to their best advantage as opportunities occur.

When an analysis indicates that a change is necessary, the best approach is a proactive one. Gather representatives of the affected groups together for a brainstorming session. These representatives may include community leaders, member of the organization leadership, workgroups, senior staff, or political leaders. A facilitator leads the session and keeps the group focused and on schedule. The session needs to have a clearly defined goal. Then the consensus accepts and ranks all ideas. The top three ideas are then critically reviewed to determine cost, effectiveness, and legality. The final result may be applied to the situation.

Because fire and emergency services organizations do not exist in a vacuum, brainstorming committees must include all external groups that have an interest in the organization or the specific change that is being considered. For example, a change in work schedules may appear to affect the members of the workgroup. However, labor representatives, family members, finance personnel, and human resources personnel also have an interest in the decision that is made and need to have some representation on the committee.

Follow-up Program Plan

The follow-up program is a formal part of the process that continues to monitor the effect of the change. The follow-up is applied to individual behavioral changes and organizational structure changes. The follow-up program becomes part of the annual performance evaluation for personnel and the periodic review of programs, operations, or policies. The change process should be viewed as cyclical rather than linear. The process is continuous. The follow-up is the feedback that takes the results and loops them back to the first portion of the process, becoming the current level of performance.

Executive Level Communications

Chief officers must be fully aware of the importance of communications in your work. You must be able to convey your thoughts accurately and sometimes quickly while ensuring that the person(s) you are speaking to understand what you want them to do.

At the executive level, however, communications may be different. You will find yourself making somewhat more formal oral presentations to the public or political groups. Your communications, oral or written, may be open to more scrutiny. To help develop your communication skills, you may want to consider taking courses in Business Communications, Interpersonal Communications, or Technical Writing at a local college or university.

Keys to Good Communications

First and foremost, you must practice good listening skills. The act of listening constitutes approximately one half of a person's average day. Listening is an active part of the communication process **(Figure 1.10)**. To ensure that you understand the information that you are receiving, you must repeat it to the person speaking to you.

Understanding the nonverbal component of the message is the next key to good communications. Nonverbal communication transmits well over half of the message. As a result, the nonverbal clues are more important than the verbal message, and the nonverbal message may overpower the verbal message. Nonverbal clues consist of kinesics (use of body motion and position), paralanguage or vocalics (vowel sounds or tones used to create the verbal message), and self-presentation (clothing, touch, use of time, and control of the speaker's environment). Understanding the importance of each of the elements of nonverbal communication will assist you in recognizing and interpreting nonverbal signals, therefore improving nonverbal communication. The non-verbal component of communication is lost in written communications such as letters and e-mails. As such, the context of a letter or e-mail can be misunderstood because of a perceived tone based upon what is written.

You must also know your audience, especially when delivering a speech or presentation to a political body or citizen group. You must use language they will understand, relating the topic to things they already know. Using jargon or slang only confuses the issue. Off-color jokes, politically incorrect comments, or disparaging remarks about others can have disastrous results. Keep on topic, be brief, and be prepared to answer questions.

Always be truthful in your remarks or comments. Never try to bluff or pretend that you know an answer when you do not. Remember that Internet search engines can rapidly locate facts and data to support or supplement your presentation.

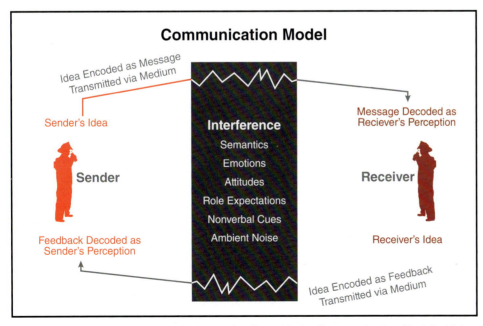

Figure 1.10 Chief officers should become familiar with the Communication Model which depicts the relationship between the six basic elements of communication.

Controversy Avoidance

As a senior fire officer, and especially as the chief of the department/organization, you must be careful in what you say and write. Use your situational awareness to prevent situations that you may regret and that may have unforeseen consequences. Things to remember:

- **Internet is forever** — Comments, information, photos, videos, and anything else that is posted on the Internet or in other social media will continue to exist in some form or location for an undetermined period of time. Removing a comment from a chat room does not make it disappear and it can still be accessed.

- **Open records** — Beginning in 1966, the U.S. federal government enacted laws based on the Freedom of Information Act. That act and the associated laws determine the records that must be provided to the public upon request. In essence, that means there is no such thing as private or personal information. The exceptions include personnel and medical records.

- **Conversations may be recorded** — Conversations, either face-to-face or over the phone can be recorded without your knowledge. Some states legally permit the recording of conversations if only one participant is aware of the recording.

- **Personal vs. public** — Although you have both personal and public lives, you must remember not to mix the two. Your personal opinions and comments should not be confused with those of your public position, especially when it comes to your political beliefs.

- **Nothing is off the record** — No matter what a reporter tells you, nothing is off the record. They may record your comments without your knowledge, take notes, or simply record your comments later. If you do not want a comment made public, do not say it.

Chapter Summary

Becoming a fire and emergency services chief officer is a journey and not a destination. You must continue to learn the best way to perform your duties, develop new skills, acquire new knowledge, and be active in your organization, community, and the fire service. Success is not guaranteed, however. External and internal forces will put intentional and unintentional barriers in your way. To overcome these barriers, you must be proactive and innovative, applying the characteristics of successful chief officers. You must be ethical in your actions and decisions, using leadership and management skills to reach the goals of your organization. Developing and applying these skills will result in an exciting journey as a senior chief officer.

Review Questions

1. What are various factors that influence the selection of a chief officer? (pp. 14-21)

2. What are some personal traits and characteristics common to successful chief officers? (pp. 22-25)

3. How do professional standards of conduct shape a chief officer's roles and responsibilities? (pp. 25-27)

4. How do education and training prepare a chief officer for the responsibilities of the job? (pp. 27-28)
5. How do experience and experiences guide the chief officer? (p. 29)
6. How can a chief officer apply best business practices from both public and private arenas? (pp. 29-38)
7. What are various skills that a chief officer should acquire to communicate successfully at the executive level? (pp. 38-40)

Human Resources Management (Levels III & IV)

Chapter Contents

III
- CASE HISTORY 45
- **Emergency Services Staffing** 45
  - Planning 46
  - Staffing Requirements 48
  - Staffing Assignments 49
- **Employment Practices** 50
  - Laws Affecting Employment 50
  - Human Resources Policies and Procedures 51
  - Employee Disabilities and Accommodations 52
  - Job Analyses and Position Descriptions 53
  - Recruitment 54
  - Employment Process 58
  - Applicant Selection 62
  - Promotions 63
  - Employee Benefits 65
  - Separation and Termination 67
- **Professional Development and Continuing Education** 70
  - Higher Education 70
  - Professional Organizations 72
  - Personal Professional Development 73
  - Succession Planning 73
  - Credentialing 73
  - Continuing Education 74

IV
- **Human Resources Demographics Appraisal** 76
  - External Community Demographics 76
  - Internal Organizational Demographics 77
  - Diversity Barriers 78
  - Affirmative Action Programs 78
  - Workplace Diversity Initiative 79
- **Labor Relations** 82
  - Negotiation Process 82
  - Incentive Programs 88
- **Training and Education Goals** 89
  - Determining Needs 89
  - Assessing Resources 90
- **Member Assistance Services** 91
  - Behavioral Health Program 91
  - Member Assistance Programs 92
  - Local, State/Provincial, and Federal Regulations 93
  - Program Appraisal 93
- **Chapter Summary** 93
- **Review Questions** 94

NFPA® Job Performance Requirements

This chapter provides information that addresses the following job performance requirements of NFPA® 1021, *Standard for Fire Officer Professional Qualifications* (2014).

Level III	Level IV
6.2.1	7.2.1
6.2.2	7.2.2
6.2.3	7.2.3
6.2.4	7.2.4
6.2.5	7.2.5
6.2.6	
6.2.7	

Human Resources Management (Levels III & IV)

Learning Objectives

After reading this chapter, students will be able to:

[Level III]

1. Identify various management concepts essential to emergency services staffing. (6.2.1)
2. Explain employment practices utilized in fire and emergency services. (6.2.2, 6.2.3, 6.2.5, 6.2.6)
3. Recognize various professional development and continuing education programs used in fire and emergency services. (6.2.4, 6.2.7)

[Level IV]

4. Describe various methods used for appraising human resources demographics. (7.2.1)
5. Explain various labor management practices relating to the duties of the chief officer. (7.2.2)
6. Identify various goals for training and educating fire and emergency services personnel. (7.2.3, 7.2.5)
7. Describe various member assistance services available to fire and emergency services personnel. (7.2.4, 7.2.5)

Chapter 2
Human Resources Management (Levels III & IV)

Case History

Nationally, fire and emergency services organization recruiting and hiring practices have been under scrutiny for many years. As a result, numerous municipalities have been faced with legal challenges to the methods they use to recruit, test, and certify potential candidates.

For over a decade, one major U.S. city faced repeated challenges because of allegations that hiring practices favored white candidates over black and Latino applicants. Although the case is still in the court system, changes in recruitment, screening, and hiring practices could be forced upon the department. The municipality has already incurred millions of dollars in legal fees and may be forced to pay many more millions in damages.

To mitigate the potential of legal actions, departments must have fair and impartial hiring practices and recruit from a representative segment of the population. Tests, both written and physical, must be job-related and designed in a way that they do not discriminate against any applicant.

People are the most valuable resource of any fire and emergency services organization. Personnel costs also constitute the largest portion of an organization's budget. Fire and emergency services functions cannot be performed without trained and organized people. Chief officers are a vital part of this effort. Chief officers must have knowledge of human resources management practices to ensure that the greatest value is derived from the organization's human resources.

 Emergency Services Staffing

One of a chief officer's most critical tasks will be to accurately analyze staffing needs and make hiring and promotional decisions based on those needs and department resources **(Figure 2.1, p. 46)**. Because the hiring and training of personnel are not quick processes, you must be forward thinking with regards to personnel planning. The following sections will explain emergency services staffing. The concepts of planning, staffing requirements, and duty assignments will be introduced.

Figure 2.1 Chief officers need to be involved in the analysis of staffing needs.

Planning

Planning is essential to human resources management for projecting needs and anticipating challenges. Although there are unforeseen outside factors that may affect the human resources plan. Chief officers should be able to identify any unforeseen obstacles that may affect human resources. These officers must have the knowledge necessary to conduct a job analysis or supervise employees who can accomplish this responsibility. This task may be contracted to an organization that specializes in job analysis and position descriptions. In small fire and emergency services organizations, the chief officer is responsible for planning personnel requirements. In large organizations, a human resources branch is responsible for planning; while in volunteer organizations, the governing body is responsible for planning personnel requirements.

Projecting Needs

The chief officer or group responsible for projecting personnel needs should collect the following information:

- Rank, function, and assignment of existing numbers of members
- Recent authorized minimum staffing levels and distribution and concentration of resources
- Current and future personnel budget, including history and current projections
- Job analysis of each position within the department/organization
- Maximum/minimum retirement ages (based on authority having jurisdiction [AHJ])
- Minimum years of service before promotion to next level (based on AHJ)
- Current retirement incentives
- Potential expansion/contraction of the service area
- Potential changes in the structure of the organization

- Potential changes in the services the organization provides
- Potential changes in the retirement system
- Time required for hiring and training new personnel (including medical testing, background checks, psychological exams, and others)
- Labor agreements
- Development and revision of job descriptions

This data should be analyzed to establish a timeline for hiring personnel by projecting personnel needs for a specific period of time. Most organizations have retirement programs with established lengths of service for personnel to reach retirement. These organizations need to make strategic plans based on these time periods with revisions every three to five years based on local circumstances **(Figure 2.2)**. Unforeseen obstacles, such as changes in the service area, can and will force the plan to be altered over time.

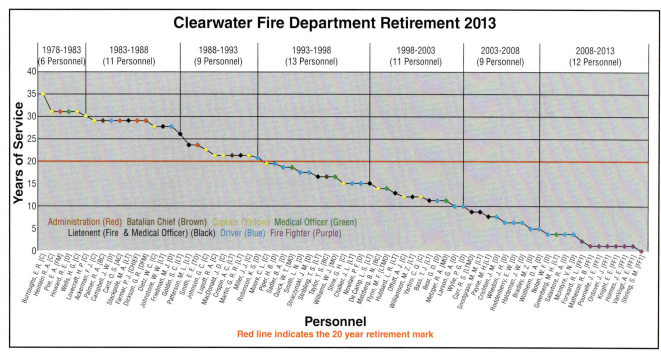

Figure 2.2 A personnel timeline to identify potential retirement periods for personnel within a fire department.

Anticipating Challenges

To anticipate unforeseen challenges, contingency plans must be developed. Some of these alterations/changes are as follows:

- **Requirements of the service area** — Alterations can include declines or increases in the population; changes in major industries or businesses; incorporation, annexation, or de-annexation of land; or other demographic factors. A shift in resources from fire suppression to emergency medical services (EMS) can also be a factor.

- **Financial resources of the governmental jurisdiction** — Recessions, depressions, or other economic factors can affect a government or locality's ability to raise funds to support a fire and emergency services organization/department.

- **Economic environment causing a change in the available pool of recruits** — Workers seeking employment during poor economic times may increase the number of applicants. Conversely, the ability to earn higher wages in private industry can result in fewer available applicants.
- **Attitude of the society toward volunteering or becoming a career firefighter/emergency responder** — Changes in personal priorities, values, or perceptions of the fire and emergency services can cause attitude changes. Events that discredit an organization can cause people to believe that the action is representative of the organization as a whole.
- **Technology or operational procedures** — New apparatus, equipment, fire-suppression agents, the installation of passive fire-protection systems, or implementation of a minimum staffing level may cause a change in personnel requirements.
- **Catastrophic events** — Challenges can include natural disasters or other incidents that result in the death or disability of members.

Staffing Requirements

Guidelines for minimum staffing levels in fire suppression, emergency medical, and special operations are found in NFPA® 1710, *Standard for the Organization and Deployment of Fire Suppression Operations, Emergency Medical Operations, and Special Operations to the Public by Career Fire Departments* and NFPA® 1720, *Standard for the Organization and Deployment of Fire Suppression Operations, Emergency Medical Operations and Special Operations to the Public by Volunteer Fire Departments*. Because local requirements and resources vary, the implementation of these standards may be based on analyses of local fire loss, target hazards, and other constraints or requirements.

- NFPA® 1710 identifies the optimum or ideal staffing levels as four members each for engine and ladder/truck companies performing fire-suppression operations.
- If the response area includes tactical hazards, high-hazard occupancies, geographical restrictions, or a high frequency of incidents, the standard raises this minimum number to six members per fire company.
- Staffing for other types of medical and special-operations companies is based on the particular situation and does not have a minimum number included in the standard.
- In the U.S., Occupational Safety and Health Administration (OSHA) regulations require all departments/organizations (including volunteer departments/organizations) to have at least four members available (2-in 2-out) before starting an interior fire attack.
- Incidents involving imminent life-threatening situations may allow for the use of fewer members as long as the operation is conducted in accordance with the requirements of NFPA® 1500 for safe operations.
- Staffing levels in Canada are determined at the provincial rather than the federal level.

NOTE: Organizations such as the Insurance Services Office (ISO) Fire Suppression Rating Schedule (FSRS), Fire Underwriter's Survey (in Canada), NIST, and Center for Public Safety Excellence (CPSE) can assist with determining needed staffing requirements.

State Occupational Safety and Health Enforcement

Federal law allows states to enforce their own safety and health regulations. The OSHA Act does not allow Federal OSHA to have jurisdiction over state and local government organizations. State-level OSHA agencies are typically provided federal funds to enforce federal regulations on the state level. However, states have no obligation to participate in this program and are free to enforce above or below established federal standards.

Staffing Assignments

Organizational staffing assignments must be based on each individual's ability to perform the job assignments (job proficiency) so that human resources are utilized in an effective manner. Some consideration may be given to seniority and policies outlined in the labor/management agreement. Assignments that result in duty or job changes are generally based on:

- Promotions
- Vacancies
- Personal requests
- Creation of new units
- Changes in services and delivery

Duty assignments should contribute to the organization's effectiveness, individual employee improvement, and should not be arbitrary. Relocating units periodically can familiarize members with the occupancy hazards, geographic response areas, and segments found in the community. These relocations involve moving a unit within its initial response area to a location that allows it to respond into adjacent response areas. After a predetermined period of time, such as 6 months, a second relocation moves the unit into the new response area **(Figure 2.3)**. The transition should be gradual, the unit should remain intact, and the justification for these moves must be clearly stated to the personnel involved.

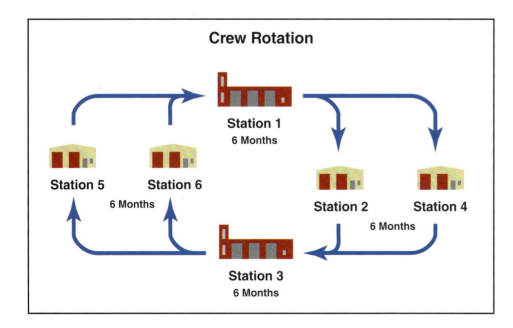

Figure 2.3 Crew rotations or relocations can help department members become familiar with the entire community, instead of just one area or district.

Some departments/organizations rotate personnel from one type of apparatus to another. Giving everyone an idea of what each crew does on the incident scene can create job enrichment, increase depth and breadth of experience, and eliminate or minimize employee burnout.

Employment Practices

Fire and emergency services organizations of all types regularly search for new personnel. Staffing polices will vary because of legal mandates and organizational past practices. This section primarily focuses on the following employment practices used in combination, industrial, and career organizations:

- Strategic and succession planning
- Attracting/recruiting diverse personnel
- Developing, retaining, and promoting qualified personnel

All chief officers need to be aware of governmental mandates and the requirements they create. Chief officers should have a basic knowledge and understanding of the following:

- Human resources function in the fire and emergency services organization
- Employment processes
- Employment laws and practices
- Interview techniques
- Applicant selection processes

Laws Affecting Employment

Federal laws that affect hiring practices in the U.S. are in the Civil Rights Act of 1964, Affirmative Action Laws created by Presidential Executive Order, Age Discrimination in Employment Act of 1967, Rehabilitation Act of 1973, Equal Pay Act, Americans with Disabilities Act, and other mandates. Similar laws serve the same function in Canada at the provincial level.

These federal laws prohibit employment discrimination and apply to almost all public and private organizations. The federal government can take legal action if these laws are violated. Groups that perceive that they have been discriminated against can bring class-action lawsuits. The best approach to the government's legal requirements is to ensure that all hiring, promoting, and assigning is based on job-related skills and requirements. Job requirements must be precise, well defined, accurately conceived, and well-structured to meet the legal test of nondiscrimination.

Employment policies and procedures should be in accordance with all applicable local, state/provincial, and federal laws, regulations, and standards as well as relevant industry codes and standards. These policies and procedures should also adhere to any applicable employment contracts or collective bargaining agreements. The organization and human resources professionals should jointly develop the employment practices policies and procedures. An employment law attorney should review these policies and procedures.

Human Resources Policies and Procedures

All human resources-related policies and procedures should be developed in conjunction with applicable federal, state/provincial, and local regulations. Additionally, some may be developed in reaction to specific incidents. Organizations should consider and establish the following policies:

- **Abuse of controlled substances** — Expectations with regard to use of controlled substances should be established in writing, provided to each member, and discussed during new employee orientation. A controlled substance policy may include drug testing, use of prescription drugs that may impair actions, use of alcohol prior to and on duty, use of illicit substances, and many others. Members who suffer from substance abuse issues may be protected under the Americans with Disabilities Act (ADA) if they have self-identified their condition prior to an infraction. Groups such as the IAFC have developed position statements regarding substance abuse policies.

- **Employee discrimination** — Discrimination, harassment, hazing, and retaliation are not acceptable and can damage a department's reputation and morale. Policies and procedures should clearly establish what constitutes discrimination and outline the penalties for violation of the policy.

- **Social media** — Clear policies and procedures should be developed to govern the use of social media while members are on and off duty, while also ensuring the member's right to free speech under the first amendment. Policies should also be written to govern the use of still and video cameras during incident operations to prevent the release of sensitive information, legal liability, and damage to the department's reputation **(Figure 2.4)**.

- **Nonviolence** — Violence, both physical and verbal, in the workplace is not acceptable under any circumstances. Policies and procedures should establish guidelines and penalties for violations. Provisions should include law enforcement in criminal investigations.

NOTE: Issues regarding individual and employee rights change; therefore, it is critical that chief officers stay up-to-date on these issues.

Figure 2.4 The introduction of digital cameras and social media have caused many fire and emergency services organizations to revise their policies and procedures about the release of photos and videos.

Employee Disabilities and Accommodations

Emergency services functions can be physically demanding. Emergency services organizations must achieve a balance between employing personnel who are capable of performing their assigned functions and while adhering to applicable regulations regarding employment of those with disabilities. Employees who cannot adequately perform their assigned functions place themselves and their coworkers at risk for serious injury or death. The following sections will describe the obligations emergency services organizations have regarding employee disabilities and accommodations.

Legal Requirements and Reasonable Accommodations

The Americans with Disabilities Act (ADA) of 1990 is a broad-reaching law that, among other things, establishes requirements for employers with 15 or more employees. The ADA defines a *disability* as "a physical or mental impairment that substantially limits a major life activity."

The law provides protections for those with disabilities in all areas of employment. An employer must provide reasonable accommodations so that individuals with a disability can perform the position's functions. The necessary accommodation should not prove to be an "undue burden" for the employer. Considerations with regard to undue burdens are generally weighed against the size and nature of the employer. For example, what may be considered an undue burden for a small business with 15 employees may not be an undue burden for a large corporation or government entity. Generally, government agencies are typically held to the higher end of this standard.

Employees may ask for accommodations that the organization does not consider reasonable accommodations. In many instances, working with the employee in a collaborative manner can arrive at a solution that is functional for the employee and more cost effective for the employer.

Fitness for Duty Considerations

While reasonable accommodations must be made under the law, firefighters have certain physical and medical fitness requirements that are considered exceptions to the reasonable accommodations rules. NFPA® 1582, *Standard on Comprehensive Occupational Medical Program for Fire Departments,* provides a list of essential job tasks and descriptions for personnel engaged in structural firefighting.

Individuals who are unable to perform these essential functions will often not apply for the position. Physical ability tests, such as the Candidate Physical Ability Test (CPAT), have been deemed valid to determine a candidate's ability to perform the physical tasks required of the position **(Figure 2.5)**. In addition, candidates must pass a medical evaluation performed in accordance with NFPA® 1582.

NFPA® 1582 provides two categories (A and B) of medical conditions that have the potential to affect the ability of a firefighter to perform the essential functions

Figure 2.5 Chief officers need to be familiar with the physical ability test used by their organization.

of his or her position. Employees with Category A conditions cannot be certified as medically fit for duty. Employees with Category B conditions can only be certified as medically fit for duty if they are able to perform the essential duties of their position without posing a risk to themselves or others.

The job analysis and position description will be a critical element in any legal challenge to an organization's hiring or employment practices. While emergency services organizations are still held responsible under the ADA to provide reasonable accommodations for employees, the courts have typically given the organizations a wide berth with regard to accommodations for essential job functions.

Job Analyses and Position Descriptions

Volunteer and combination fire and emergency services organizations should develop a job analysis. A job analysis provides valuable information for:

- Creating an interest in the organization.
- Explaining the requirements for membership to potential members.
- Providing an accurate description of the amount of commitment in work time, training, and risks.

A job analysis is the process of determining the duties of a specific position and the qualifications needed to fill that position. The analysis also provides the information necessary for the position description that is used in recruiting, promoting, and evaluating employee performance. The job analysis is also essential in worker's compensation management, rehabilitation, fitness for duty, and other considerations. Preparing a job analysis for each position in the organization is a basic function of the human resources manager or branch. The job description lists the tasks and responsibilities of the position and the minimum educational and physical qualifications and experience necessary to perform it. The professional qualifications found in NFPA® 1001, *Standard for Fire Fighter Professional Qualifications*, can be used to measure if the job analysis is complete and accurate for entry-level firefighters/emergency responders.

Because the majority of fire and emergency services organizations provide an entry-level training course, the requirements for new applicants have been traditionally very basic. The minimum entry requirements for the position of recruit firefighter generally include a minimum age requirement, educational requirements, a valid driver's license, medical and fitness evaluation, and criminal record check evaluation. In some jurisdictions, these requirements have changed as the fire and emergency services have taken on more responsibilities and training costs have increased.

Some career departments/organizations now require associate degrees in fire science, emergency medical services (EMS) certifications, firefighter certifications, and/or specialty driver's licenses **(Figure 2.6, p. 54)**. Candidates with proficiency in multiple languages may also be given preference. Health and safety concerns have driven some jurisdictions to add the requirement that applicants must not be tobacco users. The AHJ may establish increased standards directly, or the standards may be based upon a reevaluation of the jobs that members perform.

Figure 2.6 Career departments/organizations may require a variety of degrees, certifications, or licenses for personnel to possess prior to being hired or promoted.

Organizations that hire personnel for positions above the rank of firefighter/emergency responder must ensure that the job analysis includes not only the basic requirements but also the additional duties of the higher rank. For example, all applicants hired as chief officer should meet the professional requirements described in NFPA® 1021 for Level III or Level IV fire officers. For positions that a collective bargaining agreement does not cover, the job analysis may be used to determine a salary hiring range for the position.

Recruitment

Chief officers should find and recruit people who are motivated to become firefighters/emergency responders for reasons other than simply economics. *Recruiting* is the process of attracting qualified candidates to apply for available positions. Personnel should be recruited from a diverse pool of applicants capable of performing the specific tasks outlined in the job analysis.

Recruiting Sources

While governmental controls on recruiting may be different for volunteer, combination, or career organizations, the recruiting process and sources are generally the same. Career and combination organizations that pay personnel for services (full-paid, per call, stipend) must comply with AHJ requirements. Volunteer organizations do not have to comply, although the administrative body may apply the guidelines voluntarily. Based on the job analysis and resultant position description, recruiting sources may include:

- **Other fire and emergency services organizations** — Large urban career departments/organizations may use volunteer fire and emergency services organizations and small municipal departments as a source for new personnel. Ambulance services, industrial fire brigades, and public safety organizations are also sources for applicants.
- **Military** — U.S. military firefighters/emergency responders are trained to NFPA® standards and certified by two nationally recognized accrediting agencies. Generally, military veterans are familiar with discipline and risk factors.
- **Educational institutions** — Depending on the minimum educational requirements, high schools, vocational schools, community colleges, and universities are excellent sources. Athletes on sports teams are good sources for recruiting because they are likely to have the required physical abilities and an understanding of team dynamics.
- **Professional organizations** — Professional journals or newsletters provide space for recruitment advertisements. These organizations are particularly helpful when external applicants for higher ranks or specialist positions are required.
- **Hospitals and clinics** — Sources for trained personnel when the department/organization is expanding into emergency medical services.

Volunteer departments have additional sources because applicants are not dependent on the organization for full-time employment. Volunteer departments provide more than just fire protection for the community they serve; therefore, the approach to recruiting may vary from that of a career department.

Recruiting and Attracting Diverse Workforces

The fire and emergency services organization will gain the benefits of a diverse workforce through recruiting from the general population of the service area. Organizations should guard against the natural tendency to replicate its members. Define the target group and customize the message to attract members of the target group. A diverse workforce:

- Reflects the composition of the community
- Provides a better understanding of various needs and a vital connection to all segments of the community
- Sends a strong message that the fire and emergency services organization is inclusive and values the various groups in the community
- Provides all members of the population with opportunities to have a part in the community, either as a volunteer or a career public employee
- Expands the available number of applicants from which to recruit
- Helps meet any legally mandated hiring targets and prevents hiring discrimination lawsuits

Recruiting should never be represented as simply *filling a quota*. It should be communicated as an effort to attract the very best workers from each component of the population. Current organization members who are members of one or more of these groups can help tailor the message to appeal to the group. They understand the cultural customs and characteristics and can also provide positive images of firefighters/emergency responders for the community.

When targeting members of underrepresented classes, it is helpful to learn the cultural values and customs, such as religious practices, that may need to be accommodated. Bilingual recruiters and materials may also be needed. Any recruiting strategy aimed at these groups should be developed in close cooperation with members of that group to ensure the appropriateness of the message and to avoid stereotyping.

Position Marketing and Posting

The recruiting process includes knowing where to find potential recruits, marketing the organization to potential recruits, and convincing them to apply. The most appropriate recruiting method depends on the job that is available, number of positions to be filled, and need to target specific underutilized segments of the workforce. Both career and volunteer organizations should use valid marketing strategies when developing recruitment programs. Assistance can be obtained from local media, social media, the internet, advertising agencies, and colleges. Observing the successful campaigns that other organizations use, such as the military, can also be beneficial. Some general marketing methods include:

- **Advertising** — Placed in the local print media, radio and television, and state/provincial and national trade journals **(Figure 2.7)**.

- **Brochures** — Distributed at state fairs and information booths, door-to-door delivery, and direct mail.

- **Posters and banners** — Attached to apparatus, stations, and information booths.

- **Audio/visual programs** — Helpful when targeting a specific group and modified to emphasize certain aspects of the profession.

- **Public training and educational events** — Increases the visibility of the department/organization within the community.

Fire Chief
City of West Covina

Located in the beautiful San Gabriel Valley, the city of West Covina (pop. 107,000) is seeking a new Fire Chief. Serving as a member of the City's Executive Team, the Fire Chief is responsible for a Department with 82 staff, five fire stations, and a $12.1 million budget. Strong leadership, management, and interpersonal skills are required. Bachelor's degree or equivalent is required (Master's preferred) in fire science, public administration or a related field and four years' progressively responsible fire service management experience at the Battalion Chief level or higher . Salary range: $98,364–$132,792.

To apply for this outstanding career opportunity, please send your resume and cover letter by **March 29, 2004** to:

John Doe
Williard Hays & Baron
200 Stowe Avenue, Suite 255 North
Sacramento, CA 96842

Cwilliard@baroncareer.com

Call 555-665-4300 to request a detailed brochure regarding this position.

Figure 2.7 An example of a print media advertisement seeking candidates for a fire chief position.

- **Word of mouth** — Encourage members to recruit face to face with friends, relatives, and acquaintances; best used along with other methods because members tend to recruit people similar to them.
- **Executive or professional recruiting agencies** — Search the national job market for candidates, especially in the chief-officer ranks.
- **Web sites and social media** — Keep site maintained and information current.
- **Billboards** — Reaches a large number of potential applicants.
- **High school and college career days or job fairs** — Provides students with information about careers or volunteer opportunities in the fire and emergency services.

Combination and career departments/organizations' recruitment requires the creation of a hiring announcement that includes the following information:

- Accurate job description based on the job analysis
- Application closing date
- Application process
- Contact information
- Pay range or minimum salary
- List of benefits
- Equal Employment Opportunity (EEO)/affirmative action statement

Volunteer departments need to consider a slightly different approach that contains the following messages:

- **Need for volunteers** — State applicants are needed to fill vacancies
- **Personal benefits** — Describe the rewards, excitement, team spirit, and personal fulfillment that result from being a volunteer. Point out that volunteer experience can lead to a position as a career firefighter/emergency responder, particularly in combination departments **(Figure 2.8)**
- **Realities of fire fighting or emergency response** — Outline the risks, time commitment, training, and expectations of the organization

Figure 2.8 Chief officers in volunteer departments should be able to describe the rewards and benefits of becoming a volunteer firefighter to potential recruits.

Employment Process

Chief officers need to be knowledgeable of the hiring/employment process. A chief officer must be able to analyze the process and determine whether or not it is providing the quality of applicants necessary to do the job.

In career and combination departments/organizations, the hiring/employment process may be administered internally or through the AHJ's Human Resources Department. In volunteer organizations and the volunteer portion of a combination department, the governing board of the membership may administer the process. Formal rules and processes can vary greatly based on legal mandates and AHJ policies and procedures. Volunteer organizations that are not required to meet career-type hiring standards should consider applying those standards because they will attract the most qualified applicants for open positions. Standards that involve interview techniques and validated testing are good industry practices.

Organizations may even use different systems for different positions. For instance, the entry-level firefighter may be required to submit an application form and perform a physical ability test, while the applicant for chief of the department may submit a resume and undergo an assessment center screening. Elements of the typical hiring or selection process consist of application forms, tests (aptitude, personality, and physical ability), interviews, background screenings and reference checks, and medical-fitness examinations. An applicant may be eliminated at any point in the process. The applicant who successfully completes the process is offered the position and a contract or letter of acceptance is signed.

Following the common hiring steps helps ensure that the organization hires qualified personnel to perform the required duties in the position. It also ensures that personnel who are hired fully understand the expectations that the department/organization and the community have of them. The sections that follow describe the elements and levels that are common to most hiring processes.

Application Form

The application form is a questionnaire on which the applicant provides basic personal information. For some positions (such as senior management), a resume takes the place of an application form. The Human Resources Department or responsible authority compares the completed form or resume to the job specifications. Applicants who match the qualifications advance to the next level of the process.

Background Screening/Investigation and Reference Check

The Human Resources Department or responsible authority authenticates the information on the application form or in the resume (critical to the process). Because applicants sometimes overstate their qualifications and accomplishments, it is necessary to verify the information provided.

Tests

Various test formats may be used to predict the potential success of the applicant in performing the job. The EEOC requires that all employment testing be based on job-related criteria. For instance, an applicant for a clerical position can be required to take a typing test but not a test that involves dragging a fire hose. The organization must also be prepared to provide test translations and interpreters for applicants who are not completely fluent in English. Although language proficiency may be a job requirement, it cannot be a barrier in the application process. Tests that are normally used in the fire and emergency services include the following:

- **Aptitude** — Involve cognitive skills, reading comprehension, mathematical skills, and writing skills. Although the questions can be tailored to the fire and emergency services, they do not have to be. The goal is to determine the applicant's ability to perform basic mental tasks required to perform the job.

- **Personality** — Help determine if the applicant is emotionally suited for the job. These tests are usually purchased from an outside source that must also provide the analysis and assessment of the results.

- **Physical ability** — Initially consisted of elements that indicated an applicant's strength, stamina, and endurance (such as rope climbs, push-ups, sit-ups, and mid- to long-distance runs). Many have replaced these with job-related, validated physical-aptitude tests such as the Candidate Physical Ability Test (CPAT). The CPAT was developed jointly by the International Association of Fire Chiefs (IAFC) and the International Association of Fire Fighters (IAFF).

- **Assessment center** — Process in which applicants undergo a series of tests, interviews, and simulated experiences to determine their supervisory and managerial abilities; used primarily for filling upper-management positions but may also be part of the internal promotional process. Evaluators in the process are usually peers from similar fire and emergency services organizations.

Interview

The interview is an opportunity for the applicant to learn more about the organization and also an opportunity for the managers and members of the selection team to gain information about the applicant, which is not obtained in the previous elements/levels; often the most heavily weighted element of the hiring process. Many organizations use multiple interview sessions in the selection process. For instance, the interview can show the applicant's ability to communicate and respond under pressure, punctuality, personality traits, and motivations. Because this step is so important, the chief officer must develop good interviewing techniques.

An individual member of the fire and emergency services department/organization, a member of the Human Resources Department, or a selection team or committee may conduct interviews. The Human Resources Department may perform an initial screening interview before preparing a list of applicants for the department/organization to interview. Volunteer departments may require applicants to appear before the governing board for an interview.

Interview teams need to be composed of members who represent the diversity of the community. Personnel involved in the interview process should be familiar with the following interview techniques:

- How to prepare for the interviews.
- How to conduct the interviews.
- Problems to avoid in the selection process.

The type of interview that is chosen depends in large part on the policies and procedures of the AHJ, the experience of the interviewer(s), and the legal opinion of the organization's counsel. Each type of interview is based on questions and how they are asked. The three general types of interviews are as follows:

- **Structured** — Preplanned and begins with a prepared list of questions to ask the applicant. Team members may take turns asking questions based on a predetermined sequence or series of topics. The same questions are directed to all applicants providing the interviewer with a means of comparing each one to the others. It ensures against unintentional discrimination or bias.

- **Unstructured** — Lacks preplanning or prepared questions. More experienced interviewers may use this technique or it may be used for the final interview in a series of elimination interviews.

- **Semistructured** — Begins with a list of questions but allows the interviewer the flexibility of asking unplanned questions. This interview type allows the interviewer to ask the same basic questions of all applicants while tailoring specific questions to individual applicants and to build on new information.

The chief officer must be familiar with the general types of questions and the topics that can and cannot be discussed in an interview. Interview questions are intended to provide information that will assist in making a hiring decision. The questions should have a specific purpose, be job-related, and be asked of all applicants. The four general types of interview questions are:

- **Closed-ended** — Usually require a brief or "yes" or "no" answer. They are appropriate for specific aspects of the job. For example, *Do you have an emergency medical technician's certificate?*

- **Open-ended** — Allow for an unlimited response from the applicant. They are appropriate for determining ability and motivation. For example, *Why do you want to be a volunteer firefighter?*

- **Hypothetical** — Require the applicants to describe how they would respond to a certain situation. For example, *How would you handle a belligerent citizen in the fire station?*

- **Probing** — Seek to clarify a previous answer and to provide the interviewer with a better understanding (usually unplanned questions). For example, *What did you mean when you said "It was rough"?*

Questions must be job-related to prevent the possibility of discrimination. The following topics are examples of what *cannot* be asked as part of an applicant's pre-employment interview:

- Race or skin color
- National origin
- Sexual orientation
- Religion
- Political affiliation
- Debts or financial status
- Marital status
- Number and age of children

- Pregnancy or potential of pregnancy
- Physical, mental, or emotional disabilities or medical conditions
- Height and weight
- Arrest and conviction record (will be determined during the background check)
- Long-term goal for employment

While part of this information will be made available during the screening and application process, it is not part of the interview process. The information that would result from these questions has nothing to do with performing the duties of a firefighter or emergency services provider/responder. If there is any concern about the interview questions, request a legal opinion before the questions are used.

An effective interviewer should be well-prepared before the interviews. Planning ensures that the interviews provide the necessary information, are as stress-free as possible, and are an efficient use of time for all parties involved. The following tasks will help the chief officer or interview team prepare for the interviews:

- Review the application form or resume of each applicant.
- Review the job description and specifications.
- Determine the type of interview that will be used.
- Determine the types of questions that will be used. An attorney or HR specialist should review the list of questions.
- Develop the questions in written form and assign them to various team members (or ask the team members to submit a list of questions).
- Establish a time limit for each interview and prepare a schedule.
- Develop an answer form to take notes on each response.
- Select an appropriate and comfortable location for the interviews.

There are also steps for conducting a successful interview. The generally accepted interview format is as follows:

- **Welcome the applicant** — Open with a warm greeting to place the individual at ease. Introduce each team member and their position in the organization.
- **Briefly describe the organization, position, and job expectations** — Ask if the applicant has any questions about the information provided or about the selection process. Applicants may disqualify themselves once they have a clear understanding of the position or expectations.
- **Ask the questions** — Use the list of questions and start asking the questions. If a team is involved, rotate the questions around the group. Ask probing questions as necessary to clarify any points. Listen closely, take notes, and maintain eye contact with the applicant.
- **Introduce the top candidates to other members of the organization** — This step is usually reserved for upper-management positions and not entry-level applicants. These meetings may include a walk-through of the organization's facilities or a lunch meeting.

- **Close the interview** — Ask the applicants if they would like to add anything else or if they have any questions. Thank the applicants for their time and explain the next step in the process. Let them know how long it will take to make a decision and assure them that they will be contacted with a decision. Be sure to keep that commitment.

Follow-up interviews may be required to narrow the field of applicants. These interviews should follow the same pattern but with different questions. Answers from the previous interview may be used to develop new questions.

Medical-fitness examination

A medical-fitness examination must be performed once an applicant is selected. The fire and emergency services physician, the authority's medical department, or an outside provider may do the exam **(Figure 2.9)**. The information that is obtained is used not only to determine the ability of the applicant to perform the job-related tasks but also as a benchmark for future annual medical evaluations. The pre-employment medical examination should be established and conducted as per AHJ requirements and in conjunction with the requirements in NFPA® 1582, *Standard on Comprehensive Occupational Medical Program for Fire Departments*. The AHJ may require other diagnostic evaluations such as psychological testing.

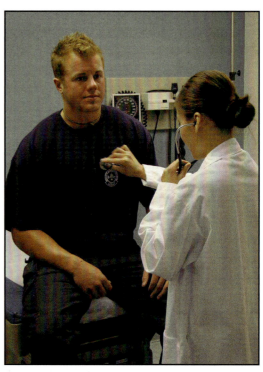

Figure 2.9 Applicants who have been selected must undergo a medical fitness examination.

Applicant Selection

When making a selection decision, the chief officer or team must determine those who are best qualified for the position. Information gathered from each step of the process is compared to the job description and specifications. Individuals who do not meet the qualifications are disqualified. In some cases, all applicants are ranked and the top candidates are placed on a list in preferred order. This list is sent to the Human Resources Department or to the governing body of the organization for approval. Offer letters are sent to the most qualified applicants. Letters of appreciation and non-acceptance are sent to the remainder. Pitfalls to avoid in the selection process include:

- **Rushing** — Occurs when pressure to fill a position is placed on the chief officer or team. If there are no qualified applicants, repeat the process rather than hiring *just anyone.*

- **Stereotyping** — Occurs when the applicant is prejudged based on considerations other than job-related qualifications.

- **Similarity** — Occurs when the interviewer selects applicants because they are *like me*. As mentioned earlier, diversity has benefits for the organization.
- **Premature selection** — Occurs when an interviewer mentally makes a selection before all the applicants have been interviewed. Consider applicants compared not to one another but to the job specifications.

Promotions

One mark of success is attaining rank through promotions. Emergency services organizations should promote based on merit and AHJ requirements. Organizations may promote strictly from within their own membership or hire qualified external candidates for specific positions. The goal of the promotional process in career, combination, and volunteer organizations is to fill the vacancy with the most capable individual whose skills, knowledge, and ability, and experience matches the duties of that position.

Promotions should be used as an opportunity to celebrate the achievements of personnel such as holding a public promotion ceremony and inviting families, elected or appointed officials, the community, and media. This event projects a positive image of the department in the community and shows personnel that the department values their contributions.

The promotion process (like the hiring process) should be based on the NFPA® professional qualifications standards as well as the internal department/organization position analysis. Candidates are tested on and judged against the level of knowledge that is required to perform the duties of the specific rank or position. In some jurisdictions, the organization is permitted to perform the testing and evaluation of the candidates internally. In others, the local government body, through the Human Resources Department, handles the promotions process. The promotion process should involve specific elements that can include the following:

- **Preparatory training** — Succession planning should prepare all personnel for advancement at least to the next level through an established career development plan.
- **Vacancy availability** — It is usually known in advance that a position will be vacated through advancement or retirement at a given time. It may be preferable to temporarily fill the position with an employee serving in an interim or "acting" capacity. Budget constraints usually do not allow an incumbent and a newly promoted person to work in the same position simultaneously. Transitions of this type are rare in the public sector but should be encouraged to reduce the loss of institutional knowledge.
- **Vacancy advertising** — Post a vacancy notice for a specific period of time in the various media mentioned previously. This period may be longer in organizations that accept external candidates to allow for publishing deadlines.
- **Applicant certification** — Certify applicants who meet the position requirements based on established criteria. Once the advertising period closes, certified applicants will move forward in the promotional process. For internal candidates, personnel records should be reviewed. For external candidates, check resumes and references and perform background checks.

- **Written examination development** — Develop a written examination that contains job-related questions. A third-party testing organization, a Human Resources Department personnel specialist, or an internal personnel committee can provide these questions. To prevent any legal issues or challenges to the promotion process, all tests should be carefully constructed to eliminate bias. The examination overseer is responsible for ensuring that all candidates are treated fairly, the timing of the test is accurate, the environment is free of distractions, and test materials are handled properly. Test security, before and after the examination, is critical to the test's success. Once the tests are graded, create a list in order of ranking based on scores. Depending on local policy, the list may include all candidates or only those scoring above a specific percentage.

- **Skills testing** — Conduct the skills-testing portion (sometimes referred to as *evolutions or practicals*) to determine how well a candidate can perform specific job-related functions. Skill testing is commonly done in examinations for driver/operator and company officer. Base the tests on NFPA® job performance requirements, time the tests, and grade students against specific criteria. Compare the results to incumbent members of the position performed under similar circumstances to ensure that the evolutions are job-related. This comparison helps establish the time for completion of each evolution.

- **Assessment centers** — Use role-playing exercises, problem-solving situations, interviews, and other exercises that show the candidate's ability to reason and respond under pressure. Select assessment-center evaluators from organizations and departments that are generally equivalent in size and types of operational systems used. These assessors should be trained in the selection process to help ensure the validity of the test. Assessment centers are more expensive and time-consuming than a simple written examination but are worth the effort and should be used for promotional examinations.

- **Applicant interviews** — Conduct interviews as part of the promotion process for higher ranks, specialized positions, new positions, and vacancies that are open to external candidates. See details of the interview process in the Employment Practices section.

- **Successful candidates posting** — Post the names of the successful candidates in rank order (depending on the local promotion policy) following the written examination. Posting test results or scores may be considered an invasion of privacy based on applicable laws. This list may become invalid once the position is filled, which is the case when only one vacancy exists, or it may remain in effect for a specified period of time when there are multiple potential vacancies within a specific rank. Some organizations allow the chief/manager to select from the top three to ten candidates on the list regardless of ranking on the list. Other variations exist for filling the vacancy once the list is certified.

- **Challenges** — Provide a specific (not open-ended) challenge period for candidates to review their examinations and challenge any questions that concern them.

All promotional activities should adhere to department policy, labor contracts, and all local, state/provincial, and federal laws regarding employment practices. Adhering to these policies, procedures, and regulations will help prevent challenges to the promotional process and will preserve the reputation of the department.

Employee Benefits

Members in career departments and some volunteer departments are provided monetary compensation and other benefits for their service. A quality benefit package is often a determining factor in a candidate's decision to accept employment.

Quality benefits come at a significant cost to the organization. A good benefits package can cost the organization 40% or more of the employee's salary and represents a large portion of the overall budget. Most benefits are reserved for the organization's full time employees. The definition of full time can vary between organizations but is typically 75% of a full time equivalent (FTE) position or greater.

Benefits typically offered as part of a benefit package include the following **(Figure 2.10)**:

- **Annual leave** — Paid time off that may or may not accrue from one year to the next. Generally, employees may use this leave in any manner they wish with supervisor approval.

- **Sick leave/Dependent sick leave** — Paid time off to be used for non-job-related illness or injury. Depending on the organization, sick leave may also be used to care for ill or injured members of the employee's immediate family. Some regulations such as The Family Medical Leave Act (FMLA) are federally mandated.

- **Bereavement leave** — Paid time off to make funeral arrangements and/or to attend memorial services for family members.

- **Retirement/Pension contributions** — The employer pays into a managed retirement program in the employee's name. The contribution is typically a percentage of the employee's pay and the employee may or may not be required to also contribute depending on the program. Defined benefit plans are traditional pension plans where the employee receives a set amount each month upon retirement. Defined contribution plans establish a set amount that will be contributed each month and the funds available upon retirement will depend on the performance of the investment.

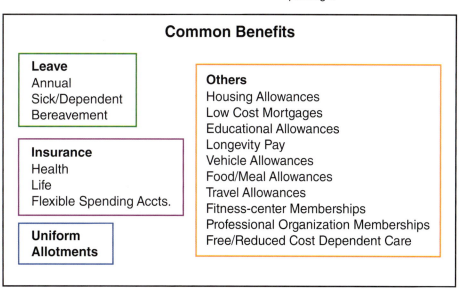

Figure 2.10 Common benefits found in fire department benefits package.

- **Health Insurance** — Contribution toward the purchase of health insurance for the employee. The employee may or may not be required to contribute depending on the program. Often, the employee also has the option to provide coverage for immediate family members at an additional cost.
- **Life Insurance** — Employer paid insurance premium payable upon the death of the covered member. Often, the provided coverage is 1-2 times the employee's annual salary. The employee is often provided the opportunity to purchase additional coverage in addition to that of the employer.
- **Flexible spending accounts** — Accounts that allow the member to contribute pretax funds toward healthcare and dependent care costs.
- **Uniform allotments** — Payments to employees for the purchase and maintenance of clothing required to perform their daily functions.
- **Other benefits** — Other benefits can include any of the following:
  - Housing allowances
  - Low cost mortgages
  - Educational allowances
  - Longevity pay
  - Deferred compensation
  - Vehicle or vehicle-use allowances
  - Food/meal allowances
  - Travel allowances
  - Fitness-center membership
  - Professional organization membership
  - Free or reduced cost dependent care

In volunteer organizations, the members may be paid per call, enrolled in a state-pension program, or workers' compensation. The governing body (federal, state/provincial, or local) or labor/management negotiations usually determine benefits. Chief officers are involved as both beneficiaries of the benefits and representatives of management who must determine which benefits employees will receive.

Most benefits are not transferable from one organization to the next. In Oklahoma, for example, a retired career firefighter who is receiving a pension cannot work in another career department within the state. In Ohio, pension, accrued annual and sick leave, and other benefits remain with the firefighter when transferring from department to department within that state. In the California state pension system, retirees cannot work more than 960 hours per year and cannot fill a position that is typically budgeted. Chief officers need to be aware of the laws within their own state/province or region and plan accordingly.

Benefit Needs Analysis

The organization's benefit package should be routinely reviewed to ensure that the benefits provided are cost effective and are of actual use to employees. From these benefit reviews, needs can be determined for future revision. A diverse group of the organization's members should participate in any benefit review because some groups of members may rely more on the benefits than other groups. Employee surveys may also help determine which benefits are used and what additional benefits may be needed.

In order to offer a benefit package that is competitive with other departments and organizations, it may be necessary to perform a benchmarking study. This study requires the organization to take stock of the benefits they offer and compare those benefits to organizations that have similar characteristics.

Benefit reviews may indicate that it is necessary to stop offering a certain benefit such as a complimentary health club membership. If the department provides quality exercise equipment, members may not use the health club membership. The funds set aside for the unused benefit might be better used to provide another benefit identified in the needs analysis.

Improving or Modifying Benefits

Managing of an organization's benefit package is a continuing process and involves significant planning. Some benefits are often negotiated as part of the collective bargaining process. Others are identified in the needs assessments mentioned previously. Employees should be given plenty of notice regarding any changes to the benefits package so they can plan and make needed arrangements. Good communication is necessary in any change to the benefits package, especially if employees may view the change as a reduction in their benefits.

Separation and Termination

Emergency services organizations and personnel responsible for their human resources administration must prepare for every member's end of service. That end may come in the form of death or disabling injury, through transfer or administrative dismissal, through normal retirement, or through leaving the department/organization for employment elsewhere. The department/organization's chief officers must be prepared to respond appropriately in each of these situations.

Line-of-Duty Death

The line-of-duty death (LODD) of a department member is one of the most difficult situations for any organization to handle **(Figure 2.11)**. The organization must establish procedures and a protocol for providing the necessary support to the family, friends, and coworkers. This support is in addition to the formal investigation into the cause of the death, which is part of the post incident analysis. Establishing a stress crisis intervention program and training members in its use is an important step. Providing grief counseling through the member assistance program (MAP) is also helpful.

Figure 2.11 A funeral for a firefighter who died in the line-of-duty.

Standard procedures should be developed to guide the organization through such a crisis. For those departments/organizations that do not have formal programs developed, the chief officers should provide leadership in assisting the bereaved. This assistance may take the form of assigning a member to act as liaison between the family and the department/organization, providing a burial team, helping with benefits, and remaining in contact for at least a year following an employee's death.

NOTE: The National Fallen Firefighters' Foundation (NFFF), International Association of Fire Fighters (IAFF), and the International Association of Fire Chiefs (IAFC) have extensive resources available for the development of LODD policies and procedures.

Some organizations have a clergy member perform the duties of chaplain. A member of a local interfaith organization or member of the organization who is also ordained in a specific faith may fill this position. A chaplain can provide valuable assistance to coworkers, family, and responders who have experienced the death of a member of the organization.

Disability

Disabling injuries may occur at any time, both on and off duty. Some will result in the employee being placed on disability leave or light duty until fully recovered and certified to return to duty. In other instances, the employee may never be able to perform the duties of an emergency responder again. In such cases, the organization's leadership will be faced with assignment or employment decisions relating to this person.

State/provincial and local workers' compensation laws, labor/management agreements, and/or other policy guides should dictate the organization's actions regarding disabilities. Some policies require complete termination of employment, while others allow some flexibility in providing alternative assignments (restricted duty) or employment to the injured employee. Regulations or policies often require the organization to provide reasonable accommodation to the employee to perform the requirements of their position. Alternative employment allows the knowledge and skills of the employee to be used in other productive ways such as training, education, prevention, planning, administration, or communications. Some governmental authorities permit the injured person to transfer to other departments or agencies such as building inspections or plans review.

The department/organization must be fair and equitable in its handling of disability injury employment decisions. If it is necessary to terminate the employee because of disabilities, then the department/organization might provide formal assistance similar to those for line-of-duty-death situations. Chief officers must be compassionate in their dealings with the injured firefighter/emergency responder, family, friends, and coworkers.

Termination

An employee may be terminated in two ways: personal choice or administrative action (dismissal). Personal choice termination is voluntary based on the desires of the individual. The individual may choose to seek employment with another fire and emergency services organization, seek other types of employment, or move to another jurisdiction. Dismissal may be the result of a disability injury, a loss of funding for the position, or disciplinary actions. The reason for dismissal and the process for terminating employment must be well documented.

Open communications and a positive work environment are the best tools for dealing with voluntary resignations. Providing feedback on the employee's work, providing reasonable compensation, and satisfying the needs of the employee (part of retention) help prevent voluntary resignations.

Dismissals are a last resort. Training, coaching, and mentoring should be used to help employees maintain the level of performance that the department requires. Layoffs due to the loss of funding may be beyond the control of chief officers, but the effect can be reduced through planning. Creating a contingency plan and budget can help the organization respond to changes in the economic environment. Alternatives to layoffs such as reducing work hours, not filling vacant positions, and assigning multiple functions to individuals may be appropriate within the limitations of law, contract, or other guidelines and requirements.

Termination/dismissal as a form of discipline should occur only when all other actions fail or when a significant rules infraction has occurred. A chief officer's first duty in this case is to attempt to alter the behavior or change the situation that required discipline. Discipline should be commensurate with the offense, up to and including termination.

Thorough documentation is critical in these instances. A detailed list of offenses or infractions must be maintained along with documentation regarding corrective action and efforts to improve the employee's performance in accordance with the AHJ's policies and procedures. This documentation will be required should the employee appeal their termination or take legal action.

Retirement

Chief officers need to use a member's retirement to celebrate and acknowledge the individual's contributions. This recognition is an intangible benefit to the retiring member, a morale boost to the rest of the organization, and shows that the administration values the member's employment. Proactive organizations make preparations for retirements and attrition through succession planning and budgeting.

Exit Interview

Obtaining answers to the following questions can benefit the organization:

- Why is an individual leaving?
- What positive and negative experiences has that person experienced?
- What changes should be considered to improve the work environment?
- Has the organization met the employment needs of the individual?

The interview should follow the format used in the initial interview of the hiring process. Questions should be developed in advance and should also include some flexibility in the event the answers lead in a different direction. The exit interview can provide part of the feedback necessary to evaluate the strength and weaknesses of the organization. The responses are going to be subjective, potentially tainted with bias, and possibly angry. Evaluating the answers needs to be a careful process and may require the assistance of human resources specialists.

Professional Development and Continuing Education

Professional development and continuing education programs are part of the succession planning of the organization, underlie the promotions system, and strengthen the retention process. Organizations that provide the programs and encourage participation in them are focused on the future needs of the organization and its membership. Setting realistic goals for each member's professional development is a critical component of the program. The following sections will highlight professional development and continuing education in greater detail.

NOTE: The IAFC *Officer Development Handbook* is a good resource for the creation of any professional development or continuing education program. This text is accepted industry-wide as a guide to officer development.

Higher Education

Many municipalities now require a minimum of a bachelor's degree and in some instances a master's degree to be considered for a chief-level position. Some municipalities require an associate's degree or a certain level of college credit to be a firefighter candidate. The following sections will discuss levels of higher education and types of degree programs.

Fire and Emergency Services Higher Education (FESHE)

The National Fire Academy (NFA) sponsors the Fire and Emergency Services Higher Education (FESHE) network of emergency services related education and training. FESHE has developed model course outlines that are widely used for associate's and bachelor's level fire and emergency services degree programs. FESHE participants were instrumental in the development of the National Professional Development Model and meet annually on the campus of the NFA to share information and industry best practices.

Levels of Education

There are several levels of higher education with different credit requirements and focuses **(Figure 2.12)**. Levels of higher education include the following:

- **Associate's** — A degree program requiring two academic years of study usually offered through community colleges. The focus of an associate's degree is typically to provide the student with technical knowledge and skills to be successful in the workforce. Because their student population is typically working adults, courses are frequently offered in nontraditional manners such as at night, on weekends, on alternating shifts, or partially or totally online.

- **Bachelor's** — A degree program requiring four to five academic years of study. Bachelor's degree programs provide technical knowledge and skills, theory, and general education courses. Many bachelor's programs are designed to incorporate courses taken at the associate's level – shortening the time required to complete the degree program.

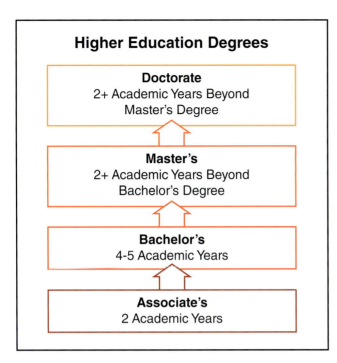

Figure 2.12 The four higher education degrees: associates, bachelor's, master's, and doctorate.

- **Master's** — A degree program requiring two or more academic years of study beyond a bachelor's degree and includes a thesis, creative component, or some other significant original work. Master's degree programs expose students to theory and relevant research intended to expand on their firm foundation of knowledge in the field.

- **Doctorate** — A degree program requiring two or more academic years of study beyond a master's degree. Doctorate, or terminal, degree programs are the highest level of study. These programs allow the student to focus on a specific topic and require a major original academic work called a dissertation.

NOTE: Degrees at all of these levels are currently offered in both traditional classroom environments and online. The courses are often offered on a variety of schedules, especially associate's degrees which may be offered at night, on weekends, on alternating shifts, or partially or totally online.

Types of Degree Programs

There are a wide range of academic degree programs available for emergency services professionals **(Figure 2.13, p. 72)**. Students should choose a degree program that fits their interests and professional goals. Degree programs offered for emergency services professionals include the following:

- **Fire Science/Technology** — A general degree program for fire service professionals. Courses can include: fire behavior and combustion, fire protection systems, fire administration, strategy and tactics, legal issues, and various others.

- **Fire Protection Engineering** — An engineering-focused degree program. Courses can include: thermodynamics, fire protection systems, fire service hydraulics, and additional general engineering courses.

Figure 2.13 Examples of degree programs commonly available to fire and emergency services personnel.

Academic Degree Programs

Fire and Emergency Services Related
- Fire Science/Technology
- Fire Protection Engineering
- Fire Administration
- Emergency Medical Technology
- Emergency Management/Homeland Security

Others
- Public Administration
- Business Administration
- Public Health
- Political Science
- Law

- **Fire Administration** — A professionally focused degree program. Courses can include: budgeting and finance, legal issues, personnel administration, program evaluation, and public management.

- **Emergency Medical Technology** — A technical focused degree program leading to a degree and certification as a paramedic. Courses typically include a traditional paramedic curriculum in addition to emergency services administration courses.

- **Emergency Management/Homeland Security** — A professionally focused degree program. Courses can include: mitigation, preparedness, response, recovery, community relations, populations at risk, regulatory risk analysis, and many others.

Other degree programs are available that do not provide a specific emergency services focus. Such degree programs can include the following:

- Public Administration
- Business Administration
- Public Health
- Political Science
- Law

Professional Organizations

Membership in professional organizations can provide benefits to employees and the organization. Chief officers and other department members personally benefit from associations with other people who have the same interests, concerns, and commitment to the fire and emergency services. Meetings, workshops, seminars, conferences, and conventions provide an opportunity to gain knowledge, establish professional networks, and learn about new techniques and equipment. The department benefits when this information is brought back and shared it with the department/organization. The experience may help renew the attendees' enthusiasm for the fire and emergency services.

Chief officers need to budget for members to belong to various professional organizations and attend state/provincial, regional, and national meetings. Because it may be cost-prohibitive to send all members to conferences, the most qualified people should be selected to go to the most beneficial events. This process should be done fairly and equitably to ensure that opportunities are provided for all participants.

Personal Professional Development

Professional development may take other forms, which are all available to chief officers and members. Other suggested forms of professional development are as follows:

- **Observation** — Involves the activity of visiting other fire and emergency services organizations and observing their operations. Observation provides a wider view of the services and helps to create and enhance professional networks.
- **Participation** — Involves the individual in an activity outside the organization. This may include membership in a civic organization, nonprofit organization, or assisting in an assessment center.
- **Reading** — Provides the individual with a wealth of knowledge from trade and professional journals and participating in fire and emergency services related Internet list-serves.
- **Analysis of past performance** — Provides the individual a form of self-evaluation that can lead to personal growth. Reviewing previous performance evaluations can determine if any improvements have occurred. Personal goals are then set for meeting any perceived deficiencies.
- **Innovation** — Gives the individual an opportunity to identify a problem and then attempts to solve it creatively. This exercise can lead to a solution or a better understanding of the problem.
- **Publication** — Involves writing articles for professional journals or other publications. This requires the writer to learn more about a topic in order to create a new viewpoint or technique and add to the body of knowledge available to the fire and emergency services.

Succession Planning

Succession planning is a proactive approach that ensures that personnel hired, trained, and promoted today will have the skills to meet tomorrow's challenges. It involves matching the job requirements with the skills of the position applicants. Professional development and continuing education plans should be developed in conjunction with succession planning to ensure they complement one another.

Key facets of succession planning are identifying talent and providing opportunities for personal and professional growth. Good succession planning constantly develops leaders and provides regular opportunities for advancement. This planning maintains morale and retention because employees can see a clearly defined career path. Employees also appreciate that the organization is willing to invest time and resources to develop them personally and professionally. Opportunities for advancement and growth should be made available for all members to avoid the appearance of favoritism.

Credentialing

Several credential programs are available that are intended to reflect the personal and professional accomplishments of chief officers while also improving the knowledge, skills, and abilities of the designees. While these credentials are an honor to have, they also require the applicants to improve themselves personally and professionally.

Executive Fire Officer Program (EFOP)

The National Fire Academy (NFA) conducts the Executive Fire Officer Program (EFOP), a course of study that leads to the Executive Fire Officer (EFO) designation. This program provides chief officers and other fire and emergency services leaders with the opportunity to develop leadership and management skills. The EFOP is a four year course of study. Each course requires an applied research project before credit will be awarded.

Applicants to the program must be a chief officer or future leader in the organization and must have a bachelor's degree from a regionally accredited institution. Applications must include an essay, a letter of intent, a letter of support from the applicant's supervisor, and a resume. Once accepted, the NFA provides free courses and pays travel costs.

Chief Officer Designations

The Center for Public Safety Excellence (CPSE) administers the Chief Fire Officer (CFO) and Chief Emergency Medical Services Officer (CEMSO) designation programs. These programs require applicants to develop a professional portfolio that highlights accomplishments in the areas of training, education, personal professional development, and professional competencies. Applications are peer reviewed and the applicant must complete an oral interview process.

After successfully completing the program, a chief officer is awarded the appropriate designation in recognition of the accomplishment. The designation must be renewed every 3 years. The program also provides an ethical code of conduct that each participant must adhere to in order to retain the appropriate designation. A renewal fee is also required with the reapplication.

The Institution of Fire Engineers (IFE) also provides credentialing. The IFE program has similar criteria to the CPC and includes a reciprocal agreement with the CPC.

Continuing Education

Continuing education programs should involve all members at all levels of the organization. Initially, training (gaining vocational skills) is the primary type of learning for firefighters/emergency responders. Once these skills become second nature or the member promotes to supervisory or management levels or moves into a specialty function, education (gaining of academic knowledge) becomes more important. To meet this need, the department/organization must make available the education necessary to perform the new duties.

Training Program Development

Because each employee has different levels of education, training, and experience, continuing education should not take a one-size-fits-all approach. Individual continuing education plans should be developed with each employee to ensure they are following a planned and focused approach to their development. Chief officers can support these continuing education in the following ways:

- Encourage members to apply for and participate in continuing education **(Figure 2.14)**.
- Provide a flexible work schedule to allow members to attend classes.

Figure 2.14 Chief officers should encourage their subordinates to seek further education, training, and degrees.

- Work with the labor organization to include educational requirements for advancement and compensation in the labor/management agreement.
- Provide compensation for completion of educational programs.
- Provide financial assistance to offset tuition costs.

Agency Mission and Goals

Continuing education efforts should be conducted in conjunction with the mission and goals of the organization. All continuing education should fit into each employee's career development plan and mirror the succession plan. Continuing education and professional development activities should be periodically reviewed to ensure they are meeting the organization's stated mission and goals.

Needs Assessments

Needs assessments should be conducted regularly to identify gaps in continuing education and professional development. These assessments should also determine if the educational and development opportunities are providing the intended outcomes and meeting the organization's needs. The succession plan will be a key source of information when conducting the needs assessment. Costs should be compared with outcomes to ensure that limited funding is creating the greatest effect.

The needs assessment can also identify instances where employees are not pursuing continuing education and professional development. It may be necessary to offer incentives to achieve the desired result, if funds are available.

IV. Human Resources Demographics Appraisal

Human resources demographics consist of data that characterize the people who compose the available workforce in an area. The data include statistical categories such as age, sex, ethnicity, religion, and race among others. It is also a good management practice to advocate and pursue a diverse workforce. Outside agencies, such as the jurisdiction's legal department or professional membership organizations, can aid in tracking and learning about these laws and ordinances. The first steps are to understand the composition of the external community that provides the available work force and then the internal demographics of the organization.

Demographics not Discrimination

Chief officers must understand and abide by the laws that govern employment, promotion, and termination proceeding. The U.S. Government enacted the Civil Rights Act of 1964 (Title VII) to prohibit employment discrimination based on an individual's race, color, religion, sex, or national origin. This act led to the establishment of the Equal Employment Opportunity Commission (EEOC) and affirmative action programs. In addition, the following U.S. acts protect against discrimination in the workforce:

- Age Discrimination in Employment Act of 1967
- Rehabilitation Act of 1973 (amended in 1993)
- Equal Pay Act of 1963
- Family and Medical Leave Act (FMLA)
- Fair Labor Standards Act (FLSA)
- Other mandates including Presidential Executive Orders

Similar acts and orders have been adopted in Canada such as the Canadian Human Rights Act of 1985 that created the Canadian Human Rights Commission and Equal Wages Guidelines of 1986. Other programs intended to provide a diverse workforce have replaced some of the federally mandated programs in both nations.

External Community Demographics

Demographics vary regionally and between urban, suburban, rural, and frontier areas. Chief officers should research the community that the department/organization serves to determine the exact composition of the population.

Sources for demographic data on the national, state, and local levels in the United States are the U.S. Census Bureau, U.S. Department of Labor, U.S. Department of Health and Human Services, and state, regional, and local government agencies. In Canada, the sources include the Canadian Census Bureau and provincial, regional, and local agencies. The most recent data were compiled following the 2010 U.S. census and the 2011 Canadian census. Information is also available in almanacs that are privately published and accessible through public library systems, the Internet, or at retail outlets. These censuses indicate that the U.S. and Canadian population is continuing to rapidly diversify.

Once the demographics of the local service area are determined, the chief officer will be able to focus recruitment efforts on each segment of the population. Recruiting then becomes a proactive rather than a reactive approach to managing diversity within the workforce. Recruiting a diverse workforce is important for many reasons, including the following:

- Reflects the composition of the community
- Provides a better understanding of various needs and a vital connection to all segments of the community
- Sends a strong message that the organization is inclusive and values the various groups in the community
- Provides all members of the population with opportunities to have a part in the community, either as a volunteer or a career public employee
- Expands the available number of applicants from which to recruit
- Helps meet any legally mandated hiring goals and prevents hiring discrimination lawsuits

Internal Organizational Demographics

Many fire and emergency services organizations in the U.S. have introduced programs designed to meet the basic legal requirements of the Civil Rights Act, EEOC, and affirmative action programs. These programs do not necessarily mean that most organizations truly reflect the demographics of the communities they serve, but rather that they have removed the formal barriers to employment of underrepresented groups. Chief officers now have local records available to appraise their own organizations' diversity and compare the organizational diversity with their service communities diversity. Volunteer organizations need to identify underrepresented groups and remove barriers to their inclusion in the organization.

Many career organizations may not have achieved diversity within the various ranks of the organization. A diversity appraisal should be conducted within the organization. Analysis of the data will help focus attention on the need for professional development, mentoring programs, career planning sessions, and personnel incentive programs. It will also help to improve the overall morale of the organization when all members realize that the administration equally values them and they have an equal opportunity to advance.

Internal diversity within the ranks and positions of the organization is an ethically sound goal to achieve. It makes the best use of the talents of each individual, regardless of heritage or background, because it ensures that promotions are based on experience, ability, and knowledge. Each individual must also be given the opportunity to acquire the skills and knowledge needed for advancement.

Diversity within fire and emergency services organizations has numerous advantages:

- **Ability to recruit the best available personnel** — Targeting the entire, diverse workforce in the community or service area means that the pool of highly desirable and eligible workers is increased.
- **Improved image of the organization** — As the organization becomes more diverse, its image in the eye of the public improves, increasing the goodwill between the organization and various cultural groups.

- **Increased personnel morale** — The membership recognizes that opportunities based on ability improve morale for all members of the organization.
- **Increased creativity and innovation in the organization** — The diversity of backgrounds and experiences provides greater opportunity for creative and innovative development.
- **Improved problem solving** — Diversity of the membership increases the perspectives available for problem solving.
- **More organizational flexibility** — The need to respond to the desires of a variety of people causes the organization to try a variety of solutions to challenging situations.
- **Increased opportunity** — Diversity creates a work environment that is based on equal opportunity so that all members have opportunities to reach their full career potentials.
- **Improved overall capability** — Diversity allows the organization to deliver a full range of services to the entire community.

Diversity Barriers

Overcoming diversity barriers requires the commitment of all chief officers and members of the organization. The resulting change in the organization's culture will establish the leadership, membership, and organization as symbols of progressive management. Diversity also creates some challenges. The more diverse the workforce is, the greater the potential is for conflicting values, needs, and expectations among personnel. This potential for conflict is not as an insurmountable barrier or even a negative situation; but one that requires capable management, understanding, cooperation, and a desire for a positive outcome. Diversity contributes to improved services delivery. Some aids to overcoming diversity barriers include affirmative action programs and the Workplace Diversity Initiative (WDI). These will be discussed in greater detail in later sections.

A diversity program is a continuing process meant to create an environmental and cultural change in the organization. A culturally diverse organization is a goal that can be attained over time.

Affirmative Action Programs

Affirmative action programs stem from equal employment opportunity (EEO) laws, rules, and regulations. They are government-initiated and mandatory under certain circumstances. The programs are based on a statistical comparison of various demographic groups within the community. Affirmative action programs may contain goals and timetables designed to bring the level of representation for minority groups and women into parity with the community's available labor force. Changing the number of women, minorities, and persons with disabilities in a particular organization is the goal of these programs.

Affirmative action programs apply to those groups defined in Title VII of the 1964 Civil Rights Act. Where appropriate (and subject to legal interpretation), agencies may set affirmative action employment goals to increase the numbers of people from protected classes to include but not limited to:

- Women
- African Americans
- Native Americans
- Hispanics
- Asian Americans
- White males
- People with disabilities

Workplace Diversity Initiative

Fire and emergency services leaders are encouraged to establish a *Workplace Diversity Initiative (WDI)*, which is a long-term strategy to manage the differences and similarities of employees in order to promote productivity, quality, and fairness in the workplace. Such an initiative can overcome barriers and facilitate the integration of underutilized segments of the population into the fire and emergency services. The U.S. National Institutes of Health (NIH), under the direction of the Office of Equal Opportunity and Diversity Management (OEODM), originally developed a WDI to meet internal requirements. The initiative is a formal program that institutionalizes diversity within the organization.

Workplace diversity initiatives are voluntary, proactive programs. A WDI seeks to address issues related to human resources, internal communications, interpersonal relationships, conflict resolution, quality, productivity, and efficiency. Its main focus is to improve organizational performance and community acceptance through respecting, valuing, and using the differences people bring to the workplace. The WDI is a long-term process that seeks to identify and change the organization's culture. The final goal of the WDI is to create a work environment that appreciates and respects the diversity of the members of the organization. To accomplish this goal, the organization must foster a positive culture through managed change.

Comparison between EEO/Affirmative Action Programs and Workplace Diversity Initiatives (WDIs)

To appreciate the advantages of a WDI, it is necessary to understand what it is and what it is not. Confusion is sometimes created when the term is used in conjunction with EEO and affirmative action programs.

Mandated EEO/Affirmative Action Program	Voluntary Affirmative Action Program and WDI
• Can be mandatory	• Is voluntary
• Has legal, social, and moral justifications	• Has productivity, efficiency, and quality benefits
• Focuses on race, gender, and ethnicity	• Focuses on all elements of diversity
• Changes the mix of people	• Changes systems/operations
• Gives the perception of preference	• Gives the perception of equality
• Is short-term and limited	• Is long-term and ongoing
• Is grounded in assimilation	• Is grounded in individuality

The steps for a WDI model consist of the following:

- Organize for change.
- Identify the current culture.
- Raise cultural awareness.
- Manage diversity.
- Evaluate the program's results.

Organize for Change

The initial step in the WDI is to establish a diversity team or committee. This group needs to be representative of the current diversity of the organization, including race, religion, gender, age, and sexual orientation. Representation from all ranks, job functions, and the labor organization need to be included. The team/committee is given the challenge to create a diversity program within a specific timeframe. Management support in the form of empowerment, resources, and employee and management participation must be provided to the team in order for it to be successful. Allow the team to develop specific objectives such as the following:

- Identify the current culture of the organization.
- Identify the current culture of the community.
- Act as a resource for questions regarding EEO and diversity issues.
- Market the organization's role in promoting cultural diversity.
- Develop a recruiting, training, and promoting process that ensures cultural diversity.
- Establish a monitoring process for the program.

Identify the Current Organizational Culture

To manage change, the team must determine the present cultural makeup of the organization, which can be accomplished through organization-wide anonymous surveys. This information must be anonymous to ensure that the respondents are honest and information is not perceived as a potential threat to the individuals. These data are used to create a demographic portrait of the organization. It is also important to obtain a demographic analysis of the community or service area to determine the potential labor market for recruiting new personnel.

At the same time, conduct an organizational survey of cultural attitudes. An outside firm or human resources specialist who is capable of writing and analyzing this type of survey may be the best approach. This analysis provides a basis for diversity awareness training that will be provided to the organization's membership.

Raise Cultural Awareness

Because diversity awareness training is unique and somewhat sensitive, it is advisable to seek outside assistance for instruction. This assistance could come from the jurisdiction's Human Resources/Personnel Department, a state/provincial or federal agency, a nonprofit agency, or a private contractor. The provider needs to be fully competent in cultural diversity issues, including generational diversity. Diversity awareness training is not a one-time event. It should become part of the annual training cycle as well as the initial entry-level training program. Include proven concepts about diversity in the training such as the following:

- Develop awareness and skills for working in a diverse environment.
- Explain how diversity benefits the organization.
- Identify the behavioral changes needed to create a nonthreatening environment.
- Demonstrate how biases, cultural misconceptions, and stereotypes affect interpersonal relations.
- Explain the need for respectful relations between members of the organization.
- Use case studies, role-playing, and group discussions to address various job situations involving diversity issues.

Provide diversity awareness training to all organizational personnel. Organizational officers must be able to recognize situations involving diversity issues in order to reduce potential conflict and effectively manage diversity in the organization. Besides improving conflict management skills for officers, diversity awareness training helps to do the following:

- Create a positive work environment.
- Increase unity of purpose and professionalism in the organization.
- Increase trust, communication, and respect between members.
- Reduce stress and stress-related illnesses and injuries.
- Improve productivity and group problem-solving skills.
- Increase understanding and respect for other cultures both inside and outside the organization.
- Increase the accuracy of employee job performance evaluations.

Manage Diversity

Creating a workplace diversity team and an awareness program are only the beginning of the initiative process. The major element of the WDI is *managing diversity* within the organization, which is defined as the process of creating and maintaining an environment that allows all employees to develop their full potential in line with the goals of the organization. While the WDI development process is managed by the diversity team, managing diversity within the organization is the responsibility of all departmental officers. Diversity must be supported and championed by the organization's chief officers.

Evaluate Program Progress and Success

A reduction in discrimination claims, personnel disputes and conflicts, and improved morale, show the internal success of the WDI. Constant monitoring can include, periodic interviews, and discussions during job-performance evaluations. Success will also become evident through the change in perception that the community and media have of the organization, and the increase of a diverse workforce.

Labor Relations

In the early 20th century, public-sector workers began to organize into labor organizations in order to gain better salary levels and some of the same benefits that private-sector workers enjoyed. Labor organizations that handle the collective bargaining for the membership represent many fire and emergency service personnel in career, industrial, and combination departments/organizations.

The leadership of both the fire and emergency services organization and union should work jointly to provide the members with a safe work environment. Budgets are prepared with the cooperation of the labor organization to create an atmosphere of transparency. Grievances are dealt with through an established process resulting in fair and equitable resolutions.

Chief officers' involvement in the bargaining unit often vary by department. Chief officers in career departments are sometimes in the position of representing the management perspective while still being members of the bargaining unit. Some organizations exclude only the chief/manager and one designated assistant. In others, all chief officers are excluded from the bargaining unit or are included in their own chief officers' organizations. Chief officers, especially the chief of the department, must be knowledgeable in the labor/management process, laws governing it, and principles of negotiations. Keys to any labor/management relationship are employee involvement and participation.

Negotiation Process

Although labor organizations exist in both public and private sectors and are responsible for negotiating member benefits with management, there are differences between the two environments where they exist. First, in the public sector, the fire and emergency services organization is the primary provider of fire protection in the community or response area, which means it is often the only source of fire or rescue services available to the public. Second, these fire and emergency services are extremely vital to the public, which is one of the reasons why governments hesitated in giving public-sector employees the right to organize and bargain collectively and also why public-safety employees have seldom been given the right to strike, a tool that most private-sector labor organizations still have. Depending on state laws, the degree to which employment issues are negotiable can vary significantly.

A third difference is that public-sector collective bargaining is more likely to involve the courts. In recent years, there has been an increase in court involvement in public-sector collective bargaining. Finally, the law governing collective bargaining in the public sector is not as uniform as laws governing the private sector. State/provincial laws now cover most collective bargaining in the public sector.

In the collective-bargaining process, management and labor organization teams develop an agreement that the membership votes on to approve or reject. In the public sector, the process does not end there. The local governing body, the state/provincial legislature, or whatever body holds ultimate responsibility to the public has to ratify the agreement. Negotiation elements include open communications and a description of the negotiation process.

The labor organization uses a different strategy during negotiations according to the IAFF. In the private sector, labor organization representatives often argue that there is too much of a gap between the department/organization's profits and workers' wages, salaries, and benefits. Since there is no profit motive in the public sector, that argument is not effective for the labor negotiators. Instead, they often argue that the public-sector employees are worth more than they are paid. This argument is usually based on a market survey of similar delivery areas with similar types of departments/organizations. Nevertheless, the labor organization's negotiations goal is still the same: improvement in the employees' situations. This goal, in turn, affects recruiting, morale, retention, and discipline.

Regardless of the strategies used, the purpose of labor/management negotiations is to create a contract between the organization's management and the employees who the labor organization represents. That contract defines the responsibilities and obligations of both parties to the agreement and specifically defines employee wages, salary, benefits, and working conditions. The sections that follow describe the open communications necessary for negotiations and the steps of the negotiation process.

Open Communications

The negotiating process (also known as the *collective bargaining process*) is basically one of communication. Good communication is vital at all times, not just at the bargaining table. Both sides have to make certain the messages they transmit are the ones received; otherwise misunderstanding occurs **(Figure 2.15)**. The process can break down because people are individuals with internal barriers of communication based on different attitudes, experiences, values, beliefs, biases, and assumptions. Those same barriers can prevent the message from being received as intended. Other barriers, such as being defensive or preoccupied, may affect the receivers. They may also have emotional blocks or hold stereotyped views that get in the way of understanding. Their expectations could prevent them from receiving the message accurately.

Figure 2.15 Chief officers and other members of a labor/management meeting.

The IAFF has suggestions for solving communications problems that are valid for both sides of the negotiation process. Three ways are suggested as follows:

- **Ensure quality communications** — Negotiators must think before speaking. They must select the right words and phrases, and use the right voice inflections and facial expressions to ensure the message is delivered as intended.

- **Understand the audience** — Communicators have to understand their audience. If the senders know to whom the message is intended, they can tailor it to make certain it is received and understood correctly.

- **Hold two-way dialogues** — Negotiators relay the message and then use questions to ensure that the other side understands. They listen for feedback, watch for nonverbal signals, and focus on the context as well as the content of the message.

Bargaining Session Schedule

Bargaining sessions are usually scheduled after the labor organization issues a formal call for proposals, typically about 60 days before the bargaining sessions are expected to begin. These dates are arbitrary and should provide sufficient time before the end of the existing contract to complete negotiations. Some negotiations begin as early as 9 months before the end of the contract. Current contracts are normally extended without a formal call for negotiations. Schedule sessions when all negotiators can be present and follow the schedule rigorously once agreed upon. Allow time for offering proposals, studying proposals, and offering counterproposals for both sides. The longer negotiations take, the greater the cost in time and effort on the part of both parties.

Contract Content

The agreement that negotiators work on usually covers the five following areas:

- **Routine clauses** — Constitutional items such as the preamble and purpose of the agreement, terms the agreement covers, reopening conditions, and amendments.

- **Clauses affecting labor organization security** — Items that describe the bargaining unit the agreement covers. These list the steps by which a labor organization is recognized as an employee representative.

- **Clauses describing the rights and prerogatives of management** — Items that recognize that management has the right to decide matters the agreement does not cover.

- **Sections that describe how the organization will handle employee grievances** — Items regarding discipline, termination, and the process for filing a grievance.

- **Sections that list the conditions of employment** — Areas such as wages, salaries, and noncash benefits; hours, holidays, vacations, and leaves; apprenticeships and training; hiring and firing; safety; and strikes and lockouts.

Representation

Bargaining teams usually represent labor and management. *Team composition:*

1. **Management team** — The IAFF suggests that this team be composed of a high-ranking personnel officer, financial expert or budget analyst, and attorney. The chief/manager of the organization or another upper-level official should also be on the management team for consultation and advice.

2. **Labor organization team** — The organization selects or elects a team. It may include the president of the organization, members with experience in bargaining, and the organization's legal counsel.

Preparation

Preparation is the key to success in the process. Both labor and management need to gather information that will support their positions. Collect data throughout the year. Examples of important data are as follows:

- **Wages** — Know what wages firefighters/emergency responders earn in nearby organizations and what they earn in similar organizations around the country.
- **Costs** — Know how much current wages and noncash benefits cost the authority and how much of an increase the authority can afford.
- **Current contract** — Gather information on the effectiveness of the current contract. Analyze the provisions of the current contract and identify any problems involved in its operation. Provisions that are not effective become items for negotiations during the next bargaining session.
- **Employee grievances** — Include any new grievances that have developed during the contract period.
- **Previous bargaining sessions** — Be aware of the history of previous bargaining sessions with the labor representatives.
- **Labor organization team** — Learn as much as possible about the members of the labor negotiating team (backgrounds, personalities, and negotiation styles).

Proposal Presentation

Management should enter the bargaining session with proposals to present to labor negotiators as well as a list of new and continuing demands that management wants to discuss. Presenting such a list allows management to be proactive and take the initiative rather than reacting to the labor organization's proposals. In addition, it enables management to start negotiations from the same position of strength as the union and provides a number of items to negotiate as a display of *good faith bargaining*.

Contract Issues

In some states, all issues that may affect hours, wages, and working conditions must be negotiable. The following three categories of real issues are involved in contract negotiations:

- **Wages and benefits** — While the labor team attempts to get the best possible compensation for their members, the management team attempts to keep the potential increases within the ability of the jurisdiction to pay.

Both sides recognize that their demands cannot be unrealistic or their positions unyielding. Management knows that a fair package of wages and benefits helps the organization attract and retain competent employees. Most chief officers do not oppose reasonable, legitimate labor proposals. The management team attempts to start low and bargain up on these issues while the labor team starts high and is willing to bargain down to an acceptable compensation.

- **Working conditions** — Good working conditions help attract and retain capable people and increase productivity. Good working conditions also help labor leaders who prefer representing happy, satisfied employees who do not waste time with complaints and grievances about working conditions.

- **Job security and career advancement of management and labor leaders** — Members of both teams have personal incentives that also depend on successful contract negotiations. Management and labor leaders who seem to concede too much during collective bargaining might also lose their jobs. The labor organization's membership can elect new labor leaders and the administrators can be replaced. Neither side should want to hurt the other so much that one or more member are replaced.

Impasses

Despite good faith negotiations by management and labor, bargaining can hit an *impasse* (a sticking point over which neither side is willing to compromise). Fact-finding and mediation are the most common means to resolve impasses in the public safety sector. Descriptions of these two and two other methods for overcoming an impasse are described in the following sections.

Mediation. A third, neutral party talks with each side and discovers the real issues and concerns that are stalling negotiations. A mediator does the following: (1) Clarifies misconceptions that one side holds about the positions of the other and gets both sides talking again in hopes of leading them to reconciliation and a contract; (2) Often uses information from other labor disputes around the country to move one or both sides away from unrealistic and untenable positions; and (3) Can also get both sides access to high-ranking officials and smooth the way to a settlement. The results of mediation, however, are not binding on either party. The U.S. and Canadian Federal Mediation and Conciliation Services (FMCS) usually provide mediators. State/provincial agencies that have the same function can also provide mediators. The FMCS is also a good source for training.

Arbitration. Arbitrators hear evidence from both sides in the dispute and determine a binding solution. Neither management nor labor particularly likes the procedure because it takes the final decision out of their control. State/provincial laws or municipal charters or ordinances sometimes require arbitration. One form of arbitration called *final offer* arbitration involves each side offering what is supposed to be its most generous offer on each issue to be resolved. The arbitrator must choose one of the offers on each issue without compromise. The procedure theoretically forces each side to make realistic proposals while coming close to what its final offer on each issue would be. The process can use a single arbitrator or a panel. A professional organization such as the American Arbitration Association, Canadian International Institute of Applied Negotiations, or similar state/provincial organizations, can supply a list of names that both sides choose names from. The so-called *strike-off* procedure is usually used. Each side alternately strikes a name from a list of professional arbitrators until the required number is left.

Fact-finding. This method (similar to arbitration) has arbitrators look at facts and then develop suggested solutions. These suggestions are not binding. The procedure identifies facts that can convince government officials and other policy-making bodies to make concessions in return for a settlement. Neither management nor labor is forced to make a serious effort to come up with its strongest offers; therefore, the procedure may not resolve a dispute, and the suggestions might not satisfy either party.

Strike. The labor organization uses a strike as the last resort when it sees no other way around an impasse or wants to pressure management to grant concessions. Public employee strikes are against the law in most states and provinces. Bans against strikes have helped to prevent them, and their numbers have decreased significantly in recent years. Historically, fire and emergency services personnel strikes have lasted an average of 3 to 7 days. They were generally caused by the following issues: (1) problems with wages and hours, (2) disputes over job benefits, (3) unhappiness about pay parity with other internal departments such as law enforcement, and (4) unhappiness about the way management handles such labor issues as recognizing a labor organization or defining the bargaining unit. One central issue was usually the primary cause of the strike.

Employee Involvement and Participation

Collective bargaining can result in a compromise in which one side believes that it has lost in the process. This perception of a *win-lose* type of confrontation can generate resentment within the organization, with the membership and the management viewing each other on a *them-us* basis. This perception is detrimental to the working efficiency of the organization. To avoid the potential loss of organizational cohesion, chief officers should consider an alternative approach that will result in what is termed *interest-based bargaining*. This type of bargaining requires both parties (labor and management) to continually focus on the welfare of the public.

When the membership of the organization is involved in the decision-making process, both labor and management create an atmosphere of mutual trust and respect. This atmosphere improves the contract negotiations because it forces both sides to work in partnership for the benefit of the public. An example of this respectful atmosphere is the continued cooperation between the IAFF and IAFC. They have established joint-development teams that created the Candidate Physical Ability Test (CPAT) and the Peer Fitness Training (PFT) Certification Program, which provides a standard for fitness trainers that is consistent with the unique health, and fitness needs of the fire and emergency services. The PFT program is part of the IAFF/IAFC Joint Wellness/Fitness Initiative.

IAFF/IAFC Labor Management Initiative

Recognizing a need to foster better working relationships between labor and management, the IAFF and IAFC partnered to deliver targeted programs to improve communication and collaboration. The IAFF and IAFC signed an agreement outlining the components of a good labor/management relationship. Representatives of both groups are available to provide training to labor and management leaders on the process of effective and efficient labor relations.

Technical assistance is provided to organizations having labor relations issues. In these instances, IAFF/IAFC representatives facilitate discussions between labor and management to identify issues and create a plan to move forward.

Incentive Programs

Fire and emergency services organizations may use incentive programs to help ensure long-term retention of experienced members. In career, industrial, and military fire and emergency services organizations, incentives are included in the compensation package or the labor/management agreement. Volunteer incentive programs also are beneficial in retaining members in the organization. Incentive programs can include (but are not limited to) the following:

- **Direct monetary incentives** — Examples: pay per call (volunteer), pension-program participation (volunteer), longevity pay, state/province or local tax incentives (volunteer), housing allowances, tuition reimbursements, low-interest home loans, and health and life insurance.

- **Indirect monetary incentives** — Examples: free admission to public parks, gyms, libraries, and entertainment facilities; professional organization memberships and conference registrations; municipal parking permits; discounts at local businesses; and personal uniforms and equipment allowances.

- **Service recognition/award ceremonies** — Examples: pins, plaques, or certificates of recognition for long service **(Figure 2.16)**.

- **Vehicles** — Example: access to the department's vehicles along with take-home privileges.

- **Social events** — Examples: parties, special trips or events, and family-oriented events.

These programs are usually based on a minimum level of job performance. Incentive awards are established for each level. Distribution of the awards must be based on performance and participation. Otherwise, unfair distribution will be perceived as a discriminatory practice and will lower morale. Successful incentive programs include the following criteria:

- Objective and attainable measures of work performance
- Employee and labor involvement in the design and implementation of the program
- Frequent and diverse rewards
- Administration simplicity, including brief and understandable rules

- Supervisory involvement in developing the program
- Supervisory coverage in the program
- Adequate budget
- Promotion of the program
- Appropriate monitoring and appeal provisions
- Frequent redesign of the incentives to maintain interest

Figure 2.16 A chief officer participating in a recognition/awards ceremony.

Training and Education Goals

The goals established for training and education of members must meet the requirements of relevant statutes, regulations, codes and standards. These goals must also align with other organizational planning functions such as professional development plans and succession planning. It can often be difficult to strike a balance between these two obligations, especially when there are limited funds and resources available. The sections that follow will highlight needs and resource assessments for training and education of emergency services personnel.

Determining Needs

As stated previously, statutes, regulations, codes, and standards establish a minimum level of training of emergency responders. For example, many AHJs restrict operations activities in confined spaces to personnel who have been formally trained for the response. This restriction is often due to outside requirements on the organization such as OSHA regulations and NFPA® standards. Regardless of the outside training requirements, personnel should be trained to operate in a safe manner. Refer to the 16 Firefighter Life Safety Initiatives included in **Appendix B**.

The AHJ establishes minimum standards that emergency services response personnel need to learn. However, the goal should be for all responders to be trained well above any minimum standards that are established.

Initial training is just the beginning. Personnel must receive ongoing training to stay proficient in their knowledge and skills. For response areas such as EMS, personnel are often required to receive a certain amount of in-service training in order to maintain their certificate or license. When assessing training needs, both initial and ongoing training requirements must be considered.

Observations made during emergency operations are another aspect of training needs assessment. Consulting the organization's training staff should identify areas of improvement that become evident on the emergency scene. Having training staff respond to incidents puts them in a position to observe operations and identify areas for improvement. For EMS, analysis of incident run reports can identify areas of improvement that should be addressed during in-service training. If the trends are identified for individual responders, these responders should be worked with individually to ensure they are able to perform the functions of their position.

Educational needs determination will often come from professional development and succession plans. If a lack of education is noticed among personnel who are likely candidates for advancement, the organization should identify these individuals and work with them individually to establish educational goals and develop a plan for completion.

Assessing Resources

Training and education resources often can be simplified to funds, personnel, and equipment/facilities. All these resources are critical and must be considered when conducting a resource assessment.

Monetary resources are often the most important for training and education because with enough funding, personnel and equipment/facilities resources can be obtained. Working with the training division, a budget should be created that addresses critical needs that have been identified. Once these critical needs are addressed, and if funds allow, additional training and educational opportunities can be provided in accordance with organizational priorities and goals.

Personnel resources are also critical with regards to training and education. Determine if the training division's current staffing level can accommodate training needs or if outside assistance is required. Outside assistance can come from both internal and external sources. Internal sources could be temporary assignments to the training division, or company officers can assign training. External sources of training can include larger neighboring departments, community colleges, state training organizations, or related conferences.

When assessing training needs, it is also important to consider the personnel who will undergo training. If training is to be conducted while on duty, units will likely be taken out of service and neighboring stations will have to cover the shifts. Overtime payments become a significant cost factor when training is conducted during off duty hours. To prevent both of these scenarios from occurring, training could be delivered in an electronic format. Personnel can complete their training during downtime at the station Units do not need to be taken out of service, and overtime pay is not necessary.

Figure 2.17 Chief officers should take the time to inspect their department's training facilities.

The final resources that must be assessed are facilities and equipment **(Figure 2.17)**. If the current training facilities and equipment are insufficient for projected needs, improvements need to be incorporated into the budget. Major improvements such as training facilities and burn buildings need to be budgeted for over the period of several years, construction grants obtained or funded through municipal bonds or other means. If neighboring departments have adequate facilities, it may be more cost effective to negotiate an agreement for their shared use.

Member Assistance Services

Member assistance services may be provided by the local jurisdiction as part of the membership benefits package. These services may include the member assistance program (MAP) and other member incentive programs. A MAP can contribute to improved retention and morale among the membership. Some service elements may have been established by the labor/management agreement and relate only to the fire and emergency services organization. The behavioral health program and its stress crisis intervention assistance program are examples of a benefit that may be part of a labor/management agreement.

Behavioral Health Program

Stress has always been a part of the lives of emergency responders because of the high levels of uncertainty, limited control over work environments, and nature of repeated emergency calls. Add major events that exceed the normal level of stress and ability of the body to cope, and critical stress develops. Critical stress can have immediate as well as long-term debilitating effects on individuals. A behavioral health program must be part of the safety and health program of the organization and contain a stress crisis intervention assistance program. This program is intended to relieve the stress experienced immediately after incidents such as the following:

- Mass casualties
- Large life-loss incidents
- Fatalities involving children
- Fatalities involving members of the organization
- Suicides
- Incidents involving close friends or relatives
- Incidents of violence directed toward firefighters/emergency responders
- Death of a civilian as a result of emergency operations
- Incidents generating excessive media attention

The behavioral health program should include a stress crisis intervention team to provide the necessary support for affected members. The team consists of emergency services personnel, affected healthcare professionals, and clergy. Team members need to have specialized training in dealing with critical incident stress. Although participation in the program is not mandatory, pre-incident training prepares personnel for the possibility of a critical stress incident. Strict confidentiality must be maintained throughout the process.

Member Assistance Programs

Member assistance programs (MAPs) (also known as *employee assistance programs*) have been in existence for several decades. They were developed to provide organizational members and their families with tools to cope with the stress and working in a high-risk profession. Participation is usually voluntary, although it may be mandatory when a disciplinary action is involved. The programs usually are designed to improve employee productivity, behavior, and retention. MAPs should be used in a positive manner to assist employees, not as a form of punishment. Professional counseling is provided and may include topics such as:

- Finances
- Marriage/relationships
- Dependency
- Domestic violence
- Child abuse
- Anger management
- Tobacco-use cessation

The AHJ may provide MAPS as a benefit or part of the labor/management agreement, rather than from the fire and emergency services organization. Funds have to be budgeted for them as part of the compensation package. Studies indicate that as many as 80 percent of those individuals who received MAP counseling returned to full productive status within the workforce. The programs can also reduce the cost of prolonged medical care and lost-time benefits and improve employee morale. NFPA® 1500, Chapter 11, requires the establishment of a MAP within the fire and emergency services organization. The health and safety officer acts as liaison with the MAP providers.

Chief officers should communicate MAPs benefits to all personnel. When a member shows signs of stress or other emotional problems, the chief officer should recommend use of the program. The chief officer may consider allowing the employee time off to participate in the program, within the limits of the labor/management agreement. It should be emphasized that the use of employee assistance services is strictly confidential.

Local, State/Provincial, and Federal Regulations

Regulations regarding member assistance programs vary greatly depending on the jurisdiction. Chief officers must understand their local requirements and the protections afforded members under the MAP. For example, members who self-identify to the MAP that they struggle with alcohol or drug abuse issues are afforded protection for a covered disability under the ADA.

Maintaining confidentiality with regards to MAP use is critical. Lack of confidentiality can jeopardize the reputation and benefit of the MAP. It could also place the organization in a position where they would be civilly liable for release of confidential information.

Program Appraisal

Member assistance services should be periodically reviewed to ensure they are being used as desired and that members feel comfortable in participating. Any review should be conducted with personnel who administer the program. One way to determine satisfaction with assistance services and frequency of use is to solicit information from confidential questionnaires or surveys. Use records should also be reviewed to look for historical trends such as greatly increased use around the holidays or after a particular emergency incident. Analyzing historical trends can help to predict future needs and plan assistance initiatives.

Chapter Summary

The human resources program is a major segment of any emergency services organization. Goals of the program include the following:

- Provide the most qualified personnel available through a legal and effective hiring process.
- Provide retention incentives, compensation, and benefits to encourage personnel to remain with the organization.
- Fulfill the succession plan of the organization through effective promotional practices.
- Provide a framework for labor/management relations, discipline, and grievance procedures designed for the protection of employees.

Chief officers must be familiar with the various components of a human resources program and legal requirements for hiring, promoting, and disciplining employees. They should also be able to evaluate the outcome of the program. It is critical that the program be directed toward all personnel, not just the sworn personnel. Not doing so creates the perception that civilian members are less appreciated in the organization. This perception is detrimental to the concept of teamwork and results in many internal morale and operational challenges.

Review Questions

1. What are some management concepts essential to emergency services staffing? (pp. 45-50)

2. What employment practices should a chief officer apply in fire and emergency services? (pp. 50-69)

3. What types of professional development and continuing education programs are available to fire and emergency services personnel? (pp. 70-75)

4. What methods can be used for appraising human resources demographics? (pp. 76-80)

5. What processes and programs can a chief officer utilize in managing labor relations? (pp. 82-89)

6. How can the chief officer set goals for training and educating fire and emergency services personnel? (pp. 89-91)

7. What types of member assistance services are available to fire and emergency services personnel? (pp. 91-93)

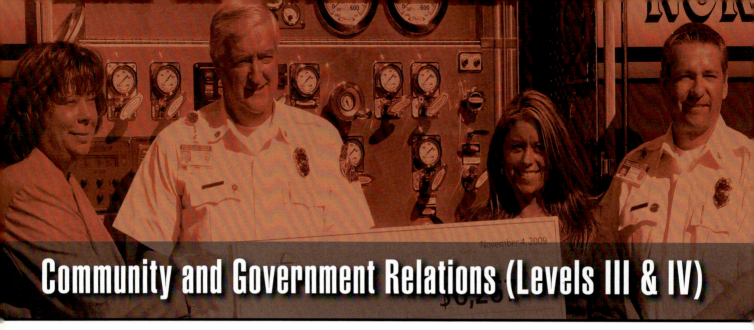

Community and Government Relations (Levels III & IV)

Chapter Contents

CASE HISTORY 99

III Service Delivery 100
- Systems-Model Approach 100
- Comprehensive-Risk Approach 101
- Types of Fire and Emergence Services 101
- Monitoring Service Delivery 103

Community Awareness Programs 103
- Community Relations Strategies 104
- Public Relations 105
- Public Fire and Life Safety Education 109
- Concerns/Complaints/Inquiries 112

IV Participation in the Political Arena 114
- Public Awareness and Acceptance 115
- Government Acceptance 116
- Interagency Relations 117
- Intergovernmental Agreements 122

Political Decision-Making Process 122
- Political Processes 122
- Political Relationships 126
- Political Resources 127

Legislation Monitoring 128
- Local 129
- State/Provincial 129
- Federal 129

Community Involvement 130
- Community Leadership 130
- Decision-Making and Goals-Setting Functions 131
- Partnerships and Programs 132

Chapter Summary 134
Review Questions 135

chapter 3

NFPA® Job Performance Requirements

This chapter provides information that addresses the following job performance requirements of NFPA® 1021, *Standard for Fire Officer Professional Qualifications* (2014).

Level III **Level IV**
6.3.1   7.3.1

Community and Government Relations (Levels III & IV)

Learning Objectives

After reading this chapter, students will be able to:

[Level III]

1. Identify various methods used for determining the fire and life-safety needs of a community. (6.3.1)
2. Describe the role of a chief officer in community awareness programs. (6.3.1)

[Level IV]

3. Explain various methods a chief officer may use for participating in a community's political arena. (7.3.1)
4. Identify various responsibilities a chief officer may assume in the political decision-making process. (7.3.1)
5. Determine ways to monitor legislation that may affect fire and emergency services organizations. (7.3.1)
6. Recognize various approaches for maintaining community involvement. (7.3.1)

Chapter 3
Community and Government Relations (Levels III & IV)

Case History

For many years, installation of fire sprinkler systems has only been required in office buildings and multi-family dwellings. These sprinkler systems are proven to save lives and extinguish fires. Beginning in 1970, the California State Fire Marshal's (CSFM) Office led a project to test the feasibility of using plastic pipe in sprinkler systems and to develop a quick response sprinkler head prototype. In 1980, the CSFM Office developed a voluntary standard for installing sprinkler systems in one- and two-family dwellings. Soon thereafter, the city of San Clemente passed the first ordinance in the nation requiring residential fire sprinkler systems for all new residences.

California continues to be proactive in supporting the development and adoption of local ordinances requiring residential fire sprinkler systems. These ordinances have emphasized the value of residential fire sprinkler systems. Having residential fire sprinkler systems ensures that occupants have adequate time to exit, and reduces the dangers to firefighters in residential fires.

In 1996, the Home Fire Sprinkler Coalition (HFSC) was formed in response to the need to inform the public about the life-saving value of home fire sprinkler protection. HFSC is a charitable organization providing independent, noncommercial information about residential fire sprinkler systems. Educational material contains detailed information about installed home fire sprinkler systems, how they work, why they provide affordable protection, and answers to common misconceptions about their operation. Target audiences are consumers, contractors, water supply agencies, and the fire service.

In 2009, the International Code Council (ICC) adopted the International Residential Code, which required fire sprinklers for all new one- and two-family homes and townhouses. The building industry strongly opposed the code change citing increased costs, accidental system discharges, and the lack of need as their primary reasons.

Because of the 2009 ICC Residential Code changes, the California State Fire Marshal, the National Fire Sprinkler Association (NSFA), and the National Automatic Sprinkler Industry (NASI) developed a program to target stakeholder groups throughout California. The program focused on the need for and benefits of residential fire sprinkler systems, including the fact that there has never been a loss of life due to fire in a sprinklered residence.

On January 12, 2010, the California Building Standards Commission approved implementation of the California Residential Code. This code included the requirement of residential fire sprinklers for all new one- and two-family dwellings and townhouse construction statewide.

Chief officers are leaders in the fire service, their fire and emergency services organizations, and their communities and service areas. Chief officers must ensure that the community is well informed and educated in the operation of the fire and emergency services organization and its ability to provide adequate service. The chief officer should recommend the level of service needed and methods for delivering that service.

This chapter will provide information that will assist all chief officers in becoming effective participants and leaders within their communities. To meet these goals, chiefs must:

- Be able to work in the political arena that influences and governs the organization and its operations
- Possess a thorough understanding of the political process to be able to participate in the political arena in a nonpartisan way
- Monitor fire service-related legislation at all governmental levels to ensure that the department is prepared to respond to new mandates, funded or unfunded
- Understand the composition of the community or service area

Service Delivery

The fire and life safety needs of a community or service area are determined through a needs analysis that is based on citizen input, legal requirements, national standards, and a hazard or risk analysis. Because communities are continually evolving, the community's fire and life safety needs must be reassessed regularly. This reassessment is part of the strategic plan for the jurisdiction as well as the emergency services organization.

In rural areas, as the population increases, the need for all fire and life-safety services increases. The population increase may result in the incorporation of villages or townships into legal jurisdictions that may form public service departments to provide fire protection and emergency medical services (EMS), law enforcement, and public works. In other situations, groups of citizens in rural unincorporated areas may form volunteer fire-protection districts or combination fire and emergency services organizations. The systems-model approach or the comprehensive-risk approach may be used to determine the services that are required in the community or service area.

Systems-Model Approach

In this approach, the appropriate input of services is balanced against the desired results. The service input consists of staffing, training, locating, and equipping the first response units. Results that the public does not want or that existing hazards do not require will not be needed as service components in the jurisdiction. For instance, a community that is located in a desert area may not require personnel trained and equipped for ice rescues. The basic elements that are always present are structural fire fighting and EMS first responder capabilities with other emergency services developing as needed.

Comprehensive-Risk Approach

The comprehensive-risk approach is based upon on a formal identification and evaluation of risks in the jurisdiction. It can be applied to emergency services and fire prevention and public education efforts. This approach compares the risk management plan developed in the jurisdiction with the services either already in place or that need to be added to mitigate those risks. The basic risk management model recommended in NFPA® 1500 for developing a plan is described in detail in Chapter 7, Emergency Services Health, Safety, and Wellness.

Once a plan is in place that identifies, evaluates, and prioritizes risks, control measures are selected to mitigate risks **(Figure 3.1)**. At this point, a cost-benefit analysis is made to determine if the potential results justify the cost of the controls. For example, it may be more cost-effective to require static fire suppression systems in structures than to staff, equip, and train additional personnel to protect rapidly developing areas of the community.

Figure 3.1 The comprehensive-risk approach is a continuous process.

In risk assumption, fire and emergency services organizations assume or take on a degree of risk. This assumption can play out in various legal and political ways. Risk assumption occurs when risk cannot be reduced, avoided or transferred. Some fire and emergency services organizations assume risk simply by their existence and agreeing to protect the public from hazards.

Types of Fire and Emergency Services

The fire service has been diversifying the types of services that it provides. Improvements in technology have helped address some of the new requirements and improved the effectiveness and efficiency of the services. Fire and emergency services organizations now provide some (or all) of the following services **(Figure 3.2, p. 102)**:

- Fire suppression
- Emergency medical response and community health
- Hazardous materials responses
- Terrorism and WMD responses
- Natural disaster response
- Technical rescue
- Communications and dispatch/telecommunications
- Fire and life safety education
- Fire investigation
- Code compliance

Figure 3.2 Examples of services provided by fire and emergency services organizations. *Structural fire fighting photo courtesy of Bob Esposito.*

Many organizations rely on automatic or mutual aid agreements with neighboring agencies. Fire and emergency services organizations may also provide the following:

- ***Community connectors*** — Links between fire and emergency services organizations and other service providers. Chief officers need to make every effort to develop these networks within the community or service area and make the public aware of the existence of other services and benefits of supporting them. Examples include the American Red Cross, emergency social services, local social services, homeless shelters, and other charitable organizations.

- ***Community service units*** — Nonemergency vehicles that respond to incidents that provide assistance with social services, grief support, information and guidance on mental health issues, support for domestic violence victims, and other social-service needs. One such unit is Care 7, a van operated by the Tempe (AZ) Fire Department and staffed with a community volunteer and one health-care provider. The purpose of Care 7 is to provide the types of services previously mentioned and assist families in starting their lives over following a fire or other emergency incident.

Citizen Corps

The U.S. government created Citizen Corps in 2002. Citizen Corps coordinates volunteer activities that help make communities safer, stronger, and better prepared to respond to emergencies. It provides opportunities for people to participate in a range of measures to make their families, homes, and communities safer from the threats of crime, terrorism, and disasters of all kinds. The Department of Homeland Security's Federal Emergency Management Agency coordinates the Citizen Corps. FEMA works closely with other federal entities, state and local governments, first responders and emergency managers, the volunteer community, and the Corporation for National & Community Service (CNCS).

Monitoring Service Delivery

Monitoring the effectiveness of the service delivery program is an ongoing process that consists of comparing the desired level of service to the actual level provided. To make this comparison, the desired level of service must be quantified. For example, the AHJ mandates that 100 percent of all target hazards shall be inspected within a calendar year. To determine the effectiveness of the program, the number of actual inspections is compared to this mandate. If the desired level of service is not consistently being met, then the reason must be determined. Once the reason is identified, a solution can be developed to eliminate the problem.

Community Awareness Programs

The fire and emergency services organizations of the service area depend upon citizens for the financial, personnel, political, and moral support necessary to operate any type of public agency. To gain and maintain this support, the community must be aware of the services that the various departments provide and the support that the departments need to meet their operational obligations. An understanding of these departments helps to justify the funding requirements and explains the actions and responses in times of crisis.

The organization's public relations and public fire and life safety branches facilitate community-awareness programs to increase the following:

1. Citizens' awareness of the fire and emergency services organization
2. Citizens' awareness of the organization's response to hazards and the associated risks for emergency personnel and for citizens
3. Public interaction with emergency responders so that public concerns, complaints, and inquiries are addressed

Community Relations Strategies

The customers within a community or service area may be very diverse in terms of age, gender, sexual orientation, ethnicity, race, religion, politics, socioeconomic level, education, and other factors. The personnel of a fire and emergency services organization must be aware of the various groups that compose their community.

Diversity can create barriers between service providers and customers because of language, culture, and values differences. These differences should be viewed as an asset to the department rather than as a series of barriers. Listening to others, being open to new ideas, and respecting differences strengthen the bonds between a department, its members, and the various elements of the community.

Language Barriers

English is the most common language in North America and a very common second language in other parts of the world. There are still groups of people who are not fully proficient in the use of English. In some areas of North America, people cluster together in communities and neighborhoods speaking their native tongue. The most common non-English language in the U.S. is Spanish, while in Canada it is French. In multilingual communities, volunteers or paid translators may be on call to assist at emergencies. They may also be used to translate written educational materials, assist in interviews, or train personnel in the cultures of various groups.

Individuals with hearing impairments may require knowledge of American or international sign languages in order to converse effectively. American Sign Language (ASL) is used in the United States and English-speaking areas of Canada. Training in ASL can be beneficial to emergency response personnel. Text telephones (teletypewriter or TTY), telecommunications devices for the deaf (TDD), and amplified phone sets are also available to assist hearing-impaired individuals in placing emergency phone calls.

Telecommunications centers may need personnel who are multilingual to take accurate information over the telephone. Emergency responders should be able to communicate with customers in the language in which the customer is most proficient. Having bilingual or multilingual members trained on each emergency response unit or providing them with a contact person who can respond as a translator are some options.

Another option is to use a *language line* available from a telecommunications provider. This line connects the caller to a translator who assists in processing the request. Public awareness and fire and life safety education materials should be produced in sufficient quantities to meet the needs of the various language groups. Braille publications may also be required for the visually impaired. Translation applications are also available for cell phones and computers. The Home Safety Council in cooperation with ProLiteracy, Fire Protection Publications (FPP), and other funding partners are involving fire and emergency services organizations in literacy programs that contain safety messages.

Cultural Customs

Fire and emergency services personnel must recognize and understand how the cultural groups in their areas use time, space, and nonverbal communications. While the dominant culture of North America values time as a precious commodity and places importance on being "on time", some cultures do not. Thus, meetings may not always begin at the specified hour and minute. This time consideration has to be taken into account when scheduling meetings with specific cultural groups.

Different cultural groups interpret nonverbal signals differently. For example, crossing one's legs and exposing the sole of the foot or shoe is considered rude in some societies. Hand gestures such as the "okay" sign, made with the thumb and forefinger of the hand, may be offensive to some cultures.

Involving members of the subject groups in sensitivity training for fire and emergency personnel is one way of connecting the groups with the department and providing training at the same time. It can be beneficial to create small workgroups representing the department and different cultural groups to discuss cultural traits, values, and characteristics.

Cultural Values

Cultural groups have unique ethical and moral values based on their own traditions. Some of those traditions are based on religious tenets, while others are based on relationships. An understanding of cultural values and traditions is important when the department wants to recruit from a particular ethnic group.

Public Relations

A public relations program markets the organization to the community. Its purpose is to acquaint the community with the department's mission and to show the department, officers, members, facilities, equipment, and operations in the best possible light. A positive public image can be the best possible tool during periods of budget cuts and layoffs. Creating and maintaining a positive public image is accomplished through the use of a media relations and public information unit and strong policy on media relations.

Public Information Officer

Large career departments may have a full-time public relations specialist on staff. This person often serves as a member of the Senior Executive Team to help ensure that manager is fully informed and directly connected to the department's leadership. Most departments depend on the department's chief or a senior staff member to fulfill the duties of the PIO. The PIO is responsible for providing information about the department and its operations to the media and the public. The PIO should know the following information:

- Mission statement of the department
- Generally recognized terminology used to describe all types of operations
- Names of television/radio/newspaper reporters, media contacts, editors, and newsroom staff
- The organization's short and long term plans
- All current community risk reduction target areas
- Deadlines for print publications and broadcast news programs
- Contact person for the various ethnic communities in the service area
- Basic marketing theory and image management
- Community calendar of events and opportunities for presentations

While the PIO is most visible to the media and public when providing emergency incident status reports, these reports are only a small part of the PIO's responsibilities. Some potential opportunities to promote the organization publicly include the following:

- Opening of a new department facility
- Hiring new personnel
- Coordinating and advertising job and career fairs
- Marketing the organization
- Announcing personnel promotions
- Displaying new apparatus or equipment
- Recognizing personal achievements of department members
- Recognizing the completion of specialized training
- Attending charitable activities
- Giving special recognition to those who retire
- Announcing changes in operational techniques
- Explaining expansion of services
- Forming joint partnerships with other public agencies or private organizations
- Giving seasonal life safety demonstrations to the public, such as candle and holiday safety.

The public should hear a positive message about the department. Because this information is not delivered instantly, there is time to develop it so that it is presented in the most professional manner possible. Every effort should be made to celebrate achievements in order to gain the best image for the department.

All statements made to the public must be factual and truthful to gain the greatest support from the customer base. Fire officers and other public officials who have attempted to hide information or distort facts have harmed their organizations and themselves.

Media Relations

Many departments have developed policies to address the relationship between the department and the media. These policies should be oriented toward having open and trusting relations between the organization and the media. When this relationship exists, members of the media can be a benefit to the department because they will be more likely to publish stories that portray the organization in a positive manner.

Media members represent the public and have a right and an obligation to access emergency incidents and other events that involve public safety officials. To reduce potential conflict between the media and fire and emergency services organization personnel at emergency incidents, the two groups should establish a media task group to create and distribute incident scene protocols for both groups. The result should be improved cooperation and communication between both groups during crisis situations.

While public safety officials and the media each have an obligation to the public, that obligation is different for each group. The fire and emergency services organization is obligated to protect the public's safety and well-being. The media is obligated to protect the public's right to know **(Figure 3.3)**. Strict ethical standards guide members of both professions. Because their obligations are different, they must be sensitive to the needs and duties of the other organization. The established protocol should be incorporated into the fire and emergency services organization's training schedule and policy and procedures manual. The media should include the protocol in its policies and instruct its employees on how to follow it. Joint training sessions can also help to refine the protocol and add to the realism of live exercises.

The protocols for media operating at an emergency incident from the chief officer's perspective include the following elements:

- **Credentials** — Properly credentialed media personnel need to be allowed access to witness and document emergency scenes in a safe manner, even when the general public has been denied access. They should identify themselves to the incident commander (IC) or PIO upon arrival at the incident.

- **Access to public property** — Media personnel have the right under normal circumstances to photograph and report events that transpire on public

Figure 3.3 A public information officer (PIO) can bridge the gap between organization's responsibility to protect the public and the media's right to provide information to the public.

property. This privilege does not permit them to do so in an unsafe or potentially dangerous manner. These personnel should not be provided personal protective equipment until they have been properly trained in its use.

- **Editorial control** — Members of the media have editorial control over their own stories including any photos and videos they take at a scene. As long as they are not creating a safety hazard to themselves or others, public safety officials should not restrict news photographers from taking photographs.

- **Deadlines** — Media representatives have the responsibility to collect and document as much information about an incident while trying to meet their agencies' news distribution deadlines. Some information may seem irrelevant, unimportant, or even improper to the chief officer, company officer, or emergency responder. News deadlines should never prevent public safety officials from taking the time necessary to first notify proper persons in sensitive situations such as personnel who were injured or killed.

- **Candid photography** — Photographing suspects or defendants in public places are neither encouraged nor discouraged. Photographs are meant to document what happened, not be staged or posed for the media. Public safety officers should go about their duties normally and should not deliberately pose a person in custody for the news media **even if requested to do so**.

Certain guidelines regulate members of the media and include the following:

- **Obstruction** — Journalists may not restrict, obstruct, or oppose a public safety officer in the lawful execution of his or her duty. The following duties of a journalist do not constitute interference: being present at an emergency incident, taking photographs and videos, and gathering information relative to the incident.

- **Crime-scene protection** — Police and fire officials may deny entrance to a crime scene or incident scene to protect evidence being collected and processed. Such a denial should be explained to the news media and access should be granted as soon as practical.

- **Safety restrictions** — Public safety officials may deny access to emergency scenes for safety reasons. When the dictates of public safety allow only limited media representation, media members may create a system among themselves in which groups or pools of media members are allowed into the scene on a rotating basis. The media representatives are responsible for policing this system themselves, and public safety officials are not responsible for settling disputes among the media.

- **Private property** — Members of the news media can photograph and witness arrests and emergencies on private property if the property owner does not object to their presence. If the owner does object, then all parties should take appropriate, courteous action to resolve the situation.

- **Patient privacy** — Emergency responders must be knowledgeable of the terms of privacy policies and laws, such the Health Insurance Portability and Accountability Act (HIPAA) and ensure that no one releases private information about patients' medical conditions.

- **Legal restrictions** — Media representatives apprehended for violating the law should be dealt with in the same manner as any other violator.

Chief officers and their staffs need to use these emergency scene guidelines and the public relations suggestions listed to develop a working relationship with the local media. Members of the organization should never attempt to censor or improperly influence the media during information gathering or before its publication, nor should any member of the organization provide classified information to the media without the permission of the organization's chief. All members must follow the organizational policy for the release of information to the public.

Social Media

Social media can assist the fire and emergency services organization in providing real-time information such as traffic alerts, weather conditions, and related safety education material to the public. It can also provide a forum for the public to interact with the department. Comments may originate from the public and from members of the department. Policies and procedures must be developed for how social media is provided and who is responsible for monitoring it.

Public Fire and Life Safety Education

Public education enhances the department's public image and provides a valuable public service. Actively seeking opportunities provide public education can generate a tremendous amount of goodwill for the organization. Two effective public education efforts are group presentations and media programs. The public fire and life safety education program should have purpose and scope statements that are included in the department's mission statement and the strategic plan.

Purpose and Scope

Fire and life safety education programs are designed to inform members of the community about the fire and life safety hazards they face and how to mitigate those hazards. These programs help them change their behavior resulting in fewer fires, injuries, and property losses within the community. Instead of attempting to educate the entire community, it is more practical and more effective to divide the community into smaller, more manageable target groups. These groups may include the following people:

- Preschoolers (**Figure 3.4**)
- School children
- Homeowners
- Senior Citizens (**Figure 3.5**)
- Apartment tenants
- People with physical impairments
- Public and private employees
- Medical and nursing facility personnel

Figure 3.4 Fire department officers providing fire and life safety education to young children.

Figure 3.5 A chief officer providing fire and life safety education to senior citizens.

- Members of religious organizations
- Members of service clubs
- Members of civic organizations

The scope of the programs should reflect the service area's needs. For example, if the community is adjacent to wildland areas or has residents in the wildland/urban interface, the programs should include information about fire-safe roofing, defensible space, and similar topics. If there are ethnic neighborhoods in the community, fire and life safety materials may need to be printed in the group's native languages. Education programs may focus on the following topics:

- Home fire-escape planning
- Babysitting safety
- Cooking hazards
- Clothing fires
- Elder care
- Juvenile fire setting
- Scald prevention
- First aid for burns
- Cardiopulmonary resuscitation (CPR) training
- Home fire-safety inspections
- Smoke and carbon monoxide detectors
- Fire extinguisher use
- Home fire sprinkler systems
- Disaster Preparedness
- Wildfire Prevention

A fire and life safety education program must be well planned and conscientiously delivered to accomplish its purpose **(Figure 3.6)**. Such programs must be based on specific, measurable goals and objectives and focused on specifi-

Figure 3.6 Chief officers should be involved in the development and implementation of their organization's fire and life safety programs.

cally identifiable groups. For example, a goal of a 50 percent reduction in fires and burn injuries to residents of senior assisted living facilities might develop into two programs; one to educate the residents and another for the staff.

Group Presentations

Opportunities to deliver fire and life safety messages to a community group are also good ways to get to know that group and to develop a positive relationship with them. Local government, civic groups, service clubs, and other community organizations are often looking for speakers to address their meetings. These engagements can provide the department with opportunities to make fire and life safety presentations.

The fire and emergency services responders who serve the local area or neighborhood should make these presentations. Presentations provide emergency-response personnel with an opportunity to interact directly with people from local neighborhoods. However, in order to maintain consistency in the message and its delivery to all of the community's neighborhoods, it may be necessary to have the department's public-education specialists make these presentations. If company officers are trained to deliver effective fire and life safety messages, the number of available speakers within the department is greatly increased. Emergency response personnel and public education specialists can make joint presentations.

Media Programs

Live and/or recorded fire and life safety messages can be very effective ways to increase public awareness and enhance the organization's public image. U.S. television and cable media are required to set aside part of their broadcast time for public service announcements (PSAs) or messages. Many fire and emergency services organizations across North America have taken advantage of these opportunities. Fire and emergency services officers may be given the opportunity to research, develop, and deliver these messages. In communities across the nation, such personnel host weekly fire and life safety programs on local public-service channels.

Newspapers and other print media also provide opportunities for departments to educate the public about fire and life safety issues enhancing the organization's public image. Service clubs and other civic organizations often provide space in their newsletters for public-safety pieces. Retail merchants may provide space in their establishments for fire and life safety education posters or other, printed public service messages. They may also allow space on their websites to advertise for the local fire department or to support fire department sponsored events.

It is important to target high-risk periods such as July 1st in Canada, July 4th in the United States, and Fire Prevention Week in the fall. Fire and emergency services organizations should also conduct a year-round program of public fire and life safety education activities. This program continually draws positive attention to the organization. Maintaining close relationships with various community groups is the best way to identify opportunities for public education.

Concerns/Complaints/Inquiries

Occasionally, a citizen may have a concern or complaint with something the department, service area, or municipality has done or *not* done **(Figure 3.7)**. The issue may involve something directly under the fire and emergency services organization's control such as burning regulations, inspections, or weed abatement programs. Questions on these issues are appropriate for department officers to answer. But the issue may also involve something outside of the organization's jurisdiction — parking regulations, for example. These concerns may be brought to the fire and emergency services organization simply because these personnel are perceived to be representatives of the jurisdiction as a whole. It may also be that the fire station is the closest government facility to the citizen's residence.

All officers must be prepared to deal with a citizen's concern in a friendly, courteous, and professional manner. If citizens are angry or upset, officers must remain calm and in control — allowing citizens to voice their concerns/complaints. However, if citizens become verbally abusive or threaten to resort to physical violence, officers should call for law enforcement assistance.

Effective listening is one of the most important skills chief officers can use when dealing with disgruntled citizens. Some citizens will be able to communicate their concerns better than others; however, chief officers must still be able to interpret what citizens mean. Chief officers should become familiar enough with their communities to understand the particular speech patterns, colloquialisms, slang, and nonverbal communication used in the community. Often, just allowing a citizen to voice a complaint calms the person and allows him or her to look at an issue more rationally. Chief officers must try to understand the true nature of a complaint in order to address it.

Once the issue has been identified, the chief officer can either resolve it or refer the citizen to the appropriate person or office. The proper resolution of all concerns/complaints/ inquiries is a duty of all department personnel. Chief officers must set a high example for customer service, develop policy to ensure that it is followed, and monitor all aspects of it.

Figure 3.7 A chief officer listening to a complaint from a citizen.

Concern/Complaint Resolution

If it is within a chief officer's means and authority to satisfy a citizen's concern/complaint, then it needs to be done as soon as possible. If the concern must be referred to a higher authority or another department or agency, the chief officer should take a personal interest in seeing that the concern/complaint is resolved as soon as possible **(Figure 3.8)**. The chief officer may need to speak on the citizen's behalf with whoever is empowered to deal with the citizen's issue. The citizen's concern becomes one of the chief officer's most important responsibilities at that moment and must remain a focus until it is resolved. However, if the concern/complaint is voiced during an emergency operation, it should not be allowed to interfere with the demands of the emergency. Resolution of the concern/complaint should wait until after the emergency incident is terminated.

To refer a citizen to the appropriate authority, a chief officer must be thoroughly familiar with the applicable organizational and jurisdictional rules and regulations. The officer should also be knowledgeable of the full range of services available to the citizens from the local AHJ. The chief officer's duty is to use every legal and ethical means within that officer's authority to satisfy the citizen's concern. The chief officer should also document the complaint and its disposition. Such documentation may prove invaluable should the issue progress to litigation.

Figure 3.8 Citizen complaints may need to be referred up the chain of command.

Member Act/Omission Resolutions

One type of citizen complaints are those that involve a member of the department. These cases must be handled with extreme care because of concerns for the department's image, the rights of all involved, and the possibility of litigation. The officer receiving the complaint must know and follow the organization's policy to the letter. In most cases, the policy requires that the complaint must be formally documented. The officer needs to elicit as much pertinent information as possible from the concerned customer regarding the alleged incident. Some departments use a standardized form for this purpose.

When this form has been completed, the officer reassures the citizen that the complaint will be fully investigated and that the citizen will be informed of the results of the investigation. The officer then forwards the complaint through channels to the appropriate individual or office.

The chief officer or company officer who received the original complaint may or may not be involved in the incident's investigation. The officer should personally make sure the complainant receives the results of the investigation. If the officer is assigned the task of contacting the complainant, care must be taken not to divulge any privileged or confidential information. Before contacting the complainant, the officer should consult with the next level supervisor, personnel department, or the jurisdiction's legal department to clarify what information can and cannot be made public.

Public Inquiries

Inquiries from the public may involve the request for information. Requests for the clarification of policies, codes and standards, or department records may be included in this category. Citizens are often not familiar with legal or regulatory language, and they simply need to know how a particular regulation applies to them. A chief officer must know the federal, state and local requirements and work with legal counsel on the release of information. These functions may be delegated to members of the staff, but the responsibility for the result remains with the chief officer.

Customer Service

How customer concerns/complaints are resolved determines to a great extent how the public views its fire and emergency services organization. All such issues should be resolved as reasonably and as quickly as possible. Policymakers for these agencies should attempt to resolve the complaints with a positive customer service approach that includes doing the following thing in this order:

1. Apologize to the customer for being inconvenienced.
2. Identify the nature of the complaint.
3. Ask the customer how they would like the complaint resolved.
4. Express to the customer what you *can* do help resolve their complaint.
    - If this is in keeping with the customer's request, then proceed to resolving the complaint.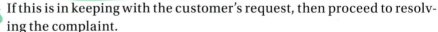
    - If this is different than what they requested, come to some mutual understanding, seek permission from a higher authority, or refer them to an official who can help them.
5. Follow through on what you agreed to do to resolve the complaint.

IV Participation in the Political Arena

Chief officers, especially those in charge of the department, should be active participants in the local political arena. These officers may also have influence at the state/provincial or national levels. They are responsible for ensuring that both private citizens and elected officials are aware of, understand, and support fire service related issues. Chief officers must also be able to establish and maintain interagency and intergovernmental relationships that aid in providing the highest level of service for the community. Chief officers must be able to accept policies or programs that the public desires even when they personally disagree with them.

All chief officers should understand the political decision-making process and how to develop strong relationships with elected officials and their designated representatives. Chief officers should also be able to monitor local, state/provincial, and national legislation that affects the fire and emergency service organization. Chief officers should be familiar with the various fire accreditation programs, how to gain accreditation, and the benefits accreditation brings. Accreditation programs include, but are not limited to, the Commission on Fire Accreditation International (CFAI) and Commission on Accreditation of Ambulance Services (CAAS). Finally, chief officers must be able to evaluate the effectiveness of the community and governmental relations.

Public officials allocate funds that fire and emergency services organizations need. Limited resources and expanded service expectations mean that fire and emergency services organizations must be aware of the views of their jurisdiction's political leaders. Chief officers must maintain public awareness of vital public safety issues and ensure that government officials are equally aware of these issues.

Chief officers must also be skilled at working with the leaders and representatives of other governmental agencies from all levels **(Figure 3.9)**. Chief officers should not give the impression that they are trying to undermine the political authority. Chief officers must be able to develop intergovernmental agreements that are necessary for providing services in an efficient and effective manner. They must accomplish all of these tasks while remaining politically neutral and unaligned.

Public Awareness and Acceptance

Good communication and positive relationships are important to keeping the public aware of fire and emergency services issues. Chief officers must be able to provide accurate, timely, and valid information to the public.

Figure 3.9 A chief officer meeting with a city manager.

Fire and emergency services related issues should be kept constantly in the public view. Alerting the public only during a crisis might create the impression that the department's administration was not prepared for the situation. The PIO can provide information through weekly news releases, press briefings, or public-access television channels. Suggested topics are as follows:

- Labor/management initiatives and agreements
- Pending local, state/provincial, or national legislation
- Firefighter/emergency responder health and safety issues and initiatives
- Requests for public involvement
- Responses to changes in the local hazards and risks
- Need for changes in fire and life safety ordinances
- Seasonal and event-related safety messages

Government Acceptance

Elected officials must balance the requirements of each segment of government against the potential outcome and cost of the service. Officials must have the most recent, accurate, and valid information on which to base their decisions. Chief officers must be capable of communicating this information to the people who make the decisions, which requires open lines of communications and positive relationships. The chief officer must not become overly involved in politically volatile issues or disputes between elected officials. If the chief officer can avoid these political entanglements, then the fire and emergency services organization should maintain a positive reputation with government officials.

One approach to good communications and positive relationship building is to provide periodic information packets to officials that contain the following:

- Executive overview of the fire and emergency services organization
- Actual and potential revenue sources
- Assessment of the community fire and life safety hazards
- Descriptions of issues specific to the department's operation
- Recommended solutions to hazard situations
- Statements of support and testimonials from private citizens

NOTE: Oral reports to officials can emphasize the importance of a particular issue.

Providing similar information on periodic basis to the general public is also a good way to establish a good relationship with private citizens. However, the public does not need to see the same level of depth and detail that public officials should receive.

The information provided on fire and emergency services related issues must be accurate, timely, valid, and thoroughly documented. Inaccurate, outdated, or inappropriate material weakens the credibility of the chief officer and the organization and may cause public officials to mistrust the chief officer. Chief officers must also present the information to the public officials in an objective manner. Information presented should be goal-oriented and focus on solutions based upon facts and should not include threats or unsupported arguments.

Many organizations provide support and assistance in presenting fire and emergency services related issues to public officials. Professional organizations that may provide data, model proposals, position papers and other assistance when preparing reports include but are not limited to the:

- International Association of Fire Chiefs (IAFC)
- Congressional Fire Service Institute (CFSI)
- International Association of Fire Fighters (IAFF)
- National Volunteer Fire Council (NVFC)
- National Fire Protection Association® (NFPA®)

Interagency Relations

Interagency relationships are important for managing incidents that go beyond what the fire and emergency services organization can handle on its own. Chief officers should establish these relationships and maintain them in anticipation of their need in the future. Interagency relationships should be based on mutual respect, common goals, open communication, and a team approach.

To accomplish a successful interagency team, the U.S. Department of Homeland Security (DHS) adopted NIMS in 2004. NIMS is the resulting incident management system developed as a result of Homeland Security Presidential Directive (HSPD)-5, *Management of Domestic Incidents*. This Presidential Directive required the creation of the National Response Plan (NRP) in 2002 (later replaced by the National Response Framework [NRF] in 2008) to integrate federal government prevention, preparedness, response, recovery and mitigation plans into one all-discipline, all-hazard approach to domestic incident management.

The NRF and National Incident Management System (NIMS) provide the incident response framework and processes to coordinate the public and private resources from multiple agencies and jurisdictions. The interagency teams created provide the following benefits:

- Establishes a common, agreed upon set of goals
- Reduces jurisdictional conflicts or turf wars
- Creates a forum to critique the team's performance in incident management
- Creates a controlled environment for the discussion of operational issues
- Encourages sharing of resources
- Builds personal and professional relationships between participants
- Increases understanding and respect between agencies

Agencies and jurisdictions that are likely to respond together should form incident management teams (IMTs). These teams should meet on a regular basis to discuss potential risks and develop a coordinated response plan for the risk. Incident management responsibilities and authority are determined and agreed upon in advance to overcome any conflict during a crisis. The responding agencies should also train together to ensure preparedness. Interagency teams and relations apply at all levels of government and apply to relations within the jurisdiction, with other emergency services, with law enforcement agencies, and with federal or national agencies.

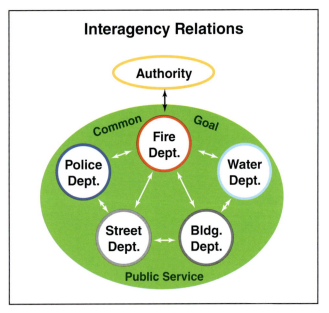

Figure 3.10 Organizations within a locality share a common authority, common goals, and dedication to serving their public.

Jurisdictions

Interagency relations are probably the easiest within a specific jurisdiction for several reasons: First, each agency has a defined set of responsibilities and there is little overlap or competition for authority (for example, only the fire and emergency services organization provides fire suppression services). Second, there is one authority that all departments answer to equally. That governing body can mediate conflicts, negotiate resolutions, provide funding, and establish policy. Third, most agencies within a jurisdiction have a common goal of providing services to the public. Finally, agency heads and management staffs have a continual working relationship with each other and may even have a shared personal life history within the community **(Figure 3.10)**.

Conflict or competition can arise between agencies because of shrinking resources that must be divided among them. As one agency expands its services, another may feel threatened. This conflict may occur when the law-enforcement agency begins to investigate suspicious fires, normally the responsibility of the fire and emergency services organization's arson investigation unit. Fire and emergency services chief officers should take the leadership in developing an IMT within the jurisdiction to address potential threats.

The composition of the team can vary depending on the organization of the jurisdiction and the services that are available. Resources, such as forensic laboratories, that can be shared. Shared resources should be identified, and policies and procedures established for their use. Because all agencies need accurate information on threats to the jurisdiction, a system for gathering, analyzing, maintaining, and sharing information should be established. The local incident management team can then become the nucleus for interagency relations with other levels of government.

Fire and Emergency Services Organizations

Most fire and emergency services organizations have a history of relations with neighboring departments. Mutual aid and automatic response agreements have created a network of organizations with compatible communications systems, centralized dispatching, joint training, compatible equipment, and standardized response procedures **(Figure 3.11)**. Between public and industrial/military fire and emergency services organizations, response plans and procedures ensure mutual support at hazardous materials incidents and other types of emergencies. Some volunteer departments have determined which department will provide heavy rescue, aerial devices, or other specialized services. The result is a more efficient and effective use of resources within the response areas.

Chief officers of the fire and emergency services organizations are responsible for maintaining this interagency relationship. They meet periodically to determine training needs, address challenges, and develop response plans. These relationships are the basis for the IMT mentioned earlier. The chief of-

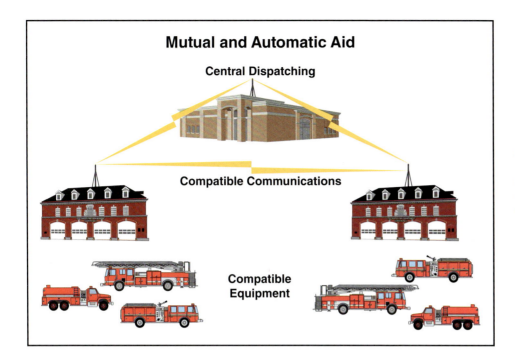

Figure 3.11 Mutual and automatic aid agreements frequently benefit the organizations and communities involved.

ficers who are also involved in the jurisdictional IMT also belong to the fire and emergency services IMT. They create mutual and automatic response agreements, monitor the effectiveness of the agreements, and apply the IMT concept to fire related issues.

State/Provincial and Local Law-Enforcement Agencies

North American law enforcement agencies have long established relationships with fire and emergency services organizations. In some regions, both are legally considered public safety officers. Chief officers must have a sound working arrangement with their law enforcement counterparts. Preincident planning is essential to joint-jurisdiction operations especially when incidents may occur on highways or involve crime scenes.

Highway incidents create potential conflict between agencies because each has certain priorities. While the fire and emergency services organization must concentrate on apparatus placement, rescue, spill or fire control, and hazardous materials cleanup; the law enforcement agency is concerned with maintaining an efficient flow of traffic **(Figure 3.12)**. At crime scenes, conflict may occur as firefighters attempt to extinguish fires and remove debris, while law enforcement officials want the scene to remain intact for evidence collec-

Competing Priorities at a Vehicle Accident

Fire Service	EMS	Law Enforcement
Spill or Fire Control	Patient Stabilization	Prevent Frurther Accidents
Patient Extrication	Patient Transport	Maintain Traffic Flow
HazMat Cleanup		Investigate Accident Cause

Figure 3.12 Examples of potential conflicts between three agencies and their priorities at a motor vehicle accident.

tion. Other issues that exist include the fire and emergency service organization's control of a contaminated area that forces law enforcement agents to remain outside the danger zones. These issues and others should be resolved before the incident occurs.

Traffic Incident Management

U.S. DOT Federal Highway Administration has developed a program to coordinate emergency responders to highway incidents. Traffic Incident Management groups are established to assist local agencies in developing procedures to educate emergency response organizations in highway safety and methods for quickly clearing incidents from the roadway.

Local law enforcement agencies are usually part of the same jurisdiction as the fire and emergency services organization. Operational coordination can be achieved through the local IMT or through direct preincident planning and training sessions. The personnel of both organizations must know the responsibilities, authority, and limitations of their counterparts. Areas of apparent conflict should be addressed and resolved during planning.

Another local relationship is between municipal fire and emergency services organizations or rural fire protection districts and county/parish law-enforcement agencies, such as sheriffs' offices. Because the two entities report to separate governing bodies, joint planning may be part of the larger state/provincial process. If not, it is up to the fire and emergency services organization to develop a relationship with this law enforcement agency.

State police, highway patrol, state marshals, Provincial Police Services (PPS) and Royal Canadian Mounted Police (RCMP) usually make up the law-enforcement agencies at the state/provincial level. The greatest point of conflict seems to occur at highway transportation accidents. Preincident planning and joint-training operations based on ICS/IMS for highway incidents will help reduce such conflict. In Canada, the occupational health and safety responsibility rests at the provincial level through workers' compensation boards and other similar organizations.

Another potential point of contact involves the local fire and emergency services units or personnel response to state-owned facilities such as offices, recreational facilities, and educational or penal institutions. Response personnel should perform preincident planning as well as preincident walk-through inspections. Fire prevention inspections and code-enforcement authorities should also be determined between state officials and the local fire and emergency services organization.

Federal Law Enforcement Agencies

In the U.S. and Canada, the federal law enforcement agencies and organizations include:

- United States
    - U.S. Marshals Service (Department of Justice)
    - Federal Bureau of Investigation (FBI)

- U.S. Coast Guard
- Military police forces
- U.S. Citizenship and Immigration Services (USCIS)
- Department of Homeland Security (DHS, various agencies)
- Bureau of Alcohol, Tobacco, Firearms, and Explosives (ATF)
• Canada
- RCMP
- Military police forces

Representatives of these agencies have offices in major cities and state capitals. Joint planning and training can be developed at the local level or through the DHS, U.S. Fire Administration (USFA), or the Canadian government. Other interagency contact between local and federal organizations includes protecting federal facilities, responding with mutual aid onto federal property, performing inspections, and responding to terrorist incidents.

Federal Agencies

Federal law-enforcement agencies are not the only national government organizations with which chiefs/managers will have relationships. In the U.S., others include, but are not limited, to the following:

- Bureau of Indian Affairs (BIA)
- Environmental Protection Agency (EPA)
- Department of Agriculture Forest Service
- Department of the Interior (DOI)
- Department of Defense (DOD)
- Department of Justice (DOJ)
- Occupational Safety and Health Administration (OSHA)
- National Institute for Occupational Safety and Health (NIOSH)
- Department of the Treasury
- Centers for Disease Control and Prevention (CDC)

Canadian fire and emergency services organizations likewise are involved with the following organizations:

- Canadian Transport Emergency Centre (CANUTEC)
- Office of Critical Infrastructure Protection and Emergency Preparedness (OCIPEP)
- Joint Emergency Preparedness Program (JEPP)
- Department of National Defense and the Canadian Forces

Relationships with federal agencies can provide increased benefits and opportunities. Information, grants, funding, equipment, and support are available both during a declared emergency and on a regular basis. IMTs can be created for response to specific types of emergencies.

Intergovernmental Agreements

Formal agreements between the fire and emergency services organization and various levels of government are important to ensure a coordinated response in time of crisis. The agreements develop as a result of IMT planning sessions and training simulations designed to recognize conflicts and support needs. Formal intergovernmental agreements should include the following items:

- Agency authority and responsibility
- Funding and reimbursement procedures
- Response procedures
- Communication systems, protocol, and procedures
- Preincident planning and training
- Post incident evaluations
- Notification procedures

Types of agreements range from local mutual aid agreements between departments to agreements between local departments/organization and the federal government in the event of a declared state of emergency. Because these agreements are legal documents, the jurisdiction's legal department should be involved in the development of them. These agreements should be reviewed and revised as needed on a periodic basis like other plans.

Political Decision-Making Process

Chief officers must understand the political process, build political relationships, and recognize and develop political resources. As part of the process, chief officers provide information to politicians and answer their requests for assistance. Understanding this process and working with it must be accomplished while remaining politically neutral.

Political Processes

The political process involves a mutually reliant relationship between elected and appointed officials, citizens, and the government bureaucracy described as follows **(Figure 3.13)**:

- **Citizens** — Elect candidates who most closely match the desires and views of the voters. Citizens express their concerns through involvement, complaints, and feedback to elected officials and the bureaucracy. Citizens provide revenue from taxes and bond issues that support government services.

- **Elected and appointed officials** — Elected and appointed officials direct the various departments to provide the necessary services. These officials' tenure in office depends upon how well they have met the desires of the citizens. Duties include:
  — Hearing and making decisions based upon complaints, concerns, suggestions, and feedback from citizens and bureaucrats
  — Creating services, programs, and policies based on the available resources

- **Government Bureaucracy** — Composed of the managers, supervisors, and members of each department. Department heads report to and may serve at the pleasure of elected officials. The careers of these heads depend on how well they accomplish their assigned duties. Duties include interacting directly with public citizens and providing information on the following:

— Services provided

— Future needs and trends

— Available resources

— Resource needs

— Potential problems

— Citizens' complaints and concerns

Fire and emergency services organization chief officers generally deal with elected or appointed local officials including:

- Mayors
- Council members
- Commissioners of municipalities
- County commissioners
- Boards of selectmen
- Boards of supervisors
- City managers (usually appointed)
- Public safety commissioners (usually appointed)
- Boards of trustees (usually appointed)

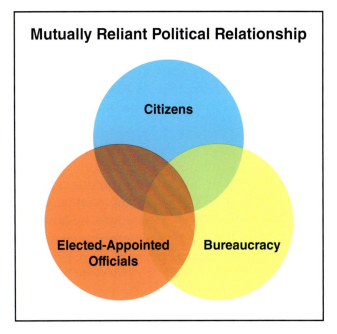

Figure 3.13 Illustrating the overlap of priorities and responsibilities within a mutually reliant relationship in an AHJ.

Chief officers who work for state/provincial governments generally interact with elected or appointed members of the legislature, executive branch, or public safety or forestry departments. At the national level, the direct relationship is with the department, bureau, or military branch to which the fire or emergency services organization reports.

The sections that follow describe elements and concepts important to understanding the political process including:

- Responsibility of elected officials
- Concept of governing
- Influence of the voting public

Responsibility of Government Officials

Many municipalities have a city manager form of government. A city/municipal council usually hires city managers. The city manager has the same responsibilities that the elected officials have plus the added challenge of maintaining a good relationship with the council. All elected officials are responsible to their constituents and this responsibility includes the following duties:

- Listening to the concerns of the citizens
- Prioritizing those concerns
- Resolving or solving those concerns
- Planning for the future

- Generating a vision for the community
- Developing goals and objectives to meet the vision
- Managing the services the government is mandated to provide
- Maintaining a viable funding base for those services
- Providing quality leadership for the governing body

Concept of Governing

Government provides services and responds to needs through sound management principles. Fire and emergency services chief officers provide accurate information, ethical leadership and sound advice to political leaders. According to the International City/County Management Association (ICMA), there are nine elements to the concept of governing. Chief officers should also apply these same nine elements to the management of their own departments. These include the following:

- Listening to the public
- Informing the public about the following:
  - Vision
  - Goals
  - Policies
  - Plans
  - Programs
  - Services
- Developing a focused vision for the future of the community
- Making decisions regarding policy, resources, and services
- Generating an ethical image of community government
- Representing local government in dealings with higher levels of government
- Monitoring the performance of the departments within local government
- Seeking feedback from citizens and adjusting resources and services accordingly
- Gaining support from community partners through partnerships with business, civic, political, and educational leaders

Influence of the Public

In a democracy, the political process depends on involvement and feedback from the public. This process starts with the portion of the public that votes for the candidates who seek election to government positions. Usually less than half of the eligible electorate members vote in any given election. Those who do participate in an election vote for the following various reasons:

- Desire for change
- Desire to prevent change
- Believe strongly in a candidate or issue
- View voting as a duty of responsible citizens

Members of a well-organized voting bloc, one with a single primary concern, can affect the outcome of an election, even if they are not in the majority. When a voting block with a single concern influences the outcome of an election,

Local

Governmental entities such as municipalities, counties/parishes, special districts, and fire protection districts create and adopt local legislation. Often, the local fire and emergency services organizations generate ordinances themselves. These ordinances consist of the following:

- Adoption of or changes to the building, fire, and zoning codes
- Adoption of collective bargaining agreements
- Policies relating to the purchase of capital items
- Changes in the tax rates or revenue sources
- Interjurisdictional agreements

At the local level, monitoring the ordinances and laws can be the duty of a liaison or fire prevention officer such as a fire marshal. Through constant contact with the governing body, this person can remain aware of the development or progress of fire and emergency services related issues. Most local newspapers print meeting agendas or pending issues before scheduled meetings. Newspapers called *Legal News* carry information on pending local or regional legislation.

State/Provincial

Laws that affect the fire and emergency services organization at the state/provincial level may originate from the fire and emergency services organization, concerned legislators, insurance industry, or other state/provincial departments such as transportation or forestry. These laws may concern items such as the following:

- Pensions
- Revenue rates and sources
- Labor or safety requirements
- Building, fire, and zoning codes in unincorporated areas
- State/provincial fire training requirements and resources
- Highway weight limitations
- Fire protection district creation

Pending legislation at the state/provincial level requires a different approach if the chief officer is not located in or near the capital city. The legislative staff usually announces pending legislation information in local or capital city newspapers or government web sites. The state/provincial fire and emergency services organization is an excellent tool for dealing with legislative issues at the state/provincial level. The chief officer could consider forming a local area or regional committee to monitor state/provincial legislation. This committee could spread the workload and provide additional people to meet with politicians. This committee might be part of the state/provincial chief officers or volunteer/career firefighters' association.

Federal

It can be difficult for a chief officer to monitor all of the potential legislation generated during a legislative calendar year. The legislative branch of government (Congress or Parliament) originates legislation at the federal/national level at the request of legislative members, from the legislative staff, governmental agencies, or through the persuasion of lobbyists, citizens groups, or representatives of professional organizations **(Figure 3.14)**. Topics of concern may include:

- Homeland security
- Revenue sources
- Grants
- Educational requirements
- Transportation and safety related laws
- Standardization of operational processes
- Hiring practices
- Other issues that apply generally throughout the nation

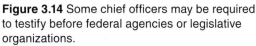

Figure 3.14 Some chief officers may be required to testify before federal agencies or legislative organizations.

Organizations already exist to help monitor pending national legislation on fire and emergency services related topics. They include CFSI, IAFC, IAFF, NVFC, and numerous other professional fire and emergency services organizations and their Canadian counterparts. These organizations also submit proposed bills to members of Congress/Parliament and provide speakers in support of bills. Local chief officers should keep in touch with these groups for the latest information on legislative changes that could affect them.

Community Involvement

Community involvement includes citizen participation in the activities, decision making, and goal setting of the department. It also means involving the fire and emergency services organization in the lives of the population in ways not directly related to the department's mission statement. Partnerships and special programs help to develop these relationships.

Community Leadership

Community leadership is a critical responsibility of chief officers. Chief officers must demonstrate concern for the overall welfare of the community. This leadership requires interest and effort extending beyond the needs of the fire and emergency services organization. The fire chief cannot be the sole supporter and advocate of community involvement and community leadership. These efforts must be tied in some way to the mission of the fire and emergency services organization. Accomplishing these efforts requires an empowering approach to community leadership that is modeled at the top and extends throughout the organization. Fire and emergency services organization members should share in the ownership of community issues and problems.

Chief officers can contribute and participate in many ways that help to build positive relationships and support for fire and emergency services organization programs. This involvement provides opportunities to interact with other current and future community leaders on a regular basis. Examples of such opportunities include, but are not limited to, the following:

- Serving on community boards and commissions
- Chairing and participating in community-wide charity and fund-raising events
- Participating in community and regional planning efforts
- Joining Rotary International, Kiwanis, or similar clubs
- Ensuring that the department is present at significant community events

The community's problems are also the fire and emergency services organization's problems. It is difficult to muster support for fire department issues if the fire and emergency services organization lacks interest in other organizations' issues. Community involvement should become a core leadership value within the fire and emergency services organization.

Decision-Making and Goals-Setting Functions

Major decisions must be made when a new fire and emergency services organization is established or an existing one alters its form. Administrative and operational policies and procedures are established, goals and objectives are created, and mission statements are written. Customers within the service area must be included in the initial planning and developing stages. Even established departments should involve citizens in the ongoing planning and decision-making process. This involvement applies primarily to volunteer, combination, and career departments. Industrial and military departments should include their stakeholders and any citizens living within or adjacent to the facility that their operations may affect. Issues that benefit from citizen involvement include, but are not limited, to the following:

- Recruiting personnel
- Locating facilities
- Financing or fund-raising
- Developing policies
- Developing multiyear plans
- Resolving personnel issues
- Determining service requirements
- Developing community emergency action plans
- Developing homeland security plans
- Developing and adopting building and fire-prevention codes
- Combining services (interagency)
- Creating mutual aid agreements
- Creating disaster drills and plans
- Serving on administrative boards or commissions

Including the public in the planning, implementation, and review of projects and programs helps gain public acceptance and provide valuable insight. Develop specific guidelines for involving the public so that all participants know the desired results, terms of service, selection criteria, expectations, responsibilities, and authorities. Most programs and projects are continuous while some are responsible for only a single event. A *sunset clause* should be included that disbands the committee or group when the project is complete.

Partnerships and Programs

Partnerships and programs that form alliances and provide services are an active approach to community involvement. These alliances can be as innovative as the department or community wants to make them. Alliances can even merge formal programs with informal programs providing an opportunity for fire and emergency services personnel to be visible to the community in nonemergency situations. Fire and emergency services organizations should actively seek such opportunities to improve services and participate as community leaders.

Partnerships

A *partnership* is a formal or informal agreement between the fire and emergency services department and other public or nonprofit agencies and private companies to provide mutual services for a common good. Partnerships provide many opportunities for fire and emergency service organization personnel to become involved in local and national projects that are normally outside the primary mission of fire and emergency services organizations. Some examples of successful partnerships include the following:

- **Toys for Tots** — Annual event that collects new, unwrapped Christmas gifts for underprivileged children. Fire and emergency service organizations have provided their facilities as collection points for many years.

- **Muscular Dystrophy Association fund-raiser** — Charitable fund-raising effort on the part of IAFF, local departments, and the Muscular Dystrophy Association (MDA) in the U.S. and Canada.

- **Immunization programs** — Immunization program delivery to babies, youth, and seniors. The IAFC is a resource for examples of such programs.

- **Cardiopulmonary resuscitation (CPR) training** — Joint training with local hospitals, clinics, and public-health departments. Statistics indicate that the larger the CPR-trained population is in an area, the greater the survival rate of heart-attack victims.

- **Project Safe Place™** — Means for youths in crisis to access a safe shelter. The project involves the national Safe Place™ organization, a local community Safe Place™ committee, a youth-serving agency with trained counselors, and a network of Safe Place™ sites where youths can gain access to the program. Fire and emergency services organizations are often key components of this partnership, offering fire stations as Safe Place™ sites, being involved in program development, and providing volunteers who transport youths to the shelter **(Figure 3.15)**.

- **Challenge the F.O.R.C.E. (Firefighters Organizing Resources for Community Enrichment)** — Summer program for middle school youth who have been identified by their teachers and counselors as potentially benefiting from participating in a structured activity. Students report to a fire station where they participate in activities designed to teach a healthy lifestyle and to provide options to students who may otherwise make poor life choices. Firefighters act as role models for the students.

- **Joint-sponsored programs** — Partner with a local corporation or business to provide a service. The corporate sponsor provides funding, advertising, and assistance for the fire and emergency services organization. Public visibility through free advertising benefits both groups.

Programs

Regardless of the type of community program in which the department is involved, the results should be the same: showing concern for the welfare of the community, actively participating in the life of the community, and being visible to the community. Community involvement programs can be informal or formal. Informal programs consist of policies within the department that encourage officers and members to become involved with the public. Formal programs are created to meet specific nonemergency needs of the public or support other agencies.

Figure 3.15 An example of a fire station serving as part of the Project Safe Place program.

Internal policies emphasize the part the fire and emergency services organization has in the infrastructure of the jurisdiction and in the community at large. Some of the policies include the following:

- Permitting and encouraging citizen groups to meet in departmental facilities
- Having an open door policy for all department facilities
- Developing and advertising the existence of a departmental Internet web site
- Providing time for members to attend civic meetings while in uniform and on duty
- Participating in nonprofit community fund-raisers
- Performing blood pressure checks at fire stations
- Participating in community events
- Encouraging chief officers to join and attend civic organizations
- Designing and designating community meeting rooms in fire stations and facilities
- Creating groups of firefighters/emergency responders who work with specific elements of the community such as the Bomberos (composed of Hispanic firefighters who work with the Hispanic community in some cities) and the school mentoring program for at-risk students
- Encouraging officers and members to serve on boards and commissions
- Providing on duty personnel and apparatus to provide standby medical assistance at local sporting events
- Establishing and supporting a Fire Explorer Post or similar youth oriented group

Policies that encourage community involvement must be fairly and equally administered. No hint of bias or partiality should exist in the choice of personnel or events to be included in the program. Care also must be taken to not compromise the security of personnel and facilities. In areas or on occasions when security is an issue, chief officers must weigh the value of the program against the potential security risks or consider alternative methods of delivery.

Formal community-based programs provide some type of service that is normally outside the primary mission of the department. These programs may include the following:

- **Youth programs** — Programs such as fire explorers, fire cadet, or junior firefighter that provide an opportunity to learn about fire fighting and emergency medical services as a future career choice.
- **Child car seat safety programs** — Inspections and installation of baby and infant seats in passenger vehicles.
- **Residential Key Box Rapid Entry** — Used to provide emergency access to homes where citizens with disabilities reside.
- **Bicycle safety training** — Classes in traffic laws and safety procedures for children riding bicycles.
- **Teen driver safety programs** — Classes promote responsible driving habits among young drivers and make them aware of the consequences of irresponsible driving behavior and providing social skills for coping with peer pressure.
- **Physical fitness programs** — Awareness programs and jogging/biking/walking events to promote healthy lifestyles. Firefighters participate with kids to promote fitness.
- **Home safety inspections** — Informational opportunities to make homeowners aware of all types of safety hazards around their homes, (usually provided at the same time home fire prevention inspections are performed).
- **Hazardous materials awareness and recycling programs** — Collection points for hazardous waste materials such as paint and batteries along with recyclables.
- **Alternative response vehicle** — Van operated and staffed with volunteers (emergency medical technician and behavioral health specialist). The unit provides grief support for families and is the liaison for the fire and emergency services organization in linking families with other social services within the city. This added service fills a gap between emergency services and the social services for individuals.

Chapter Summary

Chief officers are very much a part of their communities. As public servants, they are symbols of the fire and emergency services organization and strive to be respected leaders who are active in all aspects of community life. They also work to involve the community in the operation and life of the department. Chief officers must keep citizens informed of the activities and requirements of the departments. They should never forget that their duties are to protect and serve the citizens of their communities or service areas.

Review Questions

1. What methods can a chief officer use to determine the fire and life safety needs of a community? (pp. 100-103)

2. What is a chief officer's role in community awareness programs? (pp. 103-114)

3. How can a chief officer participate in a community's political arena? (pp. 114-122)

4. What responsibilities may a chief officer assume when making political decisions? (pp. 122-128)

5. How can a chief officer monitor legislation that may affect fire and emergency services organizations? (pp. 128-130)

6. What are some approaches a chief officer can take to stay actively involved in the community? (pp. 130-134)

Emergency Services Administration (Levels III & IV)

Chapter Contents

CASE HISTORY 139

III Public Budgeting and Finance 140
- Budget Systems and Types 140
- Budget Considerations 144
- Revenue Sources 145
- Budget Development and Management 149

Purchasing 155
- Needs Assessment 156
- Research 157
- Product Evaluation 160
- Review Product Data 161
- Acquisition Process 162
- Standardization 167

Record-Keeping Function 167
- Record Types 167
- Record Development 170
- Evaluation 172
- Revision 172
- Legal Requirements 172
- Data Analysis and Interpretation 175

Organizational Improvement 176
- Needs Analysis 176
- Gap Analysis 176
- SWOT Analysis 177
- Planning 178

IV Strategic Planning 180
- Planning Process 180
- Development 181
- Implementation 182
- Monitoring 182
- Evaluation 182
- Annual Reports 183
- Revisions 183

Operational Planning 183
- Short-Term 184
- Intermediate-Term 184
- Long-Term 185

Training Requirements 188
- Evaluation of Requirements 188
- Program Development 190
- Sources of Funding 204
- External Training Sources 204
- Training Program Evaluation 206

Community Risk Assessment and Reduction 206
- Hazard Categories 207
- High Value/Priority Exposures 209
- Creating a Written Analysis 209
- Creating a Community Risk Reduction Program 210

Chapter Summary 210
Review Questions 211

chapter 4

Key Terms

Request for Information (RFI).................159

NFPA® Job Performance Requirements

This chapter provides information that addresses the following job performance requirements of NFPA® 1021, *Standard for Fire Officer Professional Qualifications* (2014).

Level III	Level IV
6.4.1	7.4.1
6.4.2	7.4.2
6.4.3	7.4.3
6.4.4	7.4.4
6.4.5	
6.4.6	

Emergency Services Administration (Levels III & IV)

Learning Objectives

After reading this chapter, students will be able to:

[Level III]

1. Describe considerations the chief officer must take when developing a divisional or departmental budget. (6.4.1)
2. Identify various methods for developing a budget management system. (6.4.2)
3. Explain procedures for purchasing materials, equipment, and apparatus. (6.4.3)
4. Identify various methods for keeping departmental records. (6.4.4)
5. Explain ways that the chief officer manages departmental data. (6.4.5)
6. Determine various methods for developing organizational improvements. (6.4.6)

[Level IV]

7. Describe the key elements of the strategic planning process. (7.4.1, 7.4.4)
8. Explain various time frames associated with a department's operational planning stage. (7.4.1, 7.4.4)
9. Indicate the various responsibilities of the chief officer in terms of organizational training. (7.4.2)
10. Identify various components of a community risk assessment. (7.4.3)

Chapter 4
Emergency Services Administration (Levels III & IV)

Case History

Several years ago, Mesa (AZ) Fire Department decided to take part in the Center for Public Safety Excellence's Commission on Fire Accreditation International (CFAI) self-assessment program. The all-inclusive program measures all aspects of a modern fire and emergency services organization. The strategic planning necessary for this process was highly community driven in determining the levels of service for the department's standard of coverage. City officials developed budgets that met those response levels, and all line items in the budget tied back to the strategic plan and the standard of coverage.

Later, an economic downturn forced city administrators to mandate departmental cuts that could have severely affected fire and emergency services organization operations. Because the accreditation process was community driven and institutionalized within the department's organizational culture, the department made creative cuts without severely affecting response service levels.

The organization learned that in order to maintain service levels when money becomes tight, the interconnectivity of the budget, strategic plan, risk analysis, standards of coverage, and community expectations can be important.

All fire and emergency services organizations have some form of administrative framework. This framework must exist before any emergency services can be provided to the response area. The administration provides the leadership, planning, resources, and training needed for an efficient and effective department to exist. Chief officers are responsible for providing the resources required to meet the public's needs.

Level III chief officers are responsible for the budgeting and finance functions, purchasing, records management, planning, and providing organizational improvement. These functions are based on the strategic and operational planning performed by the Level IV chief officer. In addition to planning, these officers are responsible for determining and providing the department's training as well as assessing the community's level of risk and recommending ways of reducing the risk.

This chapter provides an overview of each of these topics. All fire and emergency services organizations will have some or all of these administrative programs available to them. Larger career departments may have separate sections within the administration that are responsible for providing them. Smaller volunteer, combination, or career departments may depend on outside agencies, such as municipal purchasing departments or state training agencies, to provide support. Chief officers must be aware of the functions in order to manage them internally or monitor the required support from external sources.

III Public Budgeting and Finance

Modern fire and emergency services organizations use budgets to ensure that funding is available for their expenses. The type of budget system and the funding source will vary between types of organizations and levels of government. Chief officers must be familiar with the budget types used in their jurisdiction, the legal requirements, and their responsibility for developing the annual budget. Legal mandates may exist at the national and state/provincial levels that apply to national, state/provincial, municipal, and rural departments. Budget development and management generally follows an accepted model in most jurisdictions.

Budget Systems and Types

A governmental jurisdiction budget is more than a list of projected revenues and proposed expenditures. Three vital functions that a budget performs for the government are: (1) describing and identifying the relationship between different tasks, (2) providing assistance in the decision making process, and (3) clarifying political intent.

Most budgets do the following:

- Anticipate future expenditures based on the goals and objectives of the jurisdiction or organization.
- Identify how the organization's financial resources will be utilized to further the mission.
- Review the effectiveness of past budget performance.
- Establish and reinforce governmental policy.
- Assign responsibility for the accomplishment of goals and objectives.

Many terms are used to describe budgets in the public and private sectors. The terms vary depending on the source or the organization using them. In general, the following two phrases define budgets:

1. **Budget system** — Model or format to which the budget process conforms
2. **Budget type** — How costs or revenues are divided between capital and operational purchases

Budget Systems

Budget systems are the general formats to which the jurisdiction's budget process conforms. Each system provides the same result through a variety of approaches. Some may contain elements of other systems. In some jurisdictions, the state/province establishes the budget system guidelines that the department chief and the finance officer use for their budgets. In general, chief officers may not be involved in establishing a budgeting system, although they may participate in evaluating a current system and recommending changes to the system. Typically, those systems are known as:

- **Line-item budgeting** — Consists of a list of revenue sources and a list of proposed expenditures for the budget cycle. This is also known as an *object class budget* because each line contains a specific object, such as apparatus, or class, such as salaries. For the budget to balance, revenue and expenditures must be equal. This budgeting system is the most common system used in North America. It may be applied to the entire jurisdiction or the operating budget of an individual department.

- **Zero-based budgeting (ZBB)** — Requires all expenditures to be justified at the beginning of each new budget cycle, as opposed to simply explaining the amounts requested that are in excess of the previous cycle's funding. During the budget planning, it is assumed that there is zero money available to operate the organization or program. The organization must justify the contribution that it makes to the jurisdiction. *Benefit/Variation:*

  — ZBB is generally beneficial to public organizations because expenditures can get out of control when it is automatically assumed that the amount required during the last budget cycle is the amount that will be required during the next cycle.

  — Rather than using zero as a starting point, some organizations use a predetermined percent (such as 80 percent) of the previous year's budget.

- **Matrix budgeting** — Associated with the theory of matrix departmentalization. A project manager leads members of independent units who are assigned to a project. This system is used to fund programs or projects that involve a variety of departments, divisions, branches, or sections. The project is usually for a limited duration, such as the construction of a new fire station. Project team members may come from the fire, public-works, finance, legal, or street departments. *Features:*

  — It permits double budgeting and imposes responsibility to gain consensus agreement and can be a key to collaboration between departments.

  — Funds for the project are vested in the partner departments, and allocation of other resources must be shared.

- **Program budgeting** — Often a form of line-item budgets that uses categories that are different from the classic line-item budget. In a fire and emergency services organization, each program — fire suppression, emergency medical services (EMS), fire prevention, public fire education, fire administration — is a separate category in the budget. The line-item for each program shows how much of the overall budget is allocated to that program — salaries, equipment, possible overtime. This type of budget will not have just one line, but it may be similar to a line-item budget with different subcategories for each program.

- **Performance budgeting** — Categorized by function or activity (also called *outcome-based budgets*) similar to program budgets. However, these budgets fund each activity based on projected performance. For example, the budget for fire prevention is based upon conducting a specified number of inspections in various types of occupancies. Also included in a performance budget is a breakdown of the cost of each unit of performance — per inspection, plans review, EMS call, fire call, etc.

- **Planning programming budgeting system (PPBS)** — Provides a framework for making decisions on current and future programs through three interrelated phases (planning, programming, and budgeting) consistent with the organization's predetermined goals, objectives, policies, and strategies. Its purpose is to subject the budgetary process to intense, systematic, and continuous analysis. PPBS provides an overall management philosophy and a specific management process for policy development and implementation. It translates the erratic and unpredictable aspects of routine decision making into a rational and quantified management scheme. *Effectiveness/ Development/Use:*
  - PPBS is an effort to link planning and budgeting through the development of programs that are created to achieve stated goals and objectives. The program effectiveness is determined through analysis based on cost-effective criteria.
  - PPBS was developed in the 1970s in an attempt to coordinate the planning, program development, and budget processes.
  - The U.S. Department of Defense and some industries use the PPBS. Although the military still uses the original PPBS, it has evolved into a *service based budgeting system* in some jurisdictions.

Budgets Types

Public organizations generally use two types of budgets: capital budgets (projected major purchases) and operating budgets (recurring expenses of day-to-day operation). Capital budgets may also be referred to as capital non-reoccurring (CNR) budgets. Capital and operating budgets are normally separated for the following reasons:

- **Funding** — One-time specific purpose or nondiscretionary monies fund capital purchases. One source of funds is the sale of bonds for the purchase of capital items. Separation ensures that the funds will not be used for other expenditures. Operating budgets are funded from general revenue sources such as property or sales taxes that are then assigned to the various departments, programs, or categories.

- **Decision-making process** — Capital budgets involve a listing of all potential projects and ranking them in order of priority. As a project is funded and completed, it leaves the list and a new one is added. Operating budgets generally do not require ranking because the programs they fund usually continue from year to year.

- **Planning and implementation time frames** — Capital budgets involve a longer development time and may require many years for completion. Detailed planning is critical to prevent costly errors that result in change orders to the project documents. Operating budgets are generally developed over a period of 6 months before adoption of the new budget.

A *capital budget* includes projected major purchases that cost more than a certain specified amount of money and are expected to last more than 3 years. Fire apparatus and vehicles, equipment, and facilities are typical capital items for fire and emergency services organizations **(Figure 4.1)**. Many jurisdictions have multiyear capital improvement plans/projects (CIPs) for these and other major investments such as replacing apparatus or equipment or building a

Figure 4.1 A few examples of the types of apparatus, equipment, SCBA, and facilities that are funded through capital budget line items.

new training center. Each year's capital budget represents that year's portion of the expenditures included in the CIP.

The revenues for capital purchases may come from a variety of sources. The amount may be a set percentage of the annual revenues used to operate the jurisdiction. These funds are shared between the various departments. The governing body makes the final decision on what is purchased based on each department's justification.

The organization's *operating budget* is used to pay for the recurring expenses of day-to-day operations of the fire and emergency services organization. The largest, single item in the operating budget of most career departments is personnel costs (sometimes called *personnel services*) — salaries and benefits. Personnel costs may represent as much as 90 percent of a career department's operating budget. Noncash (fringe) benefits cost some jurisdictions an amount equal to 50 percent of a person's base salary **(Figure 4.2, p. 144)**.

Operating budgets also pay for utilities, office supplies, apparatus and vehicle fuel, janitorial supplies, and other items. Contract services for the maintenance of apparatus and facilities are also a part of the operating budget.

Most chief officers are responsible for preparing budget requests to obtain the resources needed to operate their particular battalion/district, division, branch, or section. This usually involves updating the requests from the previous year's budget to reflect current needs and projecting the next year's

City of Paulstown
2013 – 2014 Annual Budget
Operating Summary Report

Fire Department

Expenditure by Category	FY2012 - 2013		FY2012 - 2013			FY2013 - 2014 Projection		
Category	FY2010 - 2011	FY2011 - 2012	General Fund	Other Funds	Total Funds	General Fund	Other Funds	Total Funds
Salaries / Benefits	13,298,622	13,133,496	13,298,622	0	13,133,496	11,929,213	0	11,929,213
Materials / Supplies	387,981	391,299	387,981	0	391,299	374,866	0	374,866
Purchased Services	41,657	40,111	41,657	0	40,111	48,233	0	48,233
Other Expenses	197,311	113,109	197,311	0	113,109	129,290	0	129,290
Non-Recurring Operating	0	5,060	0	0	5,060	10,000	0	10,000
Allocations	880,271	918,144	880,271	0	918,144	801,395	0	801,395
Department Total	14,805,842	14,601,219	14,805,842	0	14,601,219	13,292,997	0	13,292,997

Figure 4.2 An example of the summary for an operating budget.

needs. Requests from the various battalions/districts, divisions, branches, and sections are combined to form a single organizational budget request. All chief and company officers should participate in this process to share the workload and reduce the chances that something is omitted. Once a budget is approved, it is difficult to purchase anything that was not requested without the request going through a significant review and approval process.

Budget Considerations

To develop an accurate budget, the chief officer must list the types of resources that the department will need to meet its requirements to the public. These resources can be placed into six categories:

- Facilities
- Apparatus
- Equipment
- Maintenance
- Personnel costs
- Training

Facilities

Fire and emergency services organizations may have from one to multiple facilities or structures. These facilities contain space to provide:

- Apparatus, equipment, and protective clothing storage
- Maintenance
- Dispatch and communication personnel
- Training
- Living quarters
- Administrative offices

In many rural and small communities, all of these functions are contained in one fire station. In large metropolitan or urban areas, specific structures are designed and constructed to house each type of activity.

Funds must be budgeted to:
- Acquire land
- Construct facilities
- Maintain facilities
- Insure facilities
- Provide utilities, including natural gas, electricity, water, sewer, and communications

Equipment
Equipment includes all protective clothing, tools, and operating materials that the department uses. Anything the department uses during an emergency response or provides for the safety, health, and welfare of members must be included in the budget development.

Apparatus
Fire and emergency services organizations depend on a wide variety of vehicle types to provide their services. Some vehicles are designed specifically for the fire service, such as pumpers and aerial apparatus. More common vehicles include passenger cars and vans, pickup trucks, wreckers, and fuel trucks. Consulting industry standards, repair costs, and the fuel efficiency of current vehicles determine replacement cycles.

Maintenance
Facilities, equipment, apparatus, clothing, and tools need to be maintained to ensure that they are ready for use and to increase the life expectancy of the item. Cost considerations include fuel, lubricants, paint, parts, and repairs, among others.

Personnel
Personnel costs include hourly pay, pension contributions, and benefits such as health and worker's compensation insurance, and vacation/annual leave. Volunteer departments may have to pay pension contributions, health insurance, and per call wages.

Training and Professional Development
Federal, state/provincial, local jurisdictions, and organizations such as OSHA, ISO, and NFPA® may mandate and/or recommend minimum training levels for all fire and emergency services personnel. Accrediting agencies evaluate training support structure, including staff and facilities. Departments that provide specialized services require specialized training such as confined space rescue, hazardous materials incident control, and advanced levels of medical services. Professional development is essential for personnel retention and advancement within the fire service.

Revenue Sources
Revenue is required to provide the services that citizens need. The majority of jurisdictions depend on property, sales, or income taxes (or a combination of these) as the primary source of revenue. Trust funds, enterprise funds, bond sales, grants/gifts, or fund-raising activities may supplement or replace tax-based revenue **(Figure 4.3, p. 146)**.

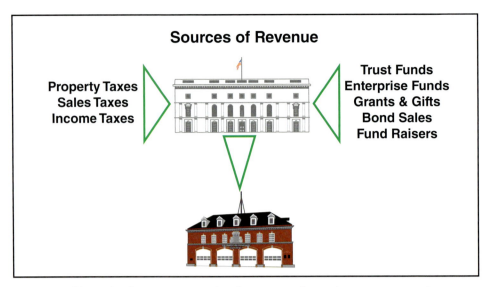

Figure 4.3 Illustrating how revenue makes its way to a fire and emergency services department.

Taxes

Traditional revenue sources include property, sales, and income taxes. These taxes tend to provide a rather stable and predictable source of revenue. However, they are not immune to changes in the economy or taxpayer revolts. Chief officers must remain aware of trends in revenue collection to develop realistic budget projections. The fire chief may need to provide justification for a tax increase based on the required level of services. Gaining public support for tax increases requires accurate data collection and public presentations that are objective and factual. Descriptions of the various revenue sources are as follows:

- **Property taxes** — Taxes increase with assessed value of property and the most recent sales price or assessed evaluations that tax assessors determine. Over the past four decades, voter initiated taxing limits have resulted in stagnation or regression in property tax revenues.

    Property taxes are subject to decisions that the governing body makes to provide economic incentives to attract new businesses. Tax increment financing (TIF) uses tax revenues to offset the cost of a project in a designated area for a specified period of time. While the TIF brings new business to the community, it also lowers the tax income of the municipality or fire district and adds to the structures that the fire and emergency services organization must inspect and protect. This TIF can significantly affect the revenues available to the fire and emergency services organization.

- **Sales taxes** — Have a greater effect on low-income consumers because they are a regressive form of taxation levied at municipal, county/parish, and state/provincial levels. Not only have attempts been made to reduce these taxes, they are susceptible to changes in the economic climate. If consumers change their purchasing habits, sales tax collections may not meet projections. Because tax revenues and budgets are established as much as 18 months in advance, the potential for changes in collections is possible. However, if there is an upturn in the economy, the potential for excess sales tax revenue increases. In areas that attract tourists or shoppers from outside the community, sales taxes spread the financial support to populations beyond the local residents. Some sales tax may be earmarked for public safety.

- **Personal income taxes** — The federal government, most state/provincial governments, and some municipal governments collect personal income taxes. Income taxes, like other forms of revenue, have been the subject of some voter concern and are directly affected by the economy and political trends. Layoffs, reductions in work hours, loss of overtime benefits, closing of businesses, and tax cuts may result in decreased revenues.

- **Special purpose tax levy** — Based on the assessed value of property specified as *millage* ($1 per $1,000 property valuation). The local government collects the levy for a specified government purpose such as the operation of the fire and emergency services organization or ambulance service. The tax levy, which runs for a specified time period, is submitted to voters for approval. Another approach is the special taxing authority used to support fire protection districts.

- **User Fees** — Collected for building permits, plans review, copies of reports, inspections/reinspections, hazardous materials responses, EMS responses, motor vehicle collision responses, and fire protection subscription services for emergency responses to support services. The individual department or the finance and revenue department may collect the fees and transfer them to the general fund, then credit them to the appropriate department.

- **Community Impact Fees** — Collected from contractors and developers to cover municipal costs that will be incurred over time.

- **Special taxing authorities** — System that provides revenue to pay for services that are provided in areas that do not have the authority to raise taxes.

Memberships/Subscriptions

Fire protection memberships and subscriptions, such as annual dues or fees that residents pay for fire protection, are used to fund rural fire and emergency services organizations. These departments are located in unincorporated areas that lack a source of tax revenue.

Trust Funds

A trustee or a board of trustees manages the assets of a *trust fund* account for the benefit of another party or parties. Applicable federal and state/provincial laws govern the funds. Funds that are derived from donations and gifts are placed into the account. They may be further divided into categories such as undesignated gifts, broadly designated gifts, and specifically designated gifts, depending on a donor's wishes. A donation may be designated to purchase a new piece of equipment, construct a new facility, or operation of the organization.

Trust funds are either *general* for perpetual and long-term trust funds or *specific* for short-term trust funds. *Perpetual* trusts are funds from which only **interest** income from the principal may be expended. *Long-term* trusts are funds from which both income and principal may be expended. Any capital spent from long-term trusts must be defined as expendable. *Short-term* trusts are funds that are spent in the current year for some expressed purpose. Trust funds are usually intended for one-time purchases and not for recurring operating expenses.

Another form of trust fund is the *employee* or *member pension* fund that provides retirees with an income based on years of service, age, and contributions. Both the jurisdiction and the member usually make contributions to the fund over the length of the member's service.

Enterprise Funds

Enterprise funds are established to finance and account for the acquisition, operation, and maintenance of government facilities and services that user fees entirely or predominantly support, such as water and sewer service fees. Enterprise funds may also be established when the jurisdiction has decided that periodic determination of revenues earned, expenses incurred, and/or net income is appropriate. Enterprise funds account for government owned utilities and hospitals. An enterprise fund often sustains or supplements the ambulance transportation component of EMS if a government agency provides the service. One fire and emergency services organization investigated the use of an enterprise fund to hire a training officer to help meet unfunded state training mandates.

An *auxiliary enterprise* is an entity that exists to furnish services to the population of a service area and that charges a fee related to the cost of the service. Auxiliary enterprise accounts are operated on an annual budget based on the estimate of operating income and expense, including bond interest expense and provisions for bond retirement if applicable. Fire protection subscriptions may be used to create auxiliary enterprise funds.

Bonds

A *bond* is a promise to repay the principal along with interest on a specified date when the bond reaches *maturity*. Some bonds do not pay interest, but all bonds require repayment of the principal. An investor who buys a bond becomes a creditor of the jurisdiction that sold the bond. The federal government, states/provinces, counties/parishes, municipalities, public corporations, and many other types of institutions sell bonds to fund programs and projects. Fire and emergency services organizations generally use bonds to purchase apparatus or construct new facilities. Fire and emergency services organizations should be aware of fluctuating bond rates that can impact the ability to make capital purchases.

Grants/Gifts

Many fire and emergency services organizations supplement their general budgets with private, corporate, or government grants and gifts to meet specific needs. In some states, a portion of all fire insurance premiums paid into the insurance industry is returned to local fire and emergency services organizations to pay for training and training-related materials.

Gifts consist of donations from life insurance policies, bequests, and in kind donations. Service clubs and other civic organizations, such as the Los Angeles Fire Department Foundation, have donated funds to purchase specialized equipment such as hydraulic rescue tools or semiautomatic defibrillators. Funds donated for capital purchases should be used for that purpose only and not for operating expenses.

Government grants, such as those provided by the Federal Emergency Management Administration (FEMA) or U.S. Department of Transportation (DOT), provide local emergency responders with the training and equipment necessary to deal with a variety of incidents. Nongovernment organizations (NGO) or nonprofit organizations provide grant money to fund programs such as civilian cardiopulmonary resuscitation (CPR) training through fire and emergency services organizations. Grant application processes can be challenging, especially for small organizations. Grant writing is highly specialized and to be successful may require a skilled professional grant writer. Chief officers may assign the task to staff members who have the skills and time necessary to perform the task or contract it to a professional service.

Some federally and state/provincial supported programs operate largely through consolidated funding streams called *block grants*. This funding is made available for defined purposes but with minimum conditions. The use of and support for block grants have increased in recent years. Block grant funding meets the need for flexibility at the program level and minimizes the bureaucratic aspects of the budgeting process. The increasing use of block grants recognizes that those who do the work and spend the funds are accountable, responsible, and best qualified to make such decisions. Block grants ensure community involvement in the application process.

Fund-Raisers

Fund-raising is most often an activity of volunteer or combination organizations that must supplement or provide their own operating revenue. Fund-raising usually takes the form of local events such as social events, bingo, raffles, and requests for donations. Some organizations have annual bean or pancake suppers that serve as public relations events as well as fund-raisers. Some fire and emergency services organizations sponsor circuses and other events and share the proceeds with the events' organizers. These cosponsored events often use phone solicitation to sell tickets and can result in negative public response focused on the department and not the telephone marketers.

Budget Development and Management

Chief officers work with company officers, other staff members, and citizen representatives to create annual budgets. Internal and external customers should be involved in the process to help ensure successful adoption. The process should be divided into understandable steps. The steps of the budget process include **(Figure 4.4)**:

1. Plan
2. Prepare
3. Implement
4. Monitor
5. Evaluate
6. Revise

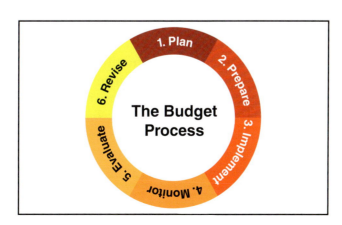

Figure 4.4 The steps of the budgeting process.

Plan

Throughout the year, the chief officers who are responsible for budget preparation should keep records and make notes on the implementation of the current budget. The budget process may begin six months to a year before the end of the current fiscal year. A jurisdiction should have a fairly clear idea of estimated revenues based upon tax projections, expected grants and subsidies from the state/provincial or federal government, expected fees for services, memberships or subscriptions, bond sales, and other sources.

Budget planning must be closely aligned with the strategic planning process. The financial resources necessary to implement elements of the strategic plan must be determined to include them into the budget process. A budget project management team evaluates the effectiveness of the current budget, determines funding requirements to meet the annual objectives of the strategic plan, and analyzes any trends that may affect the budget.

Prepare

The jurisdiction's Finance and Revenue Department estimates revenues from all sources and translates them into preliminary budget priorities. The department's chief may be informed of the general fiscal conditions and what parameters to work within during departmental budget planning and preparation sessions. The jurisdiction may require that the department submit the same budget as the current year with an adjustment for inflation. The chief may also be told to submit a budget that reflects an across-the-board increase or decrease of a specified percentage based on projected revenues that the jurisdiction's financial department determines. With this information available, the chief officers and other participants responsible for preparing the organization's budget request begin preparing a budget request proposal. In fire districts, the fire and emergency services organization or board of directors may perform the same function as a finance and revenue department.

Budget requests should *not* be inflated or overestimated. Fire and emergency services organization officers have a responsibility to make every budget request as accurate and realistic as possible and present that request in the appropriate format. This request helps the taxpayers and their elected representatives make informed decisions about how tax revenues are spent.

Next, the chief and the administrative staff must decide the level and type of services the department can and should provide during the upcoming year. The department's budget request may reflect the same services and service levels as the previous year. There may be a need to add new services or delete existing ones because of changes in the service area's needs.

The decisions regarding services and service levels must be translated into a firm program proposal and a funding request developed for each program. Each program must be described in terms of personnel, equipment, materials, and other costs. Chief officers are responsible for describing these programs and developing the funding request for each one. Some jurisdictions require the use of specific types of program justification forms in the budget development process. Chief officers must be familiar with these forms and the information necessary to complete them. See **Appendix C** for a sample justification form.

Calculating Environmental Costs

Environmental costs and benefits should be factored into the final estimate of a budget. The U.S. Environmental Protection Agency (EPA) can provide information to help determine the energy efficiency for structures.

Calculations can be made to determine:

- The reduction in specific air emissions resulting from energy conservation in facilities based on reductions in electricity and natural gas usage.
- The energy, greenhouse gas emissions, and cost savings that the conversion from incandescent light bulbs to compact fluorescent bulbs generates.
- The fuel use and air emissions from vehicle operations to determine the environmental benefits of reducing nonemergency trips, performing preventive maintenance, or purchasing more fuel-efficient vehicles.
- The reduction in greenhouse gas emissions resulting from various waste management practices, including source reduction, recycling, combustion, composting, and landfilling.
- The greenhouse gas emissions and energy effects from purchasing products produced from post-consumer recycled materials.
- The environmental benefits of using "green" janitorial products and practices.
- The cost competitiveness and environmental benefits of alternatives to food waste disposal, including source reduction, donation, composting, and recycling of grease.
- The environmental and economic benefits of purchasing computers and monitors that are registered as Electronic Product Environmental Assessment Tools (EPEAT).

Use simple and direct language to describe the requests. In the narrative description of the services and their funding requirements, the language should be written so that anyone can understand it — no acronyms or fire service jargon. Those officials who approve or disapprove these requests may have little or no knowledge of fire service terms. If a request is disapproved or reduced, it should be done on the merits of the program, not because the request could not be understood.

In most jurisdictions, funding requests for capital items are separated from operating expenses. Even though these two categories must be separated, they are submitted as part of the same organizational budget request. The first draft of the budget request is complete when all of the data are compiled and translated into specific requests for specific programs and activities. Its chances for approval are increased if the document is as complete and accurate as possible.

A complete budget contains information that supports the requests based on valid and accurate justification. The systems approach may be used to illustrate the budget. Prudent administrators also insist that each departmental budget request go through a thorough internal review before it is submitted for the jurisdiction's review.

Justifying a budget request requires documentation, data, and other supporting evidence that proves that the request is valid. Thorough research is the basis for this documentation. This information is used both to prepare the initial budget request and to justify it. Accurate research and internal records maintenance provide strong bases for both activities. Some fire and emergency services organizations actively seek citizen input and community involvement in budget preparation and review. Meeting and addressing various applicable industry standards such as NFPA®, ISO, accreditation organizations, and community expressed expectations are important in budget justifications. Sources to be researched in this effort include the following:

- **Organizational financial history** — Primary source of data to support the budget request based on the actual cost of providing the services that the jurisdiction requires. This history includes, but is not limited to, the costs of fuel, maintenance, utilities, parts, training, operating supplies, and other expenditures. It can be used to justify the operating budget or a capital request such as the replacement of an apparatus.

- **Market studies** — Surveys of similar service areas and organizations, which provide data on personnel salary increases, changes in benefits, or the hiring of additional personnel.

- **Actual equipment, material, or service costs** — Information available from vendors, reflecting the average cost of an item or product. Information may also be based on existing contracts the jurisdiction has for materials or services.

- **Government economic reports** — Information provides an idea of the cost-of-living increase based on inflation or the estimated revenue potential for the service area.

- **Insurance information** — Information from the state/provincial insurance commission, which includes fire-related claims, insurance premiums, Insurance Services Office, Inc. (ISO) rating figures, and projections based on service levels.

- **Governmental mandates** — Essential documentation when higher levels of government place requirements on local services and then fail to provide adequate funding.

- **Contractual requirements** — Contracts with the labor organization and contracts for services that the department may provide such as mutual or automatic aid response.

- **Accreditation** — When a fire and emergency services organization has achieved accreditation status, re-accreditation must occur at specific intervals. Re-accreditation requirements may trigger certain budget expenditures. These expenditures could include apparatus requirements, response times, deployment models, staffing, training levels, equipment, strategic planning issues, and other factors relating to emergency and non-emergency services and support. The fire chief can use re-accreditation to help justify budget proposals from year to year. After committing to accreditation, policy makers are commonly committed to re-accreditation as well. The accreditation process can be a factor in justifying budget expenditures.

- **Community expectations** — Community involvement in the strategic planning process is an integral part of determining the needs of the community.

The systems model can be an effective tool in the preparation of the department's budget. It can provide a visual model of the desired output, throughput, and required input in the form of all resources. Those resources can be translated into monetary values to match the costs associated with the output.

The parent organization's administrator, the department chief, or staffs of both organizations should perform an internal review of the fire and emergency services organizations budget request. At this stage, the budget is critically reviewed to determine if the data available justifies the request. It is also an opportunity to consider alternative approaches to providing the same services or alternative sources of revenue. Potential questions that the governing body may ask should be considered and accurate answers developed. After a thorough internal review, the fire and emergency services organization's budget is incorporated into the combined budget request for the parent organization. This document is then submitted to the jurisdiction's governing body for an external review.

The *external* review is the final review that the budget request document receives. The governing body of the jurisdiction schedules one or more public hearings so that the public can have input into budget decisions. The budget may be sent back to the administrator to address citizen concerns. The governing body then considers revenues and expenditures and may adjust either or both to balance the budget and meet the public's needs. When the public's concerns have been addressed and the budget is balanced, the governing body approves the budget, and it becomes law.

To replace high cost items, such as an entire inventory of SCBAs, the cost can be split over two budgets. Half of the funds would be authorized in the last month of one budget cycle, and the other half authorized in the first month of the next budget cycle. Full funding is provided within a two month period but in two separate budgets. This split can make the large expenditure more manageable for the AHJ.

Implement

Once the budget has been approved, the administrator, department heads, and supervisors have the funds to turn the budget's goals into reality. They must use their administrative and managerial skills to implement the budget. The approved and adopted budget represents a plan for the organization's operation for the fiscal year. Many chief officers take this opportunity to meet with department personnel to review the budget and explain what it means to the department's operation. In large organizations, a written or videotaped budget message from the chief may serve the same purpose. Regardless of how it is accomplished, the importance of communicating this message cannot be overemphasized.

The budget will indicate if new personnel can be hired, staff cuts will be necessary, vacant positions can be filled, or new equipment can be purchased. The budget requests that were approved or disapproved may provide an indication about how the jurisdiction perceives the services that the department provides or they may simply reflect fiscal reality. Any specific praise or criticism that the jurisdiction of the department's operation makes should be included in the budget message. The praise may be gratifying, but criticism may be more valuable. Viewed objectively, criticism can serve as a means to focus future priorities and performance within the organization.

Monitor

The budget process does not end with the implementation of the budget. It must be monitored to determine its effectiveness and prevent a budgetary crisis should the economic environment change. Typically, the individual departments within the jurisdiction are only informed of the expenditures of their allotted budgets. Some jurisdictions print and distribute monthly account statements that indicate the account balance in each program, line item, or category of the budget. The chief officer responsible for budget administration can track purchasing trends and ensure that accounts are not overspent. Computer-based accounting programs allow more frequent checks performed on a weekly or daily basis. Many departments keep such budget-accounting information in electronic form accessible to department managers. This electronic version provides more current information and eliminates the need for much of the printing and distribution that was done in the past.

When a trend appears that indicates that an account lacks sufficient funds to last the remainder of the fiscal year, the chief officer will have to determine the best option to address the problem. The legal options in order of preference include the following:

- Transfer funds from an underutilized account while maintaining a balanced total in the budget.
- Restrict further purchases from the account to an amount that can be evenly spread over the remainder of the year.
- Request a budget adjustment in the form of additional funds (supplemental appropriation) from the jurisdiction.
- Do nothing while continuing to monitor the account until it is empty or the trend ceases.

These options give the organization the ability to manage its budget efficiently. The organization will not be aware of or have any control over changes in revenue collections. It may also take a month or more for the jurisdiction to determine that a trend is developing that will result in a revenue shortfall. The individual departments may be required to take action. The decision to implement any actions must be made based on the department's primary mission. Because these actions are drastic moves and have long-range consequences, they must be made only after a risk analysis. The departments may be required to implement some or all of the following actions:

- Limit all capital purchases.
- Reduce operating services.
- Reduce or eliminate overtime pay options.
- Eliminate positions, cease hiring replacement personnel, lay off members, or make other personnel changes within the limits of the labor/management agreement.
- Close facilities.
- Eliminate preventive maintenance for apparatus, vehicles, and facilities.
- Seek alternative funding.

Evaluate

Evaluating the effectiveness of a budget involves assessing the strengths and weaknesses of programs, policies, personnel, products, and organizations to determine their effectiveness. Applied to the purchase of materials, an evaluation can be as simple as determining that the proper amount and quality of materials are available in a timely manner. When it is applied to programs and performance, the evaluation requires a cost/benefit analysis that compares the total effort necessary to produce desired results. The individual project manager, department chief, or an auditor who the jurisdiction assigns may perform the evaluation. The results of the evaluation can be used to justify program changes, additional funding for programs, or elimination of programs that are deemed cost prohibitive.

Revise

A budget may need to be revised during the budget cycle. Causes may include the following:

- Increase or decrease in revenue
- Increase in operating costs
- Budget underestimated actual costs
- Increase in service requirements
- Change in labor/management agreement
- Unforeseen or catastrophic occurrence

Because budget expenditures must align with actual revenue, the most likely result of a change will be to revise the costs of operations or capital purchases. Local ordinances or policies define the process for budget revisions. The options and actions listed in the section on monitoring can be applied to each of these reasons for revisions. All changes and revisions in the budget should be documented. These records are necessary for improving the accuracy of future budget preparations and provide a history of the current budget.

Purchasing

A budget provides the organization with the funds to purchase materials, equipment, and apparatus necessary to perform its assigned mission. Purchasing may be the responsibility of the department's supply, apparatus, or logistics chief, nonuniformed employee, or member of the jurisdiction's Central Purchasing Department.

The process for selecting and procuring apparatus, equipment, and materials must be objective, logical, methodical, ethical, legal, and repeatable. An *objective* process must be based on fact and not emotion. It must have a *logical*, stepping-stone pattern that allows each decision to be based firmly on the preceding decision. *Methodical* means that it adheres to an existing, well-established pattern that other organizations have used successfully. The process must be *ethical,* meaning that it is fair and unbiased. It must be *legal*, meeting the intent of local and state/provincial purchasing laws. It must also be repeatable so that future chief officers can perform the purchasing process.

The selection and procurement process provided in this chapter is applicable for all types of apparatus, equipment, personal protective equipment, and some expendable materials. The chief officer responsible for purchasing should use the following steps as necessary to ensure that the proper supplies are provided. These steps apply to both capital items and operating equipment and materials, although the purchasing procedures may vary as indicated later in this section. The process steps include the following:

1. Determine the needs of the department.
2. Conduct research on the equipment, manufacturers, and applicable standards/regulations.
3. Evaluate and field test proposed equipment.
4. Review product data.
5. Conduct the purchasing process.
6. Conduct acceptance procedures.
7. Inventory and issue the equipment.
8. Evaluate purchasing process and revise, if necessary.

Needs Assessment

A needs assessment takes place once during the budget preparation process and again before purchasing the approved equipment and materials. Once a list of equipment and materials is developed, it is necessary to research the quality and quantity that is available for purchase and the vendors who can provide them. The organization's needs may be determined in a variety of ways, such as the following:

- **Perform a needs assessment** — Evaluation based on the programs and services that the organization provides to the jurisdiction. Each program manager (suppression, prevention, training) can provide a list of the equipment and materials required to complete the programs during the fiscal year based on past experience and future projections. Equipment compatibility should also be determined.

- **Review standards and regulations that mandate the purchase of specific types of equipment** — Legal mandates that the local, state/provincial, or federal governments create for the operation of a fire and emergency services organization.

- **Review the current purchases** — Indicates the effectiveness of the current equipment and materials in meeting the service requirements of the response area. It also helps to determine if the correct quantities of materials are available in a timely fashion.

- **Perform a hazards analysis of the response area** — Helps to identify any changes in the service area and the need for changes in programs, services, or equipment.

- **Determine the amount of funds available in each budget account** — If an account does not contain sufficient funds to purchase the required quantity of materials, follow the options outlined in the earlier section on monitoring the budget.

Research

The time necessary to conduct research depends on the type of equipment or materials being purchased **(Figure 4.5)**. The chief officer must ensure that a sufficient amount of time is allowed to gather and evaluate the information. Expendable items such as janitorial supplies may require only a review of product literature, while apparatus or personal protective equipment may require from a few months to a year for research. The research process for capital purchases may include the following:

- Survey other jurisdictions.
- Review manufacturers' business histories.
- Request references.
- Review standards and regulations.
- Review industry trends.
- Compare various products.
- Determine equipment compatibility.
- Review purchasing ordinances and laws.
- Develop request for proposal.

Figure 4.5 Trade shows can be research opportunities for a variety of apparatus, tools, and equipment.

Survey Other Jurisdictions

Research can start with surveying the types of apparatus or equipment that other fire and emergency services organizations use. The company officer should also consider legal mandates created by the local, state/provincial, or federal governments for the operation of a fire and emergency services organization. Survey topics should include:

- Types of equipment used
- Problems encountered with the equipment
- Ability of the equipment to meet specifications
- Equipment service or maintenance difficulties
- Manufacturers' after-sales support
- Compatibility and interoperability with existing equipment and adjacent departments

Send the survey to various members of the organization, including the maintenance, training, and emergency response personnel, labor organization representatives, and the person in charge of purchasing. Allow each responder sufficient time to complete the survey. This approach provides a holistic view of the program within other departments rather than the opinion of one individual. A sample survey form used for self-contained breathing apparatus (SCBA) is included in **Appendix D,** SCBA Survey Form. This form can be used or adapted for other equipment.

Review Manufacturers' Business Histories

Review the business histories of the various manufacturers and their vendors. Annual reports, trade journals articles, financial statements, and business reports that companies like Dunn and Bradstreet publish can provide an overview of a company and provide some insight into its ability to supply the desired system or equipment. Consider the share of the market that the manufacturers hold and why they have that share.

Request References

References from other equipment purchasers are also an important source of information. Request a list of the most recent purchasers of equipment similar to the type being considered from the manufacturers. Other organizations within the area can provide these references.

Figure 4.6 Research includes reviewing applicable standards and regulations.

Review Standards and Regulations

Review all applicable standards and regulations to include the equipment's operational requirements and design and testing requirements **(Figure 4.6)**. This review aids the chief officer in developing specifications that meet or exceed the standards/regulations. It also helps the chief officer to better evaluate the products that are submitted for evaluation. NFPA® standards require an independent third party to test and certify some equipment.

Review Industry Trends

Manufacturers continually redesign fire and emergency services equipment to meet changes in the standards/regulations. Changes are also made to improve the equipment based on internal research. A chief officer should review the latest industry trends in equipment design. Trade journals, trade shows, and press releases that the manufacturers' marketing divisions produce can provide opportunities to keep up with current developments. Many online Internet sites have product reviews that may assist in the decision making process.

Compare Various Products

Competition is strong among fire protection equipment manufacturers. There are few fire protection equipment manufacturers and limited customers. Competition in the marketplace can be used to an organization's advantage when negotiating contract terms. The chief officer must compare the various products based on:

- Level of customer service
- Similar characteristics
- Sales and technical support
- Parts availability
- Length of time before equipment may become obsolete or have a major design change
- Available warranties, extended warranties, and warranty support
- Local manufacturer representation
- Location of manufacturer's repair facilities
- Manufacturer's ability to fill orders within a specified time frame

Determine Equipment Compatibility

Information relating to equipment compatibility should also be gathered during the needs assessment. Compatibility includes both physical compatibility and equipment usability. The equipment must meet the department's operational procedures without drastic changes in training and operations. For example, if a department is issuing individual respiratory protection facepieces that can be used with both self-contained breathing apparatus (SCBA) and supplied air respirator (SAR) units, compatibility concerns must be included in the evaluation.

When specifications are developed for new apparatus, height, width, length, and weight considerations must be taken into account. New apparatus may not fit into older fire station apparatus bays **(Figure 4.7)**. Local bridges, overpasses, and station driveways must be capable of supporting the weight of the new equipment. The height of new apparatus height may exceed the existing clearance under bridges and other overhangs.

Figure 4.7 Fire department officers verifying the width of a vehicle stall doorway.

Review Purchasing Ordinances and Laws

Once all of the essential data has been collected, review the jurisdiction's purchasing ordinances and laws. Purchasing requirements are binding on most state/provincial or local jurisdictions. Attempting to circumvent these laws will place the jurisdiction, department, and chief officer in jeopardy of legal action. Involving members of the jurisdiction's legal, finance, or purchasing departments in the process can prevent errors in the development of specifications or bid development.

Develop Request for Proposal, Qualifications, or Information

A **request for information (RFI)** can be used to find information needed to develop specifications. If the jurisdiction permits, a request for proposal (RFP) may be developed before sending bid notices. An RFP defines the organization's needs and allows manufacturers or their authorized vendors to determine if they can meet bid specifications. An RFP must have a specific schedule outlined, including:

- Bid dates
- Delivery dates
- Provisions for supplying equipment for scheduled evaluations
- Training dates for maintenance technicians and training officers

An RFP also allows the jurisdiction to have control over the companies that can bid, based on responses to the RFP and participation in prebid meetings. Companies are eliminated from consideration if they cannot meet delivery deadlines or provide required performance bonds, lack the established financial support to complete the contract, or have a documented history of contract violations. The RFP process reduces the number of bidders to those companies that are capable of meeting the bid specifications.

> **Request for Information (RFI)** — A request made during the project planning phase to assist a buyer in clearly identifying product requirements, specifications, and purchase options. RFIs should clearly indicate that award of a contract will not automatically follow.

A request for qualifications (RFQ) can be developed when the department requires professional services. Architects, cleaning contracts, accountants, and professional development are only a few services that may require an RFQ.

Before writing an RFP, the chief officer should consult both legal counsel and the authority's purchasing laws to determine what kinds of controls can legally be placed on bids or bidders. The selection of bidders must not be subjective or arbitrary. Sample RFP/RFQs are found in **Appendix E**.

NOTE: Fire and emergency services organizations cannot be subjective or arbitrary in the selection of bidders for fire protection equipment, apparatus, or materials: open and fair purchasing laws regulate all government organizations. Chief officers must respect these laws and operate within them.

Product Evaluation

The RFP should contain language requiring a physical evaluation of fire protection equipment and accessories that each manufacturer is planning to submit for bid. This physical evaluation allows the organization to test the proposed equipment in controlled training exercises and in actual daily operations to determine if it meets the department's needs. The physical evaluation, like the prebid meeting, should be a requirement for participation in the official bid process. Companies that do not participate should not be certified to continue the bidding process. Each manufacturer should provide a specified number of units, usually enough to outfit at least one emergency response company.

Before the actual evaluations, the manufacturer must provide training for personnel participating in the testing of the equipment. In the case of respiratory protection equipment, individual facepieces must be supplied for the testing personnel and properly fit tested. The facepieces must be provided in a variety of sizes in order to fit all possible facial configurations. A manufacturer's sales or technical representative should be present during the equipment evaluations to answer questions or provide additional training.

The physical evaluation should include both training evolutions and actual field tests **(Figure 4.8)**. The RFP must specify the amount of time that the units are needed for evaluation, specific dates and times for training evolutions, and language releasing the department from responsibility for any damage or wear to the units.

The evaluation must be based on an objective grading system. The chief officer must establish criteria and assign points based on the equipment's ability to meet the standard/regulation. Grades may be numerical from *best* to *worst,* or terms such as *excellent, good, fair,* or *poor* may be used. Include a comments section on the grade form for any additional information or opinions. A sample form for the evaluation of respiratory protection equipment is included in **Appendix F**, Equipment Evaluation Form. Evaluation criteria may include, but are not limited to, the following factors:

- Ease of donning
- Ease of doffing
- Maneuverability
- Flexibility

Figure 4.8 A chief officer monitoring the evaluation of PPE and SCBAs.

- Effect on vision
- Effect on workload
- Comfort
- Durability
- Ease of operation
- Compatibility with operational procedures

Once the controlled training evaluations are complete, the evaluation units are assigned to active emergency response companies. Depending on their activity levels, this portion of the evaluation may take a month or more. Give personnel equipment evaluation forms to complete after each use. Field evaluations under actual use conditions provide additional data for the chief officer and allow personnel who will use the final product an opportunity to take part in the selection process. Therefore, select personnel to conduct field tests who did not participate in the controlled training evaluations. The chief officer should compile and analyze the information gained from the physical evaluations. All grading forms and comments in the specifications files should be retained in case the final purchase decision is questioned.

Review Product Data

Once field evaluations are complete, the chief officer can consider other facts about the various equipment systems, materials, or apparatus. Some areas of concern and factors to consider are as follows:

- **Features** — List the various features and accessories available with the equipment.
- **Durability** — Answer questions such as the following: How sturdy is the equipment? Are plastic parts easily broken? Will the equipment withstand rough treatment?

- **Life-cycle cost** — Include the initial purchase price (which may have to be estimated based on the list price) and costs of annual maintenance, parts, and support, amortized over the life expectancy of the equipment to determine life-cycle cost.

- **Maintenance requirements** — Determine maintenance requirements. Consider the manufacturer's maintenance schedule, technician certification and training, and whether to use in-house maintenance or a manufacturer approved vendor.

- **Infrastructure** — Answer questions such as the following: What is the existing infrastructure that supports the current equipment? What changes or investments are required to redesign the equipment maintenance facility, modify existing systems, and retrofit apparatus mounting hardware?

Once all the data has been collected and reviewed, the chief officer should select the systems/equipment that best meet the organization's needs. The systems/equipment is evaluated on its ability to meet the specifications. Units that do not meet the criteria should be eliminated from consideration.

The chief officer must be fully aware of purchasing ordinances or laws in the event that specifications are too restrictive and legally prohibited. If specific equipment is determined to meet the organization's needs, thereby precluding an open-bid process, a variance or exemption from the approved purchasing process may be required from the jurisdiction's purchasing and legal departments. A variance might be necessary to standardize a specific type or brand of equipment, such as a particular model of SCBA. Documentation must support the standardization.

Acquisition Process

The AHJ adopts and regulates the purchasing procedure for fire protection equipment. Most equipment, such as SCBA, SAR systems, ventilation fans, and power extrication tools, are considered capital purchases and must have funds specifically allocated for those purposes. Other items, such as air purifying respirator (APR) cartridges, hand tools, equipment accessories, and janitorial supplies, may be purchased from operating funds. Some purchases may require a formal bid process while others may be purchased on a purchase order form. Bids are normally required on items exceeding a predetermined dollar amount. The purchasing process may consist of the following steps:

1. Determine the funds available and the source of the funds.
2. Create bid specifications based on the evaluation process.
3. Evaluate the certified bid proposals.
4. Score the bid proposals.
5. Award purchase contract.

Possible alternatives for purchasing equipment include group/cooperative purchasing arrangements and piggyback bids. Group purchasing arrangements permit small organizations to jointly purchase similar equipment while gaining the benefit of a large quantity purchase price. This arrangement is especially helpful if a department has limited staff or lacks the expertise to draft RFPs. Some small municipal and rural departments use state/provincial specifications and contracts to purchase apparatus and equipment. In piggyback bids, contract language is included to allow other departments to use existing bids for a specified time period. This language reduces the time required for preparing and accepting a bid. This language may be included in the RFP to allow all vendors equal bidding.

Alternative Purchasing Model

An example of an alternative purchasing model consists of various forms of joint purchasing agreements. For example, a group of fire and emergency services organizations within a geographic area may save money on large purchases by belonging to a purchasing organization. Another example is a group of fire and emergency services organizations entering into a contract for annual hose, ground ladder, or fire pump testing. A third example is purchasing equipment through a state/province established contract, thereby foregoing the bid process for capital items.

Funding Sources

The first step in the purchase process is to determine the funding source. Some of the more common sources were mentioned in the budget sections. Another option, based on local purchasing laws, may be available: lease or lease/purchase arrangement. Funding sources include the following:

- **Operating funds** — Designated in an annual budget for purchasing perishable or quickly consumed items. The AHJ usually determines the specific value of a purchased item.

- **Capital funds** — Designated in an annual budget for purchasing capital items, those items that are over a fixed value. These items are requested specifically during budget preparation and purchased through the bid process if approved.

- **Bonds** — Provide specific funds for specific projects or purchases. Voters must approve bonds that a jurisdiction issues and are then purchased by investors. Bonds are set for a fixed amount, a specified time period, and specific items. Bond proposals are used for high cost projects such as constructing facilities, upgrading communications equipment, or replacing the department's entire respiratory protection. Good documentation must support bond proposals, and the proposals must be justified to the population.

- **Grants** — Funds that are provided by either government agencies or nongovernment organizations. Grants provide equipment that an organization may not have the funds to purchase. In the U.S., an organization that responds to hazardous materials incidents on an Interstate highway can apply for a grant from the U.S. Department of Transportation for funds to purchase the appropriate hazardous materials response protective clothing and respiratory protection equipment. Grant funds do not have to be repaid, but the receiving jurisdiction must account for how the funds are spent and should include an accounting and oversight process.

- **Lease** — Another method of obtaining or purchasing capital items, although not truly a funding source. A *lease* may be used when equipment is needed only for a short duration or for extended evaluations. A lease may also be used as a budgeting and planning tool to spread the cost in a flexible manner.

- **Lease/purchase** — A *lease/purchase* arrangement allows the cost to be spread over several years. Purchasing ordinances and laws of the jurisdiction govern this method. In some cases, it may be illegal to encumber funds in a subsequent budget cycle, thereby preventing a lease. The chief officer must research this form of acquisition or purchase before including it in bid specifications. A cost/benefit analysis must be made to compare the direct purchase of equipment with the lease/purchase process cost.

Bid Specifications

Once the funding source is established and committed, the chief officer must develop the actual bid specifications. *Bid specifications* include the organization's specific fire protection equipment requirements and the jurisdiction's legal requirements. Most manufacturers provide sample specifications forms as a guide. The purchasing department prepares the wording of the legal requirements, sometimes referred to as *boilerplate,* which is required in all bid specifications **(Figure 4.9)**. Boilerplates define the legal obligations necessary to meet the specifications, such as vendor attendance at a prebid meeting, warranties, liability or performance bonds, specified delivery times, payment schedules, and financial statements.

> **CAUTION**
> The fire chief should be aware that manufacturer's specifications may be restrictive and violate the AHJ's competitive bidding requirements.

When developing product specific specifications, the chief officer in charge of purchasing or procurement should be aware of the legal requirements sections of the specifications and their effects on potential bidders. The specifications language must be clear and concise. Each detail of the design requirement must be included, and nothing should be assumed. Some of the items that should be included in bid specifications include:

- National Institute for Occupational Safety and Health/Mine Safety and Health Administration (NIOSH/MSHA) (current standard) or American National Standards Institute (ANSI) certification for the intended use, if applicable
- NFPA® compliance, if applicable
- Number of purchases
- Design requirements
- Delivery date
- Warranty

Purchase Order and Contract Specifications
Boilerplate

CONDITIONS AND INSTRUCTIONS

1. This purchase order was issued through the Statewide Procurement Service and is therefore subject to a fee of _____% on the total dollar amount of goods (excluding sales tax). The following exemptions apply:

    (A) Purchases from a term contract that has not yet been implemented on the Statewide Procurement Service;

    (B) Purchases from an agency-specific term contract that has not yet been implemented on the Statewide Procurement Service. Note: Fees will be invoiced monthly based on purchase order activity during the prior month.

2. This order is placed subject to shipment at prices, amounts and transportation rates not in excess of those indicated on the face of this order.

3. Each shipment must be shipped to the SHIP TO address printed on the face of this order and marked to the attention of the individual, if any, indicated in that address. Each shipment must be labeled plainly with our PURCHASE ORDER number, and must show gross, tare and net weight.

4. Complete packing list must accompany each shipment.

5. Drafts will not be honored.

6. Materials received in excess of quantities specified herein may, at our option, be returned at shipper's expense. Substitutions are not permitted.

7. Invoices in quadruplicate must be mailed on the date of shipment to the INVOICE TO address indicated on the face of this purchase order. Invoices must include the INVOICE TO name and address, the PURCHASE ORDER number, terms of payment and routing.

8. On all invoices subject to discount, the discount period will be calculated from the date a correct invoice is received in this office.

9. Each invoice must be accompanied by the following papers:

    A. Original bill of lading when shipment is made by freight or express.

    B. Signed delivery receipt when delivery is made by other means.

    C. Parcel post insurance when shipment is made by parcel post and value is over $1.00.

10. In cases where parties other than you ship materials against this order, shipper must be instructed to show our PURCHASE ORDER number on all packages and shipping manifests to insure prompt identification and payment of invoices.

11. By accepting this electronic purchase order, you agree that these CONDITIONS and INSTRUCTIONS are legally binding.

Figure 4.9 Sample bid specification boilerplate text showing the jurisdiction's legal, financial, and purchasing requirements.

- Accessories
- Training for maintenance technicians
- Training for operational personnel
- Startup parts inventory
- Acceptance testing
- Technical support
- Penalties for nondelivery

If a specific feature that meets valid operational requirements is available only from a single manufacturer, an option for bidding an equal alternative or a method to take exception to the specifications must be included. The purchasing ordinances or laws of the AHJ may prohibit restrictive bids that include too many specifications that only one manufacturer can meet. If a specific brand of equipment is the only type that meets the needs of the organization, then the jurisdiction's finance or purchasing officer may grant a variance or exemption for a sole source bid and declare that specific brand as the jurisdiction's standard.

The jurisdiction's finance or purchasing officer has to approve the specifications. Once approved, the purchasing department issues the bid requests to qualified bidders and sets a date for the opening of the bids. The purchasing department handles and returns the bids.

Evaluate and Score Proposals
Qualified bids are given to an evaluation committee or the chief officer who is responsible for evaluating them. The evaluation committee is generally made up of personnel who will be using the equipment, purchasing department representatives, and equipment maintenance personnel. Evaluation of the qualified bids is based on the original bid specifications. A matrix or spreadsheet can be created with the specific requirements listed down the side and individual bidders listed across the top. Values can be assigned to each requirement and written in the corresponding box, depending on whether the bidder exceeded, met, or failed to meet the specification.

Once the grid is filled, the scores are added. If certain specifications outweigh others, the scoring can be weighted in favor of the more important specification. For example, an integrated personal alert safety system (PASS) device on a respiratory protection unit would receive more points than a carrying case or neck strap. Scoring must be equitable and well documented. This documentation may be subject to the Freedom of Information Act and outside review. The sealed proposals are opened and ranked. The cost and the ability to meet the bid specifications determine where the proposals rank.

Award
After the bids have been reviewed and evaluated, a recommendation made to the department chief. The jurisdiction then awards a purchase contract to the supplier with the winning bid. The jurisdiction's governing body may have to approve purchases exceeding a certain value. The legal department usually writes the contract, binding the supplier to meet the specifications and the jurisdiction to pay for the goods or services. Contract administration

is the responsibility of the purchasing department on behalf of the fire and emergency services organization. The fire and emergency services organization is responsible for accepting, testing, inventorying, storing, maintaining, and placing the equipment, materials, or apparatus into service.

Standardization

Once a specific product is determined to be the most appropriate for the organization, it can be established as the *standard* for the organization, eliminating the need to rewrite specifications the next time identical equipment must be purchased. A renewable contract may be included in the bid specifications. Such a contract may be negotiated for 1 year with three subsequent annual renewals based on a set increase for inflation. Due to rapid changes in the standards/regulations for respiratory protection, protective clothing, and apparatus, the purchasing organization must be prepared to rewrite the specifications based on recent changes. The contract language should also reflect this possibility.

Record-Keeping Function

Record-keeping is just one element of the Management Information System (MIS) or Information Technology (IT) system that most organizations depend on today. Information management includes the acquisition, analysis, organization, distribution, and storage of data and information that provides managers with timely and useful information. The record-keeping function is the storing of information that the information management system generates.

Chief officers should be aware of the types of records maintained by their organization. Knowledge of the methods for developing a record-keeping system along with data collection, data analysis, legal requirements, and system maintenance are essential. Chief officers must be aware of laws that establish access to the records and the length of time records must be retained.

Record Types

The main categories of record keeping in fire and emergency services organizations include the following:

- Budget
- Inventory
- Maintenance
- Activity
- Personnel
- Training

Budget

Budget records include all the information used to create the budget, budget status reports, past budgets, and unfunded budget requests. Purchasing records, contracts, surplus sales, accounting, and other records should also be retained with this information.

Inventory

Inventory and fixed assets records should accurately include all materials, equipment, facilities, land, and apparatus that the department purchased or assigned. These records include quantities, descriptions, purchase and disposal dates, and value.

Maintenance

Maintenance records should be kept on stations and other facilities as well as on vehicles, apparatus, and certain pieces of equipment. Maintenance records are usually kept in two distinct but closely related categories: preventive and corrective maintenance.

Preventive maintenance is performed to reduce wear, avert damage from occurring, and extend the useful life of an item, vehicle, or facility. Past experience, industry standards, and manufacturers' recommendations combine to form schedules for periodic inspection and maintenance. Frequent inspection and cleaning often reveal emerging problems that are relatively easy and inexpensive to correct in their early stages. Left unnoticed and uncorrected, minor problems can develop into major breakdowns and require expensive repairs. Records that are compiled during the preventive maintenance of apparatus, facilities, or pieces of equipment can provide the information necessary to predict a trend or justify a replacement.

Corrective maintenance is always possible due to an unforeseen event. Damage may occur because of an accident, overuse, operator error, or even abuse. Damaged or nonfunctional items must be repaired or replaced as soon as possible. Deciding when or if an item should be replaced is often based on its maintenance record and life expectancy. If records show that the item is relatively new, the item should be repaired. If records show that the item is old and has a history of increasingly frequent failures or breakdowns, the item should be replaced with something newer and more reliable. In either case, the corrective maintenance record is a critical part of the decision-making process.

Activity

Activity records are maintained at the company, district/battalion, and administrative levels of the fire and emergency services organization. Each level of management supplies the next level above with accumulate information. Activity records may include but are not limited to:

- Emergency and nonemergency responses
- Surveys and inspections
- Investigations
- Training
- Communication
- Station logs

These records serve as the basis for planning and to justify budget requests. It is the historical record of all events, incidents, and projects that the department members participated in during a specific time period. The National Fire Incident Reporting System (NFIRS) is an important data collection form. Information on emergency responses is entered into this form and submitted to a national data base and used to compile trends in emergency responses. Locally, the activity reports provide the chief officer with data to determine if department goals are being met and trends are starting to develop.

NOTE: Chief officers can use established benchmarks, fractal time stamps, district response reliability, and other data to provide important data to assess performance.

Personnel

Personnel records are generally confidential aside from daily personnel attendance records and similar documents. Chief officers must keep all personnel records secure and be careful to protect confidentiality. Personnel records may be maintained at the company or district/battalion level, in the administrative office, in the medical or health and safety officer's office, or in the jurisdiction's human resources office. The types of record may include:

- Training
- Performance
- Attendance
- Health data base

Training records are essential components of a successful training program. Not only do accurate records give organizations long-term inventories of their training activities, records may also be necessary in legal proceedings and management reviews. Organizations, such as ISO, International Fire Service Accreditation Congress (IFSAC), National Board on Fire Service Professional Qualifications (Pro Board), and CFAI, may provide personnel certification and departmental accreditation reviews. The type and format of training records may vary widely depending upon the specific needs of the organization. NFPA® 1401, *Recommended Practice for Fire Service Training Reports and Records,* provides examples of training forms and other helpful information on effective management of training records.

The organization maintains a personal job performance evaluation as part of the personnel file for each member. The member's supervisor may also retain a copy for future job performance evaluations. These records are confidential.

Daily personnel attendance records are maintained to provide data for payrolls and benefits. Depending on a member's classification, a formal time card may be required as evidence of actual hours on duty. Other attendance records may be included in the company or unit logbook. Overtime and annual leave and sick leave benefits are based on information included in daily attendance records. Attendance records that support training requirements may also be retained in the training records. These records are evidence that an individual or unit has completed a specified number of hours of training in a specific topic such as respiratory protection or hazardous materials training.

NFPA® 1500 states that fire and emergency services organizations shall maintain a confidential health data base on each member. The Occupational Safety and Health Administration (OSHA) has strict requirements regarding the development and maintenance of medical records as contained in Title 29 *CFR* 1910.20, *Medical Record Keeping.*

Confidentiality is a key issue for the proper management of files and databases. The fire and emergency services organization's physician and the member are the only personnel who have access to an individual's file. The organization's physician only provides the organization with an opinion concerning an individual's ability to perform the required duties and not a detailed description of any malady. Thorough record keeping is also necessary from a legal standpoint because it supports the AHJ's position in cases involving termination, duty status, and denial of employment or membership to candidates. Award of public safety officer benefits may also depend on the availability of the member's records.

Chapter 10, Section 4 of NFPA® 1500 requires that the fire and emergency services organization maintain a confidential health file on each member. Health records need to incorporate details, pertinent information, and results of the following events:

- Any and all medical evaluations and examinations
- Fitness evaluations
- Exposures (real or perceived) to hazardous materials and toxic chemicals
- Exposures (real or perceived) to blood, body fluids, or other potentially infectious materials
- Inhalations of airborne pathogens
- Excessive exposure to noise
- Occupational injuries or illnesses

Record Development

The record-keeping system is part of the MIS, and its development should be part of the overall system. Trained professionals usually develop the MIS. Some departments may develop, operate, and manage a record-keeping system without having a MIS. Such a record-keeping system may be developed under contract with a MIS professional or internally using the project management approach. The procedures for developing a record-keeping system include defining the system requirements, planning the system, implementing the system, and completing the development project.

Define Requirements

When using the project management approach, the project manager and team members follow seven steps to determine the record-keeping requirements of the organization:

1. **Research** — Determine the legal requirements for a record-keeping system, determine the type of records that must be maintained, locate the resources (storage systems, storage models, software) for maintaining the records, and determine the financial requirements and resources.

2. **Define** — Write a preliminary definition of the project. For example: *The purpose of this project is to develop an integrated departmental record-keeping.*

3. **Establish** — Determine project objectives or outputs. These may include types of records, interrelationship of records, and access, security, and final disposal of records.

4. **Outcomes** — List in priority order the required (essential) outcomes and the desired (nonessential) outcomes. The outcome may be a system that provides accurate information upon request.
5. **Alternatives** — Generate alternate solutions through brainstorming.
6. **Evaluation** — Evaluate the various alternative solutions based on the project definition, objectives/output, and outcomes.
7. **Selection** — Select the best possible solution based on the requirements of a record-keeping system. Also determine a contingency solution.

Plan

During the planning phase, the team lists in detail what will be required for the development of the record-keeping system. Computer-based Gantt and Program Evaluation and Review Technique (PERT) charts can be used in the planning process and for monitoring the implementation phase of the project. Planning includes the following elements:

- Establish the final project objectives.
- Establish the strategy required to meet those objectives.
- Divide the project into logical subunits or steps.
- Establish performance standards or criteria for each subunit or step.
- Develop a timeline for each subunit or step.
- Create a project schedule based on the timelines of the subunits.
- Determine the cost of each subunit and the entire project.
- Determine the resources necessary for the project.
- Assign positions, duties, responsibilities, access, and authority to personnel.
- Determine the required training for implementing the project.
- Write the necessary specifications for the project.
- Determine and create the necessary policies and procedures to support the project.
- Establish a monitoring and revising process for the project.

Testing and Implementation

Prior to implementation, the system must be thoroughly tested to ensure functionality. Once resources are available, the record-keeping system can be officially implemented. Data conversion, or the entering of existing hard-copy files into computer-based files, may be required. Some hard-copy files may need to be stored in an archive or repository for records that may have historical value but are not required for daily decision making or report writing. These older files should be organized by topic, such as training, personnel, or incident, before being archived.

If a noncomputer-based, manual system is developed, current records should be sorted by topic and filed accordingly. Copies should be made of all records and kept at remote sites in the event an incident destroys the original records. The jurisdiction may have a central file storage that is available for the organization's use. Computer-based systems should have their data storage periodically backed up as a precaution.

The record-keeping system requires training for all personnel involved in the collection of data. They need to know how to fill out forms, what information to keep or discard, how to categorize the various documents, and how to cross reference the information. Computer training is also necessary to ensure that records are entered into the database correctly.

Complete

When the record-keeping system is in operation, the project management team should review the development process and make necessary recommendations to the department chief. Further, the team should establish the model for evaluating the system based on goals, process, or outcome.

Evaluation

The personnel assigned to manage the record-keeping function should periodically evaluate the system's effectiveness. During the first year of operation, evaluate the system frequently. Spot check random types of records for accuracy. If the information is integrated, then a sample file should be compared to determine if the information is identical in each of the subfiles. Annual checks of the system can be made to ensure effectiveness of the system. Revisions can be recommended based on the outcome of the evaluations.

Revision

A revision may be required if there is evidence of inaccuracies in the data-collection process, a change in data requirements, or the lack of adequate information to base decisions. If revisions are indicated, develop and implement them as soon as possible. If inaccurate data is entering the system, then training in the recognition and collection of the data may be required. For instance, if company officers are incorrectly estimating the fire loss in a structure based on square feet (or square meter) times a set value, then training may improve this skill. Accuracy of initial reports can be ensured through multiple reviews of the data as it is entered into the system. There may also be a change in the type of information that is required, such as victim demographics, which can be corrected through a change in the collection form and training in the use of the new form. Forms may need to be altered to gather additional information that aids in decision-making. In all cases, review legal requirements when the record-keeping system is developed and revised.

> **CAUTION**
> Changes in data collection requirements and maintenance process should be well thought through before implementation because they can make future comparative analysis of data difficult.

Legal Requirements

State/provincial and federal governments generally have specific laws that direct record maintenance and, in some cases, the type of information that is gathered and stored in these records. The requirements for record-keeping include the types of records, the length of retention, privacy, and who can access to some records.

Record Types

Information may have to be maintained on projects and programs that are created with funds provided through government and nongovernment grants. Various levels of government, agencies, and jurisdictions may require examples of different types of records to include:

- *Hiring records* — Applications, test results, medical evaluations, acceptance/rejection criteria
- *Promotional examinations* — Test materials, test results
- *Medical examinations/evaluations* — Personnel medical records collected throughout an individual's time with the organization
- *Exposure reports* — Actual or perceived exposures to chemical or biological hazards
- *Injury reports* — Report forms relating to all emergency and nonemergency related injuries
- *Training records* — Individual and unit training, especially training involving respiratory protection or hazardous materials certification
- *Incident reports* — All emergency-response reports; also required to be submitted to the federal government as part of the NFIRS in states/provinces that participate in the program

Retention

State/provincial laws and municipal ordinances generally dictate the length of time certain types of records must be retained and how they must be destroyed at the end of that time period. Chief officers need to know and follow the record retention and destruction schedules that apply to their organizations.

Privacy

Records that must be confidential include personnel files, administrative investigations, individual training records, and medical files; access to these files must be limited. Training records may also be considered part of an individual's personnel file that requires an organization to limit access to training records. Organizations should develop and adopt written policies that limit access to training records only to those personnel with a legal need to know.

Other personal information that is regulated to ensure privacy includes Social Security Numbers and test scores. Many organizations no longer use a member's Social Security Number for records identification, and some states prohibit its use. The practice of using other identification methods reduces the opportunity for improper use or the potential for identity theft. Laws protect the release of individuals' evaluation/testing scores. In the U.S., the Family Educational Rights and Privacy Act prohibits the release of this type of information. The Canadian province of Ontario has the Municipal Freedom of Information and Protection of Privacy Act (MFIPPA), which places the responsibility on training officers to know their duties and responsibilities under the applicable legislation within their jurisdictions. Scores and personal data are considered privileged information and are available only to management and a few other designated personnel with authorization and a specific need to know.

Public Access

While individual personnel records are confidential, other department records are not. Generally, open meeting laws and open records acts define the type of records that are available to the public and media. A jurisdiction's open meeting law will cause the official minutes and any other notes that are made as part of the meeting to be part of the public record. Care should always be taken in recording any information that might become public.

Records such as incident reports or fire investigations are available to individuals who own the involved property or are involved in the incident, unless a statute specifically indicates to the contrary. The state/province defines the exact definition and list of records that are available to the public.

Public records include virtually all records of agencies and jurisdictions within the state/province. Those records include **(Figure 4.10)**:

- Documents
- Maps
- Photographs
- Video recordings
- Handwritten notes
- Letters
- Computer data (including e-mails)
- All other records created or held by a government organization

NOTE: The Health Insurance Portability and Accountability Act (HIPAA) established the requirement for confidentiality and presents restricted access issues for records of responses to emergency medical incidents.

CAUTION
HIPAA not only covers documents relating to medical incidents. It also prohibits comments made by responders concerning patients.

Figure 4.10 A chief officer gathering a series of public records for a presentation.

Exemptions to the open records acts exist in many states, but they are limited and have been interpreted narrowly by the courts. The laws presume that all records are open and place the burden on the jurisdiction to demonstrate that any requested materials are exempt. If a public record contains both exempt and nonexempt material, the exempt portion must be removed and the remaining nonexempt material disclosed. All chief officers who are involved with the creation, storage, and distribution of records should be aware of the open records laws enforced in their jurisdiction. Federal employees must be aware of the application of the Freedom of Information Act on U.S. government agencies. Examples of exemptions are as follows:

- Medical and veterinary records and other materials involving matters of personal privacy
- Records relating to pending investigations
- Records that the federal government requires to be kept confidential such as training, promotional, and educational records
- Trade secrets and certain information of a proprietary nature
- Research data, records, or information that has not been published, patented, or otherwise publicly disseminated
- Confidential evaluations submitted to a public agency in connection with the hiring of a public employee
- Records with privacy issues that outweigh public interest need not be released, according to various court rulings

Data Analysis and Interpretation

Data are the raw materials from which information is derived. When the interpretation of data is viewed from the systems approach, data are the input portions. The system is the method that acts on or interprets data. The output is the information that results from the correction, updating, or analysis of data. The output is required for making decisions **(Figure 4.11)**.

Raw data comes from information collected on forms, in reports, on time sheets, and other sources. For instance, data contained in the average incident report includes the time of the incident, type of incident, and amount of loss. The analysis, which a computer program or manual analysis can perform, looks at the relationship between the key elements of the data and between similar information that is gathered from other incident reports. The final analysis, depending on the type of information that is desired, may include a chart that relates the types of incidents to the time of day, the loss based on the types of incidents, or the loss based on the estimated response time. The resulting information then justifies a change in operational strategy, relocation of an existing station, or change in the building code to require passive fire suppression systems in existing structures similar to those identified in the raw data.

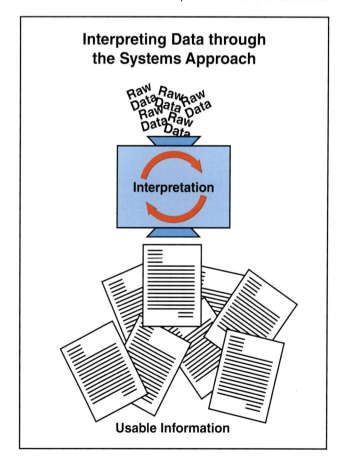

Figure 4.11 Raw data should be analyzed using a system approach that interprets the data and provides usable information.

Organizational Improvement

To provide quality services to the community, a fire and emergency services organization must continually analyze its structure, policies, procedures, and services. The results are then compared to continuing changes in the community's needs. Three analysis models can be used in this process of self review: needs analysis, gap analysis, and SWOT analysis.

Needs Analysis

A needs analysis focuses on the needs and expectations of the community. Once the needs and expectations are defined, the organization's ability to meet those needs is compared to them. These processes can occur simultaneously or in sequence.

Community Needs

To determine the community's needs, a project team under the leadership of a chief officer is formed. The team consists of community political leaders, representatives of citizen groups based on age, local, gender, and ethnicity, and stakeholders such as insurance companies and business leaders. The team uses historical data about fires, natural disasters, transportation accidents, and growth patterns to develop a list of actual and potential hazards to which the fire and emergency services organization would respond. Any expectations that the various groups have should be added to the list. For instance, ethnic groups who do not speak English as a first language or people who have vision or hearing impairments may be concerned about methods for requesting assistance. The list of needs should be prioritized based on accepted criteria that the team develops.

Meeting some of the needs or expectations may be impossible. For instance, the community may have an expectation of two-minute response times in all parts of the response area. The cost of placing fully staffed units in fire stations to provide this level of service may be too high for the community to financially fund. Likewise, the perceived threat of a terrorist attack may not justify the establishment of a Weapons of Mass Destruction (WMD) response team. Alternative solutions may need to be made such as contracting some services to other agencies or neighboring jurisdictions.

Department Capabilities

With the community needs and expectations developed, the department must analyze its capabilities. An internal project team can follow the same process as the community needs team, collecting historical data, reviewing response times and current and projected station locations, as well as analyzing the levels of training and certification provided to the department members.

The final step is to compare the department's capabilities to the community's needs to determine where the capabilities are lacking. Plans are then developed to improve or increase the organization's ability to meet those needs.

Gap Analysis

A gap analysis is used to compare the department's actual performance level to its potential performance level at both the strategic and operational levels. It identifies the areas that need to be improved such as record keeping, response times, policies and procedures, training, and resource allocation, among others.

The gap analysis process consists of the following steps:

1. Identify the existing process
2. Identify the existing outcome
3. Identify the desired outcome
4. Identify the change needed to achieve the desired outcome
5. Identify and document the gap between the current and desired outcomes
6. Develop the process or method to fill the gap
7. Define the resources needed to fill the gap

The project team should consist of representatives of all parts of the department, including the labor union, each division and shift, as well as members of the community who will be affected by the changes to the department. The analysis should have an established timeline with objectives and goals to ensure that the project is completed in a timely manner. The analysis process should become an ongoing activity performed on a set time table such as annually. Any changes should be monitored to determine if they have been effective.

SWOT Analysis

A SWOT analysis evaluates the Strengths, Weaknesses, Opportunities, and Threats that will affect the department's ability to accomplish its mission. The project management team determines the internal characteristics or strengths that give the organization an advantage in achieving its goals. The team then lists the organization's internal weaknesses or limitations that may be barriers to success. The external opportunities that will help the organization improve its service delivery are compiled next. Finally, a list of external threats that may cause the organization difficulties with meeting the mission statement as developed. **Figure 4.12** illustrates a sample SWOT matrix containing some of the following information.

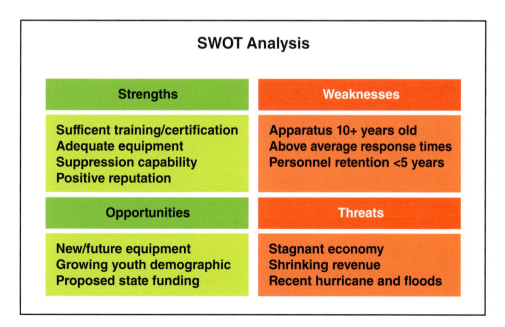

Figure 4.12 An example of a SWOT analysis matrix.

List the internal strengths and weaknesses, such as:

- **Human resources** — Levels of training or certification by division or program
- **Physical resources** — Apparatus, facilities, equipment, locations
- **Financial resources** — Revenue sources, including permanent and one-time event
- **Programs and processes** — Prevention, suppression, investigation, training
- **Past experiences** — Reputation in the community, major incidents, outreach activities

Weaknesses may include apparatus that are over 10 years old, response times that exceed the national average, or the inability to retain personnel longer than 5 years. Incidents that have detracted from the department's reputation and goodwill with the community should also be included on the list.

Next list the external opportunities and threats to the department:

- **Future trends** — Expanding area of coverage, technological changes in the fire service
- **The economy** — National, state/provincial, local
- **Financial sources** — Shrinking revenue sources
- **Demographics** — Changes in age, race, gender, and ethnicity within response area
- **Legislation** — National, state/provincial, and local that may affect the fire and emergency services organization operations
- **Recent or potential events** — Natural disasters, changes in the environment

External opportunities and threats may be difficult to recognize or predict. Including citizens and stakeholders on the planning team will provide additional ideas in these areas.

The completed SWOT analysis is then used to create the strategic plan. The department adopts and implements the completed plan. Because strategic plans extend well into the future, annual revisions and updates will be required.

Planning

Operational planning based on needs, gap, or SWOT analysis will require certain factors to be considered. These factors include:

- Benchmarks
- Code requirements
- Staffing
- Response times
- Local, state/provincial, and federal regulations

Benchmarks

Benchmarking is comparing performance to an accepted level of performance. The accepted benchmark could be a group of municipalities or service areas of similar geographic size, climate, population base, or other matching characteristics. The benchmark fire and emergency services organization should also be similar in size, structure, and type of services provided.

Code Requirements

Changes in locally adopted codes or state/provincial and nationally mandated codes necessitate changes to fire and emergency services organization policies and procedures. Consensus codes, such as those developed by NFPA®, are considered to represent *best practices*. These codes may be used in legal actions against the fire and emergency services organization or AHJ if the department is involved in an accident. Even states that have not adopted the OSHA health and safety regulations can be held liable due to the wording of the General Service Clause.

Staffing

Establishing the correct staffing level requires analyzing the types of tasks that are normally performed at various types of incidents, the number of personnel required to perform those tasks, an understanding of national staffing standards, and an understanding of the laws and ordinances that recommend minimum staffing. Ultimately, the AHJ establishes the minimum level of staffing.

NFPA® standards that provide information on staffing levels include:

- NFPA® 1710, *Standard for the Organization and Deployment of Fire Suppression Operations, Emergency Medical Operations, and Special Operations to the Public by Career Fire Departments*

- NFPA® 1720, *Standard for the Organization and Deployment of Fire Suppression Operations, Emergency Medical Operations and Special Operations to the Public by Volunteer Fire Departments*

- NFPA® 1500, *Standard on Fire Service Occupational Safety and Health Program*

- NFPA® 1410, *Standard on Training for Initial Emergency Scene Operations*

The Commission on Fire Accreditation International (CFAI) also provides systems approach to determining appropriate staffing levels for a response area. The resulting *Standard of Cover* is based on eight elements:

1. **Existing deployment** — Current station location, unit staffing, response times

2. **Community outcome expectations** — The level of coverage expected of the fire and emergency services organization

3. **Community risk assessment** — List of community assets that are at risk

4. **Distribution study** — Location of first arriving resources

5. **Concentration study** — Composition of first-alarm assignment

6. **Historical reliability** — Past history of multiple call frequency

7. **Historical response effectiveness studies** — Percentage of responses that meet current response criteria

8. **Overall evaluation** — Proposed standard of cover that is risk type listed

The analysis should result in a standard of coverage that provides an efficient use of resources. It is also a core competency of the CFAI fire and emergency services organization accreditation model.

Response Times
Response times are another statistic that can be used for operational planning and comparison. Response times are used to determine the need for new fire stations, staffing levels, and the activation of new units. Nationally recognized response time standards are available for planning purposes. At the same time, the local fire and emergency services organization's historic response times as well as those of benchmark cities can also be used in the planning process.

Local, State/Provincial, and Federal Regulations
Political governing and legislative bodies create laws, ordinances, and statutes that can affect fire and emergency services organization operations. These regulations must be constantly monitored to ensure that the fire and emergency services organization can still provide the mandated level of service or meet the legal requirements. Response times, staffing levels, safety and health are topics that these regulations may cover.

IV Strategic Planning

The department chief is responsible for determining the department's mission based on the community's needs and the goals that the jurisdiction's leaders developed. To fulfill the mission, the chief must develop and implement strategic and operational plans, establish training programs, and perform community risk assessments. The department chief does not perform all of these duties alone. Senior chief officers and staff members work closely with the chief, using accepted planning models, reviewing governmental mandates, and gathering data to support the planning process.

Fire and emergency services organizations must develop and follow a strategic plan. The department chief, assisted by a project management team consisting of community and department members, uses planning and organizing skills and the project-management process to create and implement this plan. The following section focuses on the strategic planning process and its key elements. Developing, implementing, monitoring, evaluating, reporting, and revising the plan will also be discussed.

Planning Process
Strategic planning involves defining the organization's mission and establishing objectives and action plans to develop the strategies necessary to operate successfully in the particular environment. The fire service profession is an environment that is rapidly changing in the form and severity of personal hazards. Additionally, political and economic trends continually affect the fire and emergency services professions. In recent years, the fire service has been challenged with providing additional services without increases in resources.

Developing a strategic plan from a SWOT analysis will develop objectives and strategies to reinforce the strengths, capitalize on the opportunities, and address, correct, or prevent the weaknesses and threats from affecting the department. Strategic planning differs from other types of organizational planning because of the following characteristics:

- Top management makes decisions
- It requires the total resources available to the organization

- It has a significant long-term effect on the organization
- It focuses on the interaction between the organization and the external environment

A strategic plan must have broad-based commitment and support to be effective. This support includes the department chief, the governing board, the senior staff, and the jurisdiction's political leadership. The internal customers (members), external customers (citizens), and stakeholders (labor organization) must also be involved and committed to the plan's success. For instance, the strategic plan is dependent on the resources available. If the citizens of the service area do not support the plan, they may vote to change the tax base that the department depends on to operate. Therefore, the strategic planning process is used to develop budget objectives and is essential to the budget process.

Strategic planning is part of a *strategic management* concept that includes the planning, implementing, and control functions. Without implementation and control, the plan will become a wasted effort that languishes on the shelf in the chief's office.

Development

The strategic plan is developed using a project management approach. The project manager is a senior member of the organization, usually the department chief, and the team is made up of division, branch, and section managers as well as line and staff personnel, citizens, and stakeholders. The development process involves:

- **Defining the organization's mission and vision** — This specific statement expresses the fundamental and unique purpose of the organization and identifies the customers of the organization. The vision is the department's statement to the public while the mission is the department's statement to its membership.

- **Defining the department's organizational values** — These are the foundation upon which the department was founded and state why the department was established, what it does, and how it is unique.

- **Establishing goals and objectives** — These are the end results of the activities of the organization determined in the SWOT analysis. They support the mission statement.

- **Identifying strategic alternatives** — Numerous strategies should be developed. These are rank ordered based on the established criteria and the best option is selected. Contingency plans should also be developed.

- **Formulating a strategy** — The best option is developed into a written action plan that includes resources, monitoring criteria, evaluation procedures, policies, and steps for making revisions.

Before implementing the strategic plan, the potential for conflicting goals between different units should be identified. Every aspect of the strategic plan must be compatible and/or complimentary. The goals of one division/program cannot be allowed to undermine those of another division/program.

Implementation

Once the strategic plan is adopted, it must be implemented. This task will be the responsibility of the middle and lower level chief officers, company officers, and members of the organization **(Figure 4.13)**. It can be helpful to identify a specific person to champion each of the goals.

Implementation includes the development of the operational plans to ensure the strategic plan's success. Operational plans may be long or short term and include the creation and implementation of specific projects and programs. For instance, if one of the objectives is "protecting of life and property from fire," then operational plans should include the creation of a fire suppression division. That plan should also contain the process for specifying and purchasing the necessary firefighting apparatus, a maintenance program, and a replacement program, to name a few. Visually, the result is a pyramid with the strategic plan at the top and the increasingly detailed operational plans at the base.

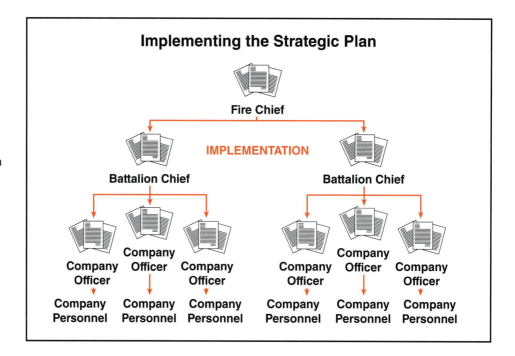

Figure 4.13 The implementation of a strategic plan from the top down.

Monitoring

The *monitoring* function, sometimes referred to as *controlling*, of strategic management involves establishing measurements against which to judge the plan's effectiveness. The measurements, based on the desired outcome of the strategic plan, are the same as those described in the following section on evaluation. The department's performance and the success of the strategic plan are one and the same. Therefore, the process will be the same.

Evaluation

The organization should evaluate the strategic plan to determine its effectiveness by comparing the actual results with the standard or criteria established to monitor success. Using one of three generally accepted performance evaluation processes (goals-based, performance-based, or outcome-based), the chief officer can determine the success of the plan:

- **Goals-based evaluations** — Determine how well a program is meeting the original goals or objectives that were established for it.
- **Performance-based evaluations** — Determine how a program actually works and highlight its strengths and weaknesses; particularly useful for long standing programs or if a program is determined to be inefficient and complaints are being generated about it.
- **Outcome-based evaluations** — Identify the benefits to the community or consumer of the service. The term *outcome* refers to the actual benefits that the community enjoys such as reduced fire loss or improved quality of life. The primary source of response data is NFIRS, which contains information collected for comparison purposes.

Annual Reports

The *annual report* is the usual method for reporting the status of the strategic plan. Annual reports are usually a legal requirement and include the previous year's activities and accomplishments. The report may begin with the mission statement and an outline of the strategic plan. Long- and short-term plans that were developed, implemented, or completed during the year may also be included with a financial audit. If laid out in a logical fashion, the report will progress from the general to the specific; that is the strategic plan to the actual results. Positive and negative results should be included along with recommendations for resolving the negative situations. Projections of the future requirements to meet the strategic plan should also be included. It can also be helpful if updates on specific elements of the strategic plan are included in agendas for department staff meetings and even labor/management meetings throughout the year.

Revisions

Strategic plans may be revised under two conditions. First, the plan should be reviewed and revised annually to maintain a consistent life cycle. If the plan is intended to encompass 10 years, then each year it is extended one more year. Second, the plan should be revised when there is a critical change in the operating environment. The increased threat of terrorist attacks has been the most obvious recent change that has influenced fire and emergency services organizations strategic plans. This threat has increased the responsibilities for responding to large-scale incidents that may include chemical, biological, radiological, and nuclear attacks.

The revision process follows the same steps as the original creation of the strategic plan. It will also require that operational plans are altered or new ones created to support the changes.

Operational Planning

The operation plans developed to support the goals and objectives of the strategic plan fall into three broad categories based on the time frame for the plan: *short-term, intermediate-term,* and *long-term* **(Figure 4.14, p. 184)**. Operational planning and budget development are linked and may be performed at the same time. The corresponding budgets, as mentioned earlier, are the *operational budget* for short-term planning and the *capital budget* for intermediate- and long-term planning.

Figure 4.14 Meeting a strategic plan requires the development of short-, intermediate-, and long-term goals and objectives.

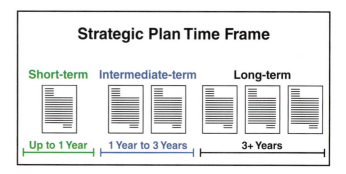

Short-Term

Like the operational budget, the short-term plan is usually a year in length. It focuses on all the projects, programs, and activities that will occur within the budget or calendar year. The plan may include the evaluation, procurement, training, and implementation of a new type of ventilation equipment or procedure. It may also include a plan to provide all annually mandated training such as respiratory protection or hazardous materials training.

The division, branch, or section responsible for a specific function usually develops the short-term plans. They may also be the result of a project management process involving representatives from all the units that will be involved with the implementation of the plan.

Intermediate-Term

Intermediate-term plans cover periods of one to three years and are more specific than the long-range and strategic plans. This flexibility is necessary to meet the potential challenges that occur with budget shortfalls, changes in personnel, changes in service level demands, and external political pressures. For example, the plan to replace a specific number of aging apparatus may have to be altered with the loss of supporting revenues. Examples of intermediate-term plans include:

- Preventive maintenance **(Figure 4.15)**
- Reorganization
- Resource allocation
- Equipment replacement

Figure 4.15 Fire apparatus undergoing preventive maintenance.

Preventive Maintenance

Apparatus preventive maintenance plans are usually based on the manufacturer's recommended service schedule, trucking industry standards, or local maintenance histories. The plan should include a fixed schedule for oil and fluid changes, brake and tire inspections, electrical systems inspections, and other operating systems inspections. The schedule should include the ability to alter the plan based on alternative milestones such as mileage, engine hours, or calendar dates. Maintenance costs should also be included and recommended replacement review dates set. Computer programs are available to assist in developing and monitoring the apparatus preventive maintenance plan. Maintenance records should be retained for the life of the apparatus.

Reorganization

Changes in the operating environment may mandate changes in the organization's structure. Changes of this type require time to plan and implement, and they fall into the intermediate-term planning cycle. If major changes are indicated, the plan may have to be implemented in phases, such as shifting hazardous materials response responsibilities from all fire companies to a single unit or branch.

Resource Allocation

The allocation of resources may change based on the operating environment, governmental requirements, or changes in operating standards. Standing plans can be developed for incidents that require more than one response assignment or contingency plans can be developed for shifts in the location of target hazards. Government mandates for increased inspections of public facilities may require a shift in personnel from other functions or duties. Adoption of NFPA® standards, such as 1500, 1710, and 1720, may require the reassignment of personnel to meet minimum staffing level. Each potential change should have a plan prepared to ensure that the change has the desired results.

Equipment Replacement

All equipment eventually needs to be replaced. Physical deterioration, contamination, mechanical damage, and aging technology cause equipment and apparatus to be replaced. Cleaning, inspection, maintenance, and replacement schedules can be developed based on criteria similar to that used for apparatus: manufacturer's recommendations, industry standards, age, condition, and local history.

Replacement plans should include the ability to replace small portions of the equipment over a set period to spread the cost out over time. For instance, if the organization's personal protective clothing is to be replaced, a 10-year replacement cycle (based on the manufacturer's recommendations) would result in 10 percent of the clothing being replaced per year. Spreading the plan out also permits periodic reviews of technology changes, making the plan more flexible.

Long-Term

A long-term plan may have a set duration, usually greater than three years, or be an open-ended, ongoing plan similar to the life cycle of the strategic plan. A long-range plan outlines the accomplishment of a goal or set of goals over a number of years into the future, usually in a specific area, such as fire station relocation, apparatus replacement, real estate purchases for future facilities, and additions to the service area. It assumes that current knowledge about future conditions is sufficiently reliable to make such long-range decisions.

Codes and Standards

Long-term planning requires a thorough knowledge of the applicable codes and standards adopted by the local jurisdiction. The chief must know NFPA® 1500, 1710, and 1720 and the Codes of Federal Regulations as they apply to response times and minimum staffing levels. Other standards that effect planning include apparatus and equipment designs, training, technical rescue, and hazardous materials.

Codes and standards can be used as references in developing and justifying budgets, writing specifications, and creating local standard operating procedures (SOPs). A good policy is to annotate long-term plans with the appropriate code or standard that justifies it.

Capital Improvements

Capital improvements generally include the construction and renovation of facilities. Because they are paid for with capital funds, they must be specified in advance, including an estimated cost. A capital improvement plan (CIP) should be developed annually, prioritized, and submitted to support the capital budget. Capital items may include but are not limited to the purchase of:

- Apparatus and equipment
- Construction of new facilities
- Major facility renovations
- Installation of a mandated apparatus exhaust capture system in apparatus bays

Developing a CIP requires projecting needs well into the future. The replacement of some items, such as roofs, can be predicted based on industry standards while other requests can be based on maintenance records that show a trend in cost increases.

Real Estate

Decisions on the locations and construction of fire stations and other facilities should be considered a long-term infrastructure investment and commitment. Stations may have a life expectancy of 50 years or more. Stations tend to remain in the same location even though the neighborhood may change, the population shift, or the target hazards close or relocate.

A project management team should be established to create the station location plan. This team determines the optimum location for all facilities based on:

- Population density
- Target hazard
- Response times
- Access
- Land use
- Land cost
- Other criteria

NOTE: Computer models can assist in determining the proper location for facilities.

The plan should focus on changes that could result in the need to acquire new property, close existing facilities, recommend road access changes, and deal with changes in resource allocation, such as staffing urban stations during workdays and suburban stations at night and on the weekends.

Once the plan is completed and approved, the land can be acquired for construction of the station. Advance planning can allow the land to be purchased economically, before area development increases property values. After the land is acquired, a sign may be displayed on the property identifying it as a future site of a fire station. This identification can help prevent neighborhood issues in the future opposing the use of the site for a fire station or other department facility.

Land must also be acquired for administrative, training, supply, and maintenance facilities. Existing facilities may become outdated as the size of the department increases. Locating training and maintenance facilities near major highways or near the geographic center of the department's coverage provides easier access to them. Consolidation of functions is another consideration that should be made in location planning.

Apparatus Replacement

Because apparatus are expensive, replacement plans must be made well into the future. Although there is no industry standard for apparatus replacement, the preventive maintenance schedule, local history, mileage, engine hours, and vehicle condition can be used to establish a schedule **(Figure 4.16)**. Some departments replace apparatus every five years while others operate vehicles that are 20 to 30 years old. Technological changes, safety requirements, increasing operational costs, and increases in the amount of equipment carried on the vehicle can be used to justify a shorter operational life for emergency response apparatus.

The replacement plan can be linked to the capital budget, capital improvement budget, or other funding source. It is also possible to use a lease or lease purchase agreement with manufacturers if capital funds are not available. Leasing is subject to local or state/provincial purchasing laws that may prevent encumbering funds beyond the current fiscal year.

Figure 4.16 A new mini-pumper being brought into service to replace an older apparatus.

Staffing Needs

Volunteer, combination, and career departments face the challenge of maintaining a minimum staffing level to provide the required service level. Planning to meet this level means:

- Establishing the number of people required to perform various tasks
- Allowing personnel to fill vacant positions (annual leave, holidays, illness, and injuries)
- Projecting the number of retirements and promotions in the future
- Allowing for the time to recruit, hire, and train new personnel

Retention is another challenge for all types of departments. The costs of recruiting, hiring, and training personnel must be spread over the length of their service time. Ensuring that personnel will stay 20 years or more is essential to keeping these costs down and maintaining the required minimum staffing level.

Training Requirements

Training ensures that operations are conducted in a safe, effective, consistent, and efficient manner. The terms *education* and *training* are often used interchangeably in the fire service. They are, however, different in their meanings. *Education* generally means the acquisition of knowledge, usually through academic means such as university or college courses. The fire and emergency services organizations provide *training* that primarily consists of vocational or technical skills.

The training function is generally the responsibility of a chief officer, although a Level II officer may be assigned the duty. The training function officer, especially in a new organization, must be able to:

- Evaluate the organization's training requirements
- Develop a training program
- Determine funding sources
- Determine alternative training sources
- Evaluate the training program

Evaluation of Requirements

Six criteria generally determine training requirements:

- Legal mandates
- Building and fire codes
- Training standards
- Community needs
- Hazards assessment
- Risk analysis

The chief officer must collect the necessary data to evaluate each requirement during the planning stage of the training program development process. Anytime an organization's performance at an incident comes under public or legal scrutiny, the training levels of the members involved in the incident will probably come under some degree of review.

Legal Mandates

Legal requirements for fire and emergency services organization training exist at federal, state/provincial, and local levels. Requirements include the type of training, length of training, minimum medical standards, certification testing, and recertification requirements. Each legal requirement must be thoroughly researched to determine how the organization may best meet it.

- **Federal** — Requirements from the national government include training for hazardous materials responses, respiratory protection training, maritime training, and airport/aircraft incident training as well as incident management training.
- **State/provincial** — State requirements usually include basic firefighter training, apparatus driver/operator training, inspector/investigator training, instructor training, and fire officer training.
- **Local** — Locally required training may be based on the adoption of NFPA® standards or building and fire code requirements.

Building and Fire Codes

Locally adopted building and fire codes regulate the construction, renovation, use, and safety features of the structures within the response area. Training programs in the interpretation and application of these codes should be developed and presented. Firefighters, instructors, and fire and life safety inspectors are the intended audiences for these programs.

Training Standards

Training requirements are also determined by the locally adopted NFPA® 1400 series standards, the NFPA® 1000 professional qualifications standards, and NFPA® 1500. These standards establish the minimum level of training that fire service personnel must have to safely perform their duties. The 1400 series defines the methods used to provide the training. Although not mandated, training programs should meet the guidelines for adult and vocational training.

Community Needs

The service area's needs may also dictate the types of training that the fire and emergency services organization requires. Community involvement in the strategic planning process and the development of the organization's mission statement provides an indication of the required training for the organization. The local service area also indicates the level of service and training the population is willing to financially support. If the cost of the service and level of funding do not match, then an alternative revenue source or service level must be determined. In no case should safety be compromised due to the lack of financial support.

Hazards Assessment

A *hazards assessment* is a review of the types of occupancies and facilities within the service area and the types of hazards each creates for the community and the fire and emergency services organization. The assessment may indicate the presence of large quantities of:

- Combustibles (lumberyards or paper processing plants)
- Hazardous materials (petroleum processing or chemical plants)

- Life safety hazards (nursing homes or hospitals)
- Wildland urban interface areas (quantities of dry underbrush or trees)

The department's emergency response, water supply, staffing, and training requirements are based on the hazards assessment. Training based on the hazards assessment may require training in topics such as:

- Building construction
- Private alarm and fire suppression systems
- Weapons of mass destruction (WMD)
- Hazardous materials, container and label recognition
- High-angle rescue
- Marine fire fighting
- Aircraft fire fighting
- Wildland fire fighting
- Medical first responder training

Risk Analysis

A risk analysis can determine training requirements by identifying the level of risk that the department is willing to accept in order to protect the lives and property of the community or service area. Traditional operational strategies may contribute to hazards and increase the risk in some cases. Training that is required to meet this model includes a thorough understanding of:

- Fire behavior
- Building construction
- Types and application of extinguishing agents
- Use of personal protective equipment
- Basic fire fighting strategy and tactics

The model gives the following decision making directions to fire officers:

1. *We will risk ourselves a lot, within a structured plan, to save a savable life.*
2. *We will risk ourselves a little, within a structured plan, to save savable property.*
3. *We will not risk ourselves at all to save lives or property that is already lost.*

Program Development

Training must be effectively managed if it is to be successful in achieving its goals and objectives. The following sections suggest steps to follow as the training manager fulfills the many roles and responsibilities included in managing and supervising training programs. These roles and responsibilities include the following:

- Training program design
- Developing training policies, records, and standards
- Determining organizational training needs
- Recruiting and selecting instructors

- Scheduling training programs
- Evaluating training programs and instructors
- Providing budget and resource management

Program Design

Designing the overall training program is a critical step toward its success. The design and structure of a training program can either contribute to its effectiveness or fail to meet the organization's needs. Most organizations appoint an individual to perform the role of training manager who is responsible for designing or overseeing the design of a program that meets organizational goals and objectives. The training manager follows two basic steps when designing a training program: identify its purpose and consider program design factors. Several goals and components are identified and discussed for each design process step.

The first step identifies the *purpose* of the training program. For example, a fire training manager responds to NFPA® 1201, *Standard for Developing Fire Protection Services for the Public,* which states the purpose of fire and emergency services organization training as follows: *The fire department shall have a training program and policy that ensures that personnel are trained and competency is maintained to effectively, efficiently, and safely execute all responsibilities . . .* This purpose can be applied to any fire and emergency services organization. The training goal is to meet the following requirements:

- Develop and maintain the skills that all personnel need to perform their specific jobs in the organization.
- Instill the organization's values and culture in every member.
- Ensure the program meets the multiple requirements of local, state/provincial, and federal agencies.
- Provide quality programs that challenge personnel. Training that is too easy tends to cause participants to discount its importance.
- Provide opportunities for professional growth that prepare personnel for future responsibilities at the next organizational level *before* being promoted to the position.

The second step considers several factors in the actual design of the training program. Whether the design is for a new program or a modification of an existing program, the following factors have a direct effect on the structure and scope of the training program:

- **Organizational and personnel training needs** — The training manager must ensure that the program provides adequate and appropriate training to meet the needs of each section or division within the organization. This program includes providing the necessary support resources such as supplies, equipment, and instructional personnel. These programs should be scheduled or designed around work schedules so all personnel can attend.
- **Needs analysis** — Have a method or policy in place for performing a needs analysis to identify the most critical training needs. With multiple training topics and requirements, all of which have high priorities, implement policies to ensure that the training program addresses the topics that the needs analysis identifies.

- **Basic program philosophy** — Develop the training program's basic philosophy and strive to meet it. This philosophy must provide a customer service approach to the development and delivery of training. For example, determine what programs meet the training needs of personnel. Every training program has internal customers with specific needs:
  - Organizational personnel need training in order to perform the skills required to do their jobs — their needs vary based on their jobs.
  - Driver/operators of pumping apparatus need different skills than driver/operators of aerial apparatus, and all driver/operators need different skills than officers.
- **Overall organizational strategic goals** — Ensure that all personnel have the skills necessary to meet the organization's strategic goals. Every organizational function must be focused on helping that organization meet its strategic or performance goals. A training program is no different. Well trained personnel who have the skills necessary to perform their jobs achieve goals. If a strategic goal is to keep all personnel in their response areas as much as possible while training, the training program must ensure that training can be delivered to personnel in appropriate locations. These skills are developed as a result of a well designed, well managed training program.
- **Program and administrative structures** — Provide a clear line of authority and accountability for achieving an organization's training goals. Identify the individual who is in charge of managing and leading a training program. *Examples:*
  - NFPA® 1201 requires the fire chief to appoint a training officer for the fire and emergency services organization. This officer is responsible for developing training goals and performance objectives, ensuring training equipment operation and facility availability, coordinating training schedules, selecting instructors, and evaluating program success.
  - In large organizations, the training program structure may include other training staff who report to the training manager such as instructors, curriculum developers, media specialists, administrative clerks, and other support personnel.
  - In small organizations, the structure may identify one person who is charged with performing all tasks associated with training.
- **Appropriate training policies and procedures** — Develop and adopt appropriate training policies and procedures that answer the *who, what, when,* and *where* questions about training. It may be necessary to develop and adopt other policies based on local needs. A training issue that requires consistency over time with different work groups is an appropriate issue for a policy. These policies/procedures can answer the following questions:
  - Who is responsible and accountable for developing, delivering, and evaluating training?
  - Who is required to attend training programs?
  - Who is responsible for ensuring that training goals are achieved?
  - Who is responsible for evaluating the training program, the instructors,

and the participants?
- Who is expected to deliver training sessions?
- Who is responsible for acquiring resources?
- What are the training priorities?
- What is the mission of the training program?
- What are the job requirements and prerequisites for instructors?
- What are the minimum hours of training required for all positions?
- What are the topics and skills to be taught?
- When is training to be conducted?
- What training reports are required to be kept? Who keeps them? When are they due?
- How will the members' training hours be recorded or logged?
- Where is training to be held?

- **Program evaluation process** — Evaluate the courses, the instructors, the learners, and the entire program. Instructors evaluate individual courses and learners, and training managers evaluate instructors and the entire program (such as recruit firefighter training). The training manager may include program evaluation in the program design and may prevent problems and identify information that must be collected, such as the following:
  - What elements of the program must be evaluated (such as prerequisites, learner demographics, sequence of courses, use of time, and costs)?
  - When are these elements evaluated?
  - Who collects the data needed?
  - Who analyzes the data and formulates recommendations for changes?
  - How are the recommendations implemented?

- **Resources required to meet goals and objectives** — Resources are essential to the delivery of any training program. Failure to adequately plan could result in failure to meet learning objectives, program delays, and increased costs. Consider the following:
  - Who is responsible for logistics?
  - What equipment or apparatus is needed?
  - How many instructors are needed?
  - Do the instructors need to be certified in the topics they teach?
  - What handouts, workbooks, or texts are needed?
  - What sites or locations can be used?
  - What scheduling conflicts are there for the same resources or like resources?
  - What outside organizations are needed?

Program Design Tips

The following design tips ensure an effective organizational training program:

- Focus on the needs of the customer. For the training organization, the customer includes all organizational personnel or members who attend training.

- Design the program so that training is visible within the organization. Training should be seen as well as heard! Publicize training activities so that all personnel are aware of training opportunities and associated organizational training goals and objectives.

- Design the program so that accountability for achieving training goals is clearly established and communicated. Accountability goes beyond the training manager. It extends to every supervisor responsible for ensuring that assigned personnel are trained. Individuals must be held accountable for their own skills. The training program's design must clarify responsibility and accountability through both policies and training classes.

- Deliver quality training classes and drills. Quality is more important than quantity. Personnel want training that is challenging, enjoyable, and will enhance their skills and knowledge. Training should not be scheduled or required simply to add hours to a ledger. Rather, training programs must ensure that personnel can do their jobs effectively, efficiently, and safely.

Course Selection

Once training topics have been identified, the chief officer in charge of training must then prioritize them. The topics will then be converted into actual courses. A consideration in prioritizing training topics is to ensure that instructors attend programs to maintain their technical skills and professional certifications. While there is no specific process or set of steps for prioritizing topics, the chief officer can categorize them into the following three areas:

- **Must-know topics** — Enable personnel to perform their jobs effectively, efficiently, and safely based on standards and policies; for example: the proper use of SCBA is a *must-know* topic because it is essential for effective job performance and the safety of personnel. NFPA® Standards 1500, 1001, and 1404, as well as OSHA regulations, require SCBA training. This training has a higher priority than training on the proper use of a fire hose washer.

- **Need-to-know topics** — Enable personnel to perform their jobs based on job descriptions and responsibilities; for example: using a fire hose washer may be part of a firefighter's job, but it is not a component of firefighting effectiveness or safety. Cleaning hose is a necessary part of equipment maintenance and readiness, so it is considered a *need-to-know* topic.

- **Nice-to-know topics** — Supplement or complement personnel jobs; for example: fire service history is a *nice-to-know* topic and receives a low priority because it does not contribute to fire fighting effectiveness or safety nor enhance equipment effectiveness.

Certain jobs may affect the prioritization of training topics. For example, driver/operators have different training priorities than firefighters or officers. When prioritizing training topics, chief officers need to ask the following questions:

- What topics are required for personnel to achieve the organization's mission or program goals?
- What topics are required for personnel to perform jobs effectively and safely?
- What topics do the laws and standards mandate?
- What topics do internal customers perceive as most important?
- What topics are priorities of the organization's administration?

Based on the answers to these questions, training managers must establish training priorities and program goals that meet the needs of the organization. There is no set formula for establishing priorities and goals. Every organization has different needs that require different priorities and goals.

Topics are then developed into courses that provide the training in an understandable and efficient manner. Training officers may be responsible for developing course outlines or syllabuses, presentation timelines and formats, and local certification criteria. Professionally developed curriculum and certification standards are also available from organizations that develop training materials and certify personnel and programs.

Training vs. Certification vs. Accreditation

The fire service uses a number of terms to describe its training programs and their results. Sometimes these terms are misunderstood or misinterpreted, confusing the public and even fire service members. Training is the act of instructing firefighters and firefighter candidates in the knowledge and skills required to perform their duties. Certification is a result of that training. Individuals are tested to a set of established criteria to determine how well they can apply the knowledge and perform the skills. Accreditation is bestowed on the training agency or fire and emergency services organization for developing the required training and certification programs needed to provide the services to the community. An outside agency determines certification and accreditation.

Facility Types

Training facilities cover a wide range of designs and types. They may be permanent, mobile, or acquired (through private owner donations before demolition and removal). These facilities may be used for a variety of training evolutions. Chief officers should consult NFPA® 1402, *Guide to Building Fire Service Training Centers*, which details the types of structures that may be used for training. NFPA® 1403, *Standard on Live Fire Training Evolutions*, is essential for planning and implementing live fire or burn training in permanent and acquired structures. Training facilities require a minimum infrastructure to support the facilities, props, and training evolutions.

To properly support an organization's training program, a permanent training facility has to provide an infrastructure that consists of the following:

- **Adequate water supply** — Water volume and pressure required to support training operations based on the number of attack and backup hoselines used (required by NFPA® 1142, *Standard on Water Supplies for Suburban and Rural Fire Fighting*). Adequate water supplies are also needed for potable water, to support sprinkler and water spray systems with necessary volume and pressure, and to supply water for other types of exercises that may take place at the site.

- **Fuel source** — Flammable or combustible liquid, liquefied petroleum gas, or natural gas piped to a training prop from a main supply **(Figure 4.17)**.

- **Breathing-air supply** — Supplies include replacement breathing-air cylinders, a portable breathing-air compressor, a piped breathing-air distribution system from a centrally located compressor, a fixed or portable cascade system, or a supplied-air system **(Figure 4.18)**.

- **Equipment decontamination area** — Area designated for the washing and cleaning of personal protective clothing, hoses, nozzles, and other equipment. Contaminated wastewater is piped to the water decontamination system.

- **Apparatus staging, approach, and operational area** — Parking area (concrete surfaces capable of supporting apparatus) for units not involved in the training. The area provides short travel routes to designated training props and space to park apparatus as though it is at an emergency incident.

- **Communications system** — Radio frequency dedicated for the training function or two-way communication devices with limited range. All personnel engaged in training exercises must have contact with one another. Include the incident safety officer and the individual assigned to the fuel shutoff valve control in the communication loop.

- **Water decontamination system** — A system that separates and removes contaminates using oil separators, containing contaminated water in a pond that separates the oil and water through natural processes (ponding), adding hydrocarbon-eating bacteria into water to destroy the oil (bacterial breakdown), or using a combination of these processes. Decontaminated water returns to the system for use in further training exercises.

- **Weather (wind direction and air speed) monitoring equipment** — Equipment installed at the facility's highest point to determine the wind effect on burning materials and foam solution streams and to plan attack tactics to take advantage of it.

- **Environmental controls** — Other less obvious environmental controls include the following:
    - Natural gas or environmentally friendly fuels
    - Nonporous concrete surfaces to prevent soil contamination
    - Protocols to determine the effect of weather (temperature extremes, wind direction, etc.) on training exercises
    - Noise pollution controls such as mandatory hearing protection

Figure 4.17 A training facility that uses flammable gas from a large storage tank (circled in yellow) to operate its fire training props (circled in red).

Figure 4.18 The air cylinder reservicing equipment at a fire department training facility.

- **Security** — Fences, controlled access gates, guards, and lighting to secure the site from public access to prevent vandalism and injury to the public **(Figure 4.19, p. 198)**. Also provide evacuation signaling system and automatic fire detection and alarm system.

- **Location** — Site that provides adequate space for the various types of training that are required to meet the organization's needs. Other considerations include a site that is easily accessible from all areas of the organization's coverage and is also remote from other occupancies such as airports or schools that may be affected by live burns.

Permanent facilities should provide the variety of training scenarios that are required to meet the training needs of the department. Because state-of-the-art training facilities can be expensive, it may be necessary to develop the site in stages, providing sufficient space for expansion. Basic training site needs include the following:

- **Classrooms** — Room(s) that provide a comfortable learning atmosphere with minimal distractions **(Figure 4.20)**. Rooms may be part of a larger structure that includes demonstration rooms, training simulators, toilets, and administrative offices. Audiovisual equipment, computer systems, and Internet access may be included in the rooms as well as chalkboards, dry-erase boards, and easels/pads.

- **Parking areas** — Basic parking requirements are generally based, at a minimum, on the local building code. Include parking and easy access for apparatus in the requirements.

- **Driving courses** — Simulated streets, alleys, parking lots, cul-de-sacs, and dead-end driveways should be provided for driver/operator training. Include burn and collapse structures for added incident realism. Include parked vehicles, overhead wires, and other obstacles to simulate an actual driving situation.

- **Burn and smoke buildings** — Structures that are specifically designed for use in live-burn exercises must provide a safe yet realistic training experience for students. Smoke buildings are enclosed structures that are designed to acquaint students with the skills required to function safely in smoke-obscured atmospheres. Use nontoxic or artificial smoke and monitoring equipment, including closed circuit television or thermal imaging equipment, to track and locate students in the structure **(Figure 4.21)**.

- **Transportation incident props** — Training props representing commonly encountered transportation/vehicle accidents. Use props for extrication training, hazardous-materials spill control, and Class A and Class B foam training **(Figure 4.22)**. Props may include wrecked or overturned vehicles, collapsed structures, confined spaces, or simulated trenches, depending on the level of rescue training required and tools available to personnel.

Specialized sites for aircraft, marine, and petrochemical training and wildland burn areas may be required if the service area contains those hazards. Class B foam training props selected for a training facility should reflect the types of hazards located within the jurisdiction. Not all of these props are

Figure 4.19 Fire department training facilities should be surrounded by a fence with controlled access gates.

Figure 4.20 A training facility should have one or more classrooms.

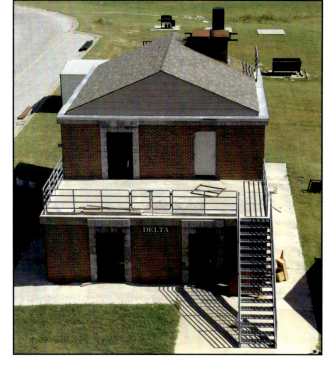

Figure 4.21 An example of a live-burn building at a fire department training facility.

Figure 4.22 Some fire department training facilities are equipped with railcar fire trainers.

required at most training facilities. Petroleum and chemical manufacturers within some jurisdictions may be able to provide out-of-service facilities for training purposes. These out-of-service units have to meet the requirements of NFPA® guidelines in order to be acceptable for training. These specialized sites and props are described as follows:

- **Specialized training props** — Most airport fire fighting organizations have burn pits with a simulated aircraft made of heavy gauge steel. Major universities and seaboard jurisdictions have access to simulators for training in maritime fire fighting. The remaining types of transportation props are found at most municipal and state fire services training facilities. Transportation props require the same safety and environmental requirements of exterior props that use foam concentrates/solutions.

Chapter 4 • Emergency Services Administration (Levels III & IV) **199**

- **Flammable and combustible liquid/gas training props** — Props designated for flammable and combustible liquids and gases include the following:
  — Pits to simulate unignited and ignited fuel spills
  — Aboveground storage tanks: vertical, horizontal, cone top, internal floating roof, external floating roof
  — Overhead flanges
  — *Christmas trees* (piping network, equipped with a shutoff valve that resembles a Christmas tree and used to simulate gas pressure fires)
  — Liquefied petroleum gas (LPG) facilities
  — Loading docks
  — Pump islands
  — Pump stations
  — Chemical plant processing facilities

- **Hazardous materials training areas** — Simulated hazardous materials and training foam concentrates are used in training exercises. All training areas must be within a levee system to contain runoff water until it is decontaminated. Props used for hazardous materials training may include some of those described in the previous section. They may also include the following:
  — Chemical processing facilities
  — Chemical storage tanks
  — Chemical stage areas (small container and drum)
  — Chemical spill pits

- **Wildland training areas** — Organizations that have primary responsibilities for protecting rural, suburban, and urban-interface areas from wildland fires should develop training areas specific to their needs. NFPA® 1402 does not address this type of facility, but a few suggestions are as follows:
  — Areas may be available on unused military bases, national and state/provincial parks, industrial parks, or other large open spaces.
  — Live-fire exercises could be included with controlled burns (with proper precautions).

Portable or mobile training facilities can prove more economical and flexible than permanent facilities for fire and emergency services organizations that serve large geographic areas. Mobile training units consist of trailer- or vehicle-mounted classrooms, computer-controlled simulators, smoke trailers, and fire behavior (flashover) simulators. They may be used to supplement or replace a permanent facility or as a temporary facility before a permanent structure is built. Fire or incident simulators that are designed for teaching tactics, strategy, and incident command may be part of the permanent facility or constructed as a mobile unit. These units may be the property of the state/provincial training organization or a regional university. Another approach is to construct portable training props that can be disassembled and transported in a light truck or van. These props can be used in fire stations or school classrooms at locations distant from the permanent facility.

Structures that are acquired for live burns such as vacant houses or retail buildings present a unique challenge to the chief training officer. The structures must be in compliance with local air quality ordinances, air management district requirements, and the requirements of NFPA® 1403 before they can be used for any live-fire exercises. The chief officer delegates the responsibility for ensuring that the requirements of NFPA® 1403 are met to the organization's health and safety officer. The acquired structure must be inspected and repairs made before any training take place.

The use of technology-based training is gaining in popularity, requiring both infrastructure and technicians to support it. Many organizations employ web-based, video-based, and other forms of technology training to educate their personnel.

Personnel

Training structures do not take the place of certified and skilled training personnel. The chief officer must ensure that the training staff is capable of providing the level of instruction that the organization requires. Effective instructors can teach, lead, motivate, inspire, and change the attitudes of an organization. Selecting competent instructors is a key management function of the chief training officer **(Figure 4.23)**.

Figure 4.23 Potential instructors being interviewed by a chief officer.

The chief officer determines the instructors' roles in the organization and the qualifications required to teach training programs. Establishing their positions in the organizational structure gives importance to the instructor role. Instructors are critical parts of program planning. They also act as intermediaries between administration and personnel in training. Instructors not only teach job knowledge and skills, but they are active in applying knowledge and skills on the job at various ranks or positions. Their experiences are critical components to their qualifications.

Few instructors are qualified to teach all topics. Instructors tend to specialize in certain areas and become proficient in teaching knowledge and skills specific to their areas of experience and expertise. The chief officer should base instructor selection upon the topics to be taught and the designated instructor roles in the organization and training program.

Instructors must have credibility with the personnel being trained. Personnel perceive that instructors have credibility when they display technical proficiency and evidence of formal training and education and demonstrate instructional experience. Rank, reputation, and respect among organizational members also indicate credibility.

A person must also be a qualified instructor such as meeting the Instructor I requirements of NFPA® 1041, *Standard for Fire Service Instructor Professional Qualifications*. If no personnel meet these requirements, chief training officers should provide instructor training programs. Instructor certification, instructor training program resources, and information are generally available from local, state/provincial, or regional training organizations.

Scheduling

The chief officer also schedules the training programs or courses. Providing a training schedule enables unit supervisors to assign personnel to training with minimal interference with or effect on daily duties. Training schedules for volunteer fire personnel allow them to integrate required training with regular employment responsibilities and personal activities. Posted training schedules provide training topics, dates, times, and locations. The organization may also post schedules to notify potential instructors of upcoming classes that are available for them to teach. When developing training schedules, the chief officer should consider the following factors that affect unit supervisors, personnel, and instructors:

- **How will the training schedule affect other job activities?** — Personnel have responsibilities other than attending training: inspections, incident responses, special events, and annual leaves. Some responsibilities may have a higher priority to the organization *at the moment* than training, and the chief officer must be aware of these other activities when creating the training schedule.

- **When are instructional resources (including instructors) most readily available?** — When sharing training resources such as classrooms, burn building, or driving courses with other organizations, chief officers must make cooperative arrangements, consider weather that may cause cancellations and rescheduling, and coordinate timely arrival and departure of class participants. Chief officers must also consider instructor schedules and conflicting assignments. Instructors may not always be available for assignments at certain times of the day or week, and available instructors may not be qualified to teach certain topics in some programs.

- **What is the most appropriate time for training?** — When a training program must be taught outdoors, it is best to schedule training when the weather is suitable. Evenings and weekends may be the best time to schedule some training.

- **How quickly must the training be completed?** — An organization's administration may want a specific training program completed immediately in order to fulfill a regulatory requirement. To meet immediate training needs, the chief officer can plan several program offerings in several time frames; that is, maximize the times and opportunities for personnel to complete the training. The chief officer can reprioritize other organizational activities and training programs where possible. For most training, programs may be scheduled over longer time periods and more frequently throughout the year so personnel can take advantage of required programs at their convenience.

- **How can technology-based training be used in place of traditional forms of training?** — Technology-based training, such as using Internet-based programs, Skype, and Smartboards, can provide training at multiple locations at convenient times. This form of training reduces out-of-service time, the fuel costs, and interruptions.

Developing a training schedule is not always a simple process. Responding to all the factors mentioned is taxing. Chief officers should establish guidelines that outline steps that provide consistency to the planning or scheduling process. Steps that assist in developing a training schedule include:

Step 1: Develop a consistent procedure for creating and publicizing training schedules:

- Consider the time period needed for training. A training schedule may cover 1 month, 6 months, or 1 year. The longer the time period a training schedule covers, the easier it is for personnel to prepare for training, but the greater the likelihood the schedule will have to be modified because of the following events:
  — Unforeseen activities
  — Extreme weather
  — Annual leaves
  — Other circumstances
- Ensure that all personnel are aware of and have access to the schedules. This awareness is especially important in a volunteer organization, where personnel must plan their personal lives around the organization's activities.
- Create schedules for time periods most convenient to all personnel.

Step 2: Assign one individual to create and keep record of training schedules — Whether the chief officer or another individual plans the schedules, one person should be responsible for the following activities:

- Tracking schedules
- Handling cancellations
- Rescheduling
- Sharing of time slots or facilities with other organizations

Step 3: Schedule a reasonable amount of training programs within a given time period:

- Do not schedule too much training in any given period and do allow for unforeseen circumstances. There should be enough time left open in the training schedule so that it can be modified without requiring a major change in the overall annual training plan.
- Schedule multiple sessions to ensure that all personnel have access to training.
- Allow for travel to and from the training site, setup time for instructors and evaluators, and cleaning or restocking time for classes that follow one another.

Step 4: Schedule all resources in a timely manner and confirm that these resources are available:

- Confirm that instructors are available and aware of the classes or topics they are to teach.
- Confirm that equipment or vehicles are available when needed.
- Reserve facilities so that use does not conflict with other training.

Step 5: Publish and distribute schedules:

- Distribute schedules to all personnel who require the training, those who will deliver the training, or those the training will affect.
- Post training schedules in areas that are accessible to all members of the organization.
- Post training schedules online, including dates, locations, times, and units assigned.

Step 6: Develop alternate plans — Developing lesson plans and instructor guides for others to use helps in reducing the chances of having to cancel training. Consider events that may prevent the scheduled training from being delivered such as the following:

- Instructor illness or injury
- Equipment failure or required emergency use
- Other organizational priorities
- Weather conditions

Sources of Funding

Potential funding sources for fire and emergency services organization training programs are the same as the organization's funding. These sources include the operating or program budget, grants from government and nongovernment agencies, and private sources such as fund-raising activities. Additional funds for training and education have been made available to fire and emergency services organizations since September 11, 2001. Chief officers should pursue all potential funding sources to ensure that the required level of training is provided.

External Training Sources

The majority of fire and emergency services organizations rely on some form of external training to supplement internal training programs. Contracts or partnerships can be used to establish relationships with various outside sources. Sources include colleges, North American fire training associations, regional programs, national courses, and private training centers.

Colleges/Universities

Community colleges, universities, and vocational/career technical schools may be sources for outside training. Some educational institutions have permanent fire service training facilities and programs. Those institutions that do not have fire service programs have classrooms, chemistry laboratories, and demonstration facilities that may be used for presentations. Many institutions have interactive television (ITV) facilities that can be used to access regional or national training seminars. Courses in non-fire related subjects such as communication, report writing, and management may also be available through these sources.

Even if training sessions are not conducted at a college campus, the college might accredit courses taught off campus that benefit the students and the courses' credibility. When considering college-level courses, the providing institution should be recognized and accredited by a regional (U.S.) or national/provincial (Canadian) accrediting agency. This accreditation allows credit hours to transfer from one academic establishment to another, provides portability between degree programs, and sanctions the quality of the education received.

North American Fire Training Associations

The majority of states and provinces in North America have fire and emergency services training associations that operate facilities providing on-site training for career, combination, and volunteer departments. Some facilities are located on state university property and operated as an outreach program of the school. Others are independent agencies of the state/provincial government. In any event, the facilities are available to provide all levels of training and certification for fire service personnel. Chief officers should encourage their training divisions to use state/provincial training programs whenever possible because most have programs that will enhance any department's training effort.

Regional Training Programs

Regional training programs and facilities provide localized resources to large or remote geographic areas or areas with high population density. An example of a regional training center is the Northern Alaska Regional Office of Fire Service Training (FST), located in Fairbanks, Alaska. It serves fire and emergency services organizations in the northern region of Alaska. Others exist in British Columbia and Connecticut.

The U.S. National Fire Academy (NFA) developed the Training Resources and Data Exchange (TRADE) program as another regional training approach. This program is a regionally based network designed to foster the exchange of fire related training information and resources among federal, state, and local levels of government. The TRADE system includes ten regional networks that correspond to the existing federal regional boundaries. These networks provide a mechanism for the exchange of resources and materials within and among regions.

Seminars

An alternative to conducting in-house training is to contract with an instructor to conduct a particular seminar for the fire and emergency services organization in its local community. Specialty subjects, including leadership and management, lend themselves to this approach.

National Courses/Curriculum

Courses and curriculum material are also available from NFA. The federally funded program provides training opportunities on and off campus and includes courses in management, inspections, investigations, and other fire service related topics. Weekend courses are available for members of volunteer departments. Chief officers should check with their appropriate state training agency because the NFA has given them most of the courses.

Private Sources

Partnerships with businesses in the response area may also result in joint training opportunities. Private sources for training vary regionally but may include the following:

- **Hospitals or medical centers** — Emergency Medical Technician/Emergency Medical Services (EMT/EMS) training
- **Fire alarm companies** — Alarm systems operation
- **Fire-suppression systems companies** — Operation of various types of permanent fire suppression systems
- **Retired senior and volunteer professionals (RSVP)** — Business management theory and application as well as organizational performance audits that retired business professionals provide that the Corporation for National and Community Service sponsors in the U.S.
- **Railroad companies** — Operations involving railroads and crossings
- **Electric power companies** — Operations involving downed power lines and other electrical equipment
- **Trucking companies** — Safe operation of heavy trucks

Training Program Evaluation

Evaluation is essential to the success of a department's training program. The training program's goals and objectives form the basis for evaluation. Goals and objectives identify what the training program is to accomplish. The program's success is determined by how well the program achieves its goals and objectives.

Evaluating the training program includes determining the satisfaction level of program customers. Personnel participating in an *effective* training program appreciate the time they spend there and the information they learn. Participants are the first to recognize an ineffective or inappropriate training program and will make their displeasure known. The evaluation process is identical to the process for evaluating the organization described previously.

The training program evaluation process also includes surveys of supervisory personnel such as incident commanders, supervisors, and program managers. These supervisory personnel work with the individuals who complete the training programs. They are aware of the skills and attitudes these individuals display on the job. Supervisory personnel provide invaluable information about the successes and results of training programs.

Community Risk Assessment and Reduction

The terms *hazard* and *risk* are often used interchangeably; however, technically, they describe two different things. The term *hazard* usually refers to the source of a risk. A *risk* is the likelihood of suffering harm from a hazard. Risk can also be thought of as the potential for failure or loss. *Risk* is the exposure to a hazard. A *hazard* is a condition, substance, or device that can directly cause an injury or loss.

Assessing the potential risks to a community or service area involves:

- Applying a risk management model

- Determining the existing and potential hazards
- Cataloging and inspecting private fire protection systems in local facilities
- Determining the available water supply sources in the area
- Recognizing the types of building construction that are prevalent in the area
- Evaluating the existing and potential mutual aid agreements from regional fire and emergency services organizations

This information is critical in the development of a fire prevention and life safety program that the organization manages. Thorough research, data collection, and data analysis provide a framework upon which to build the program.

Fire Service Vulnerability Assessment Project

The National Fallen Firefighters Foundation (NFFF), U.S. Fire Administration (USFA), and Honeywell International, Inc. formed a joint venture called the Fire Service Vulnerability Assessment Project (VAP). Its objective is to help meet the USFA's goal of eliminating all preventable firefighter line of duty injuries and deaths.

The project will result in a free, online VAP survey. This survey will allow fire chiefs to identify community risks, resource deficiencies, and safety gaps that can result in firefighter injuries and deaths. Alternatives to risk reductions for each area of vulnerability will be provided when the survey is completed. The VAP is specifically intended to reduce firefighter casualties and is comparable to a community risk reduction model.

Hazard Categories

The two broad community risk categories are divided into four specific subcategories: behavioral, intentional, natural, and occupancy related. Not all of these hazards will result in fires or emergency incidents, but all are potentially life-threatening to the service area's population. A fire prevention and life safety program can be designed to reduce the threats that many of these hazards pose.

Behavioral

Behavioral hazards result from the perceived careless actions of individuals or groups. Examples include storing ignitable liquids improperly, smoking in bed, and driving while under the influence of alcohol or drugs. While the first example may be addressed with a strong inspection and code enforcement program, all three behaviors may be altered through a public fire and life safety education program. Collecting data on these hazards involves reviewing the organization's response history and categorizing the types of responses and the causes. Additional data sources include the local Red Cross and safety council, national safety organizations such as the Home Safety Council (HSC), Centers for Disease Control and Prevention (CDC), and the medical profession.

Intentional

Intentional hazards result from actions that are meant to cause property destruction or life loss. These hazards may include, but are not limited to, vandalism, arson, or terrorism, and the reasoning may include revenge, anger, or personal gain. An effective fire cause determination or investigation program helps to pinpoint the causal factor and provide evidence for a judicial case. Inspection and public education can also reduce the potential for such incidents. If the public is aware of a trend, they can provide information that may prevent future incidents. Data is gained through the review of previous investigations, an understanding of the local society that may indicate the existence of gang or criminal activity, or information from national sources that may provide trends that are similar to local events.

Natural

Natural hazards consist of incidents that are generally out of human control, such as tornados, hurricanes, earthquakes, floods, landslides, and forest fires. Many of these incidents may be regional in nature, although some have occurred in unexpected areas. Most natural disasters would not be considered disasters if humans had not chosen to build, live, work or travel there. Human activities can even exacerbate the severity of some natural events, such as landslides, floods, and forest fires.

Fire and emergency services personnel may not be able to prevent the effects of natural hazards, but they can reduce the consequences. Building and fire codes, along with zoning restrictions (those that prevent structures from being built in natural hazards prone areas), can help reduce the potential effects of these hazards. Public fire and life safety education and disaster response training programs can help reduce the number of deaths and injuries. An example of this education is to remind drivers not to enter rapidly moving water crossing roadways. Information on these types of hazards may be obtained from the National Weather Service, historical documentation sources, and local geographical and population spread data, which may be available through the library system or agencies of the local government. The effect that natural disasters have on the infrastructure of fire and emergency services organizations is often overlooked in the planning stage.

Occupancy Related

The local or state/provincial building codes determine the occupancy use categories for structures such as assembly, residential, commercial, etc. Each of these categories is not only a criterion for building construction but also an indication of the potential hazard the structure presents. The building department inspectors or plans review personnel usually determine an occupancy's designation. The fire and emergency services organization is responsible for ensuring that the owner/occupant adhere to building code requirements. This adherence is accomplished through the enforcement of the jurisdiction's adopted fire code. The fire prevention division may also be responsible for the duties normally assigned to a building department, including plans review.

The first step in determining occupancy related hazards is to understand the building, fire codes, and locally adopted amendments. The next step is to survey all structures (except single-family dwellings) and list the types of occupancies and hazards they create. This data can then be included in a community or service area hazards assessment and used to develop a complete fire prevention and life safety program.

Although single-family dwellings may be exempt from mandatory fire and life safety inspection requirements, they may be included in two programs that can reduce loss. (On military installations, single-family dwellings can be inspected.) First, a voluntary home inspection program can be established that doubles as a public education opportunity. Fire service personnel visit every home in their response area and offer voluntary home safety surveys. The surveys include the distribution of safety-related information, suggestions for safe storage of ignitable liquids, home escape plans, and tests of smoke detection equipment. Some jurisdictions even provide free smoke detectors or replacement batteries to residents of target areas. Target areas are determined by factors such as the frequency of fires, the economic status of the residents, and the age or infirmity of the residents.

The second program is a physical survey of all residential neighborhoods in the response area to determine the potential risks from natural hazards. Streets and highways are designated and marked as escape routes, recommendations for sheltering in place are made, and an inventory of the number of potential evacuees is developed. Facilities within the neighborhood, such as schools and recreation centers, may be designated as evacuation sites and stocked with the appropriate supplies. Company officers may assist emergency planners to gather information on the neighborhoods. Emergency planners and managers use this information to establish a state/provincial, regional, or national plan for the evacuation of large numbers of people in the event of a major natural disaster, terrorist attack, or act of war.

High Value/Priority Exposures

During the risk analysis, some structures or elements of the infrastructure may be designated as high value and/or high priority exposures. These structures or elements do not contain or create hazards themselves. Their location may place them adjacent to a hazard, such as a dike that may collapse during a flood. High value structures are those that have a high financial value or contain a large number of people, posing a high life loss risk. High priority exposures are things that are basic to the community, such as a source of fresh water, a telecommunications system, or electricity. For instance, a cyber-attack on the financial institutions might prevent citizens from making electronic transactions or getting cash from automatic teller machines (ATMs). All of these exposures should be considered in the risk analysis.

Creating a Written Analysis

When the risk analysis is completed, the information must be compiled into a written report for presentation to the leadership of the jurisdiction. The goal of the report is to assist the decision makers in determining if the resources are available to eliminate or control the hazards. The report must be clear, concise, and accurate.

The report should consist of:

- A list of the potential hazards in the service area — in order of severity and frequency, beginning with the greatest risk.

- A list of the current resources that can respond to the hazards — include personnel, apparatus, equipment, funding, and outside contractors.
- Describe the types and amount of resources that are lacking.
- Provide a solution for the difference between *current* and *required* resources.
- Provide one or two alternate solutions to the problem.

Authors of the original reports usually provide executive summaries to supervisors or administrative bodies. These summaries are attached to the fronts of the reports or papers. An *executive summary* is a brief review of the key points in a report, a technical paper, specifications, or an analysis. It ensures that the essential information contained in the report is read, and it acts as an attention-getter that may spur the audience to read the full report. It also provides senior management with the main points necessary when justifying the report to the media, public, or legislative body.

Creating a Community Risk Reduction Program

The analysis of the community risk assessment can then be utilized to create a community risk reduction program. Resources should be acquired and prioritized to address each level of risk found in the community. Policies and procedures must be written describing the risk reduction approaches to be followed. Personnel must be trained on any new procedures or equipment required by the program. The program must be monitored to ensure resources are utilized effectively and risks are reduced. If discrepancies are found, adjustments must be made to the program.

Chapter Summary

All chief officers must be familiar with the budgeting process and methods used in their jurisdiction. They must also be able to analyze current conditions, processes, and policies and determine if the department is able to meet community needs and expectations. Chief officers must be able to apply various planning models to create operational and strategic plans for the department. Planning is the key to maintaining a successful fire and emergency services organization.

Review Questions

1. What considerations should the chief officer take when developing a divisional or departmental budget? (pp. 140-149)
2. What is the process for developing a budget management system? (pp. 149-155)
3. What procedures should the chief officer follow when purchasing materials, equipment, and apparatus? (pp. 155-167)
4. How does the chief officer keep successful departmental records? (pp. 167-175)
5. What methods can the chief officer use to collect and analyze departmental data? (p. 175)
6. What tools can the chief officer use to develop improvements to the organization? (pp. 176-180)

7. What key elements comprise a department's strategic planning process? (pp. 180-183)
8. What are the various time frames associated with a department's operational planning stage? (183-188)
9. What are the responsibilities of the chief officer in terms of organizational training? (pp. 188-206)
10. What are the various components of a community risk assessment? (pp. 206-210)

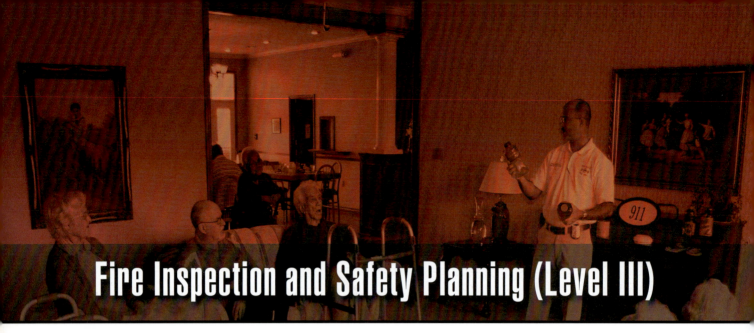

Fire Inspection and Safety Planning (Level III)

Chapter Contents

CASE HISTORY 215	**Fire Inspection Programs** 226
III Fire Prevention and Life Safety Planning 216	Selection and Design 227
Needs Identification 218	Alternatives 229
Program Selection 220	Implementation 230
Program Design 222	Evaluation/Revision 231
Implementation 223	Public Awareness and Acceptance 231
Evaluation 224	**Chapter Summary** 232
	Review Questions 232

Chapter 5

NFPA® Job Performance Requirements

This chapter provides information that addresses the following job performance requirements of NFPA® 1021, *Standard for Fire Officer Professional Qualifications* (2014).

Level III

6.5.1

6.5.2

Fire Inspection and Safety Planning (Level III)

Learning Objectives

After reading this chapter, students will be able to:

[Level III]

1. Describe the various processes used to develop a fire prevention and life safety program. (6.5.2)
2. Identify various actions taken for developing a fire inspection program. (6.5.1)

Chapter 5
Fire Inspection and Safety Planning (Level III)

Case History

During a band performance, pyrotechnics ignited foam insulation lining the walls and ceiling of the platform that was being used as a stage at a New England nightclub. The fire spread quickly along the foam-lined walls and ceiling, smoke emerged from the exit doorways in less than one minute, smoke dropped to near the dance floor, and flames broke through the roof in less than five minutes. One hundred people lost their lives in the fire and hundreds were injured.

Based on NIST recommendations, the following actions were identified to avert a similar scenario from occurring again:

- Model code adoption and enforcement
- Sprinklers installed in all new nightclubs and existing nightclubs with occupancies of greater than 100 people
- State and local authorities adopt and aggressively enforce the existing provisions of the code

This incident shows the significance of a routine annual inspection program. Part of the mission of every fire chief is to deliver quality timely emergency services. Establishing a fire prevention program creates a best practice approach to firefighter safety and citizen safety.

Because the majority of fire related deaths and injuries occur before emergency responders arrive at an incident, fire and emergency services organizations must identify and develop programs that can reduce these casualties and injuries. A fire prevention and life safety effectiveness model is one method for developing a program that ensures that the personal and physical losses due to fire are kept to a minimum. Effective fire prevention programs are traditionally based on elements that can include the following **(Figure 5.1, p. 214)**:

- **Engineering** — Building design that an adopted building code requires
- **Inspections** — Enforcement of building and fire codes in selected occupancies
- **Investigation** — Fire cause determination
- **Education** — Fire prevention information and training for the public

Figure 5.1 The four basic elements of an effective fire prevention program: Engineering, Investigation, Inspections, and Education.

This chapter explains how chief officers can use methodical approaches to create a fire prevention and life safety program or evaluate the effectiveness of an existing one. The chapter also addresses critical components in the development, implementation, operation, and evaluation of fire inspection programs.

Fire Prevention and Life Safety Planning

The terms *fire prevention and life safety* describe a proactive approach to reducing the loss of life and property, meeting the organization's mission, and reducing community risk. These programs are composed of:

- Preincident plans
- Inspections
- Investigations
- Public fire and life safety education elements

While investigation occurs after an incident, it is included as a function of prevention because it can provide vital data that can be used to:

- Alter behavior
- Influence legal or judicial changes
- Modify codes
- Identify trends

The majority of fire and emergency services organizations provide one or all of these components of the program. Chief officers may manage the overall development and evaluation of fire and life safety plans and programs. However, these duties may be delegated to other personnel such as a fire marshal. A law, a charter, or an ordinance usually requires the establishment of the office of fire marshal within the jurisdiction. All chief officers should have working knowledge of fire prevention and life safety programs and the processes used to develop them.

An **effective fire prevention and life safety program** can be built on the following elements:

- **Engineering/Technology** — Use of construction techniques that reduce the potential for fire or other hazards. The jurisdiction's building code and the plans review and permit processes control and influence construction. This control may be the responsibility of the fire or emergency services organization.

- **Enforcement** — The creation and application of codes, laws, ordinances, and regulations to reduce risk.

- **Education** — Provides public fire prevention and life safety information to the population through brochures, presentations, and various types of activities **(Figure 5.2)**.

- **Economic Incentives/Disincentives** — Include benefits such as reduced property taxes or insurance premiums for installing fire sprinkler systems in a structure. Disincentives can include fines or other monetary penalties for noncompliance.

- **Emergency Response** — A critical aspect of risk reduction but must be coupled with the other elements to truly be effective.

Some barriers must be overcome in the development of a fire prevention and life safety program. Among these barriers is a lack of any nationally defined standard or guideline for code enforcement, inspections, investigations, or education. This lack of fire prevention and life safety standards makes it difficult for chief officers to justify budget and staffing requests to the political leaders of the jurisdiction. AHJ requirements drive many of the issues.

While minimum standards exist for staffing and workload requirements for fire suppression activities, there are not similar requirements in the fire prevention and life safety programs. Historically, states/provinces and municipalities establish the guidelines for frequency of inspections in their jurisdictions. The NFPA® is working to develop a standard for inspection programs that will address some of these issues.

Figure 5.2 A public fire prevention and life safety education presentation at a preschool.

The lack of available resources (personnel, time, and funds) is a barrier to the provision of fire prevention and life safety programs. This lack of resources is especially true in areas served by volunteer organizations. Changes to building construction and fuel loads in residences and commercial occupancies increase the challenge to fire prevention efforts. Chief officers should take an active approach to overcome these barriers and do the following:

- Be a strong advocate for prevention and education efforts within the department.
- Support the creation, adoption, revision, and enforcement of standards and codes.
- Develop inspection, investigation, and education programs based on service area needs.
- Provide professional development for fire prevention and life safety program personnel.
- Consider the development of regionalized and collaborative resources.

A consistent approach is required when developing and implementing programs. One such approach is the five-step planning process. This process provides systematic planning and action and is composed of the following steps:

- Identify
- Select
- Design
- Implement
- Evaluate

Each step consists of several fact-finding activities and a decision. The general process for fire prevention life safety program development is discussed in the sections that follow.

Needs Identification

When identifying community needs, a project-management team (including citizens and other stakeholders) should be formed to provide the necessary information for creating the fire prevention and life safety program. The team performs a risk analysis to identify the service area's needs. The legal mandates and levels of service that the population desires are added to this analysis. Once these needs are defined, the appropriate type of fire prevention and life safety program is selected to address those needs.

Not all service areas require full-time inspection or investigation programs as part of the organization's services. This may be the case in rural areas where the state/territory/province provides these functions. A community's limited ability to fund an inspection, investigation, or education program may force the organization to select the one that will provide the greatest good for the largest segment of the population. The local needs direct the selection of the specific service to be provided.

The objective of the first step in developing a program is to identify the most significant local fire prevention and life safety hazards, problems, and concerns. The following are some of the questions asked during the identification process:

- What are the major fire and life safety hazards in the service area?
- Where are the high-risk locations in the service area?
- When are the high-risk times?
- Who are the high-risk populations according to age, gender, location?
- What is the high-risk behavior?
- Why does the risk exist?

Examples of fire-related hazards include ignition sources (smoking materials or faulty electrical wiring) or behaviors (children playing with matches or persons overloading electrical outlets). Non-fire related hazards may include physical hazards such as uneven pavement (a tripping or falling risk) or overloading storage shelves that may contribute to a collapse.

Community Paramedicine

The lack of access to healthcare providers, such as in rural areas and indigent populations in urban areas, is one risk-related issue that is gaining great attention. An initiative called Community Paramedicine has emerged as a popular way to close this gap. Community paramedicine programs utilize the existing EMS infrastructure and expand the role of EMS personnel. Working with physicians and other allied health providers, community paramedicine program personnel can provide routine care that would normally be provided in a physician's office or clinic. Community paramedicine is not a one-size-fits-all approach. The approach allows communities and jurisdictions to tailor the role and scope of their personnel to meet local needs, filling in gaps in the traditional healthcare system. Examples of services that may be provided in a community paramedicine program include but are not limited to the following:

- Vaccinations
- Sutures
- Follow up care
- Mental health assessments
- Injury and illness risk identification

During the identification step, a picture of the service area's most significant fire and life safety problems will begin to emerge. Answers to two or three of the questions listed may combine to form a single problem scenario (such as *inoperable smoke alarms in single-family homes* or *burn injuries from scalds to residents of a certain neighborhood*). Maybe a single issue, such as juvenile or youth fire setting, emerges as the primary problem. In most cases, more than one hazard will be identified, which requires the development of multiple solutions to address all the hazards. If resources are not available, then the hazards must be prioritized and mitigated in order of severity or frequency. Departments that have developed "Standards of Cover" documents should use these documents to assist in determining the data that should be collected.

The information used to determine frequency and severity is based on per capita data for the service area. Examples of per capita data required to determine the needs of the community include the following:

- Total residential structure fire incidents per 1,000 residential structures
- Residential structure fires per 1,000 population served
- Residential arson incidents per 10,000 residents served
- Total fire incidents per 1,000 population served
- Hazardous materials incidents per 1,000 population served
- False alarms as percentage of total structure fire incidents

Program Selection

The objective of the selection step is to choose the best solution for the identified hazard. The most cost-effective or achievable solution becomes one of the objectives of the fire prevention and life safety program. Awareness of the problem's scope and the limitations of available resources are important if planners are to be realistic about what the program can accomplish. The questions in the selection step should focus on identifying and acquiring resources such as funds, materials, and talented people. Some of the questions considered in the selection step of planning are as follows:

- Who will the program benefit?
- What are the potential costs and benefits of various program elements?
- What resources are available within the organization and the community?

Program planners can determine the *specific objectives of the program* at the end of the selection step. Objectives need to be specific, measurable, action oriented, realistic, and in an appropriate time frame. Answers to the questions in the selection step are used to complete the design, implementation, and evaluation steps **(Figure 5.3)**. Information about major fire hazards and high-risk locations, times, victims, and behaviors is helpful when it is time to answer design step questions such as: *What program best solves the problem?* The selection and design steps are so

Figure 5.3 Fitting a program's objectives together can seem like assembling the pieces of a jigsaw puzzle.

closely related that it is sometimes difficult to distinguish one from the other. The program design should be based on specific objectives selected to address a specific local problem.

Selecting the most appropriate form of the fire prevention and life safety program may not be a simple process. The needs of the service area may appear complex with a number of priorities apparent. Inadequate funding, lack of trained personnel, or competing priorities in other areas may reduce the number of options that can be selected and successfully completed. Recognized school-based public education programs and partnerships can benefit a community's fire and life safety efforts. These programs often use teachers as public safety educators. Organizations such as the United States Fire Administration, Vision 20/20, and the Center for Campus Fire Safety provide programs that can be implemented in the community.

Once the best possible choices have been made, the chief officer or project team attempts to justify each alternative. This justification will be needed when the program is presented to the jurisdiction's political leadership for adoption. Legal mandates and local, regional, and national fire and injury data may justify the existence of a fire prevention and life safety program.

Legal Mandates

Legal mandates may exist in local ordinances, state/territorial/provincial statutes, and federal laws or rules. It is often required for the AHJ to appoint a fire marshal and that a fire prevention and life safety program be established. To establish a fire prevention and life safety program, it may be necessary to simply research and collect the legal requirements and present them in a logical objective manner to the political leadership of the jurisdiction.

Data Collection

Quality data should be obtained to support the legal requirements and provide greater justification for the program. These data are based on local, regional, and national fire incident reports and information gathered from insurance carriers. Comparisons between fire losses from before the implementation of an inspection program and after the program has been in place for a period of time can demonstrate the effectiveness of inspections. Evaluations of programs in similar jurisdictions can also support the program request. To justify an investigation program, make a comparison between the number of fires with known causes and those that were suspicious, and show any trend or increase in certain types of fires or targets. Regional and national statistics on intentionally set fires (as well as intelligence reports from law-enforcement agencies) are available to the chief officer from organizations such as USFA and NFPA. Statistics concerning other injuries and risks are also available from HSC/Safe Kids, Safe Community Foundation (Canada), and similar organizations.

Accurate data is a critical component in gaining approval for a public fire prevention and life safety education program. The results of the needs analysis, local, regional, and national statistics on similar hazards (and the solutions that were developed to meet them), and the goals and objectives of the proposed program can be used as justification. All presentations should be objective, understandable and supported by facts.

To gain approval for the establishment of a fire prevention and life safety program, the chief officer must use all logical, available information to develop the request. Program costs and desired outcomes must also be provided. For instance, the justification for a school-based education program can include local and national statistics on fires involving children; the costs of property losses, medical treatments, rehabilitation sessions, and program actions for emergency responders; and a comparison of these costs to the program costs.

Program Design

The design step is the bridge between selecting a fire prevention and life safety program and actually implementing it. The objective of the design step is to develop the most effective means of delivering the program's elements to the public. Some questions asked during the design step of planning can include the following:

- Which elements are necessary to meet the needs of the fire prevention and life safety program?
- What is the best organization and application of resources?
- What are the goals and objectives that must be met?

After answering these questions and others, program planners are ready to design a program and determine how to produce the program materials. The question to answer at the end of the design step is: *Do we approve or revise the fire prevention and life safety program?*

Developing the program requires the jurisdiction to officially approve the design. This approval is vital to the success of the program because two of the elements (inspection and investigation) may involve the issuance of citations, warrants, and physical inspections on private property. This step also includes creating a contingency plan should the program (or part of it) not be approved. Personnel requirements also need to be addressed based on the type of program selected. Resources can often be shared between departments to make programs more cost effective.

Approvals

The chief officer should be able to gain the governing body's approval by proposing the desired outcome and the cost effectiveness of the fire and life safety program. The chief officer making the proposal should be prepared to provide as much supporting information as possible. The presentation could include visual aids that illustrate the cost comparison based on accurate data. Include public support in the form of statements (oral or written) from members of the project management team or civic leaders. If the program involves the resources of the law enforcement agency, then an agreement must be approved that outlines the authority, duties, and responsibilities of both organizations. The political leadership must have full faith and confidence in the program and desired outcomes to ensure approval.

Once the program is approved, it should be announced to the public. This announcement addresses the concerns of the organization, chief officers, program developers, and politicians for the hazards and risks that may exist in the service area. It also generates a positive image for the program and helps with public awareness and support.

Alternatives

Although alternatives may not be the most effective solutions to the fire and life safety hazards of a community, they may be necessary if the program is not approved due to cost or other issues. Alternatives include community involvement, corporate partnerships, and interagency agreements. These alternatives may require creating nontraditional approaches to the risks, such as the use of community volunteers, transferring the responsibility to another agency, or reassigning personnel on a temporary basis. To increase efficiency, some jurisdictions may look for redundancies where duplication of inspection efforts are occurring.

Implementation

Once the program is approved, implementation can begin. This implementation involves developing an organizational structure to support the program, allocating resources, and providing personnel to deliver services. The time required to establish the program varies, depending on the changes that are necessary to accommodate the new services within the existing organizational structure. One approach is to implement the program in phases or stages, such as hiring new personnel or reassigning existing personnel and training them to meet a limited objective of the program. Once this stage is complete, hire additional personnel or begin implementing a second portion of the objectives.

Organizational Structure

The implementation of a fire prevention and life safety program requires the creation of a formal organizational structure within the existing organization. In small organizations, one person may provide the entire program function. Large organizations may have programs that consist of a variety of chief officers managing different elements of the program. Other organizations might use civilian managers in these positions. Within the individual elements, company officers or nonemergency and specialist personnel may perform the duties of investigators, inspectors, or educators. In some instances, the program may be supplemental so that another function (such as fire suppression) with emergency personnel is responsible for both tasks. The structure needs to have clearly defined responsibilities, authorities, and lines of communication.

Resource Allocation

Resources required for a new program can be estimated based on program costs in similar service areas. This information can be acquired for evaluation from the USFA, insurance bureaus, professional organizations, or surveys of other fire and emergency services organizations. Consider the requirements and costs for the following resources:

- Personnel (including wages, benefits, and training)
- Office space
- Codes, standards, and research materials
- Computer hardware, software, and support
- Data storage
- Education props and tools

- Vehicles
- Educational materials

Funding sources generally come from the operating or program budget (which covers personnel, training, and materials) and the capital budget (which covers facilities and infrastructure). Grant or gift money may be available for special projects, such as distributing residential smoke alarms in target neighborhoods or creating educational material in Braille for the visually impaired. Donations and gifts can also be solicited from various nonprofit organizations to assist with program implementation.

Personnel Selection

Staffing is a local option based on the community's needs and organization's size. Personnel sometimes come from within the organization and are selected and reassigned based on their abilities to fulfill particular functions. New personnel may be hired for specialized tasks, such as inspections, public education presentations, plans review, or investigations. This process takes time and should be accounted for in the planning. Training has to be provided and scheduled. New curriculums may have to be developed.

An alternative to creating a new curriculum is to use state/territorial/provincial, regional, or National Fire Academy courses in the desired subject. These training opportunities are often offered at low or no cost to the department and should be incorporated into the department's training program. Personnel at lower levels in the organization should also be encouraged to pursue these training opportunities. Another alternative is to provide training through college or university fire science programs. Just as volunteers can be used for other programs in the fire and emergency services organization, they can be valuable to fire and life safety programs as well.

Evaluation

The final step is to evaluate the program to determine its effectiveness. Evaluation data also assist in budget justification for continued operations and funding. Accurate evaluation of the fire prevention and life safety program depends heavily on the ability to monitor the program and its elements. The effectiveness of the program becomes apparent through the evaluation of the data gathered while monitoring the program and determining indicators. A process for monitoring the program is established as part of the program's policies and procedures.

Data Monitoring

Criteria are based on the desired outcome of the program elements. Data that may be gathered for evaluation include the following:

- **Inspection element data**
  - Inspection reports
  - Violations reported
  - Citations written
  - Appeals based on citations

- Complaints or comments from external customers
- Incident report reviews

- **Investigation element data**
    - Incident reports that involve suspicious or intentional fires
    - Investigation reports of suspicious or intentional fires
    - Unusual number of fires with undetermined cause
    - Surveys of witnesses who have been interviewed
    - Surveys of company personnel who work with investigators
    - Observations of investigators
    - Court document reviews (cases that result from investigations)
    - Conviction rates and comparisons to similar jurisdictions
    - Reviews of existing policies and procedures
    - Comparisons with policies and procedures in similar jurisdictions
    - Reviews of complaints or review-board records

- **Public education element data**
    - Incident reports for specific types of occupancies or target groups
    - Return visits to the target group to reemphasize the topic
    - Skills tests (such as ability to perform CPR, demonstrating how to crawl under smoke) during presentations
    - Surveys or questionnaires based on information included in the presentations

The information gathered from monitoring the program is used to evaluate its effectiveness. General sources of feedback include surveys or questionnaires filled out by external customers, focus groups to solicit concerns from the customers, and requests for community involvement. Improvements in electronic survey applications allow surveys to be distributed to larger group of respondents. Together, these pieces of information provide a fairly accurate overview of the program.

Indicators

Using good evaluation techniques should provide an accurate picture of the program's effectiveness. The effectiveness of an inspection program can be determined using indicators, such as a decrease in the number of fires in commercial buildings compared with the preinspection fire record or the number of fires that installed sprinkler systems extinguished. If an inspection program has been in effect for some time, it may only be necessary to evaluate changes that have occurred, such as adding inspections of nursing homes or inspections based on fire code changes.

The investigation program and its process can be evaluated for effectiveness using the list of data collected through the monitoring phase. Depending on the original criteria, some indicators of effectiveness may be as follows:

- Decrease in intentionally set fires
- Increase in conviction rates for intentionally set fires
- Decrease in property loss due to suspicious or intentional fires

- Increase in accurate fire cause determinations
- Increase in community support of fire prevention programs

Evaluating data gathered during the monitoring phase of the public education program element helps the chief officer determine the program's effectiveness. The length of time required to evaluate this element of the program varies, depending on the specific hazard or the desired outcome. If a long-range goal is to change hazardous behaviors that cause fires, the gathering of incident reports to substantiate this reduction may take years. Presentations that focus on seasonal incidents (such as fires in Christmas trees) will also take years to show a trend because the incidents/events are annual occurrences. A specific situation, however, that requires an immediate response (such as a series of fires caused by the improper use of electrical extension cords) may show an immediate change following expanded media coverage. The same may be true of a concentration of juvenile/youth firesetter programs following a series of suspicious fires involving youth in a specific neighborhood.

An accurate evaluation depends on having clearly defined program outcomes, quantifiable measurements, and accurate, detailed data collection and retention. The resulting information and recommendations should be included in program reports to the chief officer in charge of the fire prevention and life safety program as well as community leaders. The results of the evaluation phase indicate whether the program needs to be altered in any way. If no revisions are required, the program should continue in its present form with constant monitoring and evaluating. Personnel should publicly acknowledge and celebrate the success of the program and its participants. They should also thoroughly investigate and resolve negative indicators through the revision phase established for the program. Negative perceptions on the part of the community can lead to the loss of faith in the program and its process.

Fire Inspection Programs

Fire inspection programs have been a traditional component of the fire service for decades. Fire inspections and code enforcements were outgrowths of major catastrophic fires that resulted in high life or property loss. Some organizations provide inspection services at the company level as part of their normal duties. Other organizations also provide personnel to work with the jurisdiction's building or plans review department, while a few organizations have complete responsibility for the duties of the building department. The chief officer or fire marshal evaluates the advantages and disadvantages of each level of service during the development of a fire inspection program.

A five-step process can be used to create a new inspection element or expand the existing service to include additional services. A risk analysis provides the raw data for identifying the service area's inspection needs. The most effective and resource-efficient solution is then selected, alternatives are identified, resources are gathered, and the inspection element is implemented. A process for evaluating and revising the inspection element is also developed.

Selection and Design

A fire inspection division typically consists of one service or a combination of inspection/enforcement, plans review, and building code enforcement services. Selecting the appropriate approach to fire inspection depends on the needs of the service area, resources available, and decisions of the project management team. If the jurisdiction has a building official or department, the chief officer should work closely with that individual or department to ensure coordination in the code enforcement process. A strong personal and professional relationship also improves the possibility for code adoption, alterations, and approval.

Inspection/Enforcement

Inspection/enforcement services involve the physical inspection of certain occupancy classifications on a periodic basis **(Figure 5.4)**. The authority to perform such inspections is found in the jurisdiction's fire code or local ordinances. Chief officers should establish guidelines based on code requirements for the frequency of inspections. The owner/occupant is also required by law to comply with the requirements made by the inspector.

Inspections should be performed in a consistent manner, regardless of the occupancy type or level of hazard. This consistency prevents any appearance of preferential treatment or discrimination on the part of the inspector. It also ensures accurate and effective inspections are performed.

Figure 5.4 Regular fire inspections of buildings can reduce the risk of fire in those buildings.

The occupancy classifications that must be inspectioned vary based on the AHJ. Occupancies may be classified differently depending on the fire code that the AHJ adopts. Examples of occupancy classifications that typically require inspections include the following:

- **Public assembly** — Theaters, arenas, places of worship, large-area tents, convention centers, and restaurants
- **Educational** — Public and private schools, colleges, and universities
- **Institutional** — Hospitals, clinics, correctional facilities, nursing homes, and day-care centers
- **Residential** — Multifamily dwellings, hotels, and motels (does not include the individual living quarters)
- **Business** — Office buildings, fire stations, and police stations
- **Industrial** — Automobile assembly plants
- **Manufacturing** — Machine shops
- **Storage** — Warehouses
- **Mercantile** — Retail shops and malls
- **Special properties** — High-hazard properties such as lumberyards, chemical plants, petroleum processing facilities, and aircraft hangars

Fire codes, local ordinances, and organizational resources impact the frequency and type of inspections. Prioritization of these inspections often comes from the risk analysis. Most occupancy types are inspected annually, although some sites may require semiannual or biannual visits. Other inspections can be made when the following situations occur:

- Alterations made to the structure
- Occupancy use changes
- Building/fire code changes
- Structure is vacated
- Emergency response is made to the structure
- Complaint filed
- Owner/occupant request

Plans Review

Plans reviews conducted by fire and emergency services personnel help to ensure that fire prevention and life safety requirements of the building code are properly applied to new construction and structural renovations **(Figure 5.5)**. It also provides the fire and emergency services organization with an opportunity to identify any changes that have occurred in the structures they must protect.

The fire and emergency services plans review officer may hold a liaison position in the building official's office. This officer needs to be trained in plans review procedures and knowledgeable about fire and building codes. The fire inspector may be responsible for reviewing and issuing permits for the private fire protection systems plans. In other jurisdictions, depending upon the size and knowledge of staff, such plan reviews may be contracted

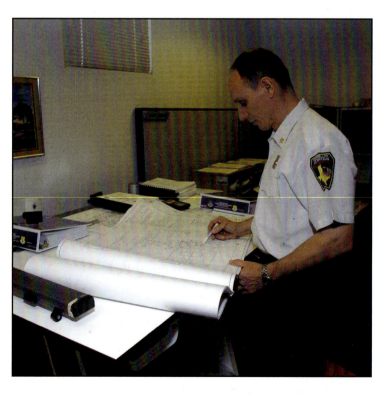

Figure 5.5 A plans examiner reviewing a set of blueprints (plans) for a construction project.

out to qualified private consultants. The jurisdiction can establish a standard list of requirements that apply to each plans review. A few examples of these requirements include the following:

- Visual address format and location
- Key lockbox for access requirements **(Figure 5.6)**
- Dumpster® placement (required distance from building)
- Computer-aided design (CAD) building plans for fire and emergency services department/organization prefire planning

Building Code Enforcement

The fire and emergency services organization may also be responsible for administering the building code through plans review, inspection, and permitting. Nonemergency personnel who are experts in the process may be hired to perform the tasks. A chief officer may be in charge of the unit or may only be responsible for overseeing the review of fire protection systems.

Figure 5.6 Some jurisdictions require businesses and government facilities to install key boxes to assist fire and emergency services in gaining access to the structures during an emergency.

When a separate department provides the building code enforcement function, coordination must occur between the fire and emergency services organization and code enforcement agency. This coordination ensures that there is continuity in services rendered and that decisions made are consistent between departments. It also ensures that the requirements and needs of the fire and emergency services organization are incorporated in building design.

Alternatives

Because code inspections are performed on private property and code violations may cost the owner/occupant to make changes, the program must have the official approval of the jurisdiction. This approval, by ordinance or model fire code adoption, provides the fire and emergency services organization with the authority of law to perform the inspections and require the alterations. It also sends a message to citizens that the code enforcement policy is not arbitrary but is intended for their own safety and well-being.

Chief officers need to be prepared to propose, justify, and defend the adoption of a model building and fire code. Model codes, which in most states or territories can be amended to meet local needs, are a standardized approach to providing engineered fire prevention and life safety in new and renovated structures. The codes also provide the inspector with a set of standards to evaluate the safety of occupancies. All states and territories in the U.S. and all provinces in Canada have building and fire codes that have been legally adopted. See **Appendix G**, Model Building and Fire Codes, for more information on building and fire codes.

If a jurisdiction does not approve the creation of an inspection program, then some other alternatives need to be developed. Alternative solutions may include the following:

- Place the code enforcement authority within the law enforcement agency.
- Provide voluntary inspections at the request of owner/occupants.

- Provide inspections only when complaints are made regarding a specific occupancy or structure.
- Develop a partnership with insurance firms to provide the inspections.
- Allow for or contract with other governmental agencies for code enforcement inspections.

These choices are not equivalent to the formal, authorized fire inspection function of the department. However, they will have some success in addressing code violations and focus citizen attention on the need for a program.

Implementation

Once selected and designed, the program must be put into operation. The chief officer or team establishes a timeline for implementation, determines resources, creates an organizational chart, and assigns tasks. Resources, including funding, personnel, training, and equipment need to be identified and allotted to the project.

Implementing a fire inspection and code enforcement element creates a need for personnel resources. An estimate of the resources required should be included in the initial proposal before adoption to provide the jurisdiction's political leadership with an idea of the personnel resources required and the options available. Program staffing may be accomplished through a number of methods including but not limited to the following:

- **Full time** — Career or paid personnel assigned full-time to the inspection function
- **Part time** — Career or paid personnel who perform the inspection function in addition to other duties
- **Nonemergency** — Personnel who are tasked specifically for the inspection function and may not be trained firefighters or emergency responders
- **Emergency** — Company personnel or emergency responders who perform the inspection function as a part of their duties
- **Volunteer** — Community volunteers who have a background in building construction or plans review and perform the inspection function without pay

An inspection unit may consist of a chief officer as the fire marshal, an assistant, one or more plans reviewers, one or more inspectors, and administrative/clerical personnel. In small organizations, the inspection function may be given to a company officer who reports directly to the organization's chief/manager. How personnel are organized in the inspection function depends on the resources available to the unit.

An appeals or review board also needs to be established. This board is usually composed of individuals representing the building trades, owners/occupants, and architects in the community. Their responsibility is to hear appeals to code violation citations and mediate resolutions. Descriptions of the board, its establishment, its rules of operation, and its authority are found in most model building and fire codes.

Evaluation/Revision

Close monitoring and evaluation of the inspection program will indicate the need for any revisions. Revisions to the inspection program that the evaluation step indicates are intended to bring the actual outcomes in line with the desired outcomes. The results of the evaluation may indicate that a revision is necessary and may include a change in the code, realignment of resources, or better public awareness and acceptance processes (among others).

The evaluation may indicate the need to amend the current fire prevention code to improve the outcome of inspections. To make this revision, the chief officer collects the necessary data to support an amendment. The amendment is written with input from citizens and stakeholders. Because the amendment requires a change to the law or ordinance, the jurisdiction's legal department is also involved. When the amendment request is formally presented to the jurisdiction's political leadership, the chief officer must be confident that it is justified and supported by citizens and stakeholders.

Evaluation may also indicate that a lack of resources contributed to an unacceptable outcome. If a specific resource is lacking, the chief officer can focus on providing that element. This element may require:

- Additional training
- Hiring additional personnel
- Altering work schedules
- Seeking grants or gifts
- Implementing an alternative inspection program

Inspection programs require the complete support of the service area for it to be successful. If evaluation indicates that this support is missing from the program, then a more effective approach to public awareness needs to be taken.

Public Awareness and Acceptance

A fire prevention inspection program is founded on the willingness of citizens to:

- Permit inspections of private properties.
- Submit to restrictions and controls on their environments and behaviors based on interpretations of the building and fire codes.
- Agree to alter anything that does not meet code requirements.

To achieve these compliances, the inspection program must have community involvement and communication. The amount of each determines the amount of public awareness and acceptance.

Citizens must be involved in the development of these programs to achieve "buy in" from the community. Community leaders and representatives involved in the process need to fully endorse and support the program. They also need to be involved in creating and implementing the appeals process.

Open communications also help to ensure the success of the program. First, the initial adoption of the fire prevention code needs to be well publicized. Announce all public meetings for citizens to review and comment on the proposal, and schedule meetings to ensure maximum attendance. This process may require that multiple meetings take place at various times and locations. Encourage the media to broadcast the event live to the service area.

Next, the public education program can market the benefits of the inspection program to the public. Use brochures, posters, public service announcements, and articles in the media to describe the advantages of a thorough inspection program. The USFA and other organizations have information and materials that can assist in this educational campaign. Finally, the inspections themselves depend on good communications.

The owner/occupant of the occupancy should be contacted before the inspection to make an appointment. During the inspection, the inspector should explain to the owner/occupant the fire and safety hazards that are uncovered and how they can be removed. To set the right tone, inspectors should make positive statements regarding the conditions whenever they are appropriate. Once the inspection is complete, the applicable code requirements should be written and explained. Finally, inspectors should set a time for reinspection, which the code requires to ensure compliance. Always encourage questions and explain the appeals process in detail. Neither the inspector nor the owner/occupant should perceive the inspection and code enforcement process as adversarial. Public awareness and acceptance demand that customers view inspections as life safety benefits that they are involved in creating.

Chapter Summary

Fire and emergency services organizations can significantly reduce the number of fires and emergency incidents and the resulting fatalities, injuries, and property losses through the delivery of carefully designed fire prevention and public life safety programs. Once needs have been identified, organizational personnel, community stakeholders, and other civic leaders can develop a program tailored for the community. Once approved and implemented, fire and emergency services organization personnel should frequently evaluate the program to ensure it is meeting its intended goals. The inspection component is another important aspect of the fire prevention and life safety program. Inspections ensure that adopted codes and standards are adhered to. This inspection component ensures that occupancies are safe places to live and work and provides a consistent avenue for enforcement.

Review Questions

1. What are the processes used to develop a fire prevention and life safety program? (pp. 216-226)
2. What are the various procedures involved in developing a fire inspection program? (pp. 226-232)

Emergency Services Delivery (Levels III and IV)

Courtesy of Ron Jeffers.

Chapter Contents

CASE HISTORY 237

III Resource Planning 239
Mutual and Automatic Aid Agreements 239
Joint Training Requirements 239

Incident Action Plan 240
IAP Development 242
IAP Forms 243

Post Incident Analysis 244
Types of Post Incident Analysis 245
Development Procedures 246
Incident Data 247
PIA Critique 248
Recommended Changes 248
Documentation 248
Final Reports 249

IV Comprehensive Disaster Plan 249
Disaster Types 250
Interagency Relations 254
Jurisdictional Authority 254
Emergency Operations Center 256
Resource Allocation 256
Plan Implementation 257
Incident Termination 258
Recovery and Rehabilitation 259

Incident Management System 260
Components/Operational Positions 260
Integrated Communications 263
Unified and Area Commands 263

Chapter Summary 270
Review Questions 270

chapter 6

Key Terms

Area Command..263
Emergency Operations Center (EOC)....256

Unified Command.....................................263

NFPA® Job Performance Requirements

This chapter provides information that addresses the following job performance requirements of NFPA® 1021, *Standard for Fire Officer Professional Qualifications* (2014).

Level III	Level IV
6.6.1	7.6.1
6.6.2	7.6.2
6.6.3	

Emergency Services Delivery (Levels III and IV)

Learning Objectives

After reading this chapter, students will be able to:

[Level III]

1. Describe various methods used to plan for additional mutual aid and training resources. (6.6.3)
2. Identify the various components of an incident action plan (IAP). (6.6.1)
3. Describe the process of completing a postincident analysis (PIA). (6.6.2)

[Level IV]

4. Explain ways to develop a comprehensive disaster plan. (7.6.1, 7.6.2)
5. Identify the various elements that comprise the Incident Management System (IMS). (7.6.1, 7.6.2)

Chapter 6
Emergency Services Delivery (Levels III and IV)

Courtesy of Ron Jeffers.

Case History

On February 7, 2010, a major explosion occurred in a power plant under construction near Middletown, Connecticut. The blast killed six workers and injured 50 others. Having multiple contractors working on the project made it difficult to determine the number of workers on-site and if any were missing. An Urban Search and Rescue team attempted to locate possible survivors trapped in the rubble.

The magnitude of the damage, the unknown number of potential victims, and the possible presence of hazardous materials caused the activation of the state Incident Management Team (IMT) plan. Fire, law enforcement, and emergency managers combined to form a unified command tasked with rapidly assembling and deploying assets to safely approach the scene. As the incident expanded, many state and federal organizations joined the command based on needs assessments and protocol that the Command staff identified. The IMT developed Incident Action Plans (IAP) for every operational period to safely evaluate and oversee the tactics and tasks carried out over the 17-day period.

Delivering emergency services is one of the primary functions of all fire and emergency services organizations. The variety and types of services depend on the needs of each individual community or service area. The hazard, risk, or needs analysis that was discussed in previous chapters of this manual determine the needs. Following the thorough analysis of the service area and the creation of a prioritized list of needs, the department prepares the mission statement listing the goals and objectives to meet those needs.

NFPA® 1021 assigns emergency services delivery duties to both Level III and Level IV chief officers. The Level III requirements include managing multiagency planning, deployment, and operations as follows **(Figure 6.1, p. 238)**:

- **Planning process** — determine the need for additional resources beyond what the local department provides
- **Deployment** — prepare an action plan so that the required resources are determined, assigned, and mobilized to resolve the incident
- **Operations** — develop and conduct post incident analyses of single and multiagency incidents

Figure 6.1 Chief officers may manage multi-agency fire incidents. *Courtesy of Ron Jeffers.*

While these requirements focus on multiple-agency operations, most chief officers will be responsible for incidents involving single- or multiple-fire company operations. The basic skills required for both large and small incidents are the same, which include:

- Understanding strategy and tactics
- Following incident management systems
- Planning
- Analyzing
- Coordinating

NFPA® 1021 states that Level IV chief officers must be able to develop a comprehensive plan to resolve major disasters quickly and effectively. The plan integrates other agencies' resources to rapidly and effectively mitigate the effect on the service area.

The Level IV chief officer responsible for these duties must have knowledge and understanding of all of the following:

- Jurisdiction's major incident policies and procedures
- Physical and geographical characteristics of the service area
- Service area demographics
- Incident management system
- Local communications systems
- Contractual and mutual aid agreements that are in effect and the local, state/territorial/provincial, and federal regulations that govern such operations
- Resources that are available

III. Resource Planning

Chapter 4 presented the concept of developing plans to match the community's needs to the fire and emergency services organization's resources. The fire and emergency services organization may be unable to meet the needs with current resources, which may require additional planning. Alternative methods must be developed with supporting policies, procedures, agreements, and training for the worst possible emergency.

Mutual and Automatic Aid Agreements

Based upon service area needs determined during needs assessment (see Chapter 4), jurisdictions and organizations may enter into mutual aid or automatic aid agreements to meet needs that they cannot meet individually. At this level of planning, many jurisdictions have come together and expanded the planning and resource development to include regional and state level special response teams. These teams include, but are not limited to, hazmat, technical search and rescue, and other specialized response needs.

Depending on population density and the geographic arrangement of communities and jurisdictions, most fire and emergency services organizations share common boundaries with other similar organizations in the surrounding area. Industrial fire brigades or military fire and emergency services organizations may also be within or adjacent to a municipality's boundaries. Each of these organizations is a potential mutual/automatic aid partner for a major emergency. They are also potential resources for services that the local fire and emergency service organization do not provide, such as aircraft fire fighting or hazardous materials response teams.

Mutual Aid

Most North American fire and emergency services organizations have mutual aid agreements with neighboring departments and other agencies. While these agreements may be verbal, a written agreement is preferred. This arrangement allows each organization to provide services on a more cost-effective basis. Each department agrees to send assets when requested. The response may be optional if department chiefs determine that it will endanger their ability to protect their communities.

Automatic Aid

Many organizations have automatic aid agreements with neighboring communities in which the closest appropriate resources are dispatched to the incident regardless of jurisdiction. These agreements may also provide for automatic *move-up* or temporary resource allocation for communities that are involved in large-scale or long-term operations. Personnel and apparatus are moved into vacant facilities where these resources assume the responsibility for incidents in that area.

Joint Training Requirements

Joint training agreements may take many forms. For instance, a large metropolitan fire and emergency services organization may have a contract to provide recruit training to firefighter candidates from surrounding smaller suburban departments. This approach is both economical and ensures operational consistency when mutual aid is needed.

Joint training can also include members of other municipal departments who may respond with or assist fire and emergency services personnel. For example, public works department heavy equipment operators may participate in collapse building or trench rescue training.

Joint training for major incidents involving multiple departments or agencies can increase efficiency of all responders. This training has become common place in many urban areas, including representatives from all levels of government. Joint multiagency training is based on the Incident Management Team (IMT) concept.

Incident Action Plan

An incident action plan (IAP) is a written plan for the safe and efficient resolution of an emergency incident. The IAP establishes the strategic decisions, assigned tactical objectives, and support requirements for an emergency incident or preplanned event involving the management of multi-agency planning, deployment, and operations.

The incident commander (IC) must create an action plan and communicate it to those who will implement it. An IAP is an integral part of the incident command system (ICS), and implementing the plan affects how emergency resources are organized. All incident personnel must function according to the IAP.

The initial IC takes the first steps in creating an IAP that can evolve as the incident expands to involve more resources. The initial IC identifies the incident priorities, determines the objectives, and identifies the overall strategy for dealing with the incident, and establishes the tactics for meeting that strategy.

Written IAPs should be required in the following situations:

- Multiagency incidents
- Hazmat incidents
- Confined space incidents
- Multijurisdictional incidents
- Incidents lasting more than one operational period that require changes in shifts of personnel, units, or equipment

IAPs usually contain these elements:

- **Tactical worksheet** — Basis for the development of an IAP
- **Incident Briefing** — Serves as an initial action worksheet (ICS 201 Form)
- **Incident objectives** — Should be SMART: Specific, Measurable, Action-oriented, Realistic, and Timeframe (ICS 202 Form) **(Figure 6.2)**
- **Organization** — Description of the ICS table of organization, including the units and agencies involved (ICS 203 Form)
- **Assignments** — Identifies specific unit tactical assignments divided by branch and division (ICS 204 Form)
- **Support materials** — Includes site plans, access or traffic plans, locations of support activities (staging, rehabilitation, logistics, etc.), and similar resources

INCIDENT OBJECTIVES	1. INCIDENT NAME Billings Warehouse	2. DATE PREPARED 1/25/2007	3. TIME PREPARED 0925

4. OPERATIONAL PERIOD (DATE/TIME)
1/25 0915 to Completion

5. GENERAL CONTROL OBJECTIVES FOR THE INCIDENT (INCLUDE ALTERNATIVES)
Contain fire to northwest corner of warehouse area
Use building fire suppression system to control and eliminate fire
Remove smoke and fire gases from structure to minimize damage to structure
Remove water from fire area
Conduct search of fire area when safe

6. WEATHER FORECAST FOR OPERATIONAL PERIOD
Clear, 35 F, Wind out of southwest at 5 mph, humidity 10%

7. GENERAL SAFETY MESSAGE
Be aware of potential roof collapse hazard
Respiratory protection & pass devices required in all operational areas.
ISO's assigned to all branches
Rehab located at corner of B-C

8. ATTACHMENTS (IF ATTACHED)
- ☐ ORGANIZATION LIST (ICS 203)
- ☐ ASSIGNMENT LIST (ICS 204)
- ☐ COMMUNICATIONS PLAN (ICS 205)
- ☐ ORGANIZATION LIST (ICS 203)
- ☐ ASSIGNMENT LIST (ICS 204)
- ☐ COMMUNICATIONS PLAN (ICS 205)
- ☐ _____
- ☐ _____
- ☐ _____

202 ICS 3-80	9. PREPARED BY (PLANNING SECTION CHIEF) J. E. FORTNEY	10. APPROVED BY (INCIDENT COMMANDER) E. C. KIRTLEY

Figure 6.2 An example of an incident objectives form.

- **Safety message** — Information concerning personnel safety at the incident; may also be part of the incident safety plan developed by the incident safety officer (ICS 208 or 208H Form).
- **List of departmental resources** — Initially, these resources will be the first assignment personnel and apparatus that are at the incident, in a staging location, or en route.
- **Mutual Aid/Automatic Aid Resources** — Contact information, radio frequencies, and resources from mutual or automatic aid units, departments, or organizations that can provide assistance should also be listed.

NOTE: Additional resources are generally listed on the preincident plan for the specific location. These specialized units may be needed to control a specific hazard, such as hazardous chemicals at the site or a complete assignment used to fill a second or higher alarm.

The plan is divided into operational periods consisting of specific time intervals. Operational periods may be as short as 2-hours or as long as 24-hours. The duration of the operational periods may vary, depending on the complexity and type of incident, the estimated time to terminate the incident, the number of involved units and agencies, and environmental and safety considerations.

The written IAP is maintained at the incident command post and updated or revised as warranted or at the end of the specified time interval. At the end of the incident, the plan is used as part of the post incident analysis and critique. A written IAP must also have an ICS 205 Incident Radio Communications Plan and an ICS 206 Medical Plan.

IAP Development

The incident commander (IC) develops the IAP through a series of steps. These steps are:

- Understand the situation
- Identify the incident priorities
- Determine the incident objecties
- Develop the plan
- Prepare and disseminate the plan
- Execute, evaluate, and revise the plan

Understand the Situation

The first step in IAP development is to understand the situation based on the initial dispatch information, knowledge of the structure or site, an understanding of fire behavior, and the type of hazard. The IC must be able to predict what may happen based on what has happened and the amount of time the incident has been developing. IAPs should be used for any type of emergency incident.

Identify the Incident Priorities

The IC determines the incident priorities that then serve as the basis for decision making for the entire incident. From these priorities, the strategy and its supporting tactics are developed. The acronym LIPS stands for **(Figure 6.3)**:

- Life safety
- Incident stabilization
- Property conservation
- Societal restoration

NOTE: Life safety includes both civilians and emergency responders.

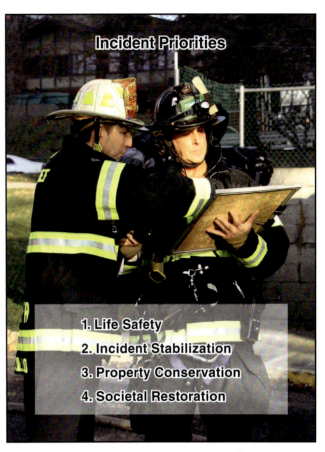

Figure 6.3 The incident commander must determine the incident priorities for each incident. *Courtesy of Ron Jeffers.*

Determine the Incident Objectives

Incident objectives are developed from what the incident priorities are determined to be. These objectives assist the IC in determining the strategy and tactics to be applied to the incident.

Develop the Plan

The IAP is based on the information gathered about the incident. For small incidents, the IC can observe the situation, mentally develop the plan, and assign resources as needed. At an exterior fire involving Class A materials, the IC can direct members of his or her own crew to apply an extinguishing agent efficiently to control the spread of embers.

Prepare and Disseminate the Plan

The plan must be communicated to all units and individuals operating at the scene before they receive a work assignment. This communication may be done in person or radio. Incident personnel must function within the IAP's scope; actions taken outside the IAP's scope are called freelancing and may place responders in jeopardy and reduce operational effectiveness. Fire officers should follow agency's standard operating procedures. Incident personnel should work toward achieving the incident objectives, strategies, and tactics specified in the plan.

Execute, Evaluate, and Revise the Plan

All command personnel must be briefed on the IAP through an operational briefing. When all personnel understand their positions, roles, and functions in the ICS, resources can be used to safely, effectively, and efficiently accomplish the plan. The IC uses Command and general staff to monitor and evaluate the operation's progress. If the current tactics are not achieving the incident objectives, then the plan must be revised. It may be necessary to shift from an offensive, interior attack strategy to a defensive, exterior strategy. All units must be notified of the change in strategy and their withdrawal monitored.

IAP Forms

Written IAPs should be developed using the NIMS-ICS forms. The IC can use these forms to list incident information, look at it quickly, and maintain control of the plan. NIMS-ICS forms include:

- ICS Form 202, Incident Objectives
- ICS Form 203, Organization Assignment List

- ICS Form 204, Assignment List
- ICS Form 205, Incident Radio Communications Plan
- ICS Form 206, Medical Plan
- ICS Form 207, Organizational Chart

Some of these forms are specific to certain types of operations, but most are generic and intended for use with any type of emergency incident. **Table 6.1** identifies the purpose of commonly used ICS Forms.

Table 6.1 Common ICS Forms and Their Purpose

ICS Form	Form Title	Purpose
202	Incident Objectives	Lists clearly stated and measurable objectives to be achieved in the specific time interval
203	Organization Assignment List	Lists descriptions of the ICS table of organization, including the units and agencies that are involved
204	Assignment List	Lists specific unit tactical assignments divided by branch, division, and group
205	Incident Radio Communications Plan	Lists the basic radio channel assignments for use during the incident
206	Medical Plan	Provides information on the location and staffing of the incident medical aid station, types of ambulance resources available, locations of on-site ambulances, and contact information for hospitals that are available
207	Organizational Chart	Provides information on the response organization and personnel staffing

Post Incident Analysis

Following most emergency incidents, a post incident analysis (PIA) of the event is made to determine the operational strengths and weaknesses of the incident response. Large multiagency incidents may result in multiple levels of government evaluating the cause of the incident and steps that emergency responders took to control it. The evaluation can help determine how they could have been better prepared or more effective.

Single-agency incidents are also analyzed to determine the effectiveness of the organization's strategy and tactics and the existence of any safety-related conditions. The organization can require additional training, allocate additional resources, or generate appropriate policy and procedure changes to resolve any apparent deficiencies. This section explains:

- Developing post incident procedures
- Gathering information for the analysis
- Critiquing the analysis
- Recommending changes
- Creating reports on the analysis of the incident and process

Types of Post Incident Analysis

The United States Fire Administration (USFA) divides PIAs into two categories: informal and formal. While PIA formats vary, they are simply variations of these two categories.

Informal

The informal PIA or debriefing is normally held at the company level, although multiple units may be involved. A company officer or incident commander leads the debriefing immediately after incident termination. Weather permitting, the debriefing may be held at the incident scene **(Figure 6.4)**. Being on scene permits crew members to walk through the site, point out physical barriers, describe actions, and observe conditions that may not have been evident to them during the incident.

Figure 6.4 An informal PIA or debriefing following a high-rise incident.

If weather or fireground conditions are too hazardous to permit an on-scene debriefing, then it can be held upon return to quarters. In either case, the debriefing should be held as soon as possible. Informal debriefings are a learning exercise for all crew members. They can be especially helpful for newly hired personnel or recent transfers to the company as a means of helping them learn their duties and become part of the team.

Informal debriefings do not normally need to be documented. However, near-miss situations, incidents resulting in injuries, or incidents that may require a change in SOPs or training should be documented.

Formal

The formal PIA is a detailed review and analysis of large-scale or tactically-challenging incidents. These incidents normally involve a large-scale response and/or assistance from other outside agencies. Incidents requiring a formal PIA may include:

- Natural disasters
- Terrorist attacks
- Mass casualty incidents
- Major fires
- Incidents resulting in multiple injuries or deaths
- Incidents resulting in firefighter line-of-duty deaths
- Building collapse
- Hazardous material incidents
- Confined space rescue
- Transportation disasters
- Large-scale wildland fires

A chief officer who was not involved in the incident usually facilitates a formal PIA. All participants, or their representatives, meet to discuss the strategy and tactics used, problems encountered during the incident, and any SOPs or training changes that should be made to address any deficiencies.

Development Procedures

The procedures for conducting a PIA should be outlined in each organization's policy and procedures manuals. The PIA process should ensure that the analysis is used consistently and results are applied to correct deficiencies or celebrate successes. Developing the analysis procedures is similar to developing any policy or procedure. Consider these actions in the development process:

- Seek full participation and input from each organization's membership
- Define goals
- State the purpose clearly
- Assign authority for making the analysis
- List types of data to be collected
- List and provide materials for the analysis
- Explain how the analysis will be used
- Establish methods for record keeping
- Establish implementing, monitoring, evaluating, and revising procedures

Once PIA procedures are developed, they should be tested to ensure that they meet the desired goals. Testing may occur as part of a training exercise or following an actual incident. When testing is complete and the PIA procedures are determined to be accurate and effective, they must be implemented, continuously monitored, evaluated for strengths and weaknesses, and revised as needed.

Implementation

Disseminating notice of the PIA policy and procedures is the first step in the implementation process. Members of each organization and agency that are subject to the policy must be informed of its development and its effective date. The next step is to provide training to the personnel who will use the analysis policy. Role-playing and exercise critiques help personnel learn what to look for at incidents and how to provide that information to the ISO or other officers responsible for the analysis. When training is complete, the policy is implemented.

Monitor, Evaluate, Revise

Because PIAs help monitor and evaluate operational procedures and activities, the monitoring and evaluating of the process must be based on sound criteria to be used as standards. A third-party reviewer can increase objectivity through periodic evaluation of the results of the analysis. Any PIA policy revisions must be communicated to the organizations' membership before they are implemented. Some monitoring and evaluating criteria questions are as follows:

- Is the process objective?
- Does it provide the type of information needed for the analysis?
- Are the results valid?
- Do the results accurately indicate any weaknesses?
- Have the weaknesses been corrected through policy/procedure corrections or training?

Incident Data

The officer assigned to this part of the analysis must gather and record data objectively. The PIA is not intended to place blame or punish personnel for perceived infractions of policies or procedures. It should be used to improve the effectiveness and efficiency of responders and to increase scene safety. Two primary areas of analysis are the application and effectiveness of the operational strategy and tactics and personnel safety.

Evolution of the Incident

The officer assigned to coordinate the development of the strategy and tactics section of the PIA may be a member of the Command staff, a section chief, or other officer from the incident. A clear description of the site before the incident is required as a matrix over which to lay the development of the emergency and the actions of the responding units and agencies.

The chief officer gathers information to recreate the events that took place during the incident. Information relating to that specific incident is gathered from these sources:

- Interviews of witnesses and participants **(Figure 6.5)**
- Media observations (photographs and video)
- Operational procedures contained in the IAP
- Communication logs and tapes
- Preincident site plans and inspections
- Structural reports
- Owner/occupant statements

Figure 6.5 A company officer describing part of an incident to the chief officer managing a PIA.

Safety Issues

According to NFPA® 1500 and NFPA® 1521, the incident safety officer (ISO) is responsible for collecting safety related information for a PIA. This officer collects the data from witnesses, participants, reports, incident action and safety plans, and communication logs and tapes. The officer then analyzes the data, reconstructs the incident, and provides recommendations to the organization's health and safety officer and the organization's chief/manager. The primary concerns for this portion of the analysis are to find answers to the following:

- If standard operating procedures/guidelines were followed
- If accidents, injuries, or fatalities were due to deviations from established procedures
- If hazards were properly identified and mitigated
- If procedures need to be reviewed or changed based upon the incident

The department's health and safety officer also evaluates the use of personal protective equipment, the personnel accountability system, rehabilitation operations, hazardous conditions, and any other issues that pertain to personnel safety at the incident. A written report containing recommendations is created and forwarded to each organization's chief or manager.

Personnel safety must be a major responsibility within each element of the ICS structure and should get considerable attention before, during, and after any emergency incident.

PIA Critique

A PIA critique is generally held involving all participating units and agencies **(Figure 6.6)**. The goal of the critique is to acknowledge any weaknesses and strengths evident in the analysis. It is not intended to find blame or punish anyone or any unit. Safety issues are highlighted as well as strategic and tactical concerns.

Recommended Changes

When the analysis and critique are complete, each organization's chief/manager or administrative staff makes any necessary changes to the operational strategy, tactics, policies, and procedures. Changes to written policy and procedures are announced to each organization's membership. Any weaknesses in skills must be corrected with additional training, which may be applied to the units that participated in the operation or each organization.

Documentation

Formal PIAs must be documented to include reports and logs compiled during the incident by the command and general staffs. A checklist of documents should be created to assist in gathering the necessary reports.

Incident Reports

Incident reports provide a basic description of the event. They include detailed information such as dispatch, arrival, and return to service times, unit assignments, fireground descriptions, and command decisions.

Informal Debriefing Records

Informal debriefing records are based on the individual unit discussions that the company officers have gathered. These records include a description of crew members' actions and their observations of the event from their location and perspective.

Critique Records

The records developed during the formal critique are also maintained with the other documents. These records may include documents that the other agencies compiled from all levels of government, automatic and mutual aid agreements, the incident action plan, and the safety plan.

Reimbursement Logs

Large-scale incidents may require the purchasing or leasing of equipment or hiring people with specials knowledge or skills. The state/provincial or local AHJ purchasing/leasing policies must be followed and exact records kept of all expenditures. These records will include contracts, sales receipts, agreements, and time sheets indicating hours worked.

Figure 6.6 A chief officer listening to two company officers describing their units' roles in an incident.

Records Management
Copies should be made of each document collected and can be used for report writing, meetings, and research. Originals are maintained in a file in the department headquarters or the AHJ's finance office. A log or list of each document should be maintained to ease locating the original and identifying the copies.

Final Reports
Two types of reports are made on the PIA: (1) Results of the analysis, focusing on the specific incident and the recommended changes or additional training and (2) Effectiveness of the PIA policy and recommendations for any changes to it. Both reports contain the same general information parts: executive summary, statement of events, strengths and weaknesses, and recommendations for changes. The organization's chief or emergency services manager and the appropriate members of the administrative staff need to receive copies of the report. Further distribution is at their discretion or as defined in local protocols.

IV Comprehensive Disaster Plan
Most incorporated communities in North America have legally mandated disaster plans. The fire and emergency services response plan is one element of the community disaster plan. A part of this plan is concerned with the potential risk that large, severe hazards pose. The role of the fire and emergency services organization's chief is critical to the success of the local Emergency Operations Plan. The chief officer and other governmental leaders must work cohesively to develop, write, and practice the plan.

The comprehensive disaster preparedness or response plan is essential to communities and service areas of all sizes. The fire and emergency services organization is usually responsible for developing their portion of the community's plan. Chief officers should work with representatives of other jurisdictional departments and agencies, other levels of government, and citizen representatives to create a plan that will:

- Meet the needs and expectations of the service area
- Explain how to prevent potential disasters
- List the resources needed to respond to potential disasters
- Explain how to restore the affected area in a minimum amount of time
- Establish a protocol for coordinating the activities of all emergency responders
- Provide a plan that is simple yet flexible

Because no plan, no matter how comprehensive, can address all possible situations, the plan needs to be generic enough so that it can be modified to meet as many potential threats as possible. To develop such a plan, chief officers and emergency service managers must:

- Recognize the types of disasters or hazards that are likely to occur in their areas
- Understand the importance of interagency relations
- Determine jurisdictional authority
- Plan resource allocations
- Understand incident prevention measures

Organizations involved in emergency management should divide the process into four phases:

- **Mitigation/prevention** — Activities performed before an emergency event to reduce the probability of occurrence or extent of damage; includes performing hazard analyses, strengthening codes and regulations, and developing plans to lessen or eliminate negative effects.
- **Preparedness** — Activities taken before an event occurs to protect a community; includes identifying hazards, gathering intelligence data, developing response plans, identifying/allocating resources, and establishing interagency agreements.
- **Response** — Actions performed during an event that save lives and protect property and the environment; includes implementing plans, deploying resources, and interacting with emergency operations centers **(Figure 6.7)**.
- **Recovery** — Activities that take place after the emergency event is stabilized to return a community to normal; includes performing cleanup and disposing of debris, restoring utility/transportation services, and rehabilitating affected areas.

Disaster Types

Disasters are any occurrences that inflict widespread destruction or distress. They may affect humans, animals, properties, the economy, or the environment. Some disasters are predictable, allowing for some degree of preparedness, while others are instantaneous. The direct result of a disaster may be devastating yet repairable over the short term. Other results may be long term or even go unrealized for years or decades. Disasters can be categorized by their cause: natural, human-caused, or technological.

Figure 6.7 Fire fighting can be just one part of a fire department's response to a larger disaster. *Courtesy of Bob Esposito.*

Natural

All regions of the world are subject to some form of natural disasters. Some areas are more prone to specific types, but the potential for these types are everywhere. Examples of natural disasters may include **(Figure 6.8, p. 252)**:

- Tornados
- Hurricanes
- Floods
- Droughts
- Wildland and wildland/urban interface fires
- Landslides
- Avalanches
- Earthquakes
- Snow and ice storms
- Temperature extremes
- Environmental epidemics (respiratory diseases such as sinusitis, environmental asthma, and allergies)

Humans cannot prevent most disasters, but the effects can be controlled to varying degrees. Preparation/prevention methods include:

- Implementing land-use controls such as zoning ordinances that prevent building on ridgelines or in flood plains and building codes that require earthquake resistant construction in earthquake prone areas
- Using early warning systems (available through improved weather-forecasting technology) as a way to reduce human losses during natural disasters
- Assisting in preincident planning to ensure that the appropriate controls are in place

  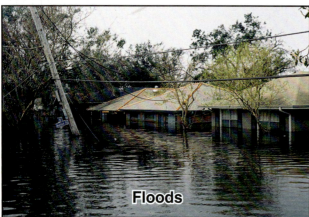 

Figure 6.8 Examples of damage caused by different types of natural disasters. *Hurricane and flood photos courtesy of Chris Mickal/District Chief, New Orleans (LA) FD Photo Unit.*

- Developing multi-agency response plans to deal with the aftermaths of disasters
- Developing contingency plans should emergency service organizations become disaster victims

Human-Caused

Humans may cause intentional or accidental disasters. The purposes of some intentional incidents are to destabilize governments, make political statements, or gain personal fame/power. Firesetters may set fires in a park or trash container that could spread to surrounding structures or forested areas. Other may be the result of human error or failure. Types of disasters that have human causes may be classified as arson, human error, terrorism/war, civil disorder, and political instability.

- **Arson** — Arson fires are usually small-scale events involving single structures, vehicles, or Dumpster® trash containers which can escalate into disasters. Some causes of arson fires are greed, revenge, crime concealment, or the desire for attention. Preparation/prevention methods include:
  - Developing fire prevention and cause determination programs to reduce the likelihood of arson-caused disasters.
  - Developing preincident response plans based on potential arson targets in the service area.

- **Human error** — Fires that occur because of human action or inaction but are not premeditated are defined as human error. Some examples might include failure to completely extinguish a camp fire or collisions of large vehicles or machinery such as cargo ships. Methods of disaster preparation and prevention include:
  — Recognizing that human error is difficult to prepare for or eliminate.
  — Being aware of the potential and prepare for the possibility.

- **Terrorism/war** — The U.S. Federal Bureau of Investigation (FBI) defines terrorism as *"the unlawful use of force or violence against persons or property to intimidate or coerce a government, the civilian population, or any segment thereof, in furtherance of political or social objectives."* Numerous acts of terrorism have occurred throughout the history of the U.S. and Canada **(Figure 6.9)**. Planning for potential terrorist attacks typically focuses on the types of weapons that attackers might have access to and use. Preparation/prevention methods include:

  Figure 6.9 The aftermath of the bombing of the Murrah Federal Building in Oklahoma City, OK. *Courtesy of Mike Wieder.*

  — Preparing for potential threats through awareness, training, planning, and equipping. Some organizations are prepared for some of these events through their abilities to deal with hazardous materials incidents.
  — Gathering information from the U.S. Department of Homeland Security (DHS) regarding response to terrorism and available resources to assist with training and equipping personnel and organizations for such events.

- **Civil disorder** — Civil disorder can result from peaceful protests turning violent or destructive, or the disorder may begin as a riot. Civil disorder usually occurs as a response to perceived injustices or governmental decisions on controversial topics like human rights or environmental policy. Protests may result in arson and other property damage or injuries and fatalities. Preparation/prevention methods include:
  — Focusing preparedness plans on an awareness of the potential and ability to respond to any type of incident.
  — Preparing fire and emergency service organizations to be targets of civil disorder because they are symbols of government.
  — Developing policies for responding to and dealing with civil disorder before such events occur.

- **Political instability** — The risk of widespread governmental failure or collapse rarely occurs in a democratic society. However, should it occur it can create chaos and severely impede emergency response. Preparation/prevention methods include:
  — Recognizing the importance of multiagency preincident planning and disaster preparedness.
  — Preparing through awareness, training, planning, and equipping to ensure the population's safety.

Technological

Technological disasters involve the failure of technology on a widespread basis covering large geographic areas. An example would be the 2003 electrical power grid failure in the northeastern parts of the U.S. and Canada. The costs in lost productivity and tax revenues have indirect effects on fire and emergency service organizations that depend on tax revenues for funding. Preparation/prevention methods include:

1. Preparing to respond to disasters and reduce the effects on service areas.
2. Conducting essential preincident planning with other agencies to reduce the long-term effects of these and other disasters.

Interagency Relations

A comprehensive community disaster plan depends on the ability of local agencies to work together. Strong relationships between agencies that may be involved in multiagency incidents must be the goal of all chief officers and emergency service managers. These relationships are based on open communications, understanding, and mutual respect.

Developing a comprehensive community disaster plan begins with the formation of an interagency planning team. The steps outlined in the Unified Command (UC) part of the Incident Command System section are applicable to the disaster plan, too. The same agencies are involved in this planning process. Each agency has a stake in the results and has valid input into developing the plan. Part of this planning process involves determining jurisdictional authority at all types of incidents.

Jurisdictional Authority

Jurisdiction can be illustrated in two ways: vertical or horizontal **(Figure 6.10)**. *Vertical jurisdiction* involves multiple levels of government. For instance, the municipal fire and emergency services organization responds to a hazardous materials spill that leaks into a river. While the fire and emergency services organization is in initial command of the incident, the arrival of state water resources agency personnel may mean that its jurisdiction takes priority. State authority may be overridden when representatives of the U.S. Environmental Protection Agency (EPA) arrive on the scene.

An example of *horizontal jurisdiction* is an incident that covers multiple jurisdictions such as a wildland fire that crosses county or state borders. Agencies from different states must agree who will be in charge of the operation or form a multi-agency emergency scene management team to provide a Unified Command (UC) system. The Federal Emergency Management Agency (FEMA) recommends the creation of area contingency plans (ACPs) to prepare for responding to multijurisdictional incidents.

The National Incident Management System (NIMS)-based ICS/UC can be used as the model for response management in the ACP to ensure an effective response. Consider the following items when developing ACPs:

- Jurisdictional responsibilities
- Roles of all governmental levels in the UC (federal, state/provincial/territorial, and local)

- Relationship between the Federal On Scene Coordinators (FOSC) and other officials who also have decision-making authority but are not part of the UC
- Financial agreements
- Information dissemination
- Communications
- Training and exercising
- Logistics
- Lessons learned

An important application of the ICS/UC concept to a response action can be seen in federal or provincial response to major disasters for the purposes of assisting local governmental agencies. Legislation has been created in both the U.S. and Canada that allows the highest levels of government to provide federal/provincial resources response to mitigate the consequences of a disaster.

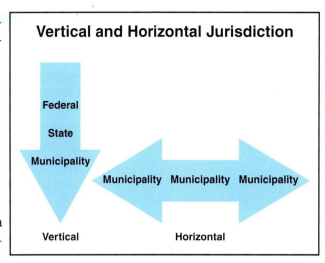

Figure 6.10 Illustrating the concepts of vertical and horizontal jurisdiction.

The Robert T. Stafford Disaster Relief and Emergency Assistance Act established the U.S. federal government programs and processes for providing disaster and emergency assistance to states, local governments, tribal nations, individuals, and qualified private nonprofit organizations. The provisions of the Stafford Act cover all hazards including natural disasters and terrorist events. Relevant provisions of the Stafford Act include the following:

In the United States a process for Governors to request Federal disaster and emergency assistance from the President. The President may declare a major disaster or emergency:

(1) *If an event is beyond the combined response capabilities of the State and affected local governments; and*

(2) *If based on the findings of a joint Federal-State-local Preliminary Damage Assessment (PDA), the damages are of sufficient severity and magnitude to warrant assistance under the Act. (Note: In a particularly fast-moving or clearly devastating disaster, DHS may defer the PDA process until after the declaration.)*

   a. *If an emergency involves an area or facility for which the Federal Government exercises exclusive or preeminent responsibility and authority, the President may unilaterally direct the provision of emergency assistance under the Stafford Act. The Governor of the affected State will be consulted if practicable.*

   b. *DHS can pre-deploy personnel and equipment in advance of an imminent Stafford Act declaration to lessen or avert the effects of a disaster and to improve the timeliness of disaster response.*

   c. *When an incident poses a threat to life and property that cannot be effectively dealt with by the State or local governments, the Governor may request the Department of Defense (DOD) to use its resources after the incident occurs but prior to a Stafford Act declaration to perform any emergency work "essential for the preservation of life and property" under Section 403 of the Stafford Act.*

Emergency Operations Center (EOC) — Facility that houses communications equipment, plans, contact/notification list, and staff that are used to coordinate the response to an emergency.

Emergency Operations Center

When major disasters occur in the U.S., most metropolitan areas activate an **emergency operations center (EOC)** **(Figure 6.11)**. The EOC provides the leadership of the jurisdiction and involved agencies with a protected site from which to manage the incident. The space usually contains individual workstations that are permanently assigned to the various agencies, such as the mayor/city manager, police/law enforcement, fire, medical, EPA, or DHS. Communications systems connect each agency with the central telecommunications and dispatching system. This system provides the jurisdiction's senior management with the ability to command and control operations that are widespread or complex.

The on-site IC or UC staff members constantly provide accurate reports on the incident to the EOC. EOC staff members, in turn, provide resources, contact higher levels of government, and coordinate the activities of agencies that do not have representatives at the incident CP. The use of Internet links between mobile CPs and the EOC as well as video imaging of the incident increases the ability of commanders at both sites to determine the appropriate actions to control the incident. Hazardous materials data, weather reports, and other information can be transmitted to the IC accurately and rapidly from the EOC. Coordination and communication between EOCs at the local, county, state/territorial/provincial, regional, and national levels is critical during major events.

Figure 6.11 An example of an emergency operations center (EOC).

Resource Allocation

Because the scope of a disaster is much wider than a normal incident, more resources are needed. During community disaster planning, resources are identified and assigned based on the type of disaster that could strike the community or service area. The list of resources is maintained at the EOC and in the mobile CP or individual vehicles assigned to district/battalion/division chief officers.

If assistance from the state/territorial/provincial or U.S. or Canadian federal government is requested, then additional resources are made available. In the U.S., the following special teams are available to the FOSC, if needed: *(← Federal on Scene Coordinator)*

- U.S. Coast Guard (USCG) National Strike Force
- EPA Environmental Response Team
- EPA Radiological Emergency Response Team
- Scientific Support Coordinators (National Oceanic and Atmospheric Administration [NOAA] in coastal areas and EPA inland)
- USCG National Pollution Funds Center
- USCG District Response Group
- U.S. Navy Supervisor of Salvage (U.S. Department of Defense)

Depending on the magnitude and scale of the incident, the FOSC may appoint one or more persons to be in charge of hazardous materials spill management, public affairs, media relations, Congressional liaison issues, and legal advice. These persons report directly to the FOSC and support, advise, and keep other key functional managers informed. In disasters where criminal activity is suspected, the FBI may take the lead in investigation, public affairs, and media relations. If the disaster causes multiple deaths and health concerns, representatives from the U.S. Department of Health and Human Services (DHHS) will play a key role in the recovery effort. In the case of terrorist-related incidents, DHS is available to provide support or take command of the incident. In most cases, these agencies will have representatives at both the EOC and the incident CP.

Plan Implementation

Like the multi-agency emergency incident management plan, the comprehensive disaster plan requires preparedness to be effective. Agencies must understand the plan, recognize their role, commit resources, and train in implementing the plan. Guidelines for the implementation of the plan must establish under what conditions the plan is activated, who may declare that a state of emergency exists, and the steps each agency takes to fulfill their responsibilities to the plan.

A state of emergency requiring the activation of the comprehensive disaster plan may occur before the incident, during the incident, or after the incident. The type of incident and its severity determine when the plan is activated. Consider these activation guidelines:

- **Before the incident** — The plan is implemented when there is a strong indication that a potential disaster is about to occur, such as when the NOAA predicts that conditions are favorable for a tornado, hurricane, flood, or other similar type of situation. Efforts focus on preparing for the disaster through evacuation, reinforcement of levies, or relocation of resources. The EOC is staffed throughout the incident and well-coordinated on-site incident CPs are established as needed during and after the incident.

- **During the incident** — The plan is implemented when an emergency rapidly overwhelms existing resources or threatens to involve exposures or hazards. The IC will usually determine if the plan needs to be implemented based on the development of the existing incident. The EOC is activated and staffed to provide support to the on-site commander.

- **After the incident** — The plan is implemented after the disaster has occurred and subsided. These incidents include earthquakes or explosions that are instantaneous and provide no indication that they are about to occur. The EOC is activated as soon as it is safe for participating agencies to travel to the center. Incident CPs are established as needed in affected areas.

All comprehensive disaster plans and multi-agency emergency incident management plans include contingency plans. Contingency plans include these items:

- Alternate communication systems
- Alternate EOC locations
- Secondary resources
- Temporary authority over agencies that do not have representatives at the EOC
- Alternate authority for disaster management in the event the EOC cannot be activated

Training in the activation of the comprehensive disaster plan is essential and must be repeated at least annually or when there is a change in personnel in various agencies. Post incident analyses need to be made of both actual incidents and training exercises. Training exercises need to be as authentic as time, resources, and safety will allow. The element of surprise is not a factor since planning for large-scale training exercises does not permit it. However, the type of disaster and the scope of the event can be kept secret until the exercise begins, which provides a certain amount of surprise for the participants.

As part of any disaster exercise, the emergency medical and health care services need to be involved. Hospitals and emergency care facilities must be prepared to receive large numbers of casualties, some of whom may be contaminated. DHS recognizes emergency room personnel as first responders and has established requirements for respiratory protection as well as personal protective clothing when handling contaminated casualties. Because of this requirement, hospital personnel must be informed and permitted to practice working in these protective ensembles.

Incident Termination

In major disasters, the incident may terminate in phases with personnel, units, or agencies released when they are no longer needed. Phases of termination depend on the type and magnitude of the disaster. In an aircraft crash, for example, the initial fire fighting units may be released when the danger of a fire reigniting no longer exists. Medical personnel remain until all victims or human remains have been recovered. FAA investigators remain until all information and debris have been recovered and removed from the site. The full scope of the incident lasts from the actual crash until the site is hazard-free and can be returned to the owner's control. With tornados or earthquakes, the incident lasts until all post incident rehabilitation is complete. The agency having ultimate authority determines when incident termination can be declared.

Recovery and Rehabilitation

Fire and emergency services organizations are generally responsible for the control of the incident. In the community disaster plan, they can also play a part in the recovery and rehabilitation of the affected area. Recovery and rehabilitation of the affected area and services focus on security, debris removal, and restoration of services. Fire and emergency services organization personnel can assist in these duties as long as they do not interfere with the organization's emergency response requirements.

Security

Law enforcement, military personnel, or private security firms normally provide site security. Fire and emergency services organization personnel may staff roadblocks, provide auxiliary lighting, and remain in the affected area to keep unauthorized persons out of the area.

Debris Removal

Debris removal is usually the task of public works personnel or private contractors. If debris is blocking access or creating a safety hazard, fire and emergency services organization personnel can use power tools that they are trained to operate and remove it. Care must always be taken when working around downed power lines. Only personnel who are trained to operate heavy equipment such as bulldozers and dump trucks should operate them. Fire and emergency services organization personnel can assist with directing vehicle movements in the damaged area.

> **CAUTION**
> To avoid compromising evidence, debris removal must be closely coordinated with law enforcement personnel or other investigative agencies.

Restoration of Services

The first objective is the restoration of the fire and emergency services organization which requires staffing and re-equipping apparatus and facilities that the incident may have depleted or damaged. Once units are ready to respond to new incidents, they may assist in the restoration of other services. This assistance may take many forms, including the use of:

- Apparatus pumps
- Water tanks
- Hose lines to provide water to the affected area
- Generators and auxiliary light units for scene lighting
- Medical first aid stations
- On-site communication services to responders and victims

Incident Management System

An Incident Management System prevents officers from becoming overwhelmed during incidents. It also provides firefighters with a command structure that gives order and structure to their roles and helps to ensure their safety. ICS, as a major part of IMS, is designed to be applicable to small, single-unit incidents of short duration as well as complex, large-scale incidents involving numerous agencies and mutual aid units over a long duration and requiring a unified command (UC) structure. Generally, the public associates multi-agency incidents with large-scale events, such as the September 11, 2001, terrorist attacks or the 2011 Texas wildland fires. These events are certainly symbolic of the need for coordination between various emergency service agencies. At the same time, multi-agency incidents occur daily in communities of all sizes. Traffic accidents on interstate highways result in joint operations between state police, local fire and emergency services organizations, ambulance units, and highway maintenance crews. Meth lab fires in structures require a close relationship between law enforcement and fire officials.

To improve the efficiency of all responding agencies, a multi-agency pre-incident emergency scene management system, including coordination, planning, and training, must be established between agencies within the jurisdiction and with outside agencies representing all levels of government. Additional elements of ICS include:

- Components/operational positions
- Integrated communications
- Unified command
- Implementation
- Incident action plan development
- Command transfer
- Resource accountability
- Incident termination

Components/Operational Positions

ICS builds from the ground up and is the basic operating system for all incidents within a jurisdiction. The transition from a small-scale incident to a large and/or multi-agency operation requires minimal adjustment for any of the agencies involved. The following components work together interactively to provide the basis for clear communication and effective operations:

- Common terminology
- Modular organization
- Integrated communications
- Unified command structure
- Consolidated action plans
- Manageable span of control
- Predesignated incident facilities
- Comprehensible resource management

To understand the application of ICS, chief officers need to be aware of the five major strategy level position descriptions within the ICS structure, which are:

- Command
- Operations
- Planning
- Logistics
- Finance/Administration

NOTE: The incident commander has responsibility for these positions unless they are delegated to other members of the Command staff or response personnel.

ICS combines Command strategy with organizational procedures. While designed primarily for use at fire incidents, much of the organizational design is applicable to other types of emergency incidents that may be encountered, including hazardous material incidents, EMS incidents, specialized rescue situations, and other types of incidents.

Command

The IC is in overall command of an incident and ultimately responsible for all incident activities, including the development and implementation of a strategic plan **(Figure 6.12)**. This process may include making critical decisions and being responsible for their results. The IC has the authority to call resources to the incident and to release them from it. The IC is responsible for:

- Assessing priorities
- Creating incident objectives
- Determining strategic goals
- Developing an IAP
- Assigning tactical objectives
- Developing appropriate organizational structure
- Managing incident resources
- Coordinating overall emergency activities
- Ensuring responder safety
- Coordinating activities of outside agencies
- Authorizing the release of information to the media

Figure 6.12 An incident commander at a large scale incident. *Courtesy of Ron Jeffers.*

If the incident's size and complexity require it, the IC may delegate authority for various duties to others who, together with the IC, form the Command staff. The larger and more involved the incident, the more the IC's duties can and must be delegated to other members of the Command staff. Positions within the Command staff include the safety officer, liaison officer, and public information officer.

Of these three, the incident safety officer (ISO) is the most commonly implemented position. An ISO is appointed to monitor activities at incidents that are involved with life-safety/hazardous situations **(Figure 6.13, p. 262)**. The ISO plays a vital role in the IMS. The ISO must have the authority from the organization's chief and the Incident Commander to immediately suspend, termi-

Figure 6.13 An incident safety officer (ISO) at a confined space incident.

nate, or alter any operation that jeopardizes personnel safety. The ISO is responsible for the development of the incident safety plan and post incident safety analysis. Chief officers filling the ISO position need to be familiar with NFPA® 1500 and NFPA® 1521, *Standard for Fire Department Safety Officer.*

Operations

The operations section chief reports directly to the IC and is responsible for the direct management of all operations that directly affect the primary mission of eliminating the hazard. The Operations Section chief develops the strategy and directs the tactical operations to meet the incident objectives that the IC devises. The Operations Section may be subdivided into as many branches as needed.

Planning

The Planning Section is responsible for the collection, evaluation, dissemination, and use of information concerning the development of the incident. The Planning Section is also responsible for maintaining the status of all resources assigned to the incident. Command will use the information that the Planning Section compiles to develop incident objectives and contingency plans. Specific units under Planning include the Resource Unit, Situation Status Unit, Demobilization Unit, Documentation Unit, and any technical specialists whose services are required.

Logistics

The Logistics Section is responsible for providing the facilities, services, and materials necessary to support the incident. There are two branches within Logistics: Service Branch and Support Branch. The Service Branch includes medical, communications, and food services. The Support Branch includes supplies, facilities, and ground support (vehicle services).

Finance/Administration

The Finance/Administration Section has the responsibility of tracking and documenting all costs and financial aspects of an incident. The Finance/Administration Section is usually activated only on large-scale, long-term incidents. Day-to-day mutual aid responses are usually considered reciprocal and do not require interagency reimbursement.

Integrated Communications

Communications during an emergency incident take a variety of forms. Face-to-face, verbal communication is clearly the best, but the size and complexity of the operation may necessitate also using telephone and radio communication. Mobile and portable radios are normally the primary communications media. The radio communications system needs to reflect the size and complexity of the incident. Routine, day-to-day incidents can usually be handled on a single channel, but larger incidents may require using several channels to allow for clear and timely exchanges of information. Separate channels may be needed for command, tactical, and support functions.

All radio communications should be transmitted in plain English (*clear text*). Codes, abbreviations, and acronyms should not be used because they may not be universally understood. Any misunderstanding can add to the confusion that is often a part of emergency operations, especially those involving more than one agency.

Personnel need to exercise proper radio discipline and follow all protocols. Transmissions should be confined to essential information and kept as brief as possible. Personnel transmitting long messages need to pause at frequent intervals to allow others to transmit with high-priority traffic. Emergency transmissions always have priority over other traffic, and other personnel need to avoid transmitting whenever individuals declare they have emergency traffic. Local protocols dictate how messages are phrased. However, in ICS, personnel should be addressed by their assigned ICS position. The incident commander is always called *IC* or *Command*. The incident name may be included (*Warehouse IC* or *Warehouse Command*) if more than one incident is in progress.

Unified and Area Commands

The key to the success of any multi-agency emergency incident is the existence of a **unified command (UC)** system or structure or **area command (AC)** system based on the ICS model. For complex or large-scale incidents, unified command is essential. Chief officers who are responsible for the coordination or development of a multi-agency plan need to review the ICS materials that are available from the Incident Management System Consortium (IMSC) as well as other materials available from the Department of Homeland Security (DHS). The steps for designing a unified command (UC) system or structure or area command (AC) system include development, implementation, monitoring, evaluating, reporting, and revising. Chief officers must also know how to operate within the UC structure.

In multijurisdictional and multi-agency situations, the UC structure provides greater efficiency and effectiveness. In this instance, UC replaces the single IC with a team of commanders composed of Command personnel from

---

Area Command (AC) — Area Command is an expansion of the Incident Command function and is primarily designed to manage a very large incident that has multiple incident management teams assigned. However, an Area Command can be established at any time that incidents are close enough that oversight direction is required among incident management teams to ensure conflicts do not arise.

Unified Command (UC) — In the Incident Command System, a shared command role in which all agencies with geographical or functional responsibility establish a common set of incident objectives and strategies. In unified command there is a single incident command post and a single operations chief at any given time.

the different jurisdictions and agencies who work together to fulfill the action plan's goals and objectives **(Figure 6.14)**. Team managers know the roles of their own agencies as well as the roles of the other organizations. This unified approach also helps keep the different agencies informed and provides for the best utilization of all the responding organizations.

In UC situations or models, there is usually a principle leader from the standpoint of oversight, depending on the type of response and the lead agency. All agencies should be integrated into the command structure at the level that they can effectively contribute.

Fire and emergency services organization managers need to understand the significance of the team or multi-agency partnership in providing emergency services within the community or service area. The UC system not only increases the effectiveness of the organizations, it also helps promote greater safety through mutual understanding of other agencies' operational goals and procedures. Finally, it provides a cost effective means for using all available resources, including professional skills, personnel, apparatus, equipment, supplies, time, and finances. The team approach has the following advantages:

- **Increased effectiveness of the operational objectives** — The term used to describe this increase in effectiveness is *synergy*, meaning the team as a whole is more effective than the individuals working alone.

- **Leadership stability** — Team leadership remains fairly consistent and focused on the operational goals and objectives, even with changes in the personnel of the group.

- **Increased involvement and representation** — Chief officers and managers of other agencies have a reason to participate in the emergency planning process. The benefits to participation and representation in the multi-agency planning and UC process include increased community image, an opportunity to generate ideas and have input, and justification for budget and policy requests.

- **Increased productivity** — This increase is not only felt at the emergency incident but also in the multi-agency planning, training, or supporting phases as the resources of each organization and participant are applied to the process.

- **Enhanced credibility** — Personal as well as organizational credibility is increased for the chief officer and the agency. Participation demonstrates to other members of the emergency services community and to the public that incident command is not a one-person show but rather a team effort.

- **Networking opportunities plus a professional support system for each participant** — Emergency service managers are able to use their interagency relationships to increase their professional knowledge and skills in areas that are normally closed to them.

- **Improved planning decisions** — Group decisions have the benefit of a variety of viewpoints and increase the quality of the final plan.

- **Variety of solutions** — Members of the group tend to provide a wider variety of solutions based on personal experience, knowledge, and resources.

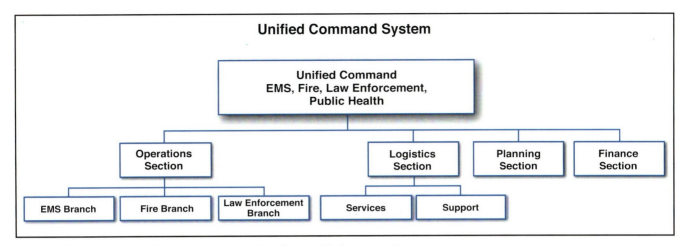

Figure 6.14 An example of an organizational chart for a unified command.

The functions of a UC include:
- Providing overall response direction
- Coordinating effective communication
- Coordinating resources
- Establishing incident priorities
- Developing incident objectives
- Develop strategy to achieve objectives
- Assigning objectives to response structure
- Reviewing/approving incident action plans
- Ensuring integration of response organization
- Establishing protocols

Developing Unified Command Systems

Developing multi-agency emergency incident management systems, partnerships, UC systems, and other interagency procedures follow the general principles of program development previously mentioned. Successful interagency efforts have the following qualities:

- The plan is implemented at the operational level.
- Midlevel managers and chief officers meet with their counterparts in other agencies on a regular basis.
- Personnel are trained on the operational procedures of the plan.
- Communications systems between agencies are frequently tested.
- Trained and certified personnel are in place or developed to meet desired objectives.
- All resources needed to meet objectives are in place or obtained.
- Participants in the plan develop good relationships with each other, show one another proper respect, and use good etiquette to maintain a good rapport.
- The multi-agency concept is understood among the interacting agencies.

The first step in developing the multi-agency incident management system is to identify the potential participants. This list should not consist solely of managers from within the jurisdiction. Representatives from each level of government and each affected agency need to be included. One approach is to begin with a meeting of the elected or appointed leaders (or their representatives) of the various jurisdictions: mayors, city managers, county/parish commissioners, governors, and federal agency/department representatives. This group determines the overall strategic plan for meeting the service area's emergency service needs. They also appoint the emergency service managers from their jurisdictions to serve on the multiagency planning committee. The multi-agency planning committee then applies the planning model mentioned earlier in this manual and takes these steps:

- Identify the current hazards.
- Assess the levels of risk.
- Identify and state how each organization responds to each type of hazard.
- Provide legal justification for each agency's authority over certain situations.
- Explain operational policies and procedures that are used when dealing with the hazards.

The next step is to generate an inventory of the resources that each organization can provide to include **(Figure 6.15)**:

- Adequately trained personnel
- Apparatus
- Facilities
- Materials
- Communications
- Equipment

Next, compare the resource requirements of each hazard with the resources of each organization. The synergy mentioned earlier begins to take effect as the resources begin to fit together like pieces of a puzzle. Where resources are lacking, sources such as other agencies or private vendors, are identified, and procedures are developed to acquire those resources.

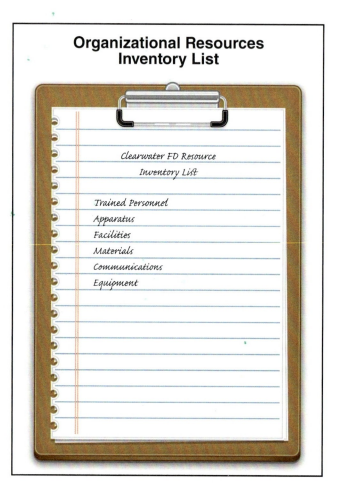

Figure 6.15 An example of the types of resources an organization can bring to a unified command.

The final step is creating the multiagency preincident plan based on:
- Potential hazards
- Available resources
- Operational constraints
- Legal and procedural constraints
- Overall strategic goals

Each agency receives a rough draft of the plan for review and comment. When each organization has had the opportunity to recommend changes or additions to the document, the committee generates the plan in its final form. A timeline for implementation is developed and each agency is assigned the tasks required to make the plan operational.

Implementing Unified Command Systems

To implement the multi-agency incident management system, each agency must train its personnel to understand and use the plan. Each agency must provide the logistical resources that were assigned to it in the plan.

Training begins with inventorying existing skills, identifying skills that must be acquired or improved, and then applying these skills in multi-agency training sessions. Cross training with members of other agencies is vital to understanding the operational procedures of each organization. This training provides for succession of trained personnel to fill Command vacancies if the leadership of a participating agency is incapacitated. When internal training is completed, then interagency training begins, which include these requirements:

- **Training to agreed standards** — Training in the use of similar equipment, terminology, procedures, and processes is critical.
- **Exercising management functions** — Each agency and unit must know its responsibility, role, and authority at a multi-agency incident. Personnel assignments must be based on skills and ability.
- **Gaining and maintaining proficiency in assigned tasks** — Personnel must be thoroughly trained in the duties that they are expected to perform. Continuous practice is essential to maintaining high skill levels.
- **Exercising operational functions** — Exercising is the constant practice of using all the tools and equipment that will be required at the emergency incident.
- **Practicing preincident planning through multi-agency drills** — Periodically, a full-scale drill with the participating agencies needs to be held **(Figure 6.16, p. 268)**. This drill is an opportunity to monitor the effectiveness of the training and proposed response. Consider these factors:
  — Drills need to focus on the activities that occur at the command and operational levels; large-scale training of this type is costly and can be unproductive unless properly planned, conducted, and evaluated.
  — Command scenarios (tabletops or computer-generated simulations) can assist managers in solving large-scale situations. These solutions can then be applied in a single exercise involving representatives of the various agencies and units.

An inventory of available resources provides an indication of the ability of participating agencies to meet identified hazards. The lack of certain equipment, such as chemical protective suits, may prevent the fire and emergency service responders of one agency from fulfilling the objective of controlling an incident. However, the multi-agency system can provide the required equipment from other agencies that possess such equipment. The equipment, its condition, and its location need to be recorded and included in the resource list for use in all Command vehicles and at key locations of participating agencies. Logistical requirements can be met through combined funding requests, such as federal grants or surplus materials/equipment purchases, reducing the time that it takes to acquire the materials/equipment. Two approaches to logistical storage are:

1. **Centralized** — Centralized storage facilities for interagency materials/equipment provide accessibility to all users, but a single incident can destroy all materials/equipment.

2. **Dispersed** — Small groupings of materials/equipment dispersed around the response area can prevent the potential destruction that a single incident can cause, but increases the security requirements at each site.

Figure 6.16 Personnel from multiple agencies participating in a high-rise drill.

Monitoring, Evaluating, Revising Unified Command Systems

Because major multi-agency incidents are infrequent, monitoring the effectiveness of the multi-agency emergency incident management system requires adaptability. The planning committee needs to meet periodically to review the post incident analyses of each incident that involves joint responses. These incidents include transportation incidents, crime scenes, and hazardous materials incidents. Deficiencies need to be evaluated so that recommendations for revisions can be made to the participating agencies.

Continuous monitoring of the system requires all levels of each agency to meet frequently with their counterparts. These meetings help establish and maintain formal and informal lines of communication between the agencies. In an emergency, personnel can relate better to people they are familiar with and who know their organizations, objectives, resources, and limitations.

Equipment, especially communications equipment, must be tested periodically and maintained in a constant state of readiness. A monthly test of the multi-agency emergency notification system needs to be performed to ensure that the UC system can be instituted and staffed in a minimal period of time. Any changes to the call list must be made immediately.

The multi-agency planning committee needs to review and evaluate the plans at least annually to determine changes in requirements, resources, or protocols. When changes are identified, the development process starts over. Evaluating the plan's effectiveness requires the use of a model, such as the systems analysis model. A comparison is made between the goals and objectives defined by the multi-agency incident management plan and the actual application of the plan. Changes in funding, legal requirements, personnel, hazards, or levels of acceptable risk indicate the need for an evaluation of the plan.

Detailed records must be kept to justify any changes or alterations to the system. The planning committee is responsible for revisions to the system. Suggested revisions should not be implemented without the knowledge and authorization of the participating agencies or jurisdictions. External influences (legal, logistical, or even political) that the committee is unaware of may prevent an agency from agreeing with the recommendations.

Reporting on Unified Command Systems

Reports regarding the multi-agency emergency scene management system should be provided to all participating agencies and jurisdictions annually and following any major application of the system or change in the system. These reports should contain:

- An executive summary
- An overview of the system to include the participating agencies and their responsibilities
- A description of the application of the system at specific incident
- The post incident analysis of any incident
- Recommendations for changes based on the evaluation

To maintain public support for the system, issue a press release during the planning process, following system activation, and following any application of the system. The public must be aware of the existence of the system and the benefits it provides. All customers and stakeholders must be informed of the system to ensure continuing support and participation.

Operating within Unified Command Systems

Chief officers must be prepared to operate within a UC structure in accordance with established protocols. Responsibilities of a chief officer in a UC structure may include but are not limited to:

- Developing or assisting in the development of the incident action plan
- Implementing or expanding the incident management system
- Tracking resources
- Transferring command or their part of the command to subsequent commanding officers **(Figure 6.17)**
- Terminating the incident and demobilizing resources

Figure 6.17 An incident commander briefing his replacement on what has already happened at a structural fire. *Courtesy of Ron Jeffers.*

Chapter Summary

Chief officers should be motivators in the establishment of community emergency services, multi-agency emergency scene management systems, and comprehensive disaster plans. As leaders in these activities, they can ensure that effective and efficient services are provided to their service areas. The key to each of these activities is an understanding of and adherence to the Incident Command System and the National Incident Management System. They provide a consistent and reliable process for controlling both large and small incidents with the resources that are available and through interagency cooperation.

Review Questions

1. What methods can the chief officer use to procure additional mutual aid and training resources for his/her organization? (pp. 239-240)

2. What are the components of an incident action plan (IAP)? (pp. 240-244)

3. What actions and elements go into the completion of a postincident analysis? (pp. 244-249)

4. How can the chief officer develop a comprehensive disaster plan? (pp. 249-259)

5. What elements comprise the Incident Management System (IMS)? (pp. 260-269)

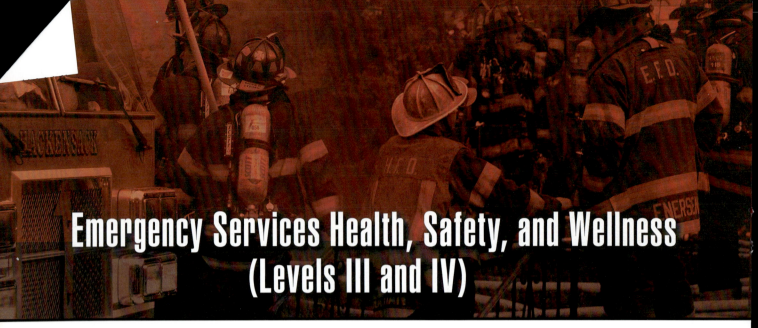

Emergency Services Health, Safety, and Wellness (Levels III and IV)

Chapter Contents

Courtesy of Ron Jeffers.

CASE HISTORY 275

III **Health and Safety Program
Development** 276
- Occupational Safety and Health Committee 277
- Health and Safety Officer Roles and Responsibilities 278
- Health and Safety Program Components 278

**Accident, Injury, and Illness Prevention
Program** 279
- Hazards/Corrective Measures Identification 279
- Program Implementation 286
- Program Monitoring, Evaluation, and Revision 288

IV **Risk Management Plan** 288
- Risk Management Model 289
- Occupational Hazards Analysis 290
- Personnel Risk Analysis 291

Plan Implementation Procedures 293
- Implementation 293
- Monitoring 294
- Evaluation 294
- Revision 295
- System Safety Program 295

Chapter Summary 296
Review Questions 296

chapter 7

Key Terms

Mobile Water Supply Apparatus 284

NFPA® Job Performance Requirements

This chapter provides information that addresses the following job performance requirements of NFPA® 1021, *Standard for Fire Officer Professional Qualifications* (2014).

Level III
6.7.1

Level IV
7.7.1

Learning Objectives

After reading this chapter, students will be able to:

[Level III]

1. Describe various ways to develop a fire department health and safety program.
2. Determine various methods for including an accident, injury, and illness prevention program in a fire department health and safety program. (6.7.1)

[Level IV]

3. Identify the various components of an organizational risk management plan. (7.7.1)
4. Describe procedures for implementing an organizational risk management plan. (7.7.1)

Chapter 7
Emergency Services Health, Safety, and Wellness (Levels III and IV)

Case History

During an annual physical examination, a firefighter/EMT underwent a cardiac stress test. The firefigher was on duty at the time and running on a treadmill in a mobile office/lab parked behind the fire station. During the test, the firefighter began to feel numbness in both arms. The monitoring physician noticed changes in the firefighter's cardiac rhythm and immediately stopped the test. On duty emergency medical personnel were summoned, and the firefighter was transported to the local hospital emergency room. At the hospital, the firefighter was transferred to the cardiac catheterization lab, where a stent was inserted in a blocked artery. After several weeks of recovery, the firefighter was allowed to return to unrestricted duty.

This incident had a positive outcome. The fire and emergency services organization involved was forced to review all aspects of its health and wellness program. This review included an evaluation of existing policies that determined the appropriate course of action in dealing with such an event. Some of the considerations were:

- Was this considered an on duty illness or injury?
- Was the required annual physical appropriate for all members?
- How does the department handle member benefits and compensation for treatment and time off?
- Does the department need to improve wellness initiatives, such as physical fitness, smoking cessation, and nutrition/dietary education?

This incident is an example of how important annual physical evaluations are in the fire service. Annual physical evaluations detect treatable ailments and prevent deaths and long term illnesses for firefighters.

Fire fighting is a high-risk profession occasionally resulting in fatalities or short- and long-term illnesses and injuries. The fire and emergency services organization's administration is responsible for ensuring the risks that firefighters face are minimized. To minimize risks, the administration must establish safe operational procedures, issue personal protective equipment, and provide health and safety programs for the organization's membership.

Some health and safety initiatives are negotiated in labor/management agreements, while the organization's administration develops and initiates others. The organization's chief must provide leadership in developing and maintaining a departmental risk management plan. Once the plan is developed, a complete health and safety program can be created.

If assigned to do so, a Level III chief officer develops, manages, and evaluates the effectiveness of the health and safety program, including an accident and injury prevention program. Each of these programs is described in this chapter.

Ⅲ Health and Safety Program Development

Developing a health and safety program is made easier if current health and safety laws, codes, and standards are used as the foundation for program development. Although these standards have requirements for the department's management, the regulations also contain significant requirements for individual members, such as complying with the occupational health and safety standards. The department's Health and Safety Officer (HSO) is assigned the duty of managing the health and safety program **(Figure 7.1)**. Information on the HSO's duties is contained in IFSTA's **Occupational Safety, Health, and Wellness** and **Fire Department Safety Officer** manuals. Unit supervisors and members must support and follow these programs to improve work environment safety and establish a safety culture in the department. The department's top management should show open and visible support of the program to encourage its success.

Important reasons for implementing an occupational health and safety program include but are not limited to:

- Fulfilling ethical obligations to prevent injuries, illnesses, and fatalities while reducing property loss

- Reducing the frequency and severity of injuries and fatalities involving vehicle collisions, personal accidents, and organizational property damage, which reduces the organizations' costs and expenditures to workers' compensation and liability insurance

- Ensuring compliance with applicable national, state/provincial, and local laws, codes, and standards

An occupational safety and health committee can be an important component of a fire and emergency services organization's health and safety program. The organization's HSO usually serves as the chair of this committee and facilitates its work.

Figure 7.1 A department's Health and Safety Officer (HSO) posting a health and safety bulletin.

NOTE: NFPA® 1021 uses the term *Health and Safety* to describe the program and NFPA® 1521 uses it to describe the position of safety officer. NFPA® 1500 refers to the *Safety and Health* Committee, reversing the term. This chapter adheres to these two variations depending on the usage.

Occupational Safety and Health Committee

According to NFPA® 1500, the safety and health committee functions as a clearinghouse for activities, problems, and issues relating to member health and safety. It may also deal with a multitude of issues. Ensuring member health and safety is a constantly changing process based upon the organization's needs and the administration's commitment to safety. Other factors that can affect the committee's success are the committee's level of activity and the examination and management of current health and safety issues within the organization **(Figure 7.2)**.

The goals of the occupational safety and health committee are to develop and recommend solutions, promote a safety culture, and empower members to practice safe behavior. The committee should not dispense disciplinary action. The activities and issues addressed must be within the committee's scope. Occupational safety and health committee members may be required to perform the following tasks:

- Identify situations that may be a source of danger to members.

- Examine and review alleged violations of the department's safety policy.

- Make recommendations to the administration on matters reported to the committee and on safety related rules and regulations that the outside regulatory agencies create.

- Evaluate organizational safety rules and regulations to ensure compliance with federal/state/territorial/provincial mandates.

- Review the annual injury and illness report for trends.

- Review health and safety inspection reports to assist in correcting identified unsafe conditions or practices.

- Evaluate incident reports to determine if the causes of unsafe acts or conditions were properly identified and corrected.

- Evaluate the accident and injury prevention program and make recommendations for improvement where indicated.

Figure 7.2 Members of a Safety and Health Committee during a meeting.

- Make recommendations to the administration and members for the improvement of members' health and safety.
- Recommend, maintain, and monitor health and safety programs and procedures.
- Review/consider information contained in reports from outside organizations to address health and safety and make recommendations to management regarding these issues.
- Document the attendance and subjects discussed at occupational safety and health committee meetings.

Health and Safety Officer Roles and Responsibilities

The HSO must apply analytical skills to the development and evaluation of a comprehensive health and safety program. NFPA® 1521, *Standard for Fire Department Safety Officer,* specifies the HSO's roles and responsibilities in the health and safety program. The HSO's roles include but are not limited to:

- Ensure safety training and education
- Manage the accident or loss prevention program
- Investigate accidents or incidents
- Maintain records management and data analysis
- Review equipment specifications and assist in acceptance testing
- Ensure program compliance
- Comply with health maintenance requirements
- Serve as internal and external liaison
- Act as infection control officer
- Develop a critical incident stress management plan
- Conduct post incident analyses
- Address workplace violence
- Advocate leadership

Health and Safety Officer Professional Qualifications
Certification of health and safety officers is strongly encouraged. There are national professional organizations and some states/provinces that offer training and certification for HSO personnel.

Health and Safety Program Components

The department's health and safety program consists of several important components to include the following:

- Risk management plan
- Accident, injury, and illness prevention program
- Medical exposure management program

- Member physical fitness and wellness program
- Employee (member) assistance program

The organization's chief is responsible for the risk management plan that will be explained in the Level IV section of this chapter. Level III chief officers are responsible for the accident, injury, and illness prevention program covered in the following sections. See IFSTA's **Fire Department Safety Officer** and **Occupational Health, Safety, and Wellness** manuals for information on the medical exposure, fitness and wellness, and member assistance programs.

Accident, Injury, and Illness Prevention Program

The accident, injury, and illness prevention program is one element of the comprehensive health and safety program. The program provides information and training to the organization's members regarding the hazards within their work environments. These environments include all facilities, apparatus, and emergency incident sites and training exercises. Hazards include:

1. Those chemicals that the organization normally uses and stores
2. Conditions that present a risk of physical injury, damage to the respiratory system, hearing loss, or other occupational illness

Although the fire chief is ultimately responsible for developing the health and safety program, the responsibility may be assigned to a Level III chief officer. The chief officer identifies the life safety hazards, develops the program, assists in its implementation, monitors its progress, evaluates its effectiveness, and recommends needed revisions. The result is a written accident, injury, and illness prevention program tailored to the organization's operations and workplace hazards.

Hazards/Corrective Measures Identification

Determining the hazards that are present in the workplace is the first step in developing an accident, injury, and illness prevention program. The hazards associated with fire suppression may be all too familiar to fire and emergency services members, while those hazards within facilities may not. OSHA's *Job Hazard Analysis* contains a comprehensive list of common workplace hazards and a description of each. Some of these hazards include:

- **Chemical** — Such as toxic, flammable, and corrosive chemicals
- **Explosion** — Resulting from chemical reaction, over pressure
- **Electrical** — Such as shock/short circuit, fire, static, loss of power
- **Ergonomics** — Resulting in strain, human error
- **Excavation** — Resulting in collapse
- **Fall** — Resulting from slip, trip
- **Fire/Heat** — Resulting in physical burns, heat exhaustion, or smoke inhalation
- **Mechanical/vibration** — Resulting in chafing or fatigue to slings, ropes, or belts
- **Mechanical failure** — Resulting from equipment exceeding its design capacity

- **Mechanical** — Resulting in crushing, cutting, tearing, or shearing injuries
- **Noise** — Resulting in hearing loss or damage
- **Radiation** — Including ionizing, nonionizing
- **Struck by** — Resulting from mass acceleration, falling objects, or vehicles
- **Struck against** — Individual initiates an action that results in contact with an object
- **Temperature extreme** — Resulting in heat stress, exhaustion, hypothermia
- **Visibility** — Lack of lighting or obstructed vision
- **Weather phenomena** — Such as snow, ice, wind, rain

Other common workplace hazards that firefighters encounter include:

- Biological exposures resulting from contact with patients
- Occupational illnesses resulting from fire station living arrangements or wearing contaminated PPE, psychological and physiological
- Emotional stress caused by the nature of emergency responses
- Workplace violence – physical and emotional

These hazards may exist en route to or at emergency incidents, during training, or while working in department facilities. Some hazards may be present in one form or another in each of these situations. After identifying and prioritizing the hazards, the appropriate corrective measure(s) can be identified. Corrective action may consist of a policy, procedure, or wearing personal protective equipment, or a combination of them.

Just as the fire and emergency services organization administration is responsible for providing a safe work environment, department members are responsible for adhering to all safety policies, following safety procedures, and using issued safety clothing and equipment. Members are also responsible for their own safety and for reporting hazardous conditions to their supervisors. Safety information is provided during entry-level training and through annual refresher courses. The organization should provide training to ensure that members are aware of their responsibilities in these areas:

- How and when to report injuries and the location of first-aid kits and facilities
- How to report unsafe conditions and practices
- Use, care, selection, and maintenance of required personal protective equipment, including respiratory, hearing, and eye protection **(Figure 7.3)**
- Proper emergency actions to include the exit routes from emergency areas
- Description of the department's comprehensive health and safety program along with the accident, injury, and illness prevention element
- On-the-job review of the requirements for safely performing initial job assignments

Fatalities

The U.S. Fire Administration (USFA) publishes an annual report, *Firefighter Fatalities in the United States*, listing the firefighter line of duty deaths (LODD) for the previous year. The data is divided into categories to include:

- Agency affiliation: career, volunteer, wildland
- Gender
- Incidents resulting in multiple deaths
- Wildland firefighting incidents
- Types of duty
  — Emergency
  — Nonemergency
  — Fireground
  — Responding to/returning from
  — After an incident
  — Training
  — Other on duty deaths
- Cause of fatal injury
  — Stress/overexertion
  — Vehicle crashes
  — Lost/disoriented
  — Caught/trapped
  — Collapse
  — Struck by object
  — Fall
  — Out of air (SCBA)
  — Other
- Nature of fatal injury
- Date, time, and state or region
- Comparison between urban and rural fatalities

Figure 7.3 An HSO monitoring a company level training exercise.

Comparing raw data listed in these reports can identify trends. For instance, the total number of fatalities has trended downward since 2004, yet the percentage of deaths resulting from cardiac arrest has remained constant. **Table 7.1, p. 282**, provides an indication of the LODDs between 1977 and 2012.

Reducing Firefighter Injuries and Deaths

In March 2004, the National Fallen Firefighters Foundation (NFFF), in cooperation with the United States Fire Administration, hosted a summit involving approximately 200 leaders from throughout the nation's fire service. Over the next three years, the organizations developed 16 strategic life safety initiatives that have been undertaken in an effort to meet the following goals beginning in 2007:

- Reduce firefighter fatalities by 25 percent over the next 5 years
- Reduce firefighter fatalities by 50 percent over the next 10 years

Advances have been made and national awareness of the problem has increased, but these goals have not been met at this time. In 2013, the NFFF formed a working group to develop a specific action plan to further the life safety initiative.

Table 7.1
On-duty Firefighter Fatalities (1977-2012)

Year	Fatalities	Year	Fatalities
1977	157	1995	103
1978	172	1996	100
1978	126	1997	100
1980	140	1998	93
1981	136	1999	114
1982	126	2000	105
1983	113	2001	452
1984	119	2002	101
1985	126	2003	112 + 1 HH
1986	121	2004	108 + 11 HH
1987	131	2005	99 + 16 HH
1988	136	2006	92 + 15 HH
1989	119	2007	107 + 13 HH
1990	108	2008	109 + 12 HH
1991	108	2009	79 + 13 HH
1992	77	2010	73 + 15 HH
1993	82	2011	64 + 19 HH
1994	106	2012	69 + 12 HH

Source: USFA Firefighter Fatalities in the United States in 2012
HH – Hometown Heroes (Fire service personnel included because of the Hometown Heroes Survivors Benefit Act of 2003.)

USFA analysis of firefighter fatalities data collected over 30 years indicates that fatalities could be significantly reduced by placing more emphasis on the following **(Figure 7.4)**:

- Proactive wellness/fitness program.
- Annual medical fitness evaluation.
- Safe driving practices.
- Enforcement of seat belt requirements.
- Ongoing incident strategy training for fire officers.
- Training designed to prevent firefighters from becoming lost inside burning buildings.

Injuries

The USFA does not issue an annual report of firefighter injuries. However, the USFA issued a report based on the National Fire Incident Reporting System (NFIRS) data collected between 2006 and 2008. This information indicates a decrease in both fireground and total injuries over that period. The report expresses the data over a variety of factors, such as cause of injury, nature of injury, and injuries by gender **(Tables 7.2a and b, p. 284)**.

Figure 7.4 Fire service fatalities can be reduced by implementing fitness, seat belt, and driver training programs.

Occupational Illness

Occupational illnesses are those diseases that are directly related to the duties and tasks of firefighters. These illnesses include cancer, respiratory ailments, stress induced ailments, and exposure to communicable diseases. Some of these health issues can be controlled through training and physical fitness. Exposures must be controlled by using personal protective equipment specifically designed to protect responders from airborne and bloodborne pathogens. Emergency medical responders are particularly susceptible to these exposures. Exposures may also occur at hazardous materials incidents or when using certain chemicals for vehicle, facility, and equipment maintenance or cleaning. Occupational illnesses may not become apparent for many years following exposure. Some personnel have not shown symptoms until long after retirement.

Motor Vehicle-Related Incidents

According to the USFA's **Traffic Incident Management Systems** (2008), 227 firefighters died in motor vehicle-related incidents between 1996 and 2006. Motor vehicle-related deaths accounted for 14 to 35 percent of total firefighter

Table 7.2a
Fire-Related Firefighter Injuries by Cause of Injury
(2006-2008)

Cause of Injury	Percentage
Overexertion/Strain	24.9
Exposure to hazard	20.0
Contact with object	15.8
Slip/Trip	12.0
Fall	10.0
Struck or assaulted	7.4
Jump	0.4
Other	9.4

Source: Fire-Related Firefighter Injuries Reported to NFIRS (2010)

Table 7.2b
Percent of Fire-Related Firefighter Injuries
by Gender (2006-2008)

Gender	Percentage
Male	95.0
Female	5.0

Source: Fire-Related Firefighter Injuries Reported to NFIRS (2010)

Mobile Water Supply Apparatus — Fire apparatus with a water tank of 1,000 gallons (3 785 L) or larger whose primary purpose is transporting water; may also carry a pump, some hose, and other equipment.

fatalities annually. Many firefighters who died in these accidents were volunteer firefighters responding to incidents in their personal vehicles. According to USFA statistics, the type of apparatus most often involved in fatal collisions included **mobile water supply apparatus**, engines/pumpers, and aircraft. More firefighters were killed in mobile water supply apparatus collisions than in engines and ladder apparatus accidents combined. Contributing factors in the motor vehicle deaths and injuries included:

- Operating the vehicle at an excessive speed
- Not wearing seat restraints
- Losing control of the vehicle

NOTE: Lack of proper vehicle maintenance is also a contributing factor in motor vehicle-related incidents.

Hearing Loss

Hearing loss is a continuing health problem for firefighters. Causes of hearing loss include:

- Exposure to apparatus audible warning devices (sirens and air horns)
- Exposure to power equipment noises
- Exposure to constant low-level noises from air-handling units or apparatus pumps

- Lack of hearing protection
- Viral diseases
- Aging process

A hearing conservation plan should be developed. Development of this plan begins with determining the types of noises that fire services personnel are subjected to and then determining what noise attenuation measures may be used to reduce the effect on the member's hearing. According to OSHA 29 *CFR* 1910.95, Occupational Noise Exposure, the department must develop a written hearing conservation plan that protects members from exposure to noises that are in excess of 85 dB (decibels) **(Figure 7.5)**. Plan development templates are available from OSHA.

Figure 7.5 A driver/operator wears a radio headset to help conserve his hearing during emergency responses.

Entry-level members are given a baseline hearing evaluation when they are hired. NFPA® 1582 recommends hearing examinations be part of the department's annual medical examination. A hearing test may also be administered upon the member's request or following any noise exposure that exceeds the established minimum level. A hearing examination should also be performed upon separation from the organization. A licensed or certified audiologist, otolaryngologist, or other qualified physician or technician should perform the audiometric tests.

Respiratory Injury or Illness

Firefighters are often exposed to various airborne hazards that can affect the respiratory system. Sources of these hazards include:

- Toxic or hazardous atmospheres found at incidents
- Concentrations of dust, paint, and other particulates produced during cleaning and maintenance
- Airborne microorganisms that may be present during medical emergencies or in the air-handling systems of department facilities

Symptoms may develop rapidly (from smoke inhalation) or slowly (from viral infections). Each situation requires a different level of personal protection and a different type of equipment. Self-contained breathing apparatus (SCBA) can provide protection against all of these circumstances. However, SCBA are generally used only as protection against toxic and hazardous atmospheres found at emergency incidents. Dust or particle masks provide the minimum level of protection and can be used in the workshop environment. High efficiency particulate air (HEPA) filter-equipped masks can be used in the shop environment as well as at the medical emergency. All masks or respiratory protection must meet the minimum requirements for the environment that the member is in at the time. NFPA® provides standards that define the selection, use, and care of all types of respiratory protection, including those associated with chemical, biological, radiological, nuclear, and explosive (CBRN[E]) incidents **(Figure 7.6)**.

Figure 7.6 Hazardous materials technicians donning SCBA as part of their chemical ensemble.

Respiratory protection plans should be based on OSHA Title 29 *CFR* 1910.134 and require the following elements:

- Selection criteria for equipment
- Inspection criteria
- Proper use policy
- Individual fit testing for members
- Maintenance schedule
- Training session
- Air-quality testing schedule
- Medical certification for those wearing the equipment

Respiratory protection equipment used in fire fighting activities must be certified by National Institute for Occupational Safety and Health (NIOSH) for structural fire fighting. Particle masks and HEPA filter masks must meet the minimum requirements that OSHA sets.

Hazardous Materials Exposure

Firefighters and emergency service personnel may be exposed to hazardous materials at emergency incidents or during non-emergency operations. Emergency incidents involving chemical spills or fires create hazards that can affect the human body through inhalation (airborne), absorption (contact), or ingestion (orally). Personnel can also be exposed to hazardous materials while cleaning and maintaining tools, apparatus and facilities.

Figure 7.7 An HSO inserting an updated safety data sheet into a fire station SDS binder.

Protection against common workplace hazards is included in the OSHA-required hazardous communication plan. The plan's purpose is to ensure that information on the hazards of all chemicals that the firefighters use is communicated to all members when the products are placed into service. Members must be made aware of where hazardous chemicals are stored and used in their work areas. They must also be informed of the requirements of the Hazard Communication Standard (Title 29 *CFR* 1910.1200), availability and location of the documentation, list of hazardous chemicals, and safety data sheet (SDS) provided with each product **(Figure 7.7)**. The SDS relays chemical hazard information from the manufacturer to the user and is maintained at the workplace where the chemical is used.

Program Implementation

Reducing accidents and occupational illnesses, injuries, and fatalities is the responsibility of all fire and emergency services organization personnel. Chief officers should lead by example and have a zero tolerance in issues affecting safety. Personal safety is a professional quality that the fire and emergency services personnel must adhere to.

Implementation of the accident, injury, and illness prevention program includes communication and training. Current members are trained in the program's requirements, policies that mandate it, and use of equipment and procedures that should protect them. New members receive a safety orientation *before* beginning work **(Figure 7.8)**. Orientation of new members, rehires, and those transferred from within the organization begins the first day in the new position.

Figure 7.8 An HSO providing a department safety orientation to new personnel.

This orientation provides an introduction of the department's policies and rules and includes a thorough safety briefing. The orientation includes a tour of appropriate facilities to acquaint members with their responsibilities and the locations of safety-related equipment. A safety orientation session describing the organization's accident, injury, and illness prevention program includes but is not limited to:

- How and when to report injuries, to include the location of first-aid facilities
- How to report unsafe conditions and practices
- Use and care of required personal protective equipment
- Proper emergency actions to be taken to include the emergency area exit routes
- Identification of the hazardous gases, chemicals, or materials involved and instructions on the safe use of PPE and emergency actions for accidental exposure
- Description of the organization's total health and safety program
- On-the-job review of the requirements for safely performing initial job assignments
- Procedures to follow if exposed to bloodborne pathogens
- Proper procedures for lifting and back care
- Proper handling and use of power tools
- Rules and regulations regarding vehicle use in emergency and nonemergency situations
- Approved safety procedures for trenching/shoring and confined-space rescues
- Safety procedures designed to provide fall protection
- Use of respiratory equipment and the type of systems used
- Proper care, use, selection, and maintenance of PPE to include its limitations

Noise level testing of apparatus, equipment, and facilities, as well as air and water quality testing in all facilities, should be conducted. Breathing air quality testing should be contracted from a certified third-party testing organization. Monthly facility safety hazard inspections should also be implemented. These inspections include but are not limited to tools, apparatus, extinguishers, protective equipment, and life-safety equipment. The HSO or a chief officer may perform an annual safety inspection.

The department should establish hose, apparatus, and equipment testing criteria based on NFPA® requirements. Third-party testing agencies, such as Underwriters Laboratories, Inc. (UL), Underwriters Laboratories of Canada (UL Canada), and Factory Mutual (FM), usually provide annual certification tests. Some testing, such as the nondestructive service testing of aerial devices, may only be required on a 5-year basis. These testing criteria are minimum recommendations, and greater safety can be provided if the testing occurs more frequently. The department's insurance carrier may also perform safety inspections. The Workers Compensation carrier may also perform an audit of the recent injuries and recommend programs, reporting, or training options.

Program Monitoring, Evaluation, and Revision

The accident, injury, and illness prevention program is continuously monitored, evaluated, and revised. The program's results are compared against the desired or planned goals, and deviations are corrected. The recognition of new safety hazards, failure of current equipment or procedures to meet the hazards, or failure of personnel to follow established procedures dictate the need for revisions to the program.

Chief officers and the HSO must continually monitor the respiratory protection plan to meet the workplace's changing challenges. Chief officers must actively pursue information regarding new respiratory protection equipment, requirements, and procedures, then provide this information to the organization. Organizations that provide this information and information on the rapidly expanding hazards to the respiratory system include the:

- NFPA®
- National Institute for Occupational Safety and Health (NIOSH)
- International Association of Fire Fighters (IAFF)
- International Association of Fire Chiefs (IAFC)
- Center for Disease Control and Prevention (CDC) provide information on new

Measurements for program effectiveness can include methods that:

- Establish a goal such as reducing back injuries by 25 percent.
- Compare the actual reported numbers of back injuries at the end of a specific time period.
- Compare the Workers Compensation costs.
- Compare the use of sick leave before and after implementation of the program.

IV Risk Management Plan

Every fire and emergency services organization should develop, implement, and use a risk management plan to guide its operations. Implementing this plan is a dynamic and aggressive process that the chief officer must monitor and revise at least annually and as needed. A sample plan can be found in Annex D of NFPA® 1500.

The terms *hazard* and *risk* can describe the hazards that exist in the community or service area and the risk that they pose to the population. The terms can also be applied to the fire and emergency services organization members in the performance of their duties and the environments to which they are exposed. The hazards are those that the individuals face while carrying out firefighting or emergency response duties. Hazards also include those found at emergency scenes and that exist in an organization's facilities, apparatus, and operations. Risks caused by the profession's high physiological and psychological nature must also be minimized.

Risk Management Model

Developing and implementing a risk management plan requires an understanding of the risk management model outlined in NFPA® 1500. The fire and emergency services and general industry have successfully used this risk management model for decades. The health and safety components of risk management have been incorporated into NFPA® 1500. NFPA® 1521 defines the role of the HSO in the risk management process.

The risk management plan described in NFPA® 1500 includes several components that can be applied to a fire and emergency services organization's operations. This plan documents that risks have been identified and evaluated and that a reasonable control plan has been implemented and followed. An effective risk management plan has a positive effect on the department from the operational, safety, financial, and liability standpoints.

The fire chief is ultimately responsible for the risk management plan. The plan may be a part of the jurisdiction's plan and may be the responsibility of that organization's health and safety manager or loss control manager. The fire chief may maintain responsibility for the review and revision or assign it to the HSO or the occupational safety and health committee.

NFPA® 1500 lists the requirements of the risk management plan. An official written risk management plan should cover the following:

- Administration
- Facilities
- Training
- Vehicle operations
- Protective clothing and equipment
- Operations at emergency incidents
- Operations at nonemergency incidents
- Other related activities.

NOTE: At a minimum, the plan should include risk identification, risk prioritization, risk evaluation, risk control techniques, and risk monitoring.

Understanding the concepts of risk management and system safety is essential to all chief officers and HSOs. These concepts are the basis for the majority of the roles and responsibilities for those officers who plan, develop, and manage the health and safety program. See Chapter 3 for details on risk management components.

Occupational Hazards Analysis

An analysis of occupational hazards begins by compiling all the hazards that firefighters commonly encounter. The chief officer may develop this compilation or delegate it to the HSO or Safety and Health Committee. There are numerous sources and methods used to develop occupational hazards lists. One method used for categorizing hazards is the one that the NFPA® uses for developing its annual fatality and injury report. The NFPA® divides hazard types into five categories. In general, common occupational hazards include but are not limited to:

- **Fireground** — fatalities and injuries that occur during fire suppression activities
- **Nonfire** — fatalities and injuries that occur during other types of emergency incidents, including hazardous materials spills and medical, rescue, or extrication incidents
- **Responding/Returning** — fatalities and injuries that result from motor vehicle or apparatus accidents **(Figure 7.9)**
- **Other On Duty** — fatalities and injuries that occur during nonemergency activities such as station maintenance, inspections, or physical fitness programs
- **Training** — fatalities and injuries that occur during training evolutions or courses

These categories are further divided by the type of injury, such as:

- Burns
- Smoke/gas inhalation
- Wounds, cuts, or bleeding bruise
- Fractures or dislocations
- Heart attack or stroke
- Strains, sprains, or muscular pain
- Thermal stress

A further subdivision of the injuries is by cause, which includes:

- Overexertion
- Contact with an object
- Fall or jump
- Struck by an object
- Extreme weather
- Exposure to fire products
- Exposure to chemicals/radiation
- Psychological and emotional stress

Figure 7.9 An injury or fatality that occurred during an automobile extrication operation would be categorized as a nonfire hazard.

Personnel Risk Analysis

Risk analysis is applied to the health and safety of the organization's personnel. Many injuries and some fatalities occur during training activities or physical fitness sessions. Risk analysis should be applied to all of the organization's nonemergency activities in order to prevent or reduce the number of occurrences.

Risk Identification

To identify the risks, the fire chief or a designated chief officer should compile a list of all of the organization's emergency and nonemergency operations and duties. This list should include the worst possible conditions or potential events, such as major disasters and multiple events. There are many sources to assist with this identification process. The first (and possibly the most effective) is the department's loss prevention data, which consists of annual fireloss reports by occupancy type, loss value, and frequency. Most departments are too small to rely on their own database for a statistically valid trend, but national averages and trends are available from NFPA® and the United States Fire Administration (USFA). National data may not be complete or accurate due to collection inconsistencies and delays of 1 to 2 years required to collect, analyze, and publish it.

The fire chief should seek input and ideas from department personnel, trade journals, professional associations, and other service providers to identify the potential risks. When using information from other fire and emergency services organizations, the fire chief should consider local circumstances that might present a different set of emergency and nonemergency operations and duties. Other risk identification sources include risk management plans developed by local industry and hazardous substance sites, vulnerability analyses, and U.S. Environmental Protection Agency (EPA) plans. Line-of-duty death (LODD) reports prepared by the National Institute of Occupational Safety and Health (NIOSH) are an excellent tool to assist chief officers in identifying hazards and risks. The reports contain recommendations that fire and emergency services organizations should implement based on the incident investigation.

Risk Evaluation

Once the fire chief or a designated chief officer identifies the risks, they can be evaluated from both frequency and severity standpoints. *Frequency,* referred to by OSHA as *incidence rate,* addresses the likelihood of occurrence. Typically, if a particular type of incident such as lifting injuries has occurred repeatedly, it will continue to occur until a job hazard or task analysis identifies the root causes and effective control measures have been implemented. In this example, the fire chief or a designated chief officer must develop and implement guidelines that:

- Describe proper lifting techniques
- Describe physical fitness requirements
- Provide mechanical aids for lifting

Severity addresses the degree of seriousness of the incident and can be measured by lost time away from work, cost of damage, cost of and time for repair or replacement of equipment, disruption of service, or legal costs. **Appendix H** contains the formula for calculating frequency and severity. The method for calculating the risk may vary from one department to another.

Risk Prioritization

The results of the frequency and severity assessments help set priorities for determining action. Risks with both a high probability of occurrence and serious consequences are considered high priority items that deserve immediate action. Nonserious incidents with a low likelihood of occurrence are lower priorities and can be placed near the bottom of the *action-required* list.

Risk Control Techniques

Once the risks are prioritized, risk control measures must be applied. When control measures have been implemented, they need to be evaluated to measure their effectiveness. Several approaches can be taken in risk control, including the following:

- **Risk avoidance** — The best risk control choice is risk avoidance by avoiding the activity that creates the risk. In a fire and emergency services organization, this approach is frequently impractical. Examples:

  — Lifting a stretcher presents a serious back injury risk, but personnel cannot avoid this risk and still provide effective service. Training in the use of safe lifting techniques and/or safer equipment would be more acceptable solutions.

  — Risk avoidance could include an organizational smoking prohibition policy, reducing the potential for lung cancer and other smoking-related illnesses among members.

- **Risk transfer** — This can be accomplished by physically transferring the risk or by purchasing insurance. Risk transfer may be difficult, if not impossible, for a fire or emergency medical services (EMS) organization. Examples:

  — Contracting hazardous waste cleanup and disposal transfers the risks to a private contractor who accepts the liability of the risks for those activities.

  — Purchasing insurance only transfers financial risk and does nothing to affect the likelihood of occurrence. Buying fire insurance for the station, while highly recommended to protect the organization's assets, does nothing to prevent the station from burning. Insurance is no substitute for effective control measures such as installing an automatic sprinkler system.

- **Control measures** — Effective control measures (risk reduction) is the most common method used for risk management. Control measures will not eliminate the risk, but they can reduce the likelihood of occurrence or reduce the severity. Effective control measures include safety, health, and wellness programs; ongoing training and education programs; and well-defined standard operating procedures or guidelines (SOPs/SOGs). Examples:

  — Changes in apparatus bay design and apparatus-backing procedures have been practical. The risks associated with backing apparatus into station bays are well-documented. The simplest solutions are improving driver/operator training, painting guide stripes on the apparatus bay floors, and a policy that requires a second person to guide the backing operation from the rear of the vehicle. A more expensive solution would be to replace older single-door stations with new drive-through stations **(Figure 7.10)**.

— Typical control measures instituted to control incident scene injuries include use of accountability systems, use of full-protective clothing, mandatory respiratory protection plans, training and education sessions, and health and wellness SOP/SOGs.

Figure 7.10 Constructing new stations with drive-through vehicle stalls would be a control measure used to reduce accidents and injuries related to backing fire apparatus into parking spaces.

Plan Implementation Procedures

Once appropriate control measures are determined, the risk management plan is implemented. Implementing the plan follows the same procedures as mentioned previously for risk analysis and program development. The fire chief or designated officer is responsible for implementing, monitoring, evaluating, reporting, and revising the plan. Administrative support is essential for the plan to meet its goals.

Implementation

Implementation of the risk management plan requires communication, training, and application. The written plan is part of the organization's SOPs/SOGs and is distributed to the organization's personnel. The distribution includes the administration and the jurisdictional publicly acknowledging the plan's importance. Administration support of the risk management plan is essential to membership acceptance and support. Communicating this support helps ensure a positive response from the internal and external customers and stakeholders.

Program effectiveness depends on proper training. Training sessions should include communicating the plan and its importance, use, and intended results. Training is organization-wide and begins in the entry-level training for new personnel. Training sessions for plan revisions and refresher training sessions are provided periodically to all organization personnel **(Figure 7.11)**.

Figure 7.11 Revisions to a department's safety program must be communicated to all department personnel.

Plan application takes place daily as officers and personnel follow the prescribed policies and procedures until the risk control techniques become second nature to all personnel. Whether these techniques involve applying proper lifting techniques when picking up heavy objects or putting on respiratory protection when entering a contaminated atmosphere, they must be performed naturally without questions.

Partnering Outside the Organization

Program implementation provides an opportunity for the fire chief to partner with other area public and private agencies to share program costs associated with annual hose, ladder, or pump testing. Regional training facilities, driving courses, or candidate testing and evaluation are also opportunities to share resources between communities or rural fire protection associations. Shared resources can result in lowered costs and lower insurance ratings.

Monitoring

The plan's effectiveness becomes evident through monitoring. This step ensures that the system is dynamic and facilitates periodic program reviews, at least annually or as needed. Any problems that occur in the process must be addressed through revision or modification of the plan. The risk management plan's intent is to develop a strategy for reducing the inherent risks associated with fire and emergency services organization operations. Every emergency services organization should operate within the parameters of a risk management plan.

Evaluation

During the evaluation process, the chief officer compares the plan's desired results with its actual results. Comparison data are derived from injury and fatality reports, amount of participation in safety training, fitness testing results, pre-employment physical fitness reports, and alterations that have been made to address preplan risks. Data sources include the following:

- Target risks or hazards
- Policies and procedures intended to eliminate the risks
- Emergency incident reports
- Daily attendance reports
- Medical leave requests
- Training records
- Physical fitness reports

The results of the comparisons, which include an increase, decrease, or no change in the risks, determine the effectiveness of the risk management plan. A decrease in the risk, indicated by a reduction in medical leave taken or lost-time injuries, indicates the plan is being effective. If there is no change or an increase in the number of injuries, then the implemented risk control techniques must be reviewed and alternate solutions applied.

It is important to determine if the cost/benefit is appropriate. The costs of the risk control techniques should be less than the cost of the results of the risk. If the cost of altering apparatus storage compartments is greater than the cost of lost-time injuries due to back strains resulting from removing equipment from the compartments, then it may not be worth the control cost.

Revision

Revision procedures are included in the risk management plan when it is developed. The revision process is similar to what the initial risk management plan followed, although it only focuses on those risks that require revision and not the entire plan. Chief officers should be aware of the reasons why revisions may be necessary and be able to recognize these reasons when they appear in the plan evaluation. Some reasons may include the following:

- Increase in injuries, fatalities, or property loss due to the target risks
- Increase in medical leave requests
- Increase in risk-related costs
- No apparent change in the risk results
- Ineffective cost/benefit
- Changes in the target risks
- Ineffective training
- New standards or regulations

System Safety Program

Another form of a risk management plan is the System Safety Program developed by the U.S. National Aeronautics and Space Administration (NASA) and used by many U.S. government agencies, including the Federal Aviation Administration (FAA). The System Safety Program covers the spectrum of safety management and assessment, from the design of equipment to the attitude of personnel and the culture of the organization. A detailed description of the System Safety Program can be found in Appendices 2 and 3 of the FAA System Safety Program. The system includes the following components:

- Hazard identification and resolution
- Design review
- System modification review and control
- Rules and procedures review
- Equipment design modifications review and control
- Procurement – timely replacement of personal protective equipment
- Facility and equipment inspections
- Member and public communications
- Safety training and education
- Emergency response planning, coordination, and training
- Safety data collection and analysis
- Occupational health, wellness, and safety
- Environmental protection

- Interdepartmental and interagency coordination
- Life safety
- Accident and post incident investigation
- Internal safety and operational audits

Within this framework, there must be documentation, accountability, and verification of results versus requirements. The systems approach provides a logical structure for problem solving, planning, and prevention. It is a tool that can be used with the risk management model to ensure an efficient and effective safety plan for the organization.

Chapter Summary

An efficient and effective fire and emergency services organization depends on a safe, healthy, physically fit, and emotionally stable membership. The administration's responsibility is to provide the membership with a safe working environment through training, education, equipment, policies, procedures, leadership, and supervision. This safe environment is accomplished through the development and implementation of a comprehensive health and safety program that contains individual components to address both the obvious and obscure hazards to the health and well-being of the members. Chief officers of all levels, along with the HSO and other department officers, must make health and safety their primary concerns. To do so, they must set the example for others to follow and ensure that all operations are performed in a way that is consistent with SOP/SOGs and safe practices.

Review Questions

1. What are various ways to develop a fire department health and safety program? (pp. 276-279)

2. What elements comprise a fire department accident, injury, and illness prevention program? (pp. 279-288)

3. What tools can the chief officer use to develop and implement an organizational risk management plan? (pp. 288-293)

4. What procedures should the chief officer follow when implementing an organizational risk management plan? (pp. 293-296)

Emergency Management (Level III)

Chapter Contents

CASE HISTORY **301**	Emergency Operations Centers (EOCs) 314
Principles of Emergency Management **302**	**Chapter Summary** 316
Emergency Management Concepts 303	**Review Questions** 316
Four Phases of Emergency Management 305	
Emergency Declaration Process 310	
Resource Integration **310**	
Types of Resources 311	
Integration Planning 314	

Chapter 8

NFPA® Job Performance Requirements

This chapter provides information that addresses the following job performance requirements of NFPA® 1021, *Standard for Fire Officer Professional Qualifications* (2014).

Level III

6.8.1

Emergency Management (Level III)

Learning Objectives

After reading this chapter, students will be able to:

[Level III]

1. Identify the principles of emergency management.
2. Identify various types of resources integrated in emergency management. (6.8.1)
3. Describe the various functions of Emergency Operations Centers (EOCs).

Chapter 8
Emergency Management (Level III)

Case History

Floods in the Southeast, tornados in the Midwest, wildfires in the West, or hurricanes on the East Coast may be part of your response during a typical year. But is your department prepared? Natural disasters and potential terrorism events have challenged the fire and emergency services for years. As a chief officer, you have the responsibility to maintain not only your department's readiness, but the ability to work with other agencies for community awareness.

- Does your department know how to request federal, state and multi-jurisdictional resources?
- At what point do you open the Emergency Operations Center (EOC)?
- Are outside agencies able to communicate and operate within your local departments?
- Are local policies and procedures in place to assist in the emergency management?
- Are your personnel trained in dealing with complex incidents with other agencies?

Fire and emergency services organizations often demonstrate their lack of planning and interoperability, directly impacting the safety of residents and emergency personnel. As chief officers, your responsibility includes understanding your local state and federal emergency management policies and procedures.

Chief level officers are likely to encounter emergency situations that require greater resources than are readily available. In these instances, it is often difficult to determine the size and scope of such incidents. Making this assessment is even more difficult when the incident crosses jurisdictional boundaries or there is an absence of a preincident plan. Emergency management is the process of managing all types of emergencies and disasters through planning and the coordination of resources. Emergency management is not just important during actual incidents. A good emergency management program can reduce the effect of large-scale incidents to a community through planning and preparedness activities.

As a fire chief, you may be the designated official responsible for emergency management in your jurisdiction. Other jurisdictions may utilize a full time emergency manager for this role. You must understand the principles of emergency management and the roles of emergency managers during a large-scale incident or disaster.

This chapter will introduce the basic principles of emergency management. It will also address resource integration and coordination during large incidents. Finally, the chapter will provide an introduction into Emergency Operations Centers (EOCs) and the role and responsibilities of chief officers during incidents.

Principles of Emergency Management

Identifying vulnerabilities and understanding their consequences are ways that emergency managers prepare for disasters. These preparations should be done in conjunction with community risk assessments and preplans. Vulnerabilities are areas of potential weakness and should be identified well before a disaster occurs. Potential vulnerabilities can include **(Figure 8.1)**:

- Areas susceptible to flooding or other effects of severe weather
- Wildfires
- Populations at risk (those with disabilities, the elderly, low income)
- Areas of industry or commerce
- Utilities (water treatment, electricity, natural gas)
- FEMA critical infrastructure (roads, bridges, ports, drainage)
- Transportation and commodity flow

Consequences are the potential results of an emergency or disaster that occur because of identified or unidentified vulnerabilities. For example, damage or disruption to a factory or other major employer can have serious and far-reaching effects for that community as a whole.

A major focus in emergency management since September 11, 2001, has been to plan for disasters and other events using an all-hazards approach. All-hazards strategies provide a coordinated approach to a wide variety of

Figure 8.1 Identifying potential vulnerabilities such as areas that may flood, elderly people, industrial facilities, and power generation plants should be accomplished before a disaster occurs. *Flooding photo courtesy of Chris Mickal/ District Chief, New Orleans (LA) FD Photo Unit.*

incidents, including weather events, earthquakes, wildfires, chemical releases, and acts of terror. Developing plans and strategies using an all-hazards approach ensures that the capabilities exist to handle any emergency.

Emergency Management Concepts

Emergency management has traditionally been seen as preparing for natural disasters such as floods, hurricanes, tornados, and earthquakes. But emergency management must also prepare for situations such as terrorist attacks and the *Columbia* space shuttle disaster recovery in 2003.

An all-inclusive list of disasters can never be completely compiled because society and civilization are constantly changing. There may be future disasters and emergencies that the emergency management profession (public or private) will face that are unknown or unimagined today. As a result, an all-hazards approach to emergency management is so important. Incidents can be categorized as emergency incidents and planned events. Emergency incidents can involve natural disasters, terrorist attacks, and many others. Planned events may include major sporting events, large scale demonstrations, political events, and concerts.

The nature of emergency management and services is such that they involve all agencies, all levels of government, corporations, the military, the community, many professions, and academic communities. Emergency management is intrinsically linked to interagency, intergovernmental, interoperability, and interdisciplinary concepts.

Interagency

When a large-scale emergency incident occurs, representatives from each relevant agency in the affected jurisdiction report to an emergency operations center (EOC) to coordinate their responses, resources, and decisions **(Figure 8.2)**. Additionally, these agencies will coordinate and communicate through an established direction, command, control, and coordination structure.

Figure 8.2 An emergency operations center (EOC) during a large-scale wildland fire fighting operation.

The response to the U.S. Pentagon on September 11, 2001, is a good example of interagency at work. Neighboring jurisdictions had a formal joint-response plan, which ensured that they had the collective capability to respond to an emergency.

Intergovernmental

Local jurisdictions or governments often depend on each other for assistance. Many emergency services organizations have long utilized mutual aid/automatic aid agreements to share resources. In the U.S., regional mutual aid has become more common. For example, through a statewide mutual aid plan, all Virginia jurisdictions have access to an available pool of public and private resources to manage emergency incidents.

Most states in the U.S. have Emergency Management Assistance Compacts (EMACs) among themselves. EMACs ensure that resources are available for a comprehensive response so that every state does not need to maintain the capability to deal with extreme emergencies alone. Any capability one member state has can be shared with another. States have the right to charge for their services and/or refuse to provide services if their resources are needed in their own states.

Hurricanes Katrina and Rita resulted in the largest deployment of mutual aid through EMAC. Emergency responders from unaffected states, civilian personnel from all disciplines, and National Guard troops were deployed in unprecedented numbers.

When local and regional resources are exhausted, assistance from the state is typically requested. When a state cannot handle an incident, the governor certifies that the state is overwhelmed and needs federal assistance, and requests a Presidential Disaster Declaration.

Interoperability

Interoperability is the ability of a system to work with and use the parts or equipment of another system. Coordinated emergency responses require effective communication systems that have this ability. Strong partnerships and effective, interoperable communications enable all emergency response organizations and personnel to respond in a coordinated, safe, and disciplined manner.

Interoperability problems at major events occur mainly in the area of communications. Other areas of interoperability difficulty include but are not limited to:

- Equipment compatibility
- Common language/terminology
- Unified command
- Joint training/drills **(Figure 8.3)**
- Standard operating procedures/guidelines (SOPs/SOGs)
- Radio discipline
- Other resource-driven factors

Figure 8.3 Several fire companies from multiple jurisdictions during a joint high-rise drill.

Interdisciplinary

All fire and emergency services and emergency responders must come together to prevent, prepare for, mitigate against, respond to, and recover from disasters. Disciplines or professions include:

- Fire/rescue
- Emergency management
- Law enforcement
- Public health
- Emergency medical services (EMS)
- Transportation
- Building safety/code enforcement
- Public works

Four Phases of Emergency Management

Emergency management activities are broken into four main areas called phases. The four phases of emergency management are:

- Mitigation
- Response
- Preparedness
- Recovery

These phases often overlap and run concurrently with one another. For example, mitigation and preparedness efforts in a community occur simultaneously. Recovery activities during a disaster often begin while response efforts are still underway. The four phases of emergency management are discussed in greater detail in the sections that follow.

Mitigation

Mitigation includes all those efforts or activities that lessen the effects or consequences of potential emergencies, such as:

- Building and fire codes
- Zoning ordinances
- Floodplain management

- Building performance standards
- Architectural design
- Structural design
- Sustainability programs
- Livability programs
- Climate monitoring
- Risk management
- Educational initiatives that improve disaster recovery capabilities

Rapid Visual Screening of Buildings for Potential Seismic Hazards

FEMA has established a program called Rapid Visual Screening of Buildings for Potential Seismic Hazards. This program can be used to identify structures that may be susceptible to earthquake damage. The assessment procedure helps users quickly identify, inventory, and rank such buildings according to their expected safety and usability during and after earthquakes. FEMA provides a handbook and training course to train individuals in performing these screenings. The Rapid Observation of Vulnerability and Estimation of Risk (ROVER) is a web-based program that aids in the performance of structural assessments.

Mitigation focuses on collaborative efforts with multiple agencies to craft strategic resolutions to an emergency. Mitigation is a scalable process that addresses simple to complex outcomes for a specific incident. It involves incident/event preplanning as well as operational/action planning once an incident occurs and is in the process of escalating.

Local mitigation programs are based on risk assessments that determine the level and type of mitigation needs present in the community. An example would be identifying clogged drainage ways and streams that could cause flooding during periods of high rainfall.

Prevention is another major aspect of mitigation and emphasizes education, personal understanding, and readiness to prevent an incident or emergency from occurring. Education on prevention activities enhances the ability to reduce risks.

Prevention-delivered strategies should implement the following six recognized elements (both tangible and intangible) of prevention:

- Tangible
  - Education
  - Engineering
  - Enforcement
- Intangible
  - Encouragement
  - Economics
  - Evaluation

The elements of encouragement, economics, and evaluation are often seen as intangible elements that add physiological and economic support to prevention efforts. The elements of education, engineering, and enforcement are viewed as tangible functions that support a safe environment through positive physical response such as:

- Public awareness, safety education, and citizen training
- Deployment of fixed intervention appliances, alarms, and warning devices
- Improved construction practices
- Code compliance

Education serves as a basis for safety initiatives, and all elements functioning together make prevention a powerful tool. Identified needs will dictate which prevention elements are used. Educational programs from federal, state/provincial, and local governments and other organizations provide citizen readiness information in areas, such as sheltering in place and evacuations, emergency notifications, and disaster kits. Unfortunately, mitigation and prevention efforts are often reactionary in nature.

Preparedness

Preparedness is a continuous process involving efforts to identify threats and consequences, determine vulnerabilities, and identify required resources before an emergency. Emergency preparedness is fundamental to emergency management. Preparedness focuses on the following life cycle domains of the security spectrum:

- Domain awareness
- Prevention activities
- Response preparedness
- Mitigation and restoration
- Recovery activities

Preparedness underpins the readiness of response agencies and communities and includes the following activities:

- Conducting research and reading
- Planning
- Gathering intelligence
- Coordinating information and activities
- Exercising (testing and practicing) plans
- Evaluating criteria
- Training and educating
- Partnering with those in the community, surrounding areas, and around the globe to extend assistance beyond usual limits
- Meeting standards of excellence and best practices

Response

Figure 8.4 One of several fire apparatus responding to a multijurisdictional incident.

Response is the activation, mobilization, and coordinated deployment and application of needed resources to address the immediate effects of an emergency **(Figure 8.4)**. Emergency services organizations operate primarily in this phase. Response efforts focus on the priorities of life safety, incident stabilization, and property conservation.

Response also includes implementation of the appropriate response plan (local, state, regional, or national). The response phase is the shortest and most intense of the phases, and it transitions into the recovery phase.

Emergency support functions (ESFs) of the United States National Response Plan (NRP) are used in state and local response plans to group emergency response concerns, functions, and capabilities of government and certain private-sector organizations into categories to provide support, resources, and services. **Table 8.1** lists the ESFs and identifies the U.S. federal department or agency that is primarily responsible for coordinating the function at a federal level during an emergency response situation. States may also have ESFs established in addition to federal ESFs in the NRP.

Table 8.1
Emergency Support Functions and Primary Responsible Federal Departments/Agencies

Emergency Support Function	Primary Responsible Federal Departments/Agencies
#1 – Transportation	U.S. Department of Transportation
#2 – Communications	National Communications System
#3 – Public Works and Engineering	U.S. Army Corps of Engineers, Department of Defense
#4 – Fire Fighting	U.S. Forest Service, Department of Agriculture
#5 – Emergency Management	Federal Emergency Management Agency
#6 – Mass Care, Emergency Assistance, Housing, and Human Services	American Red Cross
#7 – Logistics Management and Resource Support	General Services Administration
#8 – Public Health and Medical Services	Public Health Service, Department of Health and Human Services
#9 – Search and Rescue	Federal Emergency Management Agency
#10 – Oil and Hazardous Materials Response	Environmental Protection Agency
#11 – Agriculture and Natural Resources	Food and Nutrition Service, Department of Agriculture
#12 – Energy	Department of Energy
#13 – Public Safety and Security	Department of Homeland Security and Department of Justice
#14 – Long-term Community Recovery	Department of Homeland Security/Emergency Preparedness and Response/Federal Emergency Management Agency
#15 – External Affairs	Department of Homeland Security/Federal Emergency Management Agency

Response activities range from initial preemergency asset deployment to when the community or region is ready to devote full time to the recovery process. Response elements include the following:

- NIMS
- Emergency operations center (EOC)
- Logistics
- Finance
- Planning
- Operations
- Situation reports
- Public and media updates
- Search and rescue operations
- Medical needs
- Crisis counseling
- Body identification
- Resource management
- Mutual aid agreement management

Recovery

Recovery is the process of restoring and restarting life, government, and economic processes after an emergency. Short-term recovery restores vital life-support systems necessary for the general health and welfare of the community. Long-term recovery continues until the entire disaster area returns to its previous condition or undergoes improvement with new features that are less disaster-prone. Such long-term recovery can often last for several years. The following elements are part of the recovery process:

- Mass care, feeding, and sheltering of victims
- Temporary housing
- Return of basic community services
- Rebuild economic and social infrastructure
- *Continuity of Government (COG)* and *Continuity of Operations (COOP)*
- Unemployment assistance
- Crisis counseling
- Public assistance to cities and counties for streets, highways, sidewalks, and public buildings
- Donations management

Deployment on long-term incidents has historically shown to be difficult for responders' families. Departments should work to ensure families are prepared to be separated from a loved one for extended periods of time and that there is a support structure in place to assist if needed. FEMA documents and electronic resources are available that can assist in the development of family readiness programs.

Businesses affected by a disaster consider recovery as key to the return to normalcy. According to DHS-FEMA, more than 40 percent of businesses that a disaster affected never reopen. In cases of terrorism, DHS-FEMA indicates that the percentage climbs to almost 70 percent.

In the past, post-disaster reconstruction has focused on rebuilding physical infrastructure. Local livelihoods, economies, and institutions also have to be strengthened and rebuilt. Investment in the social capital of disaster-affected communities is essential to building sustainable recovery.

Emergency Declaration Process

In any incident, the law provides that a jurisdiction affected by an emergency will manage it from start to finish. If the locality or region is overwhelmed, it certifies to the state (specifically to the governor) that it cannot manage the magnitude of the emergency without the state's assistance. If there is agreement at the state level, the governor will issue a Gubernatorial Disaster Declaration/Proclamation that will release state resources (funds, equipment, or personnel) to respond to the emergency.

If the state is overwhelmed, the governor can request additional resources from the federal government. After a preliminary damage assessment report has been completed, the governor can request a major emergency declaration from the President. The President can issue a Declaration of Emergency to supplement state and local efforts to save lives and protect property **(Figure 8.5)**. The President normally acts only after the state governor has requested an emergency declaration.

Figure 8.5 This U.S. Navy vessel was part of the federal response to Hurricane Katrina in New Orleans, LA. *Courtesy of Chris Mickal/District Chief, New Orleans (LA) FD Photo Unit.*

Resource Integration

During the response phase of a disaster, resource integration is critical to ensure that operations are conducted in an organized and efficient manner. Before resources can be requested, a quality needs assessment must be performed to determine the kind, type, and number of resources required.

A phenomenon called convergence must also be considered. The tendency of many individuals or groups is to send people or supplies to an area affected by a disaster or other large-scale emergency without being requested. This convergence can be problematic because resources must be diverted from the response to managing the influx of personnel, equipment, and supplies. It is critical that resources deploy within a structured response model rather than "self dispatch" outside the agreed upon process. Resource integration, especially convergent behavior, must be accounted for in any preincident plan.

Types of Resources

Resources brought to bear in a large-scale incident can be wide-ranging. Relationships should be created with outside agencies well before an actual incident to ensure capabilities are understood and proper request channels are followed. The following sections detail resource types and responsibilities during a large-scale incident.

Fire Service

In the immediate onset of a large-scale incident, it can be assumed that local fire service resources will be participating in the initial response. Some of the first reports of incident severity will come from these assets. While these reports are beneficial, they can be limited in scope due to the size of the incident. As a chief officer, your duty will likely be to work with other agencies to analyze these numerous reports and attempt to conceptualize the overall size and scope of the incident. Preplanning with other disciplines such as law enforcement can help in conducting this assessment.

Once the incident is better understood, a decision must be made if local resources can handle the response or if outside assistance is required. While AHJ policies vary, many departments will institute a callback, or "all call", of off-duty or available personnel to assist in the response. These personnel should be directed to report to a preplanned location for assignment. All activities should be conducted in accordance with the established IAP for the incident.

If additional outside resources are required, they should be requested through the proper requisition channels. Requests should be as specific as possible to prevent confusion and to ensure the needed equipment and personnel are provided. The first requests for assistance are typically made to departments with mutual aid/automatic aid agreements. Keep in mind that if the incident is large enough in scope, neighboring departments may be unable to provide assistance. Resource requests should be directed through the EOC if one has been established. EMACs will coordinate interactions among the EOCs and prioritize the distribution of resources.

NIMS establishes criteria for the various kinds and types of resources to ensure there is continuity between what is requested and what is deployed. Fire service-related resource kind and type criteria are described in FEMA publication **Typed Resource Definitions, Fire and Hazardous Materials**, which can be downloaded from FEMA's Resource Management web page.

Law Enforcement

In a large-scale incident, local law enforcement personnel are as likely to be taxed as their fire and emergency services counterparts. Law enforcement priorities in these incidents are typically to maintain peace and manage evacuation efforts. Because there are typically many more patrol units than fire apparatus, law enforcement personnel are able to cover a larger area and can provide more reconnaissance details regarding the incident. This is especially true with regards to road access to affected locations. If a terrorist act is suspected, law enforcement personnel will also begin investigating the incident and attempting to preserve evidence.

Emergency Medical Services (EMS)

Emergency medical services (EMS) assets are also an important component in the response. If the fire and emergency services organization provides EMS services, those resources will usually be coordinated with those of that organization. If a private sector provider, a hospital, or a third service organization provides all or part of the EMS services, coordination with the managers of these assets is critical.

Coordination with local hospitals is also critical. Most hospitals have procedures to address incidents involving numerous patients. However, it may take time for equipment, supplies, and personnel to be assembled to accommodate the influx of patients. Therefore, hospitals should be notified as early as possible in the incident.

Research has shown that EMS transport needs may be overestimated. Many injured people arrive at care facilities using a private vehicle, with law enforcement, or on foot. Other "walking wounded" may refuse transport to definitive care because they are more concerned with the status of their loved ones or property. If there are substantial numbers of significant casualties, a triage area will need to be established in coordination with EMS providers.

Public Works

In large-scale incidents, public works personnel are a critical component of a successful response and recovery. Immediate tasks for these personnel are to determine and control breaches to utility services. Public works personnel are often responsible for reopening roads that are obstructed or damaged.

The easiest solution for controlling utility services breaches is often to shut off service to the affected area. Before hurricane landfall, many coastal electric providers will preemptively shut off electrical service to the area as a safety measure. Actions between public works and the fire and emergency services organization must be closely coordinated. For example, it can be detrimental if water service is shut off to an area to address a broken water main while fire suppression efforts are underway. Public safety resources must also coordinate with public works to quickly reopen affected roads and bridges and to ensure blocked or clogged storm sewers are cleared to facilitate drainage.

Community Resources

Numerous community resources are utilized in a disaster or large-scale incident to address the needs of affected citizens. Organizations such as the Red Cross are often tasked with establishing emergency shelters and providing food, clothing, and other necessities. Faith-based groups and other nongovernmental organizations (NGOs) can also provide needed assistance.

Community Emergency Response Teams (CERT) can also be deployed during these incidents. CERTs are groups of trained citizens who are able to perform basic emergency functions. CERTs operate under the direction of the incident commander within NIMS and free up emergency services personnel to handle more technical duties. Medical Reserve Corps (MRC) units may also be available to assist in the provision of emergency medical care.

Capabilities of community resources should be determined well before an incident. During the incident, these groups should be closely coordinated to prevent duplication of effort and to ensure citizens' needs are addressed in an efficient manner. Keep in mind that during the initial stages of a major event, community resources can be overwhelmed.

State/Provincial Resources

State and provincial resources can vary greatly. They should be determined in advance and factored into any planning that occurs. Some states have a full cache of supplies and equipment and are able to quickly mobilize a response cadre should a disaster or large-scale incident occur. Other states can provide emergency management personnel to assist in coordinating the response. The National Guard is a state level resource that can be quickly deployed to assist in areas, such as incident coordination, equipment provision, and supply distribution **(Figure 8.6)**.

State/provincial level coordination is critical, especially when federal resources may be needed. Coordination with state level assets should begin as quickly as possible to prevent any delay in state or federal resource deployment.

Federal Resources

Federal resources are often needed in a large-scale incident or disaster, especially if resources are not readily available at the state/provincial level. As mentioned previously, the Governor of a state must declare/proclaim a

Figure 8.6 National Guard and federal military personnel arrive in New Orleans (LA) to render aid following Hurricane Katrina. *Courtesy of Chris Mickal/District Chief, New Orleans (LA) FD Photo Unit.*

disaster or emergency and request the same declaration from the President in order to obtain federal assistance. When disasters (such as a hurricane) are anticipated, the Governor and President may preemptively issue a disaster or emergency declaration to allow state and federal resources to mobilize and stage for a speedy response.

Federal resources are diverse in nature. **Table 8.2** highlights federal resources that may be deployed in a disaster, their agency, and their capabilities. Federal Urban Search and Rescue (USAR), Disaster Medical Assistance Teams (DMATs), Disaster Mortuary Operational Response Teams (DMORTs), and others may already have a presence in the state and are often the first federal resources to arrive at an incident. These teams travel with their own supplies and equipment and are equipped to be self-sufficient for long periods of time.

Integration Planning

Perhaps the greatest determining factor in a successful response and recovery to a disaster or large-scale incident is preincident planning. Emergency managers should identify local, state/provincial, and federal resources that may be needed and to build relationships with those groups to ensure that needs can be efficiently coordinated.

Preincident planning should also involve tabletop and/or mock incident drills, training exercises, simulations, and others to provide different agencies and organizations the opportunity to work together in a controlled environment. Gaps in planning and resource availability and capability are often discovered during such drills and can be adjusted to ensure a better response during a real incident.

Emergency Operations Centers (EOCs)

An EOC facilitates incident communication, coordination, and management decision making by assembling incident management personnel at the same location. A properly designed EOC serves as an effective and efficient facility for coordinating emergency response efforts and a number of other uses, including operations, training, meetings, exercise venues, and classrooms. An EOC optimizes communication and coordination using effective information management and presentation processes.

NIMS-ICS provides EOC and operational staff members with a standardized operational structure and common terminology. Because of this standardization, NIMS-ICS provides a useful and flexible management system for incidents involving multijurisdictional or multidisciplinary responses. NIMS-ICS provides the flexibility needed to rapidly activate and establish an organizational format around the functions that need to be performed.

Managing response and recovery operations involves a tremendous amount of information. EOC staff members collect this information and support incident information and response activities. Typically, information flows in the following order:

1. An incident occurs
2. Initial response
3. Situational and resource assessment

Table 8.2
Federal Resources Deployable in a Disaster

Resource	Agency	Capabilities
Urban Search and Rescue (USAR)	Federal Emergency Management Agency	- 28 task forces - Staffed, trained, and equipped to provide search, rescue, technical, and medical capabilites
Disaster Medical Assistance Teams (DMATs)	Department of Health and Humans Services/National Disaster Medical System	- 55 teams - Staffed, trained, and equipped to be self-sufficient for 72 hours to provide medical care at fixed or temporary medical care facilities
Disaster Mortuary Operational Response Teams (DMORTs)	Department of Health and Humans Services/National Disaster Medical System	- 10 regions in the U.S. - 3 Disaster Portable Morgue Units (DPMU) - Staffed, trained, and equipped to gather data on deceased personnel and use sophisticated computer programming to match this data to recovered remains

4. Activation of the EOC
5. Notification is sent to EOC staff members
6. EOC managers evaluate status
7. The EOC is operational and an incident log is opened
8. SOPs are implemented using checklists
9. Tasks are assigned according to the response plan
10. Resources are allocated or requested (tracked in a log)
11. Performance is monitored and recorded in a log
12. Status briefings and updates are made to stakeholders
13. Information is disseminated to the public

NOTE: Jurisdictions may establish a departmental operations center (DOC) to coordinate operations during an incident or preplanned event. A DOC representative works in the EOC to facilitate the sharing of information.

Having incident decision makers from all involved agencies in the same location facilitates good communication and information sharing between organizations that may not occur in the field. The EOC coordinates resource requests to ensure that resources are acquired in the correct manner and to prevent duplication of effort. The incident commander is also able to better determine the situation and can provide direction and orders in a more efficient manner.

A chief officer may serve as the IC or be responsible for operations in the EOC **(Figure 8.7, p. 316)**. Responsibilities can vary greatly between jurisdictions, and it is incumbent on chief officers to know what is expected of them upon activation of the EOC. Regular drills and training in EOC operations will ensure chief officers operate effectively in their roles during real emergencies.

Figure 8.7 A chief officer serving in an operations position at an EOC.

Chapter Summary

Depending on the jurisdiction, chief officers may be assigned emergency management responsibilities or may operate in an emergency management function during large-scale incidents and disasters. A thorough understanding of emergency management principles and practices will go a long way towards ensuring that you as a chief officer will operate effectively in your role.

Careful preincident planning using an all-hazards approach will ensure that all contingencies are accounted for. In addition, routine exercises and drills allow for stakeholders from all responding agencies and organizations to work together and determine gaps in emergency planning and preparation.

Review Questions

1. What are the principles of emergency management? (pp. 302-310)
2. What types of resources should be integrated in emergency management? (pp. 310-314)
3. What are the various functions of an Emergency Operations Center (EOC)? (pp. 314-315)

Appendices

Courtesy of Ron Jeffers.

Contents

Appendix A
Chapter and Page Correlation to NFPA® Competencies 318

Appendix B
The 16 Firefighter Life Safety Initiatives................... 320

Appendix C
Sample Justification Form... 321

Appendix D
SCBA Survey Form 322

Appendix E
Sample Request for Proposal................................... 325

Appendix F
Equipment Evaluation Form...................................... 328

Appendix G
Model Building and Fire Codes................................. 330

Appendix H
Formula for Calculating Frequency and Severity of Risk 331

Appendix A
NFPA® 1021 Job Performance Requirements (JPRs) with Chapter and Page References
NFPA® 1021 (Level III & IV)

JPR Numbers	Chapter References*	Page References
6.2.1	2	45-50
6.2.2	2	50-63
6.2.3	2	63-65
6.2.4	2	70-75
6.2.5	2	65-67
6.2.6	2	52
6.2.7	2	70-72
6.3.1	3	99-114
6.4.1	4	140-155
6.4.2	4	149-155
6.4.3	4	155-167
6.4.4	4	167-175
6.4.5	4	167-175
6.4.6	4	176-180
6.5.1	5	226-232
6.5.2	5	216-226
6.6.1	6	240-244
6.6.2	6	244-249
6.6.3	6	239-240
6.7.1	7	276-288
6.8.1	8	302-315
7.2.1	2	76-80
7.2.2	2	82-89
7.2.3	2	89-91
7.3.4	2	91-93
7.2.5	2	88-89, 93

JPR Numbers	Chapter References*	Page References
7.3.1	3	114-134
7.4.1	4	180-188
7.4.2	4	188-206
7.4.3	4	206-210
7.4.4	4	180-188
7.6.1	6	249-269
7.6.2	6	249-269
7.7.1	7	288-296

Appendix B
The 16 Firefighter Life Safety Initiatives

The 16 Firefighter Life Safety Initiatives, also known as *Everyone Goes Home®*, are:

1. Define and advocate the need for a cultural change relating to safety; incorporating leadership, management, supervision, accountability and personal responsibility.
2. Enhance personal and organizational accountability for health and safety.
3. Focus greater attention on the integration of risk management with incident management at all levels, including strategic, tactical, and planning responsibilities.
4. All firefighters must be empowered to stop unsafe practices.
5. Develop and implement national standards for training, qualifications, and certification (including regular recertification) that are equally applicable to all firefighters based on the duties they are expected to perform.
6. Develop and implement national medical and physical fitness standards that are equally applicable to all firefighters, based on the duties they are expected to perform.
7. Create a national research agenda and data collection system that relates to the initiatives.
8. Utilize available technology wherever it can produce higher levels of health and safety.
9. Thoroughly investigate all firefighter fatalities, injuries, and near misses.
10. Grant programs should support the implementation of safe practices and/or mandate safe practices as an eligibility requirement.
11. National standards for emergency response policies and procedures should be developed and championed.
12. National protocols for response to violent incidents should be developed and championed.
13. Firefighters and their families must have access to counseling and psychological support.
14. Public education must receive more resources and be championed as a critical fire and life safety program.
15. Advocacy must be strengthened for the enforcement of codes and the installation of home fire sprinklers.
16. Safety must be a primary consideration in the design of apparatus and equipment.

Appendix C
Sample Justification Form

Grange City
PROJECT JUSTIFICATION
FY13/14 thru FY17/18

Project Title:

Department:

Department Rank:

Project Type:
    Street Improvements   Economic Development
    Sidewalks & Trees   Vehicles
    Buildings & Grounds   Equipment

Project Description:

	FY13/14	FY14/15	FY15/16	FY16/17	FY17/18	TOTAL
Grant Share:						$ 0
Motor Fuel Tax Share:						$ 0
Capital Budget Share:						$ 0
Other Funding Share:						$ 0
TOTAL:	$ 0	$ 0	$ 0	$ 0	$ 0	$ 0

Appendix D
SCBA Survey Form

1. Primary Use Applications:

Fire fighting operations	Yes	No
Rescue operations	Yes	No
HAZ MAT operations	Yes	No
Other:	Yes	No

2. What features are most important for new SCBA?

NFPA compliance	Yes	No
Capable of future NFPA upgrade	Yes	No
Comfort	Yes	No
Communications	Yes	No
Individual facepiece and sizes	Yes	No
Electronic features	Yes	No
Low lifecycle cost	Yes	No
Ease of use while wearing protective clothing	Yes	No
Ease of cleaning/disinfecting	Yes	No
Proven performance	Yes	No
Distributor service and support	Yes	No
SCBA warranty	Yes	No
SCBA maintenance requirements	Yes	No

3. SCBA working pressure:

4 500 psig cylinders:	4 500 psig	2 216 psig
• Lighter weight		
• Low profile		
• Choice of duration (30-45-60 minutes)		
2 216 psig cylinders:		
• Lightweight (composite cylinders)		
• Refill capability – cascade *vs.* compressor		
Fill station capability	4 500 psig	2 216 psig

4. What accessory options are important?

Integrated PASS alarms	Yes	No
Buddy-breathing capabilities	Yes	No
Airline capabilities for extended duration – HAZ MAT/Confined space	Yes	No
Rapid cylinder refill option	Yes	No
Communications	Yes	No
• Amplification	Yes	No
• Radio interface	Yes	No

5. How many SCBA are required?

Total number of SCBA required	
Total number of spare cylinders required	
Rated duration: 30 Minute	
45 Minute (4 500 psig)	
60 Minute (4 500 psig)	

6. How will the department pay for this purchase?

Cash purchase	Yes	No
Lease-purchase options	Yes	No
• City/county/township finance	Yes	No
• Vendor finance programs	Yes	No
Other:	Yes	No

7. How many different SCBA will be considered?

Scott Air-Pak 2.2	Yes	No
Scott Air-Pak 3.0	Yes	No
Scott Air-Pak 4.5	Yes	No
MSA MMR	Yes	No
Survivair Panther	Yes	No
Draeger	Yes	No
ISI Viking	Yes	No
Interspiro	Yes	No

8. Which SCBA distributors will be considered?

Distributor	Contact Person and Phone	SCBA Supplied

9. Who will provide SCBA training after purchase?

SCBA distributor	Yes	No
Department training officer	Yes	No

10. Who will provide service and testing of SCBA after purchase?

SCBA distributor	Yes	No
Department personnel	Yes	No

11. Who will initiate SCBA?

Record format	Department	Distributor
SCBA identification	Department	Distributor
Facepiece fit testing and records	Department	Distributor

12. Will current SCBA be:

Kept for backup/training?	Yes	No
Traded in to offset purchase price?	Yes	No
Disposed of by SCBA distributor?	Yes	No
Sold by department?	Yes	No
Donated by department?	Yes	No

Appendix E
Sample Request for Proposal

Introduction

The _____ Department is pursuing the evaluation and subsequent purchase of SCBA. To accomplish this, the department is requesting SCBA meeting the specifications shown in this request for proposal.

Through each of the major steps of the evaluation process, the SCBA evaluated will be assigned points based on a point system in the categories as follows:

    SCBA Provider Support   30 points
    Actual and/or Simulated Use Conditions   35 points
    Classroom/Maintenance   35 points

Throughout the evaluation process each evaluation team member will review the features of the SCBA submitted and complete an evaluation form. The forms will be tabulated and totaled in each category.

The evaluation process will begin with distributor presentations and training of firefighters who are assigned to evaluate the SCBA. At the time of the presentation, the supplier must submit _____ SCBA meeting the specifications shown in this request for proposal and at least one spare cylinder for each SCBA to be used by the department for the evaluation period.

Each supplier is requested to complete the attached questionnaire and return it to:

_____

(Department Contact Person and Address)

The completed questionnaire should be returned no later than_____.

Pre-Qualification Questionnaire

All questions will be answered in detail on a separate sheet.

1. Location of Corporate/Business Headquarters:

    Company Name:
    Street:
    City, State, Zip:
    Phone:
    FAX:
    SCBA Supplied:

2. Location of the nearest office or distribution center with repair capabilities. Prompt facilitation of repairs will be a critical factor in pre-qualification. Describe in this section your ability to effectively perform maintenance service and repair functions.

   Company Name:
   Name of Person in Charge:
   Street:
   City, State, Zip:
   Phone:
   FAX:

3. Provide contact individuals, titles, and phone numbers of persons within your organization who will be responsible for supporting the department through the evaluation process as well as subsequent use and maintenance of SCBA.

4. How long has your firm been in the business of supplying SCBA and service?

5. What major fire department or industrial SCBA owner does your firm currently support? How many SCBA does this department/company own? How long has your firm supported this customer?

6. Indicate the approximate number of self-contained breathing apparatus sold during each of the past two years.

7. Indicate the approximate number of self-contained breathing apparatus overhauled/serviced during each of the past two years.

8. Will you furnish a finance program for this purchase? If so, include details of program.

9. Indicate if you will provide facepiece fit testing, equipment identification, and record format. Please provide details of how each process is conducted.

10. Will you furnish a written guarantee that sufficient replacement apparatus and/or replacement parts and components will be available at your facility if requested within a minimum 24-hour period?

11. Will your firm provide support including training and technical information for the evaluation units and subsequent purchased SCBA?

12. Will you provide a written copy of the manufacturer's warranty on the entire SCBA unit? State length of standard warranty and portions of unit covered as well as all requirements for the department to remain within warranty compliance.

13. Provider must state estimated ability to meet current and future NFPA standards.

14. Include any information that may be of interest to the _____ Department in this process.

15. Prospective provider must submit "Current Customer Profile" to allow the _____ Department full range of communication with current distributor customers.

Request for Qualifications
Qualifications of Proposer Construction Manager

Instructions (Add additional pages as needed)

Provide the following information for projects completed by the Project Manager within the past five (5) years. Each project submitted should be of equal or greater scope, size, and complexity. Complete all required information and submit this form as required by the RFQ. Failure to submit a completed form may result in the submission being rejected. List no more than 5 projects: Reference Form RPQ-CM-R1 must be submitted for each Form RFQ-CM that is submitted.

RFQ Solicitation No.: _____ **RFQ Title:** _____

Name of Proposer: _____ **Name of Constr. Mgr:** _____

Project Name: _____

Project Address: _____

Owner's Name: _____ **Contact Name:** _____

Contact Telephone No. _____

Contact e-mail address: _____

Brief Scope of Project: _____

_____

Construction Value: Awarded: _____ **Actual:** _____

Basis for difference in value: _____

Project Completion Days: Projected: _____ **Actual:** _____

Number of Change Orders Approved: _____

Number of RFI's Submitted: _____

Project Type:

Design-Bid-Build   Design/Build   CM@Risk   Other: _____

Green Globe or LEED Certified Project:

YES   NO   If yes, level of Certification: _____

Was work performed as an employee of the Proposer?   YES   NO

By: _____   _____
      Signature of Authorized Officer   Date

Appendix F
Equipment Evaluation Form

Rank _____ Name _____

Date _____ Location _____

        (1) Strongly Disagree
        (2) Disagree
        (3) No Opinion or Not Applicable
        (4) Agree
        (5) Strongly Agree

1. The SCBA was easy to don.   1   2   3   4   5

_____

2. After donning, the SCBA fit comfortably.   1   2   3   4   5

_____

3. The facepiece is easy to don.   1   2   3   4   5

_____

4. The facepiece and head harness do not interfere with head protection.   1   2   3   4   5

_____

5. It is easy to breathe with the regulator undocked from the facepiece.   1   2   3   4   5

_____

6. The regulator is easy to dock/undock and remains secure.   1   2   3   4   5

_____

7. It is easy to breathe with air flowing.   1   2   3   4   5

_____

8. The purge/bypass is easy to operate.   1   2   3   4   5

_____

9. It is easy to determine when *my* PASS device activates.	1	2	3	4	5

10. The PASS device is easy to reset. 1 2 3 4 5

11. I felt balanced wearing the SCBA while:
    A. Walking 1 2 3 4 5
    B. Climbing ladder 1 2 3 4 5
    C. Crawling 1 2 3 4 5
    D. Raising arms and pulling 1 2 3 4 5

12. The air-pressure gauge is easy to read. 1 2 3 4 5

13. The low-air alarm is easy to hear and identify. 1 2 3 4 5

14. The cylinder valve is easy to turn off. 1 2 3 4 5

15. The cylinder is easy to change. 1 2 3 4 5

16. Communication is clear with the facepiece on. 1 2 3 4 5

17. The communication system is clear. 1 2 3 4 5

Total Points _____ /100 possible

Appendix G
Model Building and Fire Codes

Canadian and Provincial:
The Canadian Commission on Building and Fire Codes is responsible for development of the national model codes.

- National Codes
  — The National Building Code of Canada, 1995
  — National Fire Code of Canada, 1995
- Provincial Codes
  — Alberta Fire Code, 1997
  — Alberta Building Code, 1997
  — Quebec Construction Code — Chapter 1, Building, and National Building Code of Canada, 1995 (amended)

United States and State/Territorial:
At the time of writing, model building and fire codes in the United States are experiencing considerable change. Beginning in 1994, the consolidation of a number of model code organizations into the International Codes Council (ICC) started the process of replacing each with a single International Building Code (IBC). Over generally the same period of time, the National Fire Protection Association (NFPA) began work on a model building and fire code.

Building and fire codes in the United States are adopted at the state/territorial, county/parish, and municipal levels of government. There is no national fire code as such. The following list of applicable codes is based on the existing codes in the fall of 2003.

- Model Codes
  — NFPA 1 Uniform Fire Code, 2003
  — NFPA 101 Life Safety Code (applicable in 31 states)
  — NFPA 5000 Building Code
  — Uniform Building Code (UBC), 1997
  — Uniform Fire Code, 2000
  — NFPA National Fire Alarm Code, 1999
  — International Building Code, 2000 (will replace Standard Building Code, BOCA Building Code, National Building Code, and Uniform Building Code)
  — International Fire Code, 2000 (will replace Standard Fire Prevention Code, BOCA Fire Prevention Code, National Fire Prevention Code, And Uniform Fire Code)
- State Codes
  — Florida Building Codes, 2001
  — New York State Fire Code
  — Virginia Statewide Fire Prevention Code, 1999
  — North Carolina Fire Prevention Code, 2002
  — Idaho Fire Code, 2000
  — California Fire Code, Title 24, Part 9, 2001
  — California Building Code, Title 24, Part 2, 2001
  — San Francisco Building Code, current edition

Some states, such as New York and Wisconsin, and some municipalities, such as Chicago, New York, San Francisco, and Los Angeles, have their own locally developed codes. But most states and municipalities adopt one of the three model codes in total or in part, at which time it becomes the law of that jurisdiction.

Appendix H
Formula for Calculating Frequency and Severity of Risk

The following formulas may be used to calculate the frequency or incident rate and the severity of incidents.

The Occupational Safety and Health Administration (OSHA) calculates the frequency (incident rate) as follows:

$$N/EH \times 200{,}000 = IR$$

Where:

   N = number of injuries and/or illnesses
   EH = total hours worked by all employees during the calendar year
   200,000 = base for 100 full-time equivalent employees
       (provides *standardization between agencies and companies*)
   IR = incident rate

OSHA calculates the severity as follows:

$$LWD/EH \times 200{,}000 = S$$

Where:

   LWD = loss work days
   EH = total hours worked by all employees during the calendar year
   200,000 = base for 100 full-time equivalent employees
   S = severity rate

Another method is to assign values to the frequency and severity in the following formula:

$$R = S \times IR$$

Where:

   R = risk
   S = severity
   IR = incident rate

Assessment of Severity

8. Extreme — Multiple deaths or widespread destruction may result from hazard.
7. Very High — Potential death or injury or severe financial loss may result.
6. High — Permanent disabling injury may result.
5. Serious — Loss time injury greater than 28 days or considerable financial loss.
4. Moderate — Loss time injury of 4 to 28 days or moderate financial loss.
3. Minor — Loss time injury up to 3 days.
2. Slight — Minor injury resulting in no loss of time or slight financial loss.
1. Minimal — No loss of time injury or financial loss to organization.

Assessment of Incident Rate

7. Frequent — Occurs weekly.
6. Very Likely — Occurs once every few months.
5. Likely — Occurs about once a year.
4. Occasional — Occurs annually in the United States.
3. Rare — Occurs every 10 to 30 years.
2. Exceptional — Occurs every 10 to 30 years in the United States.
1. Unlikely — May occur once in 10,000 years within the global fire service.

Glossary

Courtesy of Ron Jeffers.

Glossary

A

Analysis — Ability to divide information into its most basic components.

Area Command (AC) — Area Command is an expansion of the Incident Command function and is primarily designed to manage a very large incident that has multiple incident management teams assigned. However, an Area Command can be established at any time that incidents are close enough that oversight direction is required among incident management teams to ensure conflicts do not arise.

B

Boilerplate — Standardized or formulaic language.

C

Customer Service — Quality of an organization's relationship with individuals who have contact with the organization. There are internal customers such as the various levels of personnel and trainees, and external customers such as other organizations and the public. Customer service is the way these individuals, personnel, and organizations are treated, and their levels of satisfaction.

E

Emergency Operations Center (EOC) — Facility that houses communications equipment, plans, contact/notification list, and staff that are used to coordinate the response to an emergency.

G

Grant — Donated funding from a government or private source, typically secured through a competitive application process; funds do not have to be repaid, and are separate from an organization's operational or capital budget.

L

Leadership — Knack of getting other people to follow you and to do willingly the things that you want them to do.

Logistics — Process of managing the scheduling of limited materials and equipment to meet the multiple demands of training programs and instructors.

M

Management — Process of accomplishing organizational objectives through effective and efficient handling of resources; official, sanctioned leadership.

Mobile Water Supply Apparatus — Fire apparatus with a water tank of 1,000 gallons (3 785 L) or larger whose primary purpose is transporting water; may also carry a pump, some hose, and other equipment.

N

Needs Assessment — Analysis identifying life-support and critical infrastructure requirements.

P

Planning Model — Organized procedure that includes the steps of analyzing, designing, developing, implementing, and evaluating instruction; a systematic approach to the design, production, evaluation, and use of a system of instruction.

R

Request for Information (RFI) — A request made during the project planning phase to assist a buyer in clearly identifying product requirements, specifications, and purchase options. RFIs should clearly indicate that award of a contract will not automatically follow.

Request for Proposal (RFP) — Public document that advertises an organizational need to manufacturers or individuals who may be able to meet that need and defines the specific requirements for an item that an organization intends to purchase through the bid process.

Risk Assessment — (1) Determining the risk level or seriousness of a risk. (2) Process for evaluating risk associated with a specific hazard defined in terms of probability and frequency of occurrence, magnitude and severity, exposure, and consequences. *Also known as* Risk Evaluation.

S

Stakeholder — People, groups, or organizations that have a vested interest in a specific issue.

Strategic Planning — Process for identifying long-term goals and objectives for a program or department, usually for a period of five years.

U

Unified Command (UC) — In the Incident Command System, a shared command role in which all agencies with geographical or functional responsibility establish a common set of incident objectives and strategies. In unified command there is a single incident command post and a single operations chief at any given time.

Index

Index

A

AC (area command), 263
Accident, injury, and illness prevention program, 279-288
    hazards/corrective measures identification, 279-286
        fatalities, 280-282
        hazardous materials exposure, 286
        hearing loss, 284-285
        injuries, 282
        motor vehicle-related incidents, 283-284
        occupational illness, 283
        respiratory injury or illness, 285-286
    implementation, 286-288
    monitoring, evaluation, and revision, 288
Accreditation
    certification vs., 195
    CFAI. *See* Commission on Fire Accreditation International (CFAI)
    Commission on Accreditation of Ambulance Services, 115
    re-accreditation, 152
    training vs., 195
ACP (area contingency plan), 254
Acronyms
    LIPS, 242-243
    SMART, 240
Activity records, 168-169
ADA (Americans with Disabilities Act), 50, 51, 52
Administration of emergency services
    budgeting and finance, 140-155
        budget considerations, 144-145
        budget development and management, 149-155
        budget systems, 140-142
        budget types, 140, 142-144
        revenue sources, 145-149
    community risk assessment and reduction, 206-210
    operational planning, 183-188
    organizational improvement, 176-180
        gap analysis, 176-177
        needs analysis, 176
        planning, 178-180
        SWOT analysis, 177-178
    purchasing, 155-167
        acquisition process, 162-167
        needs assessment, 156
        product data review, 161-162
        product evaluation, 160-161
        research, 157-160
        standardization, 167
    record-keeping, 167-175
        activity records, 168-169
        budget records, 167
        data analysis and interpretation, 175
        evaluation, 172
        inventory records, 168
        legal requirements, 172-175
        maintenance records, 168
        personnel records, 169-170
        revision, 172
        system development, 170-172
    strategic planning, 180-183
    training requirements, 188-206
        evaluation of requirements, 188-190
        external training sources, 204-206
        funding sources, 204
        program development, 190-204
        program evaluation, 206
Administrative Fire Officer (NFPA® Level III), 28
Advertising
    for position marketing, 56
    vacancy, 63
Affiliation as cause of unethical conduct, 15
Affirmative action, 50, 76, 78-79
Age Discrimination in Employment Act of 1967, 50, 76
Agency mission and goals, 75
Agreements
    automatic aid, 239, 242
    automatic response, 118
    Emergency Management Assistance Compact, 304
    intergovernmental, 122
    joint training, 239-240
    mutual aid, 118, 239, 242
AHJ. *See* Authority having jurisdiction (AHJ)
Alaskan fire service training, 205
Alternative response vehicle, 134
Amateurs seeking elected office, 125
American National Standards Institute (ANSI), 164
American Sign Language (ASL), 104
Americans with Disabilities Act (ADA), 50, 51, 52
Amplified phone sets, 104
Analysis best practices, 34
Analysis of past performance for professional development, 73
Annual leave employee benefit, 65
Annual reports, 183
ANSI (American National Standards Institute), 164
Antagonists seeking elected office, 125
Anticipating personnel challenges, 47-48
Apparatus
    budget considerations, 145
    mobile water supply apparatus, 284
    replacement planning, 187
    training facility areas for, 196
Application form, 58
Applied Research Project (ARP), 28
Appointed official political processes, 122
Aptitude tests for employment, 59
Arbitration, 86-87
Area command (AC), defined, 263
Area contingency plan (ACP), 254
ARP (Applied Research Project), 28
Arson, 252
ASL (American Sign Language), 104
Assessment
    needs assessment, 34
    for performance excellence, 31
    risk assessment, 34
Assessment center, 59, 64
Assignment List (ICS Form 204), 240, 244

Associate's degree program, 70
ATF (Bureau of Alcohol, Tobacco, Firearms, and Explosives), 121
Attendance records, 169
Audio programs for position marketing, 56
Authority having jurisdiction (AHJ)
    budget considerations, 153
    certification requirements, 28
    chief officer education and training, 27, 28
    fire prevention and life safety standards, 217
    job applicant standards, 53
    MAPS, 92
    pre-employment medical examination, 62
    product acquisition, 162
    professional standard of conduct, 27
    training and education standards, 90
Automatic aid agreements, 239, 242
Automatic response agreements, 118
Auxiliary enterprise, 148
Award ceremonies, 88
Award of purchase contract, 166-167

B

Bachelor's degree program, 70
Background screening, 58
Baldrige Performance Excellence Program, 31
Banners for position marketing, 56
Bargaining sessions, 84, 85
Basic needs as cause of unethical conduct, 15
Behavioral hazards, 207
Behavioral health program, 91-92
Benchmarks, 178-179
Benefits. *See* Employee benefits
Bereavement leave employee benefit, 65
Best practices, 29-38
    change management, 34-38
        change process stages, 34-35
        change types, 35
        follow-up program plan, 38
        process implementation, 36-38
        resistance to change, 35-36
    code requirements, 179
    current management theory, 29-32
        contingency theory, 30-31
        organizational behavior, 30
        organizational culture, 32
        quantitative management, 30
        systems theory, 30
        Total Quality Management, 31
    fire service leadership, 32-34
        environmental scanning, 32
        forecasting and trending, 32
        innovation, 33
        research, analysis, and evaluation, 34
        technology awareness, 33
    follow-up program plan, 38
    process implementation, 36-38
BIA (Bureau of Indian Affairs), 121
Bicycle safety training, 134
Bid specifications, 164-166
Billboards for position marketing, 57
Biological exposures, 280
Block grants, 149

Boilerplate, 164, 165
Bonds
    as budget revenue source, 148
    for purchases, 163
Bottom-line mentality as cause of unethical conduct, 16
Breathing-air supply at training facilities, 196
Bribery as unethical conduct, 16
Brochures for position marketing, 56
Budgeting and finance, 140-155
    budget considerations, 144-145
    budget development and management, 149-155
        environmental costs, 151
        evaluation, 155
        implementation, 153
        justification form, 150, 321
        monitoring, 154
        planning, 150
        preparation, 150-153, 321
        revision, 155
    budget systems, 140-142
        defined, 140
        line-item budgeting, 141
        matrix budgeting, 141
        performance budgeting, 141
        planning programming budgeting system, 142
        program budgeting, 141
        zero-based budgeting, 141
    budget types, 140, 142-144
    capital budget, 142-143, 183
    operating budget, 142, 143-144, 183
    records, 167
    revenue sources, 145-149
Building codes. *See also* Codes
    enforcement of, 229
    Model Building and Fire Codes, 229, 330
Bureau of Alcohol, Tobacco, Firearms, and Explosives (ATF), 121
Bureau of Indian Affairs (BIA), 121
Burn and smoke buildings for training, 198

B

CAAS (Commission on Accreditation of Ambulance Services), 115
Canada
    Canadian Human Rights Act of 1985, 76
    Canadian Human Rights Commission and Equal Wages Guidelines of 1986, 76
    federal agencies, 121
    Fire Underwriter's Survey, 48
    interagency relations, 121
    law enforcement agencies, 120, 121
    laws affecting employment, 50
    military police forces, 121
    RCMP, 121
    Safe Community Foundation, 221
    staffing requirements, 48
    UL Canada, 288
Canadian Transport Emergency Centre (CANUTEC), 121
Candid photography, 108
Candidate Physical Ability Test (CPAT), 52, 59, 87
CANUTEC (Canadian Transport Emergency Centre), 121
Capital budgets, 142-143, 183
Capital funds used for purchases, 163

Capital improvements, 186
Capital non-reoccurring (CNR) budget, 142
Cardiopulmonary resuscitation (CPR) training, 132, 149
Career advancement as contract issue, 86
Career days for position marketing, 57
Career fire departments, NFPA® 1710 staffing requirements, 48
Catastrophic events, contingency plans for, 48
Category A medical condition, 52–53
Category B medical condition, 52–53
CBRNE (chemical, biological, radiological, nuclear, and explosive) incidents, 285
CDC (Centers for Disease Control and Prevention), 121, 207, 288
CEMSO (Chief Emergency Medical Services Officer) designation, 74
Center for Campus Fire Safety, 221
Center for Public Safety Excellence (CPSE)
    CFAI self-assessment, 139
    Chief Officer Designation Program, 28
    Chief Officer designations, 74
    data analysis training, 34
    staffing requirements, 48
Centers for Disease Control and Prevention (CDC), 121, 207, 288
Centralized storage, 268
CERT (Community Emergency Response Team), 313
Certification
    of applicants, 63
    certification vs., 195
    education and training, 28
    training vs., 195
CFAI. *See* Commission on Fire Accreditation International (CFAI)
CFO (Chief Fire Officer) designation, 74
CFSI (Congressional Fire Service Institute), 117
Challenge the F.O.R.C.E. (Firefighters Organizing Resources for Community Enrichment), 132–133
Change management, 34–38
    change process stages, 34–35
        commitment, 35
        denial, 34
        exploration, 35
        resistance, 34
    change types, 35
        people, 35
        strategic, 35
        structure, 35
        technology, 35
    follow-up program plan, 38
    process implementation, 36–38
    resistance to change, 35–36
Characteristics of chief officers, 14–25
    ethics, 14–18
        causes of unethical conduct, 15–16
        Code of Ethics, 17
        ethical conduct, 15
        issues, 18
        personal ethics origins, 15
        personal justifications, 16
    leadership, 18–23
        application of theory, 20–21
        challenges and solutions, 23
        defined, 18
        management vs., 19
        principled leader theory, 20
        proactive leadership, 24–25
        skills, 19
        strong leaders, 18–19
        360-degree feedback evaluation, 21
        traits, 22–23
Chemical, biological, radiological, nuclear, and explosive (CBRNE) incidents, 285
Chemical hazards, 279
Chief Emergency Medical Services Officer (CEMSO), 74
Chief Fire Officer (CFO) designation, 74
Chief Officer Designation Program, 28
Child car seat safety programs, 134
Citizen Corps, 103
Citizen political processes, 122
Civil disorder, 253
Civil Rights Act of 1964, 50, 76, 78
Class A foam training, 198
Class B foam training, 198
Classrooms for training, 198
Closed-ended questions, 60
CNCS (Corporation for National & Community Service), 103
CNR (capital non-reoccurring) budget, 142
Code of Ethics, 17, 26
Code of Federal Regulations
    long-term planning and, 186
    29 *CFR* 1910.20, *Medical Record Keeping*, 169
    29 *CFR* 1910.95, *Occupational Noise Exposure*, 285
    29 *CFR* 1910.134, respiratory protection, 286
    29 *CFR* 1910.1200, *Hazard Communication Standard*, 286
Codes
    building and fire codes
        enforcement of, 229
        model, 229, 330
    consensus, 179
    enforcement of, 229
    long-term planning and, 186
    organizational changes to comply with, 179
    training requirements, 189
Collective bargaining, 82, 83
College
    career days for position marketing, 57
    for outside training, 204–205
    as recruitment source, 55
Columbia space shuttle disaster recovery, 303
Combustible liquid/gas training props, 200
Commission on Accreditation of Ambulance Services (CAAS), 115
Commission on Fire Accreditation International (CFAI)
    politics and importance of accreditation, 115
    self-assessment program, 139
    staffing levels, 179
Commission on Professional Credentialing (CPC), 28
Commitment to change, 35
Communication
    executive level, 38–40
    Incident Radio Communications Plan (ICS 205), 242, 244
    integrated, 263
    labor negotiation open communication, 83–84
    leadership traits, 22
    as political resource, 127
    at training facilities, 196
    as trait of good leaders, 22

Community and government relations, 99–134
    community awareness programs, 103–114
    community involvement, 130–134
    legislation monitoring, 128–130
    participation in politics, 114–122
    political decision-making, 122–128
    service delivery, 100–103
        Citizen Corps, 103
        community connectors, 103
        community service units, 103
        comprehensive-risk approach, 101
        monitoring, 103
        systems-model approach, 100
        types of services, 101–103
Community awareness programs, 103–114
    community relations strategies, 104–105
    concerns/complaints/inquiries, 112–114
        customer service, 114
        effective listening, 112
        member act/omission resolutions, 113–114
        public inquiries, 114
        resolution, 113
    cultural customs, 105
    cultural values, 105
    language barriers, 104–105
    public fire and life safety education, 109–111
        group presentations, 111
        media programs, 111
        purpose and scope, 109–111
    public relations, 105–109
        media relations, 107–109
        Public Information Officer, 105–106
        social media, 109
Community connectors, 103
Community emergency resources, 312–313
Community Emergency Response Team (CERT), 313
Community expectations of fire and emergency services organizations, 152–153
Community impact fees, 147
Community involvement, 130–134
    community leadership, 130–131
    decision-making function, 131–132
    goals-setting functions, 131–132
    partnerships, 132–133
    programs, 132, 133–134
Community leaders seeking elected office, 125
Community needs analysis, 176
Community needs and training requirements, 189
Community Paramedicine, 219
Community risk assessment and reduction, 206–210
    Fire Service Vulnerability Assessment Project, 207
    hazard categories, 207–209
        behavioral, 207
        intentional, 208
        natural, 208
        occupancy related, 208–209
    high value/priority exposures, 209
    procedure, 206–207
    program development, 210
    written analysis, 209–210
Community service units, 103
Community stewards seeking elected office, 125

Complaints from citizens, 112–114
Comprehensive-risk service delivery, 101
Concerns from citizens, 112–114
Confidentiality of records, 108, 170, 173
Congressional Fire Service Institute (CFSI), 117
Contingency plans, 47–48
Contingency theory, 30–31
Continuing education
    agency mission and goals, 75
    needs assessments, 75
    training program development, 74–75
Contracts
    content, 84
    issues, 85–86
    negotiations and, 85–86
    requirements, budgeting for, 152
Controlled substances, human resources policies and procedures, 51
Convergence, 311
Corporation for National & Community Service (CNCS), 103
Costs
    budget considerations, 152
    employee benefits, 65, 143
    environmental, 151
    government mandates, 152
    knowledge of, in negotiation preparation, 85
    life-cycle cost of equipment, 162
Counselors for improving leadership skills, 21
Courses for improving leadership skills, 21
Covey, Stephen, 20
CPAT (Candidate Physical Ability Test), 52, 59, 87
CPC (Commission on Professional Credentialing), 28
CPR training, 132, 149
CPSE. *See* Center for Public Safety Excellence (CPSE)
Credentialing
    chief officer designations, 74
    Commission on Professional Credentialing, 28
    credentialed media personnel, 107
    Executive Fire Officer Program, 74
    professional development, 73–74
Crew rotation, 49
Crime-scene protection, 108
Criticism of leaders, 25
Critique records, 248
Culture
    community relations and, 105
    customs, 105
    identifying the current organizational culture, 80
    raise cultural awareness, 80–81
    values, 105
Current management theory, 29–32
    contingency theory, 30–31
    organizational behavior, 30
    organizational culture, 32
    quantitative management, 30
    systems theory, 30
    Total Quality Management, 31
Curriculum for the fire service, 28
Customer service, 114

D

Data analysis and interpretation, 175
Data collection for fire prevention and life safety programs, 221–222
Data monitoring, fire prevention and life safety programs, 224–225
Deadlines of the media, 108
Debris removal after disasters, 259
Decision-making functions of community involvement, 131–132
Decisiveness of good leaders, 23, 25
Decontamination
    equipment, at training facilities, 196
    water system, 196
Dedication of good leaders, 23
Demographics appraisal, 76–81
    affirmative action programs, 78–79
    discrimination, 76
    diversity barriers, 78
    EEO/affirmative action programs, 79
    external community demographics, 76–77
    internal organizational demographics, 77–78
    Workplace Diversity Initiative, 79–81
Denial of change, 34
Department of Agriculture Forest Service, 121
Department of Defense (DOD), 121
Department of Justice (DOJ), 120, 121
Department of National Defense and the Canadian Forces, 121
Department of the Interior (DOI), 121
Department of the Treasury, 121
Dependent sick leave, 65
Deployment of resources to incidents, 237
DHHS (U.S. Department of Health and Human Services), 257
DHS. *See* U.S. Department of Homeland Security (DHS)
Direct monetary incentives, 88
Disability
    accommodations for, 52
    Americans with Disabilities Act, 50, 51, 52
    as cause of separation or termination of employment, 68
    defined, 52
Disaster Medical Assistance Team (DMAT), 314
Disaster Mortuary Operational Response Team (DMORT), 314
Disaster plan
    debris removal, 259
    emergency operations center, 256
    implementation, 257–258
    incident termination, 258
    interagency relations, 254
    jurisdictional authority, 254–255
    mitigation/prevention, 250
    overview, 249–250
    preparedness, 250
    recovery, 250
    recovery and rehabilitation, 259
    resource allocation, 256–257
    response, 250
    restoration of services, 259
    security, 259
Disasters
    defined, 250
    human-caused, 252–253
    natural, 251–252
    technological, 254

Discipline, dismissals, 69
Discrimination
    affirmative action programs, 50, 76, 78–79
    Age Discrimination Employment Act of 1967, 50
    demographics not discrimination, 76
    employee, 51
Disincentives for fire prevention, 217
Dismissals, 69
Dispersed storage, 268
District Response Group, 257
Diverse workforce, 55–56
Diversity in organizations. *See also* Demographics appraisal
    advantages of, 77–78
    barriers, 78
    Workplace Diversity Initiative, 79–81
DMAT (Disaster Medical Assistance Team), 314
DMORT (Disaster Mortuary Operational Response Team), 314
Doctorate degree program, 71
Documentation, post incident analysis, 248–249
DOD (Department of Defense), 121
DOI (Department of the Interior), 121
DOJ (Department of Justice), 120, 121
DOT. *See* U.S. Department of Transportation (DOT)
Driving courses at training facilities, 198
Dunn and Bradstreet, 157–158
Duties of chief officers, 3–4

E

Economic incentives for fire prevention, 217
Economics, contingency plan considerations, 47–48
Editorial control over stories, 108
Education
    assessing resources, 90–91
    associate's degree, 70
    bachelor's degree, 70
    chief officers, 27–28
    defined, 188
    degree programs, 71–72
    doctorate degree, 71
    emergency management/homeland security degree program, 72
    emergency medical technology degree program, 72
    fire administration degree program, 72
    fire prevention, 215, 217
    fire prevention and life safety programs, 225
    fire protection engineering degree program, 71
    fire science/technology degree program, 71
    higher education, 70–72
    master's degree, 71
    needs determination, 89–90
    as political resource, 128
    16 Life Safety Initiatives, 320
Educational events for position marketing, 56
EEO/Affirmative Action Program, 79
EEOC (Equal Employment Opportunity Commission), 76
EFO (Executive Fire Officer), 74
EFOP (Executive Fire Officer Program), 28, 74
Elected official political processes, 122
Electric power companies as training source, 206
Electrical hazards, 279
Electronic Product Environmental Assessment Tool (EPEAT), 151

EMAC (Emergency Management Assistance Compact), 304
Emergency management, 301–316
   concepts, 303–305
      interagency, 303–304
      interdisciplinary, 305
      intergovernmental, 304
      interoperability, 304
   emergency declaration process, 310
   emergency operations centers, 314–316
   emergency support functions and federal agencies, 308
   mitigation phase, 305–307
   preparedness phase, 307
   recovery phase, 309–310
   resource integration, 310–314
      community resources, 312–313
      convergence, 311
      emergency medical services, 312
      federal resources, 313–314
      fire service, 311
      law enforcement, 312
      planning, 314
      public works, 312
      state/provincial resources, 313
   response phase, 308–309
   vulnerabilities, 302
Emergency Management Assistance Compact (EMAC), 304
Emergency management/homeland security degree program, 72
Emergency medical services (EMS) emergency resources, 312
Emergency Medical Technician/Emergency Medical Services (EMT/EMS) training, 206
Emergency medical technology degree program, 72
Emergency operations center (EOC), 256, 314–316
Emergency response, fire prevention, 217
Emergency services delivery, 237–269
   comprehensive disaster plan, 249–259
      emergency operations center, 256
      human-caused, 252–253
      incident termination, 258
      interagency relations, 254
      jurisdictional authority, 254–255
      natural disasters, 251–252
      plan implementation, 257–258
      recovery and rehabilitation, 259
      resource allocation, 256–257
      technological, 254
   incident action plan, 240–244
      development, 242–243
      elements, 240, 242
      forms, 243–244
      incident objectives form, 240, 241
   incident management system, 260–269
      components/operational positions, 260–263
      integrated communications, 263
      unified and area commands, 263–269
   overview, 237–238
   post incident analysis, 244–249
      development, 246
      documentation, 248–249
      final reports, 249
      formal, 245
      incident data, 247–248
      informal, 245
      PIA critique, 248
      recommended changes, 248
   resource planning, 239–240
Emergency services staffing, 45–50
   planning, 46–48
      anticipating challenges, 47–48
      projecting needs, 46–47
   staffing assignments, 49–50
   staffing requirements, 48
Emergency support functions (ESFs), 308
Emotional stress, 280
Employee assistance programs, 92
Employee benefits
   annual leave, 65
   benefit needs analysis, 66–67
   bereavement leave, 65
   budgeting for, 143
   contract issues, 85–86
   costs of, 65, 143
   flexible spending accounts, 66
   health insurance, 66
   improving or modifying, 67
   life insurance, 66
   other benefits, 66
   purpose of, 65
   retirement/pension contributions, 65
   sick leave, 65
   uniform allotments, 66
Employee disabilities and accommodations, 52–53
   Americans with Disabilities Act, 50, 51, 52
   fitness for duty considerations, 52–53
   legal requirements, 52
   reasonable accommodations, 52
Employee grievances, 85
Employee involvement and participation in labor negotiations, 87
Employee pension fund, 148
Employment practices, 50–69
   applicant selection, 62–63
      premature selection, 63
      rushing, 62
      similarity, 63
      stereotyping, 62
   employee benefits, 65–67
   employee disabilities and accommodations, 52–53
   employment process, 58–62
      application form, 58
      background screening, 58
      interview, 59–62
      medical-fitness examination, 62
      overview, 58
      reference check, 58
      tests, 58–59
   human resources policies and procedures, 51
   job analyses, 53–54
   laws affecting employment, 50
   position descriptions, 53–54
   promotions, 63–65
   recruitment, 54–57
      defined, 54
      diverse workforces, 55–56

position marketing and posting, 56–57
    sources, 54–55
separation and termination, 67–69
Employment process, 58–62
    application form, 58
    background screening, 58
    interview, 59–62
    medical-fitness examination, 62
    overview, 58
    reference check, 58
    tests, 58–59
EMS emergency resources, 312
EMT/EMS training, 206
Enforcement
    building codes, 229
    fire inspection programs, 227–228
    fire prevention laws, 217
Engineering
    building codes, 215
    fire prevention, 215, 217
Enterprise funds as revenue source, 148
Environment
    changes, challenges of, 1
    costs, 151
    EPA Environmental Response Team, 257
    EPA Radiological Emergency Response Team, 257
    scanning, 32
    at training facilities, 196
    U.S. EPA. *See* U.S. Environmental Protection Agency (EPA)
EOC (emergency operations center), 256, 314–316
EPA. *See* U.S. Environmental Protection Agency (EPA)
EPEAT (Electronic Product Environmental Assessment Tool), 151
Equal Employment Opportunity Commission (EEOC), 76
Equal Pay Act, 50
Equal Pay Act of 1963, 76
Equipment
    budget considerations, 145, 152
    decontamination area at training facilities, 196
    evaluation form, 160, 328–329
    replacement, planning for, 185
Ergonomics, 279
ESFs (emergency support functions), 308
Ethics, 14–18
    causes of unethical conduct, 15–16
        affiliation, 15
        basic needs, 15
        behaviors violating ethical standards, 16
        bottom-line mentality, 16
        exploitive mentality, 16
        self-esteem, 15
        self-gratification, 16
    ethical conduct, 15
    importance of, 14–15
    personal ethics origins, 15
    values, 15
Evaluation
    best practices, 34
    budget effectiveness, 155
    fire inspection programs, 231
    fire prevention and life safety programs, 224–226
    goals-based, 183

outcome-based, 183
performance-based, 183
record-keeping, 172
risk management plan, 294–295
strategic planning, 182–183
training, 188–190, 193, 206
unified command systems, 268–269
Everyone Goes Home®, 320
Evolutions, 64
Excavation hazards, 279
Executive Fire Officer (EFO), 74
Executive Fire Officer (NFPA® Level IV), 28
Executive Fire Officer Program (EFOP), 28, 74
Executive level communications, 38–40
    controversy avoidance, 40
        Internet is forever, 40
        nothing is off the record, 40
        open records, 40
        personal vs. public, 40
        recorded conversations, 40
    importance of, 38
    know your audience, 39
    listening skills, 39
    nonverbal clues, 39
    truthfulness, 39
Executive recruiting agencies for position marketing, 57
Exit interview, 69
Experience vs. experiences, 29
Exploitive mentality as cause of unethical conduct, 16
Exploration of change, 35
Explosion hazards, 279
Exposure
    high value/priority, 209
    reports, 173
External review of budget requests, 153

F
FAA (Federal Aviation Administration), 295
Facilities
    budget considerations, 144–145
    location of, 186–187
    training, 195–201
    for training and education, 91
Fact-finding, 87
Factory Mutual (FM), 288
Fair Labor Standards Act (FLSA), 76
Falls, 279
Family and Medical Leave Act (FMLA), 65, 76
Family Educational Rights and Privacy Act, 173
Fatalities, 280–282. *See also* Line-of-duty death (LODD)
FBI (U.S. Federal Bureau of Investigation), 120, 253
Federal agencies, 121
Federal Aviation Administration (FAA), 295
Federal Bureau of Investigation (FBI), 120, 253
Federal Emergency Management Agency (FEMA)
    area contingency plans, 254
    business recovery after disasters, 310
    Citizen Corps, 103
    government grants, 149
    Rapid Visual Screening of Buildings for Potential Seismic Hazards, 306
Federal emergency resources, 313–314

Federal law-enforcement agencies, 120–121
Federal legislation monitoring, 129–130
Federal Mediation and Conciliation Services (FMCS), 86
Federal On Scene Coordinator (FOSC), 255, 257
Federal training requirements, 189
Feedback
    change process implementation, 37
    direct, 37
    survey, 37
    360-degree feedback evaluation, 21
FEMA. *See* Federal Emergency Management Agency (FEMA)
FESHE (Fire and Emergency Services Higher Education), 28, 70
Final offer arbitration, 86
Finance. *See* Budgeting and finance
Finance/Administration Section, 263
Financial resources, contingency plan considerations, 47–48
Fire administration degree program, 72
Fire alarm companies as training source, 206
Fire and Emergency Services Higher Education (FESHE), 28, 70
Fire and life safety education
    group presentations, 111
    media programs, 111
    purpose and scope, 109–111
    topics, 110
Fire inspection and safety planning, 215–226
    Community Paramedicine, 219
    defined, 216
    elements, 215, 217
    evaluation, 224–226
        data monitoring, 224–225
        indicators, 225–226
    implementation, 223–224
        organizational structure, 223
        personnel selection, 224
        resource allocation, 223–224
    investigation and prevention, 216
    needs identification, 218–220
    program design, 222–223
        alternatives, 223
        approvals, 222
    program selection, 220–222
        data collection, 221–222
        legal mandates, 221
        objectives of the program, 220
    programs for, 216
    resources, lack of, 218
Fire inspection programs, 226–232
    alternatives, 229–230
    background, 226
    evaluation/revision, 231
    implementation, 230
    public awareness and acceptance, 231–232
    selection and design, 227–229
        building code enforcement, 229
        inspection/enforcement, 227–228
        plans review, 228–229
Fire protection engineering degree program, 71
Fire Protection Publications (FPP), 105
Fire science/technology degree program, 71
Fire service emergency resources, 311
Fire service leadership, 32–34
    environmental scanning, 32
    forecasting and trending, 32
    innovation, 33
    research, analysis, and evaluation, 34
    technology awareness, 33
Fire Service Vulnerability Assessment Project (VAP), 207
Fire Suppression Rating Schedule (FSRS), 48
Fire Underwriter's Survey, 48
Firefighter Fatalities in the United States, 280–282
Fireground hazards, 290
Fire/heat hazards, 279
Fire-suppression systems companies as training source, 206
Fitness for duty
    employee disabilities and accommodations, 52–53
    Joint Wellness/Fitness Initiative, 87
    medical-fitness examination, 62
Flammable training props, 200
Flexible spending account employee benefit, 66
FLSA (Fair Labor Standards Act), 76
FM (Factory Mutual), 288
FMCS (Federal Mediation and Conciliation Services), 86
FMLA (Family and Medical Leave Act), 65, 76
Follow-up program plan, 38
Forecasting, 32
Foresight of proactive leaders, 24
Formal PIA, 245
FOSC (Federal On Scene Coordinator), 255, 257
FPP (Fire Protection Publications), 105
FSRS (Fire Suppression Rating Schedule), 48
Fuel source at training facilities, 196
Funding
    budget revenue sources, 145–149
        bonds, 148
        enterprise funds, 148
        fund-raisers, 149
        grants/gifts, 148–149
        memberships/subscriptions, 147
        taxes, 146–147
        trust funds, 147–148
    capital purchases, 142
    operating budgets, 142
    for purchases, 163–164
        bonds, 163
        capital funds, 163
        grants, 163
        lease, 164
        lease/purchase, 164
        operating funds, 163
    for training, 204
Fund-raising, 149

G

Gap analysis, 176–177
Gifts as revenue source, 148–149
Goals, 75
Goals-based evaluations, 183
Goals-setting functions of community involvement, 131–132
Good faith bargaining, 85
Government. *See also* Politics
    acceptance of chief officers, 116–117
    bureaucracy political processes, 122–123
    concept of governing, 124
    economic reports, 152

grants, 149
mandates, costs of, 152
public influence, 124–125
responsibility of government officials, 123–124
types of individual seeking office, 125

Grants
as budget revenue source, 148–149
for purchases, 163

Greenhouse gas, 151

Group presentations, 111

H

Hazard
all-hazards strategies, 302–303
assessment for training, 189–190
behavioral, 207
defined, 206, 289
hazards/corrective measures, 279–286
    fatalities, 280–282
    hazardous materials exposure, 286
    hearing loss, 284–285
    injuries, 282
    motor vehicle-related incidents, 283–284
    occupational illness, 283
    respiratory injury or illness, 285–286
intentional, 208
natural, 208
occupancy related, 208–209
occupational, 290

Hazardous materials
awareness and recycling programs, 134
exposure, 286
training areas, 200

Health and Safety Officer (HSO)
functions, 276
qualifications, 278
risk management roles, 289
roles and responsibilities, 278

Health and safety program, 276–279
components, 278–279
Health and Safety Officer, 278
occupational safety and health committee, 277–278
reasons for, 276

Health insurance employee benefit, 66

Health Insurance Portability and Accountability Act (HIPAA), 108, 174

Health of job applicants, 53

Hearing loss, 284–285

HEPA filter, 285, 286

HFSC (Home Fire Sprinkler Coalition), 99

High efficiency particulate air (HEPA) filter, 285, 286

High school career days for position marketing, 57

Highway incidents and conflict between agencies, 119–120

HIPAA (Health Insurance Portability and Accountability Act), 108, 174

Hiring records, 173

History, financial, 152

Home Fire Sprinkler Coalition (HFSC), 99

Home Safety Council (HSC), 105, 207

Home safety inspections, 134

Homeland security degree program, 72

Homeland Security Presidential Directive (HSPD)-5, *Management of Domestic Incidents*, 117

Honeywell International, Inc., 207

Horizontal jurisdiction, 254

Hospitals as training sources, 206

HSC (Home Safety Council), 105, 207

HSC/Safe Kids, 221

HSO. *See* Health and Safety Officer (HSO)

HSPD-5, *Management of Domestic Incidents*, 117

Human error disasters, 253

Human resources management, 45–93
continuing education, 74–75
demographics appraisal, 76–81
    affirmative action programs, 78–79
    discrimination, 76
    diversity barriers, 78
    EEO/affirmative action programs, 79
    external community demographics, 76–77
    internal organizational demographics, 77–78
    Workplace Diversity Initiative, 79–81
emergency services staffing, 45–50
    anticipating challenges, 47–48
    planning, 46–48
    projecting needs, 46–47
    staffing assignments, 49–50
    staffing requirements, 48–49
employment practices, 50–69
    applicant selection, 62–63
    employee benefits, 65–67
    employee disabilities and accommodations, 52–53
    job analyses, 53–54
    laws affecting employment, 50
    policies and procedures, 51
    position descriptions, 53–54
    process of employment, 58–62
    promotions, 63–65
    recruitment, 54–57
    separation and termination, 67–69
labor relations, 82–89
    background, 82
    incentive programs, 88–89
    negotiation process, 82–88
member assistance services, 91–93
professional development, 70–75
    credentialing, 73–74
    higher education, 70–72
    personal professional development, 73
    professional organizations, 72
    succession planning, 73
training and education, 89–91

Human-caused disasters, 252–253
arson, 252
civil disorder, 253
human error, 253
political instability, 253
terrorism/war, 253

Humility of good leaders, 23

Humor as a trait of good leaders, 23

Hurricanes Katrina and Rita, 304

Hypothetical questions, 60

I

IAFC. *See* International Association of Fire Chiefs (IAFC)
IAFF. *See* International Association of Fire Fighters (IAFF)
IAP. *See* Incident action plan (IAP)
ICC (International Code Council), 99
ICMA (International City/County Management Association), 124
ICS Form 201, Incident Briefing, 240
ICS Form 202, Incident Objectives, 240, 241, 243, 244
ICS Form 203, Organization Assignment List, 240, 243, 244
ICS Form 204, Assignment List, 240, 244
ICS Form 205, Incident Radio Communications Plan, 242, 244
ICS Form 206, Medical Plan, 242, 244
ICS Form 207, Organizational Chart, 244
ICS Form 208 or 208H, Safety message, 242
IFE (Institution of Fire Engineers), 74
Illness
   occupational, 280, 283
   prevention. *See* Accident, injury, and illness prevention program
   respiratory, 285-286, 288
Immunization programs, 132
Impasses in labor negotiations, 86-87
IMT. *See* Incident management team (IMT)
Incentive programs, 88-89
Incident action plan (IAP)
   defined, 240
   development, 242-243
   elements, 240, 242
   forms, 243-244
   incident objectives form, 240, 241
Incident Briefing (ICS Form 201), 240
Incident command system (ICS). *See also* Incident management system
   forms. *See specific ICS Form*
   IAP. *See* Incident action plan (IAP)
Incident commander (IC)
   command responsibilities, 261
   incident action plan creation, 240, 242-243
Incident management system, 260-269
   components, 260
   integrated communications, 263
   operational positions
      command, 261-262
      finance/administration, 263
      logistics, 262
      operations, 262
      planning, 262
   purpose of, 260
   unified and area commands, 263-269
Incident management team (IMT)
   interagency relations, 117, 118-119
   operational coordination, 120
Incident Objectives (ICS Form 202), 240, 241, 243, 244
Incident Radio Communications Plan (ICS 205), 242, 244
Incident reports, 173, 248
Incident safety officer (ISO), 261-262
Income taxes, 147
Indirect monetary incentives, 88
Informal debriefing records, 248
Informal PIA, 245
Information Technology (IT) system, 167

Injury
   causes, 290
   hearing loss, 284-285
   prevention. *See* Accident, injury, and illness prevention program
   reports, 173
   types, 290
   USFA report, 282
Innovation
   best practices, 33
   change as opportunity for, 38
   for professional development, 73
Inquiries from citizens, 112-114
Inspections. *See also* Fire inspection and safety planning; Fire inspection programs
   fire prevention and life safety programs, 224-225
   occupancy classification requiring inspections, 227-228
Institution of Fire Engineers (IFE), 74
Insurance, budget considerations, 152
Insurance Services Office (ISO), 48
Integrated communications, 263
Integration planning, 314
Intentional hazards, 208
Interactive television (ITV) for training, 204
Interagency relations, 117-121
   community disaster plan, 254
   emergency management, 303-304
   federal agencies, 121
   federal law enforcement agencies, 120-121
   fire and emergency services organizations, 118-119
   incident management teams, 117
   intergovernmental agreements, 122
   jurisdictions, 118
   NIMS, 117
   purpose of, 117
   state/provincial and local law-enforcement agencies, 119-120
   traffic incident management, 120
Interdisciplinary, 305
Interest income from trusts, 147
Interest-based bargaining, 87
Intergovernmental agreements, 122
Intergovernmental assistance, 304
Intermediate-term plan, 184-185
International Association of Fire Chiefs (IAFC)
   Code of Ethics, 17
   CPAT physical ability test, 59
   Joint Wellness/Fitness Initiative, 87
   labor management initiative, 88
   LODD policies and procedures, 68
   Officer Development Handbook, 28, 70
   promotion of chief officers, 3
   reports to public officials, 117
   respiratory hazards, 288
International Association of Fire Fighters (IAFF)
   CPAT physical ability test, 59
   Joint Wellness/Fitness Initiative, 87
   labor management initiative, 88
   labor negotiations, 83, 84
   LODD policies and procedures, 68
   management team, 85
   promotion of chief officers, 3

reports to public officials, 117
respiratory hazards, 288
International City/County Management Association (ICMA), 124
International Code Council (ICC), 99
Internet communications are forever, 40
Interoperability, 304
Interview for employment, 59-62
closed-ended questions, 60
exit interview, 69
hypothetical questions, 60
open-ended questions, 60
preparation for, 61
probing questions, 60
promotions, 64
purpose of, 59
questions not allowed, 60-61
semistructured, 60
steps, 61-62
structured, 60
techniques, 59
unstructured, 60
Inventory records, 168, 266
Investigation, fire prevention and life safety programs, 225
ISO (incident safety officer), 261-262
ISO (Insurance Services Office), 48
IT (Information Technology) system, 167
ITV (interactive television) for training, 204

J

JEPP (Joint Emergency Preparedness Program), 121
Job analyses, 53-54
Job fairs for position marketing, 57
Job Hazard Analysis, 279-280
Job performance requirements (JPRs)
NFPA® 1021 chapter and page references, 318-319
NFPA® 1021 establishment of, 3
NFPA® 1021 standards, 27
Job security as contract issue, 86
Joint Emergency Preparedness Program (JEPP), 121
Joint Wellness/Fitness Initiative, 87
Joint-sponsored programs, 133
JPRs. *See* Job performance requirements (JPRs)
Jurisdiction
disaster plans, 254-255
horizontal, 254
for interagency relations, 118
vertical, 254
Justification form, 150, 321
Justifications for unethical conduct, 16

K

Knowledge topics for chief officers, 27

L

Labor organization team, 85
Labor relations, 82-89
background, 82
incentive programs, 88-89
negotiation process, 82-88
Language barriers, 104-105
Language line, 105

Law enforcement emergency resources, 312
Law-enforcement agencies, 119-120
Laws. *See* Regulations
Leadership
application of theory, 20-21
defined, 2, 13, 18
fire service leadership best practices, 32-34
good leader traits, 22-23
management vs., 19
personal, 23
principled leader theory, 20
proactive, 24-25
criticism, 25
decisions, 25
foresight, 24
politics, 24
problem solving, 24
skills, 19
skills improvement
counselors/mentors, 21
courses, 21
literature reading, 21
networking, 21
seminars/workshops, 21
strong leaders, 18-19
360-degree feedback evaluation, 21
Lease, uses for, 164
Lease/purchase, 164
Legal restrictions of the media, 108
Legislation monitoring, 128-130
federal, 129-130
groups influencing fire and emergency services organizations, 128
local, 129
state/provincial, 129
Level I Fire Officer
response to challenges and solutions, 23
Supervising Fire Officer, 28
Level II Fire Officer
Managing Fire Officer, 28
response to challenges and solutions, 23
Level III Chief Officer
accident, injury, and illness prevention program, 279-288
Administrative Fire Officer, 28
budgeting and finance, 140-155
budget considerations, 144-145
budget development and management, 149-155
budget systems, 140-142
budget types, 140, 142-144
revenue sources, 145-149
community awareness programs, 103-114
community relations strategies, 104-105
concerns/complaints/inquiries, 112-114
public fire and life safety education, 109-111
public relations, 105-109
emergency management, 301-316
concepts, 303-305
emergency declaration process, 310
emergency operations centers, 314-316
phases, 305-310
principles, 302-310
resource integration, 310-314

Index **349**

emergency services delivery, 239–249
    duties of chief officers, 237
    incident action plan, 240–244
    post incident analysis, 244–249
    resource planning, 239–240
health and safety program, 276–279
human resources management, 45–75
    continuing education, 74–75
    emergency services staffing, 45–50
    employment practices, 50–69
    professional development, 70–74
organizational improvement, 176–180
    gap analysis, 176–177
    needs analysis, 176
    planning, 178–180
    SWOT analysis, 177–178
proactive leadership, 24–25
purchasing, 155–167
    acquisition process, 162–167
    needs assessment, 156
    product data review, 161–162
    product evaluation, 160–161
    research, 157–160
    standardization, 167
record-keeping, 167–175
    activity records, 168–169
    budget records, 167
    data analysis and interpretation, 175
    evaluation, 172
    inventory records, 168
    legal requirements, 172–175
    maintenance records, 168
    personnel records, 169–170
    revision, 172
    system development, 170–172
service delivery, 100–103
Level IV Chief Officer
    community involvement, 130–134
    community risk assessment and reduction, 206–210
    emergency services delivery, 249–269
        comprehensive disaster plan, 249–259
        duties of chief officers, 238
        incident management system, 260–269
    Executive Fire Officer, 28
    human resources management, 76–93
        demographics appraisal, 76–81
        labor relations, 82–89
        member assistance services, 91–93
        training and education, 89–91
    legislation monitoring, 128–130
    operational planning, 183–188
    politics, participation in, 114–122
        decision-making process, 122–128
        government acceptance, 116–117
        interagency relations, 117–121
        intergovernmental agreements, 122
        public awareness and acceptance, 115–116
    proactive leadership, 24–25
    risk management plan, 288–296
    strategic planning, 180–183
    training requirements, 188–206
        evaluation of requirements, 188–190

        external training sources, 204–206
        funding sources, 204
        program development, 190–204
        program evaluation, 206
Life insurance employee benefit, 66
Line-item budgeting, 141
Line-of-duty death (LODD)
    Firefighter Fatalities in the United States, 280–282
    grief counseling, 67–68
    personnel risk identification, 291
LIPS acronym, 242–243
Listening
    chief officer skills for dealing with disgruntled citizens, 112
    executive level communications, 39
    as trait of good leaders, 23
Literature reading for improving leadership skills, 21
Local law-enforcement agencies, 119–120
Local legislation monitoring, 129
Local training requirements, 189
Location for training facilities, 197
LODD. *See* Line-of-duty death (LODD)
Logistical storage, 268
Logistics Section, 262
Long-term plan, 185–188
Long-term trusts, 147
Looking good on paper, 16
Loyalty of good leaders, 23

M

Maintenance
    budget considerations, 145
    corrective, 168
    preventive, 168, 185
    product requirement review before purchase, 162
    record-keeping, 168
Management
    defined, 17
    leadership vs., 19
    team, 85
Management Information System (MIS), 167, 170
Managing Fire Officer (NFPA® Level II), 28
MAP. *See* Member assistance program (MAP)
Market studies, 152
Maslow's Hierarchy of Need, 2
Master's degree program, 71
Matrix budgeting, 141
Measurement conversion, 6–8
Mechanical failure hazards, 279, 280
Mechanical hazards, 279
Media
    credentialed media personnel, 107
    newspapers, 111
    print media, 111
    public relations at emergency incidents, 107–109
    public service announcements, 111
    relations with, 107–109
    social media
        policies and procedures, 51
        for position marketing, 57
        public relations, 109
Mediation, 86
Medical examination records, 173

Medical Plan (ICS 206), 242, 244
Medical-fitness examination, 62
Member act/omission resolutions, 113–114
Member assistance program (MAP)
    chief officer recommendations for use of, 93
    as employee benefit, 91, 92
    grief counseling, 67
    professional counseling, 92
    regulations, 91, 93
Member assistance services, 91–93
    behavioral health program, 91–92
    local, state/provincial, and federal regulations, 93
    member assistance program, 91, 92–93
    program appraisal, 93
Member pension fund, 148
Memberships as revenue source, 147
Mentors
    for improving leadership skills, 21
    as trait of good leaders, 23
Metric conversions, 6–8
MFIPPA (Municipal Freedom of Information and Protection of Privacy Act), 173
Military veterans as fire department personnel, 55
MIS (Management Information System), 167, 170
Mission, 75
Mitigation
    of disasters, 250
    emergency management, 305–307
Mobile water supply apparatus, 284
Model Building and Fire Codes, 229, 230
Monitoring
    of the budget, 154
    risk management plan, 294
    service delivery, 103
    strategic planning, 182
    unified command systems, 268–269
Mothers seeking elected office, 125
Motor vehicle-related incidents, 283–284
Municipal Freedom of Information and Protection of Privacy Act (MFIPPA), 173
Muscular Dystrophy Association fund-raiser, 132
Mutual aid agreements, 118, 239, 242

N

NASA (U.S. National Aeronautics and Space Administration), 295
National Aeronautics and Space Administration (NASA), 295
National Fallen Firefighter's Foundation (NFFF), 68, 207, 281
National Fire Academy (NFA)
    EFOP, 74
    Executive Fire Officer Program, 28
    FESHE, 70
    sample code of ethics, 26
    training courses/curriculum, 205
    Training Resources and Data Exchange, 205
National Fire Incident Reporting System (NFIRS), 168–169, 282
National Fire Protection Association® (NFPA®). See also specific NFPA®
    occupational hazards, 290
    reports to public officials, 117
    respiratory hazards, 288
    risk identification, 291

National Guard, 313
National Incident Management System (NIMS)
    background, 117
    emergency operations centers, 314
    ICS/UC, 254–255
    purpose of, 117
National Institute for Occupational Safety and Health (NIOSH)
    interagency relations, 121
    personnel risk identification, 291
    respiratory hazards, 288
    respiratory protection equipment, 286
National Institute for Occupational Safety and Health/Mine Safety and Health Administration (NIOSH/MSHA), 164
National Institute of Standards and Technology (NIST)
    Baldrige Performance Excellence Program, 31
    staffing requirements, 48
National Institutes of Health (NIH), 79
National Oceanic and Atmospheric Administration (NOAA), 257
National Pollution Funds Center, 257
National Professional Development Model, 28
National Response Framework (NRF), 117
National Response Plan (NRP), 117
National Volunteer Fire Council (NVFC), 117
Natural disasters, 251–252
Natural hazards, 208
Needs assessment, 34, 75
Negotiation process, 82–88
    bargaining sessions, 84
    collective bargaining, 82, 83
    contract content, 84
    contract issues, 85–86
    employee involvement and participation, 87
    IAFF/IAFC labor management initiative, 88
    impasses, 86–87
    open communications, 83–84
    preparation, 85
    private sector, 83
    proposal presentation, 85
    representation, 85
Networking for improving leadership skills, 21
Newspapers, 111
NFA. See National Fire Academy (NFA)
NFFF (National Fallen Firefighters' Foundation), 68, 207, 281
NFIRS (National Fire Incident Reporting System), 168–169, 282
NFPA®. See National Fire Protection Association® (NFPA®)
NFPA® 1000, training standards, 189
NFPA® 1001, *Standard for Fire Fighter Professional Qualifications*, 53, 194
NFPA® 1021, *Standard for Fire Officer Professional Qualifications*
    duties of chief officers, 3–4
    emergency services delivery, 237, 238
    Health and Safety program, 277
    job applicant standards, 54
    job performance requirements, 3, 27, 318–319
    skills and knowledge for officers, 1
NFPA® 1041, *Standard for Fire Service Instructor Professional Qualifications*, 201
NFPA® 1142, *Standard on Water Supplies for Suburban and Rural Fire Fighting*, 196
NFPA® 1201, *Standard for Developing Fire Protection Services for the Public*, 191, 192

NFPA® 1400, training standards, 189
NFPA® 1401, *Recommended Practice for Fire Service Training Records*, 169
NFPA® 1402, *Guide to Building Fire Service Training Centers*, 195
NFPA® 1403, *Standard on Live Fire Training Evolutions*, 195, 201
NFPA® 1404, training course selection, 194
NFPA® 1410, *Standard on Training for Initial Emergency Scene Operations*, 179
NFPA® 1500, *Standard on Fire Service Occupational Safety and Health Program*
    command responsibilities, 262
    confidential health records, 170
    long-term planning and, 186
    MAP program, 92
    personnel records, 169
    PIA safety issues, 247
    resource allocation, 185
    risk management, 101, 288, 289
    Safety and Health Committee, 277
    staffing levels, 179
    staffing requirements, 48
    training course selection, 194
    training standards, 189
NFPA® 1521, *Standard for Fire Department Safety Officer*
    command responsibilities, 262
    Health and Safety Officer roles and responsibilities, 278
    PIA safety issues, 247
    risk management plan, 289
    safety officer, 277
NFPA® 1582, *Standard on Comprehensive Occupational Medical Program for Fire Departments*
    employee disabilities and accommodations, 52–53
    hearing examinations, 285
    pre-employment medical examination, 62
NFPA® 1710, *Standard for the Organization and Deployment of Fire Suppression Operations, Emergency Medical Operations, and Special Operations to the Public by Career Fire Departments*
    long-term planning and, 186
    resource allocation, 185
    staffing requirements, 48, 179
NFPA® 1720, *Standard for the Organization and Deployment of Fire Suppression Operations, Emergency Medical Operations and Special Operations to the Public by Volunteer Fire Departments*
    long-term planning and, 186
    resource allocation, 185
    staffing requirements, 48, 179
NGO. *See* Nongovernmental organization (NGO)
NIH (National Institutes of Health), 79
NIMS. *See* National Incident Management System (NIMS)
NIOSH. *See* National Institute for Occupational Safety and Health (NIOSH)
NIOSH/MSHA (National Institute for Occupational Safety and Health/Mine Safety and Health Administration), 164
NIST. *See* National Institute of Standards and Technology (NIST)
NOAA (National Oceanic and Atmospheric Administration), 257
Noise hazards, 280
Nonfire hazards, 290
Nongovernmental organization (NGO)
    emergency resources, 313
    grants, 149

Nonprofit organization grants, 149
Nonverbal communications, 39
Nonviolence in the workplace, 51
North American fire training associations, 205
Northern Alaska Regional Office of Fire Service Training, 205
NRF (National Response Framework), 117
NRP (National Response Plan), 117
NVFC (National Volunteer Fire Council), 117

O

Object class budget, 141
Observation for professional development, 73
Obstruction by journalists, 108
Occupancy classifications requiring inspections, 227–228
Occupancy-related hazards, 208–209
Occupational hazards, 290
Occupational illness, 280, 283
Occupational Safety and Health Administration (OSHA)
    incidence rate of risk, 291, 331–332
    interagency relations, 121
    Job Hazard Analysis, 279–280
    medical records, 169
    staffing requirements, 48
    state enforcement, 49
    29 *CFR* 1910.20, *Medical Record Keeping*, 169
    29 *CFR* 1910.95, *Occupational Noise Exposure*, 285
    29 *CFR* 1910.134, respiratory protection, 286
    29 *CFR* 1910.1200, *Hazard Communication Standard*, 286
    2-in 2-out, 48
Occupational safety and health committee, 277–278
OCIPEP (Office of Critical Infrastructure Protection and Emergency Preparedness), 121
OEODM (Office of Equal Opportunity and Diversity Management), 79
Office of Critical Infrastructure Protection and Emergency Preparedness (OCIPEP), 121
Office of Equal Opportunity and Diversity Management (OEODM), 79
Officer Development Handbook, 28, 70
Ohio administrative law, 25
Open records, 40
Open-ended questions, 60
Operating budgets, 142, 143–144, 183
Operating funds used for purchases, 163
Operational planning, 183–188
    intermediate-term, 184–185
    long-term, 185–188
    short-term, 184
Operations Section, 262
Ordinances, regulating chief officer selection, 14
Organization Assignment List (ICS Form 203), 240, 243, 244
Organizational behavior theory, 30
Organizational chart, 14
Organizational Chart (ICS Form 207), 244
Organizational culture theory, 32
Organizational improvement, 176–180
    gap analysis, 176–177
    needs analysis, 176
        community needs, 176
        department capabilities, 176
    planning, 178–180
    SWOT analysis, 177–178

OSHA. *See* Occupational Safety and Health Administration (OSHA)
Other on duty hazards, 290
Outcome-based budgets, 141
Outcome-based evaluations, 183

P

Parking areas at training facilities, 198
Participation for professional development, 73
Particulate masks, 286
Partnerships, 132–133
Patient privacy, 108
Payoffs as unethical conduct, 16
Peer Fitness Training (PFT), 87
Pension contributions, 65
Pension trust fund, 148
People, change type, 35
Performance budgeting, 141
Performance Excellence (PE), 31
Performance-based evaluations, 183
Perpetual trusts, 147
Personal income taxes, 147
Personal professional development, 73
Personal vs. public life, 40
Personality tests for employment, 59
Personnel
    budget considerations, 145
    budgeting for services, 143
    fire prevention and life safety programs, 224
    records, 169–170
    risk analysis, 291–293
    technology or operational procedure changes, 48
    timeline, 47
    training, 201
PFT (Peer Fitness Training), 87
Photography, candid, 108
Physical ability tests for employment, 59
Physical fitness programs, 134
PIA. *See* Post incident analysis (PIA)
Planning
    budget, 142, 150
    emergency services delivery, 237
    emergency services delivery resources, 239–240
    fire inspection and safety planning, 215–226
    human resources management, 46–48
        anticipating challenges, 47–48
        projecting needs, 46–47
    incident management system, 262
    integration, 314
    long-term, 186, 188
    operational improvement, 178–180
        benchmarks, 178–179
        code requirements, 179
        regulations, 180
        response times, 180
        staffing, 179
    operational planning, 183–188
    record-keeping system, 171
    strategic planning, 180–183
    succession planning, 73
Planning programming budgeting system (PPBS), 142
Planning Section, 262

Political bottom line as cause of unethical conduct, 16
Politics. *See also* Government
    chief officer involvement in, 24, 114–115
    decision-making process, 122–128
        dealing with government officials, 126–127
        governing concept, 124
        government official responsibilities, 123–124
        political neutrality, 126
        political processes, 122–125
        political relationships, 126–127
        political resources, 127–128
        public influence, 124–125
        types of individuals seeking office, 125
    government acceptance, 116–117
    instability, 253
    interagency relations, 117–121
        federal agencies, 121
        federal law enforcement agencies, 120–121
        fire and emergency services organizations, 118–119
        incident management teams, 117
        intergovernmental agreements, 122
        jurisdictions, 118
        NIMS, 117
        purpose of, 117
        state/provincial and local law-enforcement agencies, 119–120
        traffic incident management, 120
    public awareness and acceptance, 115–116
Pork-barrel projects, 16
Position descriptions, 53–54
Position marketing, 56–57
Post incident analysis (PIA), 244–249
    critique, 248
    development procedures, 246
        implementation, 246
        monitor, evaluate, revise, 246
    documentation, 248–249
    final reports, 249
    formal, 245
    incident data, 247–248
        evolution of the incident, 247
        safety issues, 247–248
    informal, 245
    purpose of, 244
    recommended changes, 248
Posters for position marketing, 56
Posting
    for position marketing, 56–57
    successful candidates posting, 64
PPBS (planning programming budgeting system), 142
Practicals, 64
Preincident plan, 267
Premature selection of applicant, 63
Preparedness
    for disasters, 250, 251
    for emergencies, 307
Presidential Disaster Declaration, 304
Presidential Executive Order, 50, 76
Preventive maintenance, 168, 185
Principled leader theory, 20
Print media, 111
Privacy of records, 108, 170, 173

Private property, news media access to, 108
Proactive leadership, 24–25
    criticism, 25
    decisions, 25
    foresight, 24
    politics, 24
    problem solving, 24
Probing questions, 60
Problem solving of proactive leaders, 24
Product evaluation for purchasing
    comparison, 158
    evaluation form, 160, 328–329
    generally, 160–161
    product data review, 161–162
        durability, 161
        features, 161
        infrastructure, 162
        life-cycle cost, 162
        maintenance requirements, 162
Professional development, 70–74
    budget considerations, 145
    credentialing, 73–74
    degree programs, 71–72
    higher education, 70–72
    higher education, levels of education, 70–71
    personal professional development, 73
    professional organizations, 72
    succession planning, 73
Professional organizations, 72
Professional recruiting agencies for position marketing, 57
Professional standards of conduct, 25–27
Program budgeting, 141
Programs for community involvement, 133–134
Project Safe Place™, 132
Projecting personnel needs, 46–47
ProLiteracy, 105
Promotions
    adherence to policy, procedures, and regulations, 65
    applicant certification, 63
    applicant interviews, 64
    assessment centers, 64
    challenges, 64
    to chief officer, factors to consider, 13–14
    examination records, 173
    preparatory training, 63
    purpose of, 63
    skills testing, 64
    successful candidates posting, 64
    vacancy advertising, 63
    vacancy availability, 63
    written examination development, 64
Property taxes, 146
Props for training, 198–200
Provincial law-enforcement agencies, 119–120
Provincial legislation monitoring, 129
Provincial training requirements, 189
Pseudo-managers seeking elected office, 125
Public awareness and acceptance, 115–116
Public inquiries, 114
Public property, media access to, 107–108
Public records, 174–175
Public relations, 105–109
    media relations, 107–109
    as political resource, 127–128
    Public Information Officer, 105–106
    social media, 109
Public service announcements, 111
Public training events for position marketing, 56
Public works emergency resources, 312
Publication for professional development, 73
Purchasing, 155–167
    acquisition process, 162–167
        alternative purchasing model, 162–163
        award, 166–167
        bid specifications, 164–166
        funding sources, 163–164
        proposals, evaluation of, 166
    needs assessment, 156
    product data review, 161–162
    product evaluation, 160–161
    research, 157–160
        compare various products, 158
        equipment compatibility, 159
        industry trends, 158
        ordinances and laws, 159
        references, 158
        request for proposal, qualifications, or information, 159–160, 325–327
        review manufacturers' business histories, 157–158
        standards and regulations, 158
        survey other jurisdictions, 157, 322–324
    standardization, 167
Purpose of the manual, 4

Q

Quantitative management theory, 30
Questions for interviews, 60–61

R

Radiation hazards, 280
Railroad companies as training source, 206
Rapid Observation of Vulnerability and Estimation of Risk (ROVER), 306
Rapid Visual Screening of Buildings for Potential Seismic Hazards, 306
RCMP, 121
Reading for professional development, 73
Real estate for facilities location, 186–187
Reasons for becoming chief officers, 1–2
Recorded conversations, 40
Record-keeping, 167–175
    activity records, 168–169
    budget records, 167
    data analysis and interpretation, 175
    evaluation, 172
    inventory records, 168
    legal requirements, 172–175
        privacy, 173
        public access, 174–175
        record types, 173
        retention, 173
    maintenance records, 168
    NFIRS, 168–169
    personnel records, 169–170

attendance records, 169
confidentiality, 170
medical records, 169, 170
training records, 169
post incident analysis, 248-249
revision, 172
system development, 170-172
completion, 172
define requirements, 170-171
planning, 171
testing and implementation, 171-172
Recovery
after disasters, 250, 259
business recovery after disasters, 310
defined, 309
elements, 309
Recruitment of personnel
defined, 54
diverse workforces, 55-56
position marketing and posting, 56-57
sources, 54-55
athletes, 55
educational institutions, 55
fire and emergency services organizations, 55
hospitals and clinics, 55
military, 55
professional organizations, 55
volunteer departments, 54, 55
Red Cross, 207, 312-313
Reference check, 58
Regulations
equipment, 158
fire prevention and life safety programs, 221
laws affecting employment, 50
member assistance services, 91, 93
organizational improvement, 180
promotions and, 65
purchasing decisions, 159
training requirements, 189
Rehabilitation Act of 1973, 50, 76
Rehabilitation after disasters, 259
Reimbursement logs, 248
Reorganization, 185
Reports
annual reports, 183
post incident analysis, 249
unified command system, 269
Representation in labor negotiations, 85
Request for information (RFI), 159
Request for proposal (RFP), 159, 325-326
Request for qualifications (RFQ), 160, 327
Research best practices, 34
Residential key box rapid entry, 134
Resistance to change
process stage, 34
reasons for, 35
steps to overcoming, 35-36
Resources
allocation, 185
for disasters, 256-257
emergency management, 310-314
community resources, 312-313

convergence, 311
emergency medical services, 312
federal resources, 313-314
fire service, 311
integration planning, 314
law enforcement, 312
public works, 312
state/provincial resources, 313
facilities and equipment, 91
fire prevention and life safety programs, 223-224
list of departmental resources, 242
monetary, 90
personnel, 90
planning
joint training requirements, 239-240
mutual and automatic aid agreements, 239
political, 127-128
communication, 127
educational information, 128
public relations, 127-128
training and education, 90-91, 193
Respiratory injury or illness, 285-286, 288
Response
defined, 308
elements, 309
to emergencies, 308-309
emergency support functions and federal agencies, 308
times, 180
Restoration of services after disasters, 259
Retired senior and volunteer professionals (RSVP), 206
Retirement, separation from employment, 69
Retirement contributions, 65
Revenue sources, budget, 145-149
bonds, 148
enterprise funds, 148
fund-raisers, 149
grants/gifts, 148-149
memberships/subscriptions, 147
taxes, 146-147
trust funds, 147-148
RFI (request for information), 159
RFP (request for proposal), 159, 325-326
RFQ (request for qualifications), 160, 327
Risk, defined, 206, 289
Risk analysis for training requirements, 190
Risk assessment, 34
Risk management plan, 288-296
implementation, 293-296
evaluation, 294-295
monitoring, 294
partnering outside the organization, 294
revision, 295
System Safety Program, 295-296
model, 289
occupational hazards analysis, 290
personnel risk analysis, 291-293
control measures, 292-293
frequency or incidence rate, 291, 331-332
risk avoidance, 292
risk control, 292-293
risk evaluation, 291
risk identification, 291

risk prioritization, 292
risk transfer, 292
severity of risk, 291, 331–332
Robert T. Stafford Disaster Relief and Emergency Assistance Act, 255
Rookies seeking elected office, 125
ROVER (Rapid Observation of Vulnerability and Estimation of Risk), 306
RSVP (retired senior and volunteer professionals), 206
Rushing, 62

S

Safe Community Foundation, 221
Safe Place™, 132
Safety
    community-based programs, 134
    issues during PIA, 247–248
    OSHA. *See* Occupational Safety and Health Administration (OSHA)
    restrictions at emergency scenes, 108
    System Safety Program, 295–296
Safety data sheet (SDS), 286
Safety message (ICS 208 or 208H Form), 242
Sales taxes, 146–147
SAR (supplied air respirator), 159
SCBA. *See* Self-contained breathing apparatus (SCBA)
Scheduling training programs, 202–204
Scientific Support Coordinators, 257
Scope of the manual, 4
SDS (safety data sheet), 286
Security
    at disaster sites, 259
    training facilities, 197
Selection of chief officers, 2–3, 14
Self-contained breathing apparatus (SCBA)
    determining equipment compatibility for purchase, 159
    purchasing survey form, 157, 322–324
    uses for, 285
Self-esteem as cause of unethical conduct, 15
Self-gratification as cause of unethical conduct, 16
Seminars
    for improving leadership skills, 21
    training, 205
Semistructured interviews, 60
Sensitivity training, 37
Separation and termination, 67–69
    disability, 68
    dismissals, 69
    exit interview, 69
    line-of-duty death, 67–68
    retirement, 69
    termination, 68–69
September 11, 2001, 302, 304
Service area, anticipating requirements, 47
Service based budgeting system, 142
Service delivery, 100–103
    Citizen Corps, 103
    community connectors, 103
    community service units, 103
    comprehensive-risk approach, 101
    monitoring, 103
    systems-model approach, 100
    types of services, 101–103
Service recognition/award ceremonies, 88
Short-term plan, 184
Short-term trusts, 147
Sick leave employee benefit, 65
Similarity during applicant selection, 63
Simulators for training, 199
16 Firefighter Life Safety Initiatives, 320
Skills needed by chief officers, 4, 27
Skills testing, 64
SMART acronym, 240
Social events as incentives, 88
Social media
    policies and procedures, 51
    for position marketing, 57
    public relations, 109
SOPs (standard operating procedures), 186
Special purpose tax levy, 147
Special taxing authorities, 147
Staffing
    assignments, 49–50
    budget considerations, 145
    crew rotation, 49
    long-term planning for, 188
    minimum staffing levels, 48
    operational planning, 179
    personnel records, 169–170
    planning, 46–48
        anticipating challenges, 47–48
        projecting needs, 46–47
Stafford Act, 255
Standard for organization equipment, 167
Standard of Cover, 179, 219
Standard operating procedures (SOPs), 186
State law-enforcement agencies, 119–120
State/provincial emergency resources, 313
State/provincial legislation monitoring, 129
State/provincial training requirements, 189
Stereotyping during applicant selection, 62
Strategic change, 35
Strategic management, 181
Strategic planning, 180–183
    annual reports, 183
    characteristics, 180–181
    development of, 181
    evaluation, 182–183
    implementation, 182
    monitoring or controlling, 182
    planning process, 180–181
    revisions, 183
Strike, 87
Strike-off procedure, 87
"Struck against" hazards, 280
"Struck by" hazards, 280
Structure change, 35
Structured interviews, 60
Subscriptions as revenue source, 147
Succession planning, 73
Sunset clause, 132
Supervising Fire Officer (NFPA® Level I), 28
Supplied air respirator (SAR), 159

Support materials for IAP, 240
SWOT analysis, 177–178
System Safety Program, 295–296
Systems theory, 30
Systems-model service delivery, 100

T

Table of organization, 14
Tactical worksheet, 240
Tax increment financing (TIF), 146
Taxes as budget revenue source, 146–147
    community impact fees, 147
    personal income taxes, 147
    property taxes, 146
    sales taxes, 146–147
    special purpose tax levy, 147
    special taxing authorities, 147
    user fees, 147
TDD (telecommunications devices for the deaf), 104
Teams
    change process implementation, 37
    Community Emergency Response Team, 313
    Disaster Medical Assistance Team, 314
    Disaster Mortuary Operational Response Team, 314
    good leaders as team players, 23
    IMT. *See* Incident management team (IMT)
    incident management teams, 117
    labor organization team, 85
    management team, 85
    synergy, 264
    unified command, 264
Technology
    awareness, 33
    change type, 35
    degree program, 71
    disasters, 254
    emergency medical technology degree program, 72
    fire prevention, 217
    Information Technology (IT) system, 167
    new technology and personnel changes, 48
Teen driver safety programs, 134
Telecommunications devices for the deaf (TDD), 104
Temperature extreme hazards, 280
Termination. *See* Separation and termination
Terrorism
    business recovery after disasters, 310
    defined, 253
    emergency management of attacks, 303
    September 11, 2001, 302, 304
    U.S. Pentagon attack, 304
    Weapons of Mass Destruction, 176
Tests for employment, 58–59
    aptitude, 59
    assessment center, 59
    personality, 59
    physical ability, 59
    skills testing, 64
Text telephones (TTY), 104
Them-us confrontation, 87
360-degree feedback evaluation, 21
TIF (tax increment financing), 146
Title 29 *CFR* 1910.20, *Medical Record Keeping*, 169

Title 29 *CFR* 1910.95, *Occupational Noise Exposure*, 285
Title 29 *CFR* 1910.134, respiratory protection, 286
Title 29 *CFR* 1910.1200, *Hazard Communication Standard*, 286
Title VII, 76, 78
Total Quality Management (TQM), 31
Toys for Tots, 132
TQM (Total Quality Management), 31
TRADE (Training Resources and Data Exchange), 205
Traffic incident management, 120
Training, 188–206
    accreditation vs., 195
    assessing resources, 90–91
    budget considerations, 145
    certification vs., 195
    change process implementation, 37
    chief officers, 27–28
    colleges/universities, 204–205
    continuing education, 74–75
    CPR, 132
    defined, 188
    external training sources, 204–206
    facilities, 195–201
    funding sources, 204
    hazards, 290
    joint training agreements, 239–240
    national courses/curriculum, 205
    needs determination, 89–90
    North American fire training associations, 205
    preparatory training for promotions, 63
    private sources, 206
    program design, 191–194
        administrative structures, 192
        design tips, 194
        evaluation process, 193
        needs analysis, 191
        organizational and personnel needs, 191
        philosophy, 192
        policies and procedures, 192–193
        purpose of the training program, 191
        resources required, 193
        strategic goals, 192
    program development, 190–204
        course selection, 194–195
        facility types, 195–201
        must-know topics, 194
        need-to-know topics, 194
        nice-to-know topics, 194
        personnel, 201
        program design, 191–194
        scheduling, 202–204
    program evaluation, 206
    record-keeping, 169, 173
    regional training programs, 205
    requirements, evaluation of, 188–190
        building and fire codes, 189
        community needs, 189
        hazards assessment, 189–190
        legal mandates, 189
        risk analysis, 190
        training standards, 189
    seminars, 205
    sensitivity, 37

16 Life Safety Initiatives, 320
Training Resources and Data Exchange (TRADE), 205
Traits of good leaders, 22–23
    builds trust, 22–23
    communicates, 22
    decisiveness, 23
    dedication, 23
    good listener, 23
    humility, 23
    identifies challenges, 22
    loyalty, 23
    mentorship, 23
    plans for success, 22
    sees opportunities, 22
    sense of humor, 23
    team player, 23
Transition to chief officer, 13–14
Transportation incident props, 198
Trending, 32
Trucking companies as training source, 206
Trust, as trait of good leaders, 22–23
Trust funds, 147–148
Truthfulness of communications, 39
TTY (text telephones), 104
29 *CFR* 1910.20, *Medical Record Keeping*, 169
29 *CFR* 1910.95, *Occupational Noise Exposure*, 285
29 *CFR* 1910.134, respiratory protection, 286
29 *CFR* 1910.1200, *Hazard Communication Standard*, 286
2-in 2-out, 48

U

UC. *See* Unified command (UC)
UL (Underwriters Laboratories), 288
UL Canada, 288
Underwriters Laboratories of Canada (UL Canada), 288
Underwriters Laboratories (UL), 288
Unethical conduct, causes of, 15–16
    affiliation, 15
    basic needs, 15
    behaviors violating ethical standards, 16
    bottom-line mentality, 16
    exploitive mentality, 16
    self-esteem, 15
    self-gratification, 16
Unified command (UC)
    defined, 263
    functions, 265
    implementation, 267–268
    monitoring, evaluating, revising systems, 268–269
    operations, 269
    organizational chart, 263–264, 265
    overview, 263–264
    reporting, 269
    system development, 265–267
    systems, 254
    team approach, 264
Uniform allotment employee benefit, 66
United States
    interagency relations, 121
    law enforcement agencies, 120–121
U.S. Citizenship and Immigration Services (USCIS), 121
U.S. Coast Guard (USCG)
    District Response Group, 257
    interagency relations, 121
    National Pollution Funds Center, 257
    National Strike Force, 257
U.S. Department of Health and Human Services (DHHS), 257
U.S. Department of Homeland Security (DHS)
    interagency relations, 117, 121
    terrorism, 253, 310
U.S. Department of Transportation (DOT)
    Federal Highway Administration, 120
    government grants, 149
    U.S. Navy Supervisor of Salvage, 257
U.S. Environmental Protection Agency (EPA)
    calculating environmental costs, 151
    Environmental Response Team, 257
    interagency relations, 121
    jurisdictional authority, 254
    personnel risk identification, 291
    Radiological Emergency Response Team, 257
U.S. Federal Bureau of Investigation (FBI), 120, 253
United States Fire Administration (USFA)
    Executive Fire Officer Program, 28
    FESHE curriculum, 28
    fire prevention and life safety programs, 221
    Fire Service Vulnerability Assessment Project, 207
    firefighter fatalities, 282
    Firefighter Fatalities in the United States, 280–282
    injury report, 282
    post incident analysis, 245
    risk identification, 291
U.S. Marshals Service (Department of Justice), 120
U.S. National Aeronautics and Space Administration (NASA), 295
U.S. Navy Supervisor of Salvage, 257
U.S. Pentagon terrorist attack, 304
Universities
    for outside training, 204–205
    as recruitment source, 55
Unstructured interviews, 60
Urban Search and Rescue (USAR), 314
USAR (Urban Search and Rescue), 314
USCG. *See* U.S. Coast Guard (USCG)
USCIS (U.S. Citizenship and Immigration Services), 121
User fees, 147
USFA. *See* United States Fire Administration (USFA)

V

Vacancy advertising, 63
Vacancy availability, 63
Values, ethical, 15
VAP (Fire Service Vulnerability Assessment Project), 207
Vehicle incidents
    conflict between agencies, 119–120
    deaths from, 283–284
    responding/returning hazards, 290
    training props, 198
Vehicles as incentives, 88
Vertical jurisdiction, 254
Vibration hazards, 279
Violence in the workplace, policies and procedures, 51
Visibility hazards, 280
Vision, defined, 2

Vision 20/20, 221
Visual programs for position marketing, 56
Volunteer fire departments
    NFPA® 1720 staffing requirements, 48
    personnel recruiting sources, 54–55
    position marketing, 57
    societal attitude toward, 48

W

Wages
    contract issues, 85–86
    knowledge of, in negotiation preparation, 85
War, 253
Water
    decontamination at training facilities, 196
    mobile water supply apparatus, 284
    training facility supply, 196
WDI. *See Workplace Diversity Initiative (WDI)*
Weapons of Mass Destruction (WMD), 176
Weather
    hazards, 280
    monitoring at training facilities, 196
Web sites for position marketing, 57
Wildland training areas, 200
Win-lose confrontation, 87

WMD (Weapons of Mass Destruction), 176
Word of mouth for position marketing, 57
Working conditions as contract issue, 86
Workplace Diversity Initiative (WDI), 79–81
    defined, 79
    EEO/Affirmative Action Program vs., 79
    evaluate program progress and success, 81
    identify the current organizational culture, 80
    manage diversity, 81
    organize for change, 80
    raise cultural awareness, 80–81
Workplace violence, 280
Workshops for improving leadership skills, 21
Written examination development, 64

Y

Youth programs, 134

Z

ZBB (zero-based budgeting), 141
Zealots seeking elected office, 125
Zero-based budgeting (ZBB), 141

Index by Nancy Kopper